THE SPECTRAL JEW

SERIES EDITORS

RITA COPELAND
BARBARA A. HANAWALT
DAVID WALLACE

*Sponsored by the Center for Medieval Studies
at the University of Minnesota*

Volumes in this series study the diversity of medieval
cultural histories and practices, including such
interrelated issues as gender, class, and social
hierarchies; race and ethnicity; geographical
relations; definitions of political space; discourses
of authority and dissent; educational institutions;
canonical and noncanonical literatures; and
technologies of textual and visual literacies.

The Spectral Jew

Conversion and Embodiment in Medieval Europe

Steven F. Kruger

Medieval Cultures, Volume 40
University of Minnesota Press
Minneapolis
London

The University of Minnesota Press is grateful for a grant from the Professional Staff Congress–City University of New York (PSC–CUNY) Research Award Program (2005–2006), which helped fund publication of this book.

Earlier versions of several sections of this book have been previously published in the following publications. "The Spectral Jew," *New Medieval Literatures* 2 (1998): 9–35; reprinted by permission of Oxford University Press. "Medieval Christian (Dis)identifications: Muslims and Jews in Guibert of Nogent," *New Literary History* 28 (1997): 185–203; reprinted with permission from The Johns Hopkins University Press. "Conversion and Medieval Sexual, Religious, and Racial Categories," in *Constructing Medieval Sexuality*, edited by Karma Lochrie, Peggy McCracken, and James A. Schultz (Minneapolis: University of Minnesota Press, 1997), 158–79; reprinted with permission. "Becoming Christian, Becoming Male?" in *Becoming Male in the Middle Ages*, edited by Jeffrey J. Cohen and Bonnie Wheeler, The New Middle Ages 4 (New York: Garland, 1997), 21–41; reprinted with permission. "(De)Stabilized Identities in Medieval Jewish–Christian Disputations on the Talmud," in *Making Contact: Maps, Identity, and Travel*, edited by Glenn Burger, Lesley Cormack, Jonathan Hart, and Natalia Pylypiuk (Edmonton: University of Alberta Press, 2003), 63–85; reprinted with permission of the University of Alberta Press.

Published by the University of Minnesota Press
111 Third Avenue South, Suite 290
Minneapolis, MN 55401-2520
http://www.upress.umn.edu

Library of Congress Cataloging-in-Publication Data

Kruger, Steven F.
   The spectral Jew : conversion and embodiment in medieval Europe / Steven F. Kruger.
      p.   cm. — (Medieval cultures ; v. 40)
   Includes bibliographical references and index.
   ISBN 0-8166-4061-0 (hc : alk. paper) — ISBN 0-8166-4062-9 (pb : alk. paper)
      1. Judaism—Relations—Christianity.   2. Christianity and other religions—Judaism.
3. Judaism (Christian theology)—History of doctrines—Middle Ages, 600–1500.
4. Antisemitism—Europe—History—To 1500.   5. Conversion—Christianity—
History—To 1500.   6. Religious disputations—Europe—History—To 1500.   7. Body,
Human—Social aspects—Europe.   8. Self-perception—Religious aspects—
Christianity—History—To 1500.   I. Title.   II. Series.
   BM535.K765   2005
   261.2'6'0940902—dc22   2005023757

Printed in the United States of America on acid-free paper

The University of Minnesota is an equal-opportunity educator and employer.

12 11 10 09 08 07 06   10 9 8 7 6 5 4 3 2 1

For Glenn Burger
with love

Contents

Acknowledgments

My decision, in the late 1980s and early 1990s, to direct my work toward questions of religious and sexual identity was strongly influenced by Judith Raiskin. Her example and her friendship have supported and guided me from the earliest stages of this book to its completion. Four of my teachers also contributed significantly to the inception of this project. Sherron Knopp made the Middle Ages an irresistible object of study. Donald R. Howard engaged me in my earliest discussions of English literary representations of Jews and Jewishness. David Wallace first pointed me toward historical studies of medieval Jewish-Christian relations; he has been, for more than a decade, a most generous supporter of my work. Morton Bloomfield, as a learned and sympathetic student of medieval Christian culture whose Jewishness nonetheless played an important role in his writing and his teaching, set an example that I have, if always imperfectly, tried to emulate.

This project was supported by grants from the Social Sciences and Humanities Research Council of Canada (2000–2001), the Professional Staff Congress–City University of New York (PSC–CUNY) Research Award Program (2001–2002), and the Queens College In-Residence Research Awards (2003–2004). These made possible archival work at the British Library and the Bibliothèque Nationale, and they provided for the able research assistance of Vivian Zenari and John Plews at the University of Alberta and of Robin Hizme at Queens College, CUNY. The grant of released time from Queens College facilitated the final stages of writing this book. I was able, as well, through funding provided by the Department of English at Alberta and the Ph.D. Program in English at CUNY, to benefit from the research assistance of David Watt and Drew Karpyshyn (at Alberta) and of Louis Bury, Mia Schilling Grogan, Matthew Williams, and Rebecca Williams (at CUNY).

For opportunities to present work related to this project I thank Glenn Burger, Lesley Cormack, M. V. Dmitriev, Graham Drake (and the Society for the Study of Homosexuality in the Middle Ages), Allen Frantzen, Julie Gammon, Stanton Garner Jr., Andrew Gow, Jonathan Hart, Martin Irvine, Michelle Karnes, Benny Kraut, Kathy Lavezzo, Peggy McCracken, Jacqueline Murray, Natalia Pylypiuk, Larry Simon (and *Medieval Encounters*), Patricia Skinner, Andrew Taylor, Sylvia Tomasch, David Wallace, Mary Wood, and Evan Zimroth.

During the years I have been working on this book I have been lucky to be part of several intellectually stimulating and supportive communities. Bob Tilton, Rita Connolly-Tilton, Julee Raiskin, Mary Wood, Mary Favret, Sara Blair, Thomas C. Moser Jr., and Roger Smith continue to connect me to the roots of this project in my graduate work at Stanford University. Ron Scapp and Meryl Siegman have helped me make a home in New York City, as have those sometime New Yorkers Aline Fairweather and Larry Scanlon. During my all too brief stay at the University of Alberta, I benefited from the support and encouragement of colleagues in both English and religious studies, especially Rob Brazeau, Garrett Epp, Chris Gittings, Andrew Gow, Francis Landy, Daphne Read, and Heather Zwicker. Teresa Zackodnik, Susan Hamilton, and Paul Brennan helped make Edmonton a second home.

Both at Alberta and at Queens College and the Graduate Center of CUNY, I have had more dedicated and thoughtful students than I can list here. For pointing me in some of the directions I have pursued in this book, I thank especially Lauren Baker, Melissa Jacques, Patty Milligan, Aimée Morrison, Christie Schultz, and Heather Tapley (at Alberta); Rosa Attali, Matthew Boyd Goldie, Manolo Guzmán, Wan-Chuan Kao, Sharon Kraus, Sean O'Toole, Christine Timm, Jason Tougaw, Eric Tribunella, and Richard Zeikowitz (at CUNY). Since 1988, the English department at Queens College has provided support for my work, and I thank especially Barbara Bowen, Nancy Comley, Duncan Faherty, Deborah R. Geis, Carrie Hintz, David Kazanjian, Catherine McKenna, Tony O'Brien, Janice Peritz, David Richter, Michael Sargent, Amy Tucker, and Gordon Whatley for stimulating discussions, pertinent suggestions, and intellectual comradeship. John Weir has been the best of friends, the most inspiring of teachers, and the most supportive of colleagues. The Ph.D. program in English at the CUNY Graduate Center has, under the leadership of Martin Stevens, Joe Wittreich, Rich McCoy, Bill Kelly, and Joan Richardson, also provided much support for this project, and my fellow medievalists—Professors Burger, McKenna, Sargent, and Whatley, as well as

Scott Westrem, William Coleman, Francesca Canadé Sautman, and Pam Sheingorn—have made the Graduate Center a particularly exciting place to be doing medieval studies. My colleague in women's studies at both Queens and the Graduate Center, Patricia Clough, always seems to understand where my thought is going before I do.

While writing this book, I was a member of two reading groups. The first provided the occasion for my initial encounter with Derrida's *Specters of Marx*, which now looms large in my work. For their open, skeptical, challenging discussion of such difficult texts, I thank Christopher Baswell, Larry Scanlon, Susan Crane, Peter Travis, Scott Westrem, and Sylvia Tomasch. The second group, organized by Francesca Canadé Sautman, has also provided a location for reading much work important to this project; I thank the members of that group, Professor Sautman, Rosa Attali, Glenn Burger, Susanna Byrne, Paolo Fasoli, Lía Schwartz, Patricia Sokolski, and Pascale Vassy.

Far-flung colleagues in medieval studies have expressed their interest in this project and have contributed to the completion of this book. I would especially like to thank Jeffrey Jerome Cohen, Rita Copeland, Allen Frantzen, Robert Hanning, Karma Lochrie, Larry Scanlon, D. Vance Smith, Michael Uebel, David Wallace, and Nicholas Watson.

Gregory S. Hutcheson read an early version of this book for the University of Minnesota Press and provided a generously detailed response: his comments have been at the center of my thinking as I have revised and completed the manuscript. Richard Morrison and his colleagues at the University of Minnesota Press have seen this book through the process of publication with great professionalism.

I thank the members of my family, Alice S. Kruger, Stanley I. Kruger, Susan D. Kruger, Joshua D. Kruger, Jonathan Dull, Diane Bassett, David Kruger, Jessica Kruger, Max Kruger-Dull, and Anna Kruger-Dull, for their intellectual example and their love.

I dedicate this book to my partner, Glenn Burger, without whose intellectual companionship and love my life and my work would be much the poorer. Glenn has been the first audience for this book; every page owes a debt to his insight that this dedication can but poorly repay.

Figure 1. The living cross: historiated initial "A." Codex Monacensis 23041, fol. 3v (ca. 1494–97). Bayerische Staatsbibliothek, Munich. Reproduced with permission.

INTRODUCTION

In the fine example of the late medieval pictorial tradition of the "living cross" shown in Figure 1, Jews and Jewishness are everywhere, yet at the same time everywhere under erasure.[1] The scene of the crucifixion is presided over by God the Father, surrounded by angels who hover next to and below him, holding scrolls: these represent, no doubt, not only the New Testament texts that testify to the details of the crucifixion scene (along with, perhaps, the apocryphal Gospel of Nicodemus that recounts the Harrowing of Hell, the scene at the base of the illustration) but also the prophetic texts of the "Old Testament," the Hebrew texts that, from the Christian perspective, unerringly predict the life, death, and resurrection of Jesus Christ as Messiah. Read backward from the moment of the crucifixion, a moment thought to confirm "Old Testament" prophecy of a new, Christian dispensation, these Jewish texts become something other than Jewish, incorporable now into a Christian Holy Scripture that, while acknowledging its partly Jewish origin, firmly relegates Jewishness to a past, superseded moment. Thus, in this illustration, the "Old Testament" moments visually represented or alluded to are clearly taken over into a Christian typology. Eve stands below and to the left of the crucified Christ (to the viewer's right): just between her head and her right hand, which plucks fruit from the tree of the knowledge of good and evil, is the head of the serpent, whose body coils around the trunk of the tree. The consequence of Eve's imminent eating from that tree—death for all human beings—is clearly indicated by the skull she cradles in her left hand, halfway between her naked breasts and genitals. The death that Eve's act institutes reverberates throughout the picture: in the naked bodies of the patriarchs, who kneel below Eve in the flames of hell; in Christ's naked body, dead on the cross. But of course the initiation of death is also—in the later moments represented here, the crucifixion and the harrowing—connected to its dissolution: Christ dies on the cross to defeat death, and that defeat is triumphantly depicted in the approach of Christ—still largely naked, with the wounds of the crucifixion apparent on his hands, feet, and side, but now robed and attended by angels—toward the gate of hell. The gate has fallen before his approach, crushing two animal-like demons beneath it. A ratlike demon atop hell-gate holds a pitchfork, and another demon, directly below Eve, a crook; but their defense of hell is clearly doomed, their instruments powerless before the staffs Christ and one of the angels preceding Christ carry (both staffs are surmounted by the cross). The prediction, from Genesis 3:15, that Eve ("mulierem . . . ipsa") will crush the serpent underfoot,[2] traditionally read to prophesy that a woman, Mary, will repair the injuries of Eve's fall,[3] is also depicted here: even as she sins, Eve steps on one of the defeated demonic figures. And Eve's typological fulfillment, Mary, faces her across the pictorial space.[4] Mary's face echoes Eve's, but every-thing else about her suggests a radical change. She is richly robed, not naked. Her head is crowned and haloed, not bare. Under her aegis stands the Christ of the harrowing and his attendant angels, not the souls con-signed to hell by Eve's act. She cradles near her body not a death's head but two modestly dressed women, women bound like the figures about to be freed from hell for salvation instead of eternal death. She also grasps, with her left hand, a miniature replica of the cross and the crucified body of Christ that grows at the center of a flourishing tree: here, Mary's action demonstrates that the tree of the knowledge of good and evil—which, through Eve's action, brought death into the world—becomes the life-giving tree, the cross, which, in bearing the crucified body of Christ, defeats death. Moreover, Mary's plucking the crucifix from the tree has explicitly Eucharistic resonances: indeed, in some other living cross depictions, the fruit of this tree is clearly the consecrated host.[5] Mary's tree may also evoke the burning bush of Exodus, a standard figure for Mary's virgin motherhood.[6] And at the same time, this tree may make us think of the Tree of Jesse, the genealogical tree that, in Chris-tian tradition, connects Jesus Christ to the Davidic line of inheritance through Mary.[7]

The Hebrew text—Genesis especially but also Exodus and prophetic texts like Isaiah 11:1 ("a shoot shall go out from the root of Jesse and a flower shall ascend from his root")[8]—is thus thoroughly taken up into the Christian story; likewise, all the Jewish figures in the picture are in the process of leaving Judaism behind. Thus, the righteous patriarchs, about to be released from death and hell by Christ, are also about to be drawn out of their Jewishness (consistently placed in this illustration to the left of the crucified Christ) into a new, Christian, dispensation, made possible by Christ's incarnation. The same is of course true of the other Jews in the picture—Mary, who already occupies a place diametrically opposed to the "Old Testament" figure of Eve, and Christ himself, whose body occupies center stage, the place where old, Jewish, and new, Christian, traditions meet and diverge. This body, like the "Old Testament," is marked by its Jewish origin (physically marked, we know, by circumcision), and yet, in the moment of the crucifixion, it is transformed into a new kind of body—a body to be resurrected, a body that can descend into death and hell but now to "conquer death" rather than to be conquered.

The point of the depiction of the "living cross" is to make vivid this central Christian paradox, that death is defeated through death, that Christ's crucifixion, the killing of God's son, paradoxically allows for a salvation and an eternal life previously denied human beings. If, in this illustration, the typological transformation of Eve's fall into a series of actions that repair that fall is at all unclear or obscure, the central tableau of the crucifixion reiterates that transformation in a striking way. In the picture's major conceit, the very instrument of Christ's violent death, the cross, is identified with life rather than death.[9] God the Father surmounts it, suggesting clearly that the cross is his instrument.[10] Moreover, living hands sprout from each of the cross's remaining points. From the bottom grows an arm that holds a hammer (notably, one of the instruments of the passion) aimed menacingly at the ratlike demon poised above the gate of hell;[11] this living arm, then, like the cross itself, reemphasizes the living, redemptive nature of the violence that attends Christ's death. The hand that emerges from the right side of the cross points to a scroll that evokes the new scriptures of Christianity, since immediately below rides the figure of Ecclesia, the church, on a mount clearly representing the New Testament Gospels.[12] The multiple feet of Ecclesia's multiform beast are the feet of the four creatures that traditionally represent the evangelists—a hoof (for Luke the ox), a lion's paw (for Mark), a human or angelic foot (for Matthew), and an eagle's talons (for John); the beast also has four heads, a lion's, an eagle's, an ox's, and a person's (or angel's). Carrying in her right hand a staff that echoes those held by the angel and Christ below, Ecclesia rides triumphantly forward, and she holds in her left hand a cup with which she collects the

(Eucharistic) blood coursing from Christ's side, the blood that gives her, the Church, life. But the birth of Ecclesia under the aegis of the living cross is at the same time a death for the allegorical figure who directly faces her from the left side of the cross, Synagoga. Synagoga rides not the powerful lion-eagle-ox-man of the evangelists but, as Wolfgang Seiferth notes, a "stumbling donkey whose hocks have been cut,"[13] a figure perhaps of Judaism's obstinacy in adhering to the radically limited "Old Testament" law rather than the Gospels. Indeed, as is typically the case, Synagoga here is blindfolded, unable to see the scene of the crucifixion that unfolds before her and that marks her end. While in her left hand Ecclesia extends the chalice that catches Christ's life-giving blood, Synagoga holds in her left hand a black goat's head that echoes the grotesque bodies of the demons toward the bottom of the illustration and that evokes traditional medieval associations of Judaism with animal sacrifice, devil worship, and lust.[14] Where Ecclesia grasps in her right hand the staff of her institutional power, Synagoga's staff, surmounted by the banner of her power, disintegrates: its broken form echoes the twisted forms of the demons' crook and pitchfork rather than the staffs of Christ and his angel. And, in what is perhaps the illustration's most powerful gesture, the hand that emerges from the left arm of the "living cross" wields a sword with which it stabs Synagoga in the head.

If the main argument of the "living cross" is that death finds its death in the moment of the crucifixion, then a corollary of that argument is that part of what is killed off in this moment is the prior religious dispensation associated with Synagoga; as death dies, so does a Judaism that thus comes to be identified with death. As Christine Rose notes, "the tree of Life (the cross) becomes a tree of Death for the infidel Synagogue."[15] Christ's death inaugurates eternal life: hell is broken, heaven opened, the instrument of death itself, the cross, lives on. A future of life, of salvation, of resurrection, unlike anything that has previously been available to human beings, is opened up, but not only through the death and resurrection of Christ. This event also effects, and depends upon, the death and *non*resurrection of Judaism. And yet, even as Ecclesia arises and Synagoga falls, the prior Jewish dispensation—Synagoga herself, but also the "Old Testament" texts whose meaning changes irrevocably with Christ's incarnation, the Jewish figures of the patriarchs and indeed of Mary and Christ himself—must be represented in order for us to understand the meaning of that which displaces it. Even as it is made to die, to disappear, Judaism comes to occupy our field of vision. It is this dynamic in medieval Christian thought—a dependence upon the Jewish ancestor that is simultaneously an erasure—which I hope the book that follows helps us more fully to understand. To gesture here toward my largest argument, in this illustration of the living cross, Jewishness is a *spectral* presence, strongly felt and yet just as strongly derealized.

A representation like the living cross makes no attempt to depict contemporary, late fifteenth-century European Jews. Indeed, its identification of the moment of the crucifixion with the death of Synagoga (wishfully and counterfactually) suggests that Jews cannot be part of a present, post-incarnational moment. Clearly, something other than a desire to grapple with a vital, contemporary religious competitor motivates such a representation, and in recent years much work on medieval Christian engagements with Judaism has emphasized the ways in which "the Jew" serves certain primarily ideological functions within hegemonic medieval culture. This line of inquiry has treated "the Jew" as a fantasy construction that had as much or more to do with Christian identity as it did with actual Jews and Jewish communities.[16] Thus, for instance, in his important recent book *Living Letters of the Law: Ideas of the Jew in Medieval Christianity*, Jeremy Cohen considers the long-standing Christian tradition of the "hermeneutical Jew":

> In order to meet their particular needs, Christian theology and exegesis created a Jew of their own.... Even if, in his inception, in his function, and in his veritable power in the Christian mindset, the hermeneutical Jew of late antique or medieval times had relatively little to do with the Jewish civilization of his day, his career certainly influenced the Christian treatment of the Jewish minority, the sole consistently tolerated minority, of medieval Christendom. Medieval Christian perceptions of this Jew's personality contributed amply to the significance of Judaism and anti-Judaism in Western intellectual and cultural history. Viewed more broadly, these perceptions shed light on the place and purpose of the "other" in the collective mentality of the Christian majority.[17]

As Cohen himself notes, the idea of a "theological Jew," a "juif théologique," developed by Gilbert Dahan in his magisterial *Les intellectuels*

chrétiens et les Juifs au Moyen Âge, presents a similar construction.[18] Like
Cohen, Dahan makes it clear that the constructs he analyzes do not necessarily reflect, directly or clearly, social reality; he notes a certain "schizo-
phrenic view of the Jews," a "quotidian and real Jew, with whom one willingly discusses the Bible or the sciences," on which is "superimposed
that which we have called the 'juif théologique,' an unreal Jew in whom
diverse stereotypes come to be mixed and added together, born first of all
from the reflection of theologians."[19]

Cohen and Dahan are primarily interested in medieval theological
and intellectual work, where we might expect especially abstract formulations of Jewish difference, but recent scholarship also recognizes the
prevalence of figures like the "hermeneutical" and "theological Jew" in
less elite and abstruse medieval cultural formations. Thus, in her recent
study of poetic and dramatic as well as theological texts, Lisa Lampert
takes up Cohen's "hermeneutical Jew," arguing that this figure works in
tandem with the gendered figure of the "hermeneutical Woman" to further a universalizing Christian self-definition: "The hermeneutical
Woman and the hermeneutical Jew both become associated with veiled
knowledge, a clouded seeing, and, of course, with carnality and the body
itself. Both become figured as embodied particulars in relation to a universal that transcends embodiment."[20] In work on English texts and history after the expulsion of Jewish communities in 1290, it is no surprise
that figures emphasizing the fictionality, the "absent presence,"[21] of "the
Jew" should dominate. Jeffrey J. Cohen has asked the provocative question "Was Margery Kempe Jewish?" suggesting that, in the absence of
Jews in fifteenth-century England, we might read Kempe as a "performative Jew," figured forth as Jewish by her "exorbitant voice" and unorthodox, "boystows," behavior, though herself failing to "recognize the Jewish
timbre of her voice."[22] And while the historical absence of Jews may allow
for a more uninhibited medieval fantasizing about Jewishness, it does
not necessarily lead to a monolithic stereotyping or othering of Jews. (As
Cohen's reading of Margery Kempe suggests, in such fantasy constructions, the Jew might indeed come into a certain dangerous proximity
with the Christian.) Thus, Denise L. Despres calls our attention to "the
protean Jew," arguing that, in late medieval England, Jewish figures
might operate in "markedly different ways"; as she suggests, a single,
late fourteenth-century English manuscript (the Vernon manuscript)
"provides us with important evidence of conflicting attitudes toward the

Jew, who emerges from these narratives simultaneously as intellectual, criminal, convertable [sic], and equally resistant to genuine conversion."[23] In a similar vein, Elisa Narin van Court argues that, in "textual productions which represent medieval Jews,"

> [t]here are stereotypes, to be sure, but there are also authors who return to the symbolic to re-imagine Jews and Judaism; there are texts which hold in unresolved tension mutually exclusive responses to the Jews; and there are texts which invoke the Jews as exemplars for Christian community.... In the absence of organized Jewish communities, that nearly total material absence, they remain a strong conceptual presence.[24]

And while Jewish absence does not stand in the way of Jews and Jewishness assuming and maintaining a certain cultural centrality and complexity, Jewish social-historical presence might well call forth attempts to deny or erase that presence—whether ideologically or, all too often, in actual practice. Several scholars have emphasized that, even in real historical proximity to Jews and Jewish communities, Christian understandings tend to construct an absence. Kathleen Biddick argues, in reading two Albrecht Altdorfer etchings of the Regensburg synagogue made immediately before the 1519 destruction of the synagogue and expulsion of the Jewish community, that these depictions do the work of "'disappearing' Jews," constructing a representational space "where others are reduced to ontological absence"; as their community is destroyed, historical Jews become, through the work of Christian "ethnographic" representation, "paper Jews."[25] And Sylvia Tomasch has developed the powerful notion of "the virtual Jew," which applies equally to situations in which Jews are present or absent; in either case, Tomasch argues, medieval constructions replace actuality with virtuality:

> the virtual does not refer to the actual, although this is what it claims to do. Rather, the virtual "surround[s] the realm of the actual in a system of reality," thereby creating a simulation that, by seeming to be more authentic than the actual, may be mistaken for it. When we examine the virtual Jew, for example, we see that it does not refer directly to any actual Jew, nor present an accurate depiction of one, nor even a faulty fiction of one;

instead it "surrounds" Jews with a "reality" that displaces and supplants their actuality. In fact, following the trail of the virtual guarantees that one will never arrive at the actual, for the referent of the virtual is always irretrievable. Thus, rather than being surprised at or having to explain the continuation of English reference to Jews after the expulsion, we might better acknowledge that Jewish absence is likely the best precondition for virtual presence. For wherever in Western culture Jews come to reside, they encounter the phantom that follows and precedes them. By virtue of its virtuality, therefore, "the Jew" maintains its frightful power.[26]

Such a formulation would suggest that Jews are important, even central, in mainstream Christian culture not so much because they provide a religious challenge to Christianity and its thought, and not so much because they present a real social and cultural alternative to Christian hegemony, but because—whatever the social reality of Jewish-Christian relations, and despite the complex, "protean" nature of representations of Jews—Jews and Judaism can be quite easily rendered "virtual," reduced to a nonpresence, even a nonbeing that functions to reconfirm a real, present Christianity. The notion of the spectral Jew, which is at the heart of the book that follows, is clearly related, and indebted, to notions like the "hermeneutical," "theological," "paper," and "virtual." Like these, the spectral emphasizes that the Jews we encounter in medieval Christian texts—theological, historical, polemical, autobiographical, fictional—are constructions that do not correspond in any easy way to the lived experiences of Jews, or even of the Christians who elaborated and made use of these constructions. But I want to emphasize that these constructions are also potentially "protean" and complex, not reducible, despite their constructedness, to a single form or even a single (anti-Jewish or anti-Semitic) impulse.[27] To my mind, the *specter*, standing between life and death, conjured up but not therefore necessarily in the full control of the conjurer, best suggests this potential complexity. I want to emphasize, moreover, that the lack of a clear correspondence between fantasy constructions of Jews and lived experience does not mean that these constructions do not themselves constitute a crucial part of lived experience. One critic has responded to an earlier formulation of "the spectral Jew" by suggesting that "Kruger's provocative essay is much influenced by Jaques [*sic*] Derrida's *Spectres de Marx* . . . , and in my view underestimates the extent to which Jews and Judaism were living realities for the medieval Christian."[28] Part of my response would be that "Jews and Judaism *were* living realities for the medieval Christian"— even the medieval English Christian post-1290 for whom "real" Jews were absent—but that those "living realities" were experienced as much and as importantly *through* the constructions of fantasy and ideology as in any more purely experiential realm.

That is *not* to say that the significance of the experiential—of real historical figures standing in discernible, concrete, material relations to each other—should be overlooked in favor of an analysis of figures and constructions, and their corresponding "mentalities" or ideologies. In a recent essay on the Croxton *Play of the Sacrament,* David Lawton has suggested that we have "mov[ed] too hastily from the body to notions of absence—the cultural significance of absent Jews, studied by Sylvia Tomasch in an essay on 'The Virtual Jew' and by Steven Kruger as 'The Spectral Jew.'"[29] But as I hope to show throughout this project, spectrality is not simply to be opposed to body: indeed, medieval Jews' spectrality often brings them into a particularly close relation to pure or dead body, mere materiality. More generally, while the spectral is a figure of a certain immateriality, it also remains significantly wrapped up in embodiment; without body, or something like body, how could the specter appear? In Jacques Derrida's formulation of spectrality (which will be explored more fully in chapter 1 below), "the specter is a paradoxical incorporation, the becoming-body, a certain phenomenal and carnal form of the spirit."[30]

In addition to being thought to deny the body or materiality, an idea like spectrality potentially leaves itself open to the serious charge that it levels the *differences* among interreligious interactions as these existed at different points in time and in different locations: if the medieval Jew is always, for Christians, spectral, how can we distinguish the very different dynamics of Jewish-Christian interaction in pre- and post-1290 England, or in pre- and post-1096 Northern Europe, or, at any given moment, among educated clerics, nobles in part economically dependent on Jewish communities, and those who might be in a more competitive or directly conflictual relationship to Jews? David Nirenberg—in one of the most influential and admired of recent books on medieval majority-minority relations, *Communities of Violence: Persecution of Minorities in the Middle Ages*—has emphasized the primary importance of historical specificity in considering interreligious dynamics. Strongly criticizing the approach of a certain "structuralist" intellectual history or history of discourse that would ignore the specific social circumstances in which discursive structures are embedded and played out (as claims and counterclaims that may sometimes be successful and sometimes not), he argues that, while the same discourse or representation of "the Jew"— as usurer, as literal-minded, etc.—may appear in radically different circumstances, that does not mean that the status of Jews has remained unchanged. Indeed, as Nirenberg would argue, we can only know the meaning of a particular discursive claim if we analyze its deployment in its particular historical moment.[31]

My own work in this book, with its emphasis on the operations of spectrality, will no doubt appear to belong to the "structuralist" school that Nirenberg strongly critiques. Yet I take Nirenberg's position seriously. The reappearance of particular tropes or discourses, of the "hermeneutical" or "theological" or "virtual" or "spectral Jew," does not mean that relations between Christians and Jews simply replay the same dynamic over and over.[32] Power shifts; relations among distinct religious communities become more intensely confrontational or, sometimes, cooperative.[33] The deployment of discourses—to follow Michel Foucault—is polyvalent:

> Discourses are not once and for all subservient to power or raised up against it, any more than silences are. We must make allowance for the complex and unstable process whereby discourse can be both an instrument and an effect of power, but also a hindrance, a stumbling-block, a point of resistance and a starting point for an opposing strategy.... There is not, on the one side, a discourse of power, and opposite it, another discourse that runs counter to it. Discourses are tactical elements or blocks operating in the field of force relations; there can exist different and even contradictory discourses within the same strategy; they can, on the contrary, circulate without changing their form from one strategy to another, opposing strategy.[34]

The figure of the Jew could be put to many, and conflicting, uses—and the discourses surrounding that figure were available to be taken up for

very different ends, even into counterdiscourses developed by Jews and
Jewish communities themselves (if often counterdiscourses that failed
in achieving their political goals). But it is important as well to recognize
the persistence of discourses, the remaining centrality of Jews in relation
to Christian self-construction. While we must question, as Nirenberg has
questioned, a historical master narrative that would see the emergence
of a "persecuting society" in Europe in the eleventh or twelfth or thirteenth century, and a growing anti-Semitism (replacing an earlier, less
virulent anti-Judaism) that leads to a "racist" persecution and expulsion
of Jews from a formerly "tolerant" fifteenth-century Iberia, and then,
across the centuries, to the most virulent racism of Nazi Germany's
Final Solution, we must still recognize how in fact transhistorically Jewish
figures, Jewish "specters," have survived—to feed destructive projects,
but, indeed, also projects of Christian self-construction and projects of
Jewish survival.[35]

While I recognize the force of such constructions as the "hermeneutical," "virtual," "theological," and "paper Jew," I believe (as I hope
the book that follows will demonstrate) that *spectrality* might be particularly useful in thinking the overarching dynamics of medieval Jewish-
Christian relations *and* in answering Nirenberg's call for historical
specificity. As I argue more fully in chapter 1, spectrality focuses attention explicitly on questions of historicity and historical change, on questions of pastness, presentness, futurity. And the figure of the spectral
Jew, while primarily a Christian construction, also perhaps leaves some
space for Jewish agency, for an acting within, through, and against the
hegemonic attempts to limit Jews to a position of significance primarily
for Christian projects.

In *The Spectral Jew: Conversion and Embodiment in Medieval Europe*, I
rethink the significance of Jewish presence and absence in Western
Europe during the high and late Middle Ages. While we often conceive of
Western European Christianity as monolithic, an enormously powerful
institution that formed medieval Europe in the most crucial manner—
and while there is of course some truth in such a description—it is also
true that the church and the European culture it shaped defined themselves in complex, and not always self-consistent, ways, and that crucial
to such definitions were "orthodox" Christians' attempts to place themselves in relation to other religious groups: Islam, Judaism, the pagan

cultures Christianity often had displaced, and the "heresies" orthodoxy identified within Christendom itself.

In this book I focus particularly on texts that represent or enact Christian-Jewish contact. While medieval Jewish-Christian relations are intimately intertwined with the histories of Islam, Christian "heresy," and paganism, Judaism stands in a privileged relation to Christianity, since it is out of Judaism that Christianity first arose. One might therefore expect that Christian self-understanding will particularly have to grapple with its "parent" religion. By examining texts where such grappling occurs, as well as Jewish texts that respond to or counter Christian arguments, I hope to understand more fully both the processes by which Christianity constructed itself and the ways in which Jewish self-understandings were shaped by the encounter, in Western Europe, with Christianity.

Body and embodiment were especially crucial terms in medieval Jewish-Christian interactions. Christian writers often understood the relationship between Christianity and Judaism in terms of an opposition between Jewish corporeality and Christian spirituality. In Christian polemic, we find Jews depicted as excessively corporeal and concomitantly less spiritual than their Christian counterparts. Jewish men were thought to suffer a monthly "bloody flux" that associated them, in at least certain Christian writers' minds, with menstruating ("unclean") women.[36] Jews were accused of such violent corporeal crimes as ritual murder, cannibalism, host desecration, and well poisoning—all of which were thought to threaten Christian bodies at the same time that they expressed a certain monstrous Jewish bodiliness. In the realm of intellectual difference, too, bodies were crucial: Christian exegetes understood specifically Jewish readings of scripture as overly literal, corporeal denials of the "true spirit" of the text.

At the same time, however, the medieval record of relations between Jews and Christians is filled with moments when Jews are, fictionally and in real life, decorporealized, rendered shadowy or invisible. Chronicles often fail to mention the presence of Jews in places where other evidence suggests that there were thriving Jewish communities. In a text like Peter Abelard's twelfth-century *Dialogue of a Philosopher with a Jew, and a Christian,* the Jew speaks only in the first third of the text; after that point, he is silent, essentially absent.[37] From the thirteenth century on, one increasingly common way in which Christian communities and nations dealt

with anxieties about Jews was expulsion. As noted above, England's
Jews were expelled in 1290, not openly to return until the seventeenth
century; France expelled Jews soon after, in 1306; the Iberian expulsion
of 1492 is the best known. Such actions were partly responses to corporeal fears like those sketched above, partly the result of economic calcu-
lation. In any case, this history of expulsion effectively derealized Jews
for many medieval people. But though, for instance, most English people
from the late thirteenth to the mid-seventeenth century were unlikely to
encounter Jews,[38] a threatening Jewish corporeality (though one usually
displaced from contemporary England either temporally or spatially)
continues to be an important trope in such major English texts as Chaucer's *Prioress's Tale*, Langland's *Piers Plowman*, the Croxton *Play of the
Sacrament*, the cycle drama, and, later, Marlowe's *Jew of Malta* and
Shakespeare's *Merchant of Venice*.

The *Spectral Jew* makes clear the ways in which interactions between
medieval Christians and Jews pivoted on a dynamic relation between
embodiment and disembodiment, the attribution of gross corporeality
to Jewish bodies and a concomitant attempt to make those bodies disappear. Condensed in this relation were Christian anxieties about identity—the identity both of Christendom as a whole (a body dangerously
"infiltrated" by non-Christian bodies) and of individual Christians (anxious to distinguish themselves from those believing otherwise). Further,
Jewish literature and culture, and a Jewish sense of identity, were themselves deeply marked by the dynamic movement between embodiment
and erasure: Jewish thinkers and writers had both to respond to the
accusation that Judaism was an excessively corporeal religion and to
attempt to make Jews visible in their actual embodiment, without visi-
bility becoming simply a spur to renewed violence and erasure.

My investigation of the ways in which bodiliness and disembodiment shape medieval Jewish-Christian interactions rests on a wide variety of sources: polemical Christian anti-Jewish and Jewish anti-Christian
texts; the writing of converts from Judaism to Christianity, and fragments
of accounts of conversion from Christianity to Judaism; chronicles, laws,
papal documents; transcripts of actual public disputations between
Christians and Jews as well as fictional accounts of interreligious debate.
By giving attention to such a wide range of different kinds of text, as well
as to texts written from both Jewish and Christian points of view, and
by reading these texts in both their historical-sociopolitical and textual-

literary contexts, I hope to develop as broad and deep a sense as possible of how questions of Jewish-Christian difference mattered in medieval culture. My sources also derive from a wide geographic area—England, France, Germany, Spain, and Italy—and from a broad temporal span, the eleventh to the fifteenth centuries. While there are dangers in making the purview of the project so large, I believe that doing so is fruitful—in enabling a tracing of continuities and changes over time as well as a recognition of similarities and differences across space.

I begin the investigation in the second half of the eleventh century because, as historical work has made clear, this moment is associated with a shift in both Christian and Jewish self-understanding, as well as in Christian-Jewish relations.[39] Thus, for instance, massacres of Jews associated with the First Crusade characterized the closing years of the eleventh century. While Christianity, from its beginning, expressed an uneasiness with Judaism, we can see, starting in the late eleventh century, and accelerating through the twelfth and into the thirteenth century, a growing intensity of Christian anti-Judaism. The same period was, however, also a time in which much collaborative work between Jews and Christians was ongoing: Christian exegetes consulted with Jewish biblical scholars in Paris during the twelfth century; the "renaissance" of that same period involved Jewish, Christian, and Muslim scholars working together on a massive, and deeply influential, project of recovering ancient (classical) knowledge. The period when both Christian persecution of Jews and Jewish-Christian collaborations intensified should be a particularly revealing one for the understanding of complex interreligious dynamics, and I study what I call the "long" twelfth century especially fully (it is, indeed, a period when many Jewish texts about Christianity and many Christian texts about Judaism were produced). But I also bring my investigation into the later Middle Ages, since this period is characterized by repeated attempts to remove or eliminate Jews from Christian Europe, whether through conversion, expulsion, or massacre.

In framing the project around the dynamic movement between embodiment and disembodiment, I have been influenced by recent discussions of "spectrality" and "apparitionality" in writers as diverse as Terry Castle (*The Apparitional Lesbian*), Kathleen Brogan (*Cultural Haunting: Ghosts and Ethnicity in Recent American Literature*), and Jacques Derrida (*Specters of Marx*), and I explore the usefulness of such formulations for thinking medieval Jewish-Christian relations in chapter 1, "The Spectral Jew." Spectral or apparitional figures—at one and the same time corporeally threatening and decorporealized—crystallize a dynamic in which the attempt to rid oneself of a presence perceived as dangerous is haunted by the impossibility of doing just that. "Ghosting" may operate in the realms of gender and sexuality (as we see, for instance, in Castle), race and ethnicity (as in Brogan), and (as I will argue) religion; in all these cases, the spectral works in part to solidify one's own sense of identity over against an "other." But, as Derrida emphasizes, the work of "conjuring away" a specter also "conjures it up": the very need to derealize the specter, to declare it dead, depends upon a recognition that it is in fact *not* yet dead.[40] Synagoga must be made to appear beneath the living cross if her definitive elimination through the crucifixion is to be announced. But violent as the work of conjuration may be (as when Jews were expelled from their homes in England or massacred in Northern France and the Rhineland in 1096), in its ambivalent stance between presence and absence it might open a certain space for resistance on the part of those who are "ghosted." As Castle suggests, while "the apparitional figure seem[s] to obliterate . . . the disturbing carnality of lesbian love," at the same time, it represents a "reembodiment," an "uncanny return to the flesh."[41] One persistent question in my project, then, is whether, in the space between the violent derealizing of Jewish bodies and the concomitant recognition of the presence of those bodies, we might find a place for medieval Jewish resistance to a Christian hegemony.

Chapter 2, "Body Effects: Individual and Community Identity in the Long Twelfth Century," examines how medieval understandings both of individual Christian identity and of a corporate Christendom depended in crucial ways on constructions of the body of the Jewish individual and of Jewry as a whole. The late eleventh and early twelfth centuries were a period of intensive church reform that also involved, with the First Crusade (1096), a violent reaching beyond the boundaries of Europe. The (re)formation of a medieval Christian sense of identity in this moment was, I argue, importantly dependent on a differentiation from, and sometimes a direct attack on, Jews as well as Muslims; this differentiation often operated in terms of the body. At the same time, as noted above, this moment saw significant collaboration between Jews and Christians, and I consider here the paradoxes that characterized Jewish-Christian contacts during this era. In part, I do so by turning to the extensive and varied (historiographical, autobiographical, and theological-polemical) writings of Guibert of Nogent, intensively considering how Guibert represented Western European Christians' encounters with a range of religious others—Jews, Muslims, Greek Christians, and Christian "heretics." In closing the chapter, I then look at how European Jewish writers responded to twelfth-century changes in their relationship with Christendom, attempting to reassert Jewish identity, to reconstruct and reclaim it in terms that a dominant Christian ideology would disallow, even as they represented the real destruction of Jewish communities. My discussion throughout makes clear that the differences in religious identity constructed by both Christian and Jewish writers depended significantly upon idealized and gendered imaginings of the body, with Christian chroniclers positing a heroic, masculine crusader's body over against decrepit Jewish and Muslim ones, and with Jewish chroniclers constructing both masculine and feminine models of heroic martyrdom.

Chapter 3, "Becoming Christian? Conversion and the Stubborn Body," shifts its attention from the explicitly violent confrontations of the First Crusade to the more subtly coercive relations in which Jews were often urged (and sometimes forced, as indeed during the First Crusade) to convert to Christianity. The texts of conversion are especially crucial to my project—I return to them in chapters 4 and 5—since they dramatize both the separateness of Jewish and Christian positions and the possibility of a movement between these. That is, they especially crystallize questions about religious identity and its stability or instability. Here, the Jewish body poses a real problem to Christian thinking: if Jews, in the very stuff of their corporeality, are somehow essentially different from Christians, what happens when they undergo a religious conversion? Are their bodies also converted? Or do Jewish bodies remain strange, recalcitrant to religious, moral "reform?" As we will see, such questions about bodily change also entail significant questions about the convert's gender and sexuality. To recover as full a sense as possible of the gendered, sexualized body's place in the process of religious conversion, I here bring forward a wide range of kinds of evidence—legal-juridical, medical, polemical, fictional, autobiographical—from the high and late Middle Ages. This adds up, I believe, to a compelling case for seeing bodies, genders, and sexualities as intimately involved with religious identity and conversion. In the remaining two chapters of the book, I then complement this analysis by turning to a more intensive investigation of several texts at the center of which stand questions of identity and conversion, gender, sexuality, and embodiment.

The texts considered in chapters 4 and 5 all represent direct confrontations—debates or disputations—between Jews and Christians. Many surviving medieval texts—in both Latin and Hebrew—stage fictional or allegorical debates between Jewish and Christian positions, and some of these fictions display a tantalizing connection to "real life." Thus, one literary dialogue between a Jew and a Christian was composed by the theologian Rupert of Deutz, and while we have no evidence that this text itself represents a debate that actually occurred, the Jewish convert to Christianity, Hermann of Cologne, elsewhere claims to have engaged in a public disputation with Rupert.[42] We have, moreover, surviving Hebrew and Latin accounts of a variety of historically verifiable public debates between Jews and Christians. While some of these varied debate texts are discussed in earlier chapters, in chapter 4, "Merchants, Converts, Jews: Interreligious Debate and the Troubling of Christian Identity," I turn to a more intensive consideration of this literature and what it might tell us about medieval Jewish-Christian interaction and identity formation. I examine first the clearly fictional *Dialogi* of Peter Alfonsi, an extremely popular polemic written by a Jewish convert to Christianity. While the text develops a powerful anti-Jewish and anti-Islamic argument, in focusing attention on Peter's identity as a convert, it at the same time complicates a sense of what it means to be a Christian as opposed to a Jew. On the one hand, a "conversion identity"—an identity paradoxically dependent upon a radical change in identity—is historically constitutive of both the Christian community and the Christian individual: Christianity, after all, originates in and grows by means of conversion, and individual Christian moral reform is often treated as conversion. We might, then, see the convert Peter (like the New Testament convert Saul/Paul before him) as a particularly appropriate emblem of Christian identity. On the other hand, however, an explicit recognition in Peter of the proximity of Christian identity to Jewishness might be deeply disturbing to a Christian sense of self.

A similar ambivalence characterizes the other major set of texts at play in chapter 4, the twelfth- and thirteenth-century disputations of Ceuta and Majorca, which (unlike Peter's *Dialogi*) purport to recount actual disputations between Jews and Christian merchants. A rise in Christian mercantile activity—from the twelfth century to the fifteenth, and then into "modernity"—threatened Christianity's sense of itself as a *spiritual* dispensation established over against the corporeal tradition of a super-seded Judaism, and these debates develop strategies for distinguishing *Christian* mercantilism from discredited Jewish mercantile and mone-tary practices. At the same time, however, the debates (especially the disputation of Majorca) implicate their merchant protagonists in Jewish-ness and thus fail to put anxieties about the proper *Christianitas* of mer-cantile identity wholly to rest.

The final chapter, "Staying Jewish? Public Disputation, Conversion, and Resistance," continues to examine texts generated by public debate between Jews and Christians, in this case Hebrew and Latin accounts of the church- and state-sponsored disputations held, most notably, at Paris in 1240, Barcelona in 1263, and Tortosa in 1413–14. These three debates share certain intriguing features: unlike the earlier disputational litera-ture, all focus their attention especially on postbiblical Hebrew texts, particularly the Talmud, and all have as their main Christian interlocutor a Jewish convert to Christianity. Both facts suggest that, for the Chris-tian officials who arranged and presided over these disputations, crucial to Christian self-identification remain a consideration of and confronta-tion with Jewishness (Judaism's authoritative texts) and Jewish difference (the difference that is both figured forth and overcome in the convert). At the same time, these debates bring to bear a strong pressure toward policing Jewish identity, belief, and practice, trying to ensure that Judaism take a form confirming Christian ideas of "proper" Jewishness. In the last of the debates, at Tortosa, the Christian pressure on Jewishness in-tensifies, pushing toward a full elimination of Jewish identity through conversion. In concluding *The Spectral Jew,* I look especially fully at this last disputation, examining how the pressure toward Jewish conversion builds, what its local Iberian and broader European politics are, and thinking through how spectrality—the conjuring up of a Jewish pres-ence in order to subject it to attack and a wished-for disappearance—con-tinues to operate in late medieval Jewish-Christian interactions, if dif-ferently than it did in the earlier Middle Ages. In closing, I return, too, to the difficult question of how much space might remain within late medieval Christian constructions for medieval European Jews to *stay* Jewish.

1

THE SPECTRAL JEW

THE CHRISTIAN REORGANIZATION OF HISTORY

> *It is often a matter of pretending to certify*
> *death there where the death certificate is*
> *still the performative of an act of war or the*
> *impotent gesticulation, the restless dream,*
> *of an execution.*
> —Jacques Derrida, *Specters of Marx*, 48

For medieval Christianity, one historical moment—the moment of Christ's incarnation—rewrites all of history. The point at which divinity intervenes decisively in human affairs—not just to shape or redirect them but to change them essentially—opens a new future for humanity, and whether this is thought in individual or corporate terms, with attentiveness to the personal consequences of (im)moral behavior or to the promises and dangers of apocalypse and millennium, it demands a very different relation also to present and past time. The present comes to be intimately connected to both the (past) incarnational moment and the salvific future this makes possible. Indeed, the present becomes a time of Christ's presence, with the church and its institutions (and particularly the Eucharist) maintaining the real bodily and spiritual presence of the divine in the world. And there come to be, in essence, two quite different sorts of past time: the first, the everyday past of living human beings, a past lived within the present time instituted by the

1

incarnation; but the second, a past truly past, the past of life before the incarnation, standing outside the framework of a properly Christian history.

Such a restructuring of time was commonplace for believing medieval Christians, established, early on and influentially, in Augustine's conceptualization of history as a sequence of seven days or ages. The sixth of these, initiated by Christ, is the time of the Christian present, containing all of Christian history until the end of time, the seventh day when "God will rest...and cause us, who are the seventh day, to find our rest in him."[1] The current, sixth, age, an ongoing present not to end until the world itself is ready to end, provides a premonition of future timelessness; indeed, for Augustine, during this present age "carnal man," having experienced the coming of Christ, now begins to realize his "spiritual" potential. If postincarnational history thus becomes a single, uninterrupted era of the present awaiting its future, the preincarnational becomes the realm of history proper; divided into five discrete ages, this is a realm of change and diversity, of the this-worldly ("carnal") existence that was the only possibility before the ("spiritual") potentials of the future were opened up by Christ, and it is a realm that, with the incarnation, is definitively made past.

Of course, other temporalities than this official Christian one were powerfully at play in the Middle Ages.[2] Despite the idea that the present was one continuous age—in Lee Patterson's words, "a vacant and meaningless period of time about which nothing useful can be said"[3]—events and changes *were* felt to occur. Classical literature and the historical models (both linear and cyclical) that it provided the Middle Ages were influential alternatives to an "Augustinian [historiographical] severity."[4] Other exegetical readings of history than Augustine's, particularly apocalyptic ones, "both expanded and redirected the previously definitive view of Augustine," and enabled the elaboration of alternative historical models.[5] Further, a cyclical, seasonal temporality governed much of the activity of everyday life. Still, the reorganization of history around the incarnational moment was immensely influential, and, as I will suggest here, not least in its shaping of Christian-Jewish relations.

Jews are positioned differently from any other group in relation to Christian history. As the direct precursor of Christianity, Judaism is precisely that which Christian history needs to move beyond. Indeed, the Christian incarnational reorganization of history, in working to make fully *past* that which precedes the rupture of the incarnation, operates efficiently to put Judaism to rest, to kill it off (at least, but not only, phantasmatically) and thus to make way for the new, Christian dispensation. Such an impulse is already at work in the Gospels, with their nascent (and immensely influential) typological understanding of Hebrew scripture. Pauline formulations of a "faith" that makes "the law" unnecessary, of a "carnal" and "literal" understanding superseded by the "spiritual," of an "old man" replaced by a "new," of "death" giving way to "life" definitively write Jewish law, Jewish understanding, Jewish being as the past, as an inflexible, literal-minded legalism made unnecessary by the new belief, as a blindness stubbornly resistant to spiritual enlightenment, as an immersion in the body that blocks access to salvation, as death—all ideas crucial for dominant Christian theology, and reverberating strongly in anti-Jewish polemic of the Middle Ages (and beyond).[6] (We have seen above, in the elaborate late medieval typologies of the living cross, the longevity—and capacity for innovative renewal—of such tropes.) The Christian exegetical apparatuses founded in Pauline doctrine—both simple typology and more complex, multitiered systems of allegoresis—work to rewrite all of biblical history before Christ as literally dead, significant only as it points toward the incarnational narrative that remakes all of history, or as it comments on the soul's present relation to Christ, or as it gestures toward the living history of the church's triumph in the world.[7] Significantly, Augustine's historical schema of seven ages is itself an allegorical one that transforms the letter of Genesis, the creation in seven days, into a history that reveals its goal in Christ and the post-incarnational movement to an end-time.

Christianity thus claims to recognize a new and universal structure of time instituted by the incarnation, and it claims for itself a similar universality: not just one alternative to other systems of belief, it effects a universal reorganization of human life. It is the truth breaking into a history that until then contained only glimpses of truth—that is, glimpses of the Christian dispensation to come. And that now-finished history is largely identified with Judaism. In making such claims, of course, Christianity has to address the problem of Christ's historical Jewishness, and it does so with a bold denial: Christ is presented as "divine and *human*," not as divine and *a male Jew* (as might still be read, for instance, from Matthew's account of his life). As archetypal human being, attached to all human beings, Christ supersedes his own Jewishness, and while, in relation to the "Gentiles," universalizing Christ in this way operates as a gesture of embrace, the gesture, in relation to those Jews who, after Christ, remain Jewish, is rather one of refusal and rejection.[8] Indeed, after Christ, to be properly human, to participate in Christ's powerful conflation of divinity and "humanity," to live in a present of Christ's presence, one needs specifically *not* to be Jewish, no longer to subscribe to an "old," preincarnational system, as Christ opens up for the "human" a future not before possible. To be Jewish after the incarnation is precisely not to be "human" in the ways enabled by Christ, not to participate in the dispensation of the "spirit," not to have access to the future of salvation.

The thoroughness with which Jews are repositioned by the new Christian understanding of history is made especially visible in allegorical readings that invert the biblical text's literal opposition between Jewish believers and non-Jewish unbelievers to make the believers Christian types and the unbelievers Jewish infidels.[9] I cite here just one instance, from a letter written (ca. 1040–41) by Peter Damian against "the madness of Jewish depravity and all their garrulous fabrications."[10] Addressing a "contentious Jew"[11] in order to provide "evidence for the coming of Christ,"[12] Peter presents his reading of Obadiah 18, "the house of Jacob shall be a fire, and the house of Joseph a flame; the house of Esau stubble":[13] "What is meant by the house of Jacob and Joseph but the Church of Christ? What should be understood by the house of Esau if not infidel people?"[14] Such a reading violently alienates postincarnational Jews from their sacred history, repositioning them with "infidel people" and claiming the faithful Jews of biblical tradition not for a history of Judaism but for the present time of the "Church of Christ." In such formulations, the "true Israel," *verus Israel,* becomes not the historical (Jewish) Israel, but its Christian successor.[15]

Jews, Jewishness, and Judaism, however, were not to be so easily put to rest.[16] Some Jews, of course, had refused, and continued to refuse, the "new" dispensation; Jewish communities existed alongside and within Christian communities throughout the Middle Ages, though the attempt to identify Judaism as past history was echoed in actions—forced conversions, expulsions, and massacres—intended to eliminate real Jews from the present moment. Still, majority Christian communities and institutions had to make pragmatic decisions about how to deal with Jews, and the decisions made were variously tolerant, neutral, full of hatred. The variation in Christian treatments of Jews needs to be analyzed carefully in relation to economic conditions and class divisions, tensions between secular and religious institutions, the perceived and real instabilities of Christian hegemony, the presence of Islam, "heresies," and native "pagan" traditions alongside Christianity and Judaism.[17] Here, though, I want to suggest that, despite the historical vicissitudes, and in addition to any pragmatic pressures toward or away from Christian tolerance of Jews, there was, in the basic structure of Christianity's self-definition in relation to Judaism, a strong ambivalence.[18] Despite all the pressure to disavow, indeed destroy, Judaism, Christianity also expressed a certain need to preserve Jews.

Paradoxically, this ambivalence arose from the very restructuring of history that worked to accomplish the supersession of Judaism. The argument that the incarnation marked a definitive new beginning could not be validated except in relation to certain prior claims about God's relation to humanity, and, for a Christianity that arose from Judaism, these were the claims of Jewish scripture. The self-presentation of Christianity as universal thus paradoxically relied upon the specificity of its relationship to an ancestral Judaism understood as having (if only "darkly") recognized what would be revealed with Christ's coming. Typological and allegorical readings dealt with this dependence upon Judaism by denying "true" Jewishness (that is, chosenness) to Jews; after the incarnation, this quality passed to Christians. Even so, the definition of Christianness remained dependent upon Jewishness: witness the repeated reiteration and continual development of "Old Testament" exegesis.

The actual survival of Jews complicated matters further, giving the lie to claims of their pastness, and Christian ideology developed a complex rationale that simultaneously justified Jewish survival and reaffirmed Jewish obsoleteness. It is significantly Augustine, the prime theorist of the new Christian history, who most influentially states this rationale in a double formulation that reflects the double sense of the past chosenness and present obsoleteness of Jews. On the one hand, "dispersed among all nations, in whatever direction the Christian Church spreads," Jews, "in spite of themselves," give testimony to Christian truth, "by their possession and preservation of those books" of scripture "bear[ing] witness for us that we have not fabricated the prophecies about Christ."[19] Here, Jews act as the present spokespeople for their ancestors, important for their relation to the past rather than for their own present being. In addition, however, the present condition of Jews is significant, but only as it demonstrates their true pastness, their absenting from salvific history. The divine punishment, the exile and subjugation Jews are thought to suffer because of their rejection of Christ, is read as testimony to Christian truth and Jewish error: "if they had not sinned against God by turning aside to the worship of strange gods and of idols, seduced by impious superstition as if by magic arts, if they had not finally sinned by putting Christ to death, they would have continued in possession of the same realm, a realm exceeding others in happiness, if not in extent."[20] Surviving Jews thus testify not only to the scriptural basis for Christian revelation but also to the very supersession of Judaism that survival might rather be thought to belie. This is true, too, of the role Jews are expected to have in the future, when, upon Elijah's arrival, they will have "their hearts turned by conversion."[21] The final conversion—that is, the final historical supersession—of the Jews will mark the salvific end that the incarnation has instituted if only to defer, even as it has deinstituted Judaism only to defer its final demise.

This Christian reorganization of history has had remarkable staying power—though of course its deployment in various historical circumstances has functioned in markedly different ways. We might see its most devastating recent effects in largely secularized nineteenth- and twentieth-century moves to exclude Christianity's predecessor from "modernity," which functioned, most virulently, by identifying Jews and Jewishness with racial "degenerescence," thus justifying ("eugenic") attempts to exterminate Jews altogether.[22] Marc Chagall's *White Crucifixion* of 1938 (Figure 2) gains its power at least in part by intervening in such ultimately Christian constructions of supersession. Chagall draws here on medieval and early modern traditions of representing the crucifixion, some of which—for example, the "living cross" examined above—actively show the crucifixion as the moment of Synagoga's destruction, the moment when Jews and Judaism are expelled from history.[23] In his revision of such representations, Chagall outrageously claims Jesus for Judaism—making Jesus's loincloth the fringed tallith (prayer shawl) of Jewish tradition, and surmounting the crucified figure not only with the traditional I.N.R.I. (see John 19:19: "Iesus Nazarenus rex Iudaeorum") but also with its Hebrew or Aramaic "original," "Jesus of Nazareth, king of the Jews." In so doing, Chagall rewrites the moment that institutes Christianity as a religion of supersession as precisely a moment of Judaism's continuation and continuity.[24] The past of the so-called Old Testa-

Figure 2. Marc Chagall (French, born Russia, 1887–1985), *White Crucifixion*, 1938. Oil on canvas, 154.3 x 139.7 cm. Gift of Alfred S. Alschuler to the Art Institute of Chicago. Item no. 1946.925. Reproduction courtesy of the Art Institute of Chicago. Copyright 2004 Artist Rights Society (ARS), New York / ADAGP, Paris. Reproduced with permission.

ment, as both Jesus's past and the past of the besieged shtetls of 1938, is evoked throughout the painting—in the tablets of the law that surmount the burning synagogue; in the Torah preserved (in the foreground, by the figure who moves toward the left), and in the Torah attacked, taken from the holy ark in the burning synagogue by a "brownshirt trooper,"[25] and dashed to the ground at bottom right. Yet that last Torah emanates something powerful—fire? smoke? incense?—even from its forbidden position on the ground. And what it emanates leads to Jacob's ladder, which, rather than reveal "angels of God ascending and descending" (Genesis 28:12), leads to the cross and to the strong swath of white light that cuts diagonally across the picture and connects the besieged ground of the town turned upside down, burning, destroyed, and of the ship filled with dismayed escapees, to an unseen heaven. Perhaps this band of light suggests some divine force that oversees and organizes the scene of horror, but the sole visible occupants of heaven here are a hovering group of contemporary Jews, perhaps the souls of the dead,[26] who seem as dismayed by what they witness as the fleeing, disoriented figures in the foreground. This hovering group replaces the traditional mourners at the foot of the cross—the figures actually near the base of the cross all move away from it, too immersed in their own small piece of the catastrophe to survey the wider scene around them—but these distressed, floating spirits mourn a whole complex scene of which the crucifixion is but one, if a central, element. That scene includes synchronously the Torah, Jesus, and contemporary, twentieth-century Jewish communities and Jews—the figure in the left foreground originally wore a sign that read "Ich bin ein Jude" [I am a Jew], which Chagall later removed as too explicit[27]—all under attack, framed menacingly by Soviet and Nazi armies (marked by their respective flags to the left and the right)[28] but also, in the center foreground, by an unextinguished menorah, an undying Judaism. An unambiguously Jewish past, that of the Torah; a past usually identified with the beginning of Christianity, that of the crucifixion; and a threatened Judaism of the present all participate in a staying Jewish that is not the stagnant removal from change constructed for Jews and Judaism by medieval Christianity, but a wrapped-upness in change. The fleshly, passionate bodiliness claimed by Christianity for itself—the power of an incarnation, of a suffering that might transform the world and history—is here remade as Jewish. A Jewish past, both the "Old Testament" and Jesus, that has been taken away from Jews is here revivified, reawakened *as* Jewish, to be activated in a situation of present distress.

SPECTERS OF JUDAISM

Haunting belongs to the structure of every
hegemony.
    —Jacques Derrida, *Specters of Marx,* 37

A recurring pattern in the history of the West is the declaration of a historical end that then, as it turns out, is not quite at hand. We are at such a moment presently, with the "end of philosophy," the "end of science," the "end of Marxism/communism/socialism," and the "end of history" all having been recently declared. Jacques Derrida, in *Specters of Marx: The State of the Debt, the Work of Mourning, and the New International*, presents an extended reflection on this present historical moment, and I believe that his thinking is useful as well for an analysis of the temporality of medieval Christian-Jewish relations. The terms of Derrida's own argument suggest that this might be so. In discussing Francis Fukuyama's *The End of History and the Last Man*, he calls attention to the book's status as "a gospel" and as "neo-testamentary,"[29] and he notes that Fukuyama claims to bring "good news" (57, 59–60) that, like the Gospel announcements of a new dispensation, proclaims a new structure of history; indeed, Derrida reads "This end of History" as "essentially a Christian eschatology" (60).

Derrida recognizes in the proclamation of such an end—and, by implication, in all "gospels"—a statement that performs the end that it claims to describe. That is, Fukuyama's announcement of the "end of history," the fall of Marxism and the triumph of liberal democracy, rather than being a constative speech act is a "performative interpretation . . . that transforms the very thing it interprets" (51).[30] Not primarily a response to the perception of Marxism's demise, such an announcement is rather a wishful movement toward that demise, and a movement that arises precisely because Marxism is felt—despite its "defeat"—to be still a threatening presence, still in historical play: "At a time when a new world disorder is attempting to install its neo-capitalism and neo-liberalism, no disavowal has managed to rid itself of all of Marx's ghosts" (*Specters*, 37). For Derrida, indeed, it is a sense of open-endedness, of time's unpredictable movements, of a present that is not simply self-present but rather "unhinged" and "out of joint" (17–29)—open to the insistent demands of the past and the future—that calls forth such (wishful) "descriptions" (performances) of the end. The moment when a certain historical trajectory of Marxism seems to have run its course suggests to Derrida not the death of Marxism but the renewed need to ask what might remain of the radical potential of a particular movement for social, political, and economic justice, and it is fear of the possible responses to such a question that motivates the impulse to put Marxism altogether to rest.

Another way of looking at it, and one that approaches more closely to the significance for Derrida of *specters*, would be to see Marxism—though pushed aside after the demise of Eastern European communism—as still *spectrally* present in the form of certain unfulfilled (economic, social, and political) promises. Or more accurately, since the specter is for Derrida precisely that which is *not* present, Marxism and its unfulfilled potentials "haunt" the present moment as a call from the past heard in the present and demanding a radically different kind of future (and thus also a radically different kind of present). It is this spectral disturbance of present security that performative claims of "the end" like Fukuyama's serve to deny and allay.

But for Derrida the "conjuring" of the specter—the performative attempt to put it to rest—is always ambivalent. As he points out, "conjuration" evokes a complex set of meanings: (1a) "the conspiracy (*Verschwörung* in German) of those who promise solemnly, sometimes secretly, by swearing together an oath (*Schwur*) to struggle against a superior power" (40); (1b) "the magical incantation destined to *evoke*, to bring forth with the voice, to *convoke* a charm or a spirit" (41); and (2) "'conjurement' (*Beschwörung*), namely the magical exorcism that, on the contrary, tends to expulse the evil spirit which would have been called up or convoked (OED: 'the exorcising of spirits by invocation,' 'the exercise of magical or occult influence')" (47).[31] The attempt to "conjure away," while it claims the death of the specter, always admits at the same time its continued existence, as a threat that *needs* to be exorcised, maintaining it in relation to the present even as it claims to put it to rest:

> Since such a conjuration today insists, in such a deafening consensus, that what is, it says, indeed dead, remain dead indeed, it arouses a suspicion. It awakens us where it would like to put us to sleep. Vigilance, therefore: the cadaver is perhaps not as dead, as simply dead as the conjuration tries to delude us into believing. The one who has disappeared appears still to be *there*, and his apparition is not nothing. It does not do nothing. (*Specters*, 97)[32]

The pertinence of Derrida's analysis for thinking the peculiar operations of temporality in medieval Christianity's definition of its relation to Judaism, I hope, begins to become clear. This analysis first of all calls our attention to the *performative* work of Christian historical thinking: though Judaism survives, the new temporal scheme that Christianity puts in place attempts to settle it as past, "conjure" it away, provide it once and for all with its "death certificate" (48). But the very act of conjuration

suggests that the hoped-for effect of the performative does not in fact
pertain, that Jews and Judaism are not fully past, but rather still disturbing and disruptive—"haunting"—enough to Christianity's sense of its
own hegemony to necessitate the act of conjuration. The "conjuration,"
as "the conspiracy...of those who promise solemnly...to struggle
against a superior power" (40), serves to reinforce a sense of Christian
unity over against its religious opponent, but only at the expense of
admitting the continued power of the opponent that is, in this very act,
declared dead. That is, the attempt to conjure Jews away also serves to
conjure them up, into a certain presence: defining Jews as past involves
simultaneously recognizing their (ongoing) role as Christianity's ancestor and (oedipal?) competitor.

Like any ancestor, Judaism provides Christianity with an inheritance,
which is always, Derrida suggests, spectral (not of the present, but influencing, appearing in, the present, demanding some present response)
and "heterogeneous" (resisting in its complexity any reductive response):
"If the readability of a legacy were given, natural, transparent, univocal,
if it did not call for and at the same time defy interpretation, we would
never have anything to inherit from it. We would be affected by it as by a
cause—natural or genetic. One always inherits from a secret—which
says 'read me, will you ever be able to do so?'" (16). If Christianity works
radically to reduce the "heterogeneity" of Judaism, to claim for itself the
one proper "reading" of the Jewish "legacy," and a reading that denies
validity to Jewish readings, the felt necessity of keeping Judaism and
Jews in play, to provide testimony both through the divine punishment
they are believed to be undergoing and through their preservation of
Hebrew scriptures, allows for a Jewish presence that is spectral—con-
signed to a time other than the present and yet "haunting" the present,
disrupting its "identity to itself" (xx) by bringing the past to bear on it,
and thus also suggesting, despite the insistences of Christian eschatological thinking, a future different from that securely predicted.

An admitted danger of emphasizing spectrality in our consideration of Christian-Jewish relations is that it potentially replicates the tendency of medieval Christianity (and of traditional medievalist historicism) to deny the significance of Jews and Jewish communities in their
own right. Medieval Jews are significant not only for the roles they play
in Christian self-constructions. They have a real presence and at least
some agency within Western Europe. Subject to economic, political, and

social pressures and violences, they also potentially intervene against these, shaping their lives in ways that might be disallowed by a dominant Christian culture. Still, I will insist on the usefulness of thinking the spectrality of medieval Jews and Judaism, not because this reveals everything about their relationship to Christianity and Christians—of course, it does not—but because it enables a reading of some of the complexities of that relationship, including the effects that the construction of Jews as spectral might have upon Jews as real corporeal and social presences. Such effects include both the deadly work that a culture performs upon its spectral others (not just ideological disavowal but real violence) and a space for survival and resistance that spectrality, in its ambivalence as both the disavowed and the inherited, both the absent and the present, both the bodiless and the embodied, might open up—a space, for instance, in which medieval Jews might make certain claims for their own priority and for the significance of their traditions. The specter shares this ambivalence with such other disavowed, (anti)-social categories as the polluting and the queer. In Mary Douglas's influential formulation, even while polluting entities, entities thought to disrupt social-cultural order, are met with attempts at purification and extirpation, the place of the polluted remains the place of a certain power, engendering a "danger" for hegemony.[33] Similarly, as Judith Butler suggests, "the construction of the human" operates to produce a queer "outside," "the inhuman, the humanly unthinkable," "refused the possibility of cultural articulation." But the queer space thus created is not an "absolute 'outside'"; it stands instead in a constitutive relationship to the culturally intelligible: "These excluded sites come to bound the 'human' as its constitutive outside, and to haunt those boundaries as the persistent possibility of their disruption and rearticulation."[34] As we analyze the processes by which pollution and the queer are put to rest, and specters conjured away, we must not forget to examine how occupying the space of danger or the time of the specter might also present some real, if difficult and dangerous, opportunities for disruption, rearticulation, and resistance.

Derrida's analysis and models like Douglas's and Butler's in fact help elucidate not just the general structure of medieval Christian thinking about the historicity of Jews but also more specific, historically particular aspects of Christian-Jewish relations, and I will be considering these in some detail in the following chapters. Thus, one crucial site for the elaboration of a Christian sense of Jewish otherness is, as I have argued elsewhere and will develop more fully below, the Jewish body—seen as deficient and excessive, fragmented and porous, dirty, bloody, excremental.[35] Judaism, as (from the Christian perspective) a religion dependent upon corporeal, rather than spiritual, understanding, comes to be identified with bodiliness, and with a bodiliness seen as particularly debased—disintegrating, but also threatening the integrity of other (Christian) bodies. Though embodiment might be thought to be the opposite of spectrality, medieval Christian attention to the Jewish body stands in a significant relationship to the spectral in Christian constructions of Jewish otherness. In order to affirm Christianity's definitive, spiritual turn away from materiality, mere corporeality—a turn that, of course, paradoxically involves a theology of incarnation[36]—the dead body of the Jews is summoned up as an absolute other, a body that must be once and for all buried. And Christian polemical texts indeed often conjure up this body in all its deficient-excessive physicality. But in being summoned up for burial, Jewish corporeality is also paradoxically preserved and invested with a transgressive, polluting power. In Derrida's terms, conjuring up and conjuring away are here inseparable.

In one of the most common genres of medieval interreligious polemic, the Christian-Jewish debate, the Jewish body is conjured up primarily through the voice of a Jewish spokesman whose positions are evoked in order to be put to rest. While the claim of the dialogue form is that Jewish and Christian disputants are given equal opportunities to make their case, in such Christian-authored works of debate, Jewish positions are given expression largely as questions about or objections to Christian doctrine that the Christian author or interlocutor can easily dismiss. Thus, for instance, the "dialogue" in Peter Damian's letter consists of brief, formulaic "Jewish" questions to which Peter gives much fuller responses in his own voice. The Jewish spokesman (of course, a creation of Peter's) has no opportunity for rebuttal.[37]

The conjuring up of Jews in such a work thus serves mainly to conjure them away. But, as Derrida's analysis emphasizes, the need to conjure specters away belies the claim of their death—challenging, in this case, the Christian ideology of Jewish pastness. Clearly, Christian authors who imagine Jews in debate with Christians still feel that the "superseded" ancestral religion represents a threat that must be grappled with. When Peter Damian first presents himself as having been asked by his correspondent Honestus to provide "something . . . to use in silencing, with reasoned arguments, the Jews,"[38] Peter begins to beg off, suggesting that Judaism does not provide any real challenge for Christian doctrine and that it would be more profitable for the individual Christian to look inward, to his own moral state, than to take on a debate with Judaism: "if you wish to be a knight of Christ and to fight manfully for him, as a renowned warrior take up arms against the vices of the flesh, against the stratagems of the devil, enemies, indeed, who never die, rather than against the Jews who now have been almost exterminated from the face of the earth."[39] Peter here clearly expresses the idea of Jewish pastness, but he immediately rethinks this position, recasting the "almost exterminated" Jews as in fact capable of disturbing the very foundations of Christian faith:

> Surely it is disgraceful for a man of the Church to hold his tongue out of ignorance when those outside the fold set things in a false light, and that a Christian incapable of giving an account of Christ should retreat, conquered and ashamed, as his enemies vaunt over him. One may add, that often harmful ineptitude and dangerous simplicity in such matters not only excite boldness in the unbelieving, but also beget error and doubt in the hearts of the faithful.
>
> And since certainly this knowledge relates totally to the faith, and faith is undoubtedly the foundation of all virtues, when the foundation is shaken, the whole structure of the building soon threatens to fall into ruin.[40]

To resettle this "foundation," to secure a place where believing Christians can stand firm in their belief, the threat posed by Jewishness, at first disavowed, must be acknowledged and ultimately put to rest, and this becomes the project of Peter's letter.

The structure of Peter's anti-Jewish letter itself reiterates the explicit ambivalence with which it thus opens. Having promised to provide "a few, clear statements of the prophets" by which Honestus might "win a victory over all the madness of Jewish depravity and all their garrulous fabrications," Peter introduces a Jewish presence as the object of his discourse, as its "target": "since an arrow is shot more accurately if first the target which it must pierce is set up for us to hit, I here bring on this contentious Jew, that the shafts of my words put into the air may not fly aimlessly, but in a well-aimed barrage, may rather reach the specified objective."⁴¹ Jewish presence structures the polemic, providing it with its "aim," and from here Peter directly addresses his arguments to the conjured-up Jewish persona:

> What do you have to say to that, Jew? By what shameless daring can you avoid such obvious, such divine statements? Even allowing what you blasphemously say, that Christ could invent lies about himself, if he were not God, would he be able to prophesy about himself through the lips of others before he was born? I would also like to hear how you interpret this verse: "My heart has uttered a good word, I speak of my works to the king" [Psalm 44:2].⁴² Who is this king to whom God speaks of his works? Perhaps you will tell me: "David." But read through the rest of the psalm and understand its true meaning. Continue on a little, and do not ask me, but ask the Lord himself who this king is to whom he speaks of his works. Listen to what God himself says to this king.⁴³

But while the Jew is thus insistently called upon to speak—and while Peter imagines his possible statements, even citing him here as having "blasphemously" spoken—through the whole course of this section of Peter's letter, the Jew is kept in silence. Only after Peter has essentially concluded his argument and can exhort his Jewish "interlocutor" to admit the truth of what has been proven—"Obviously, for anyone who still needs evidence after such enlightening testimony, it remains for him to request a lighted lamp to view the radiant sun at noontime. With the vision of so many heavenly stars sparkling before you, Jew, I marvel how such deep shades of blindness can hold sway, even in eyes that are totally without sight"⁴⁴—does Peter have the Jew speak in "his own" voice. The "dialogue" that ensues is thus not only one-sided but belated, occurring after the truth of Christian positions has already been "demonstrated." Further, Peter's introduction of the discussion limits it to a narrow range of material, and makes clear that its outcome is decided in advance: "now let us have a brief discourse in dialogue form, using questions and answers, on certain ceremonies about which you often inquire in great detail, and in your wordy circumlocutions bring suit in these matters; so that when all shall be to your satisfaction, you will be compelled either to agree that you have lost, or to depart in confusion because of your shameful disbelief."⁴⁵

Peter thus delimits Jewish presence and speech so that these will present no threat to Christian truths. Still, the Jewish figure remains potentially disruptive to the security and self-enclosure of Christian arguments, as the very reluctance to give him voice suggests. Even after he has successfully answered all the Jew's questions, Peter does not close his letter but feels the need to re-present the Christian argument: "But now, Jew, after such a cloud of witnesses I will compose a peroration for you. Beginning with the coming of the humanity of Christ and proceeding through the passage of time until its end, I will place before your eyes, if you are up to it, the evidence of the prophets, that you may view in summary, as it were, and in one glance everything that you saw me discussing above in a diffuse and scattered way."[46] And even after the completion of this scriptural summary (which as it recurs to the preincarnational moment of the prophets makes that moment significant only as it relates to a "passage of time" that begins with "the coming of the humanity of Christ"), Peter is not finished, but insists on presenting a further argument "from reason,"[47] which he then follows with an exhortation to the Jew, urging his conversion, his movement, that is, out of the anachronistic position of being a Jew in a present defined as essentially Christian.[48]

The Jew's words—though few and unpersuasive—are thus carefully cordoned off, presented in such a controlled manner that their potential disruptiveness is especially emphasized. Indeed, not even Peter's exhortation to the Jew sufficiently concludes the work. Peter finally abandons his address to the Jew and speaks once again to the Christian Honestus, stressing the polemical use-value of the letter and particularly of the Jew's "contribution" to it:

> in placing before you almost bare texts from Scripture, I have sent you, as it were, a bundle of arrows for your quiver. And since from the words of your opponent a good opportunity of replying is provided, I have indeed supplied the weapons. But since the contest is not imminent, I was unable to instruct you fully as to where, when unscathed, you should let loose, and where you should protect yourself with your shield. But you have at your disposal all that is necessary for such an engagement. Use the means before you as you shall judge expedient.[49]

Though Peter's letter presents "weapons" for use against the Jews, and though the Jewish figure's words are necessary for learning how to use those weapons, Jewish statements here are also explicitly recognized as dangerous, sometimes necessitating a "shield." And Peter's final words to Honestus take the form of a prayer—"Dear brother, may almighty God in his mercy protect you from the hidden snares of the enemy and bring you safely through the battles of this world to his heavenly kingdom. Amen"[50]—which, though conventional in its call for divine protection, also specifically evokes a Jewish presence engaged in "battle" with Christianity. No matter that the Jews have been "almost exterminated," that Peter carefully orchestrates their representation and speech, that they are repeatedly conjured away: as soon as they are conjured into the letter, they intrude (in Peter's Christian imagination) in ways that may not be wholly predicted or controlled.

I do not mean to suggest that works like Peter's letter open up for their readers the possibility of seeing Jews in positive terms; clearly, this is not the case. The Jew remains a specter that must be put to rest, a polluting presence whose only hope for survival is conversion—that is, a survival gained through self-erasure. But the representation of Jews here and in similar works does emphasize the anxiety provoked by Jewish presences—even unreal ones created in Christian texts and therefore under tight ideological control.

SPECTRALITY AND CONVERSION

> *Ego = ghost. Therefore "I am" would mean*
> *"I am haunted": I am haunted by myself*
> *who am (haunted by myself who am haunted*
> *by myself who am . . . and so forth).*
> —Jacques Derrida, *Specters of Marx*, 133

So far, I have mostly focused attention on the ways in which the larger historical, ideological, and social dynamics of medieval Christian-Jewish relations may be understood as "spectral," but I also want to suggest here that spectrality might be a useful way of reading psychic as well as social phenomena. Derrida's formulation in *Specters of Marx* relies, after all, on Freud as well as Marx, and particularly on Freud's analysis of "the work of mourning." Freud suggests that the formation of the ego involves a double movement of loss and preservation:

> [W]e have come to understand that this kind of substitution [of an object-cathexis by an identification] has a great share in determining the form taken on by the ego and that it contributes materially towards building up what is called its "character." . . . When it happens that a person has to give up a sexual object, there quite often ensues a modification in his ego which can only be described as a reinstatement of the object within the ego, as it occurs in melancholia. . . . [T]he process, especially in the early phases of development, is a very frequent one, and it points to the conclusion that the character of the ego is a precipitate of abandoned object-cathexes and that it contains a record of past object-choices.[51]

Derrida's reading of the ambivalent operations of spectrality—of the heir's reception of an inheritance that may be repudiated but still insists on being taken up—and my own reading of Christianity's self-positioning vis-à-vis its ancestor describe similar movements: the "triumphant mourning" for an ancestor (and rival) that results not just in putting it to rest but in making it (if only *as* repudiated) always integral to the self.

Given such an understanding of medieval interreligious relations, it is not surprising that the figure of the convert—both the Jewish convert to Christianity (who, from a Christian perspective, recognizes an emptiness in his native tradition that leads to its repudiation) and the Christian convert to Judaism (who, again to a Christian cast of mind, would wrongly revivify what has been identified as dead)—should be a particularly salient one for Christian self-definitions. (I turn to a fuller consideration of the dynamics of conversion in chapters 3, 4, and 5 below.) And in the literature of conversion we can see operating intrapsychically the kinds of spectral movements that characterize the larger social relations of Judaism and Christianity. Thus, for instance, while Hermann of Cologne, in recounting his conversion, constructs a linear narrative of supersession—tracing step by step his attraction to Christianity, his training in Christian modes of reading, his recognition of Jewish errors, all leading to a moment of enlightenment after which Hermann can never turn back to his originary Jewishness—he also makes his account oddly circular, beginning and ending it with a dream that he had before his first encounter with Christianity.[52] On the one hand, that dream serves to reconfirm the linearity of the movement away from

Judaism: Hermann shows, in retrospect, that the "material" (Jewish) interpretation originally given the dream was erroneous and that in fact it predicted the "spiritual" movement of his conversion. But the return to the dream also emphasizes the ways in which Hermann's new Christian identity continues to depend upon his original Jewish status. As convert, he is always defined by Jewishness, even after this is definitively given up, a fact that the opening of Hermann's autobiography makes clear in how it names its author-subject: "I, a sinner and unworthy priest, Hermann, once called Judah, of the Israelite people, the tribe of Levi, born of my father David and mother Sephora in the city of Cologne."[53]

Perhaps unsurprisingly, then, considering the complex depiction of converted identity in even such an orthodox Christian apologist as Hermann of Cologne, the convert from Judaism to Christianity him- or herself becomes a particularly vexed figure for medieval Christianity. Emphasizing on the one hand the triumph of Christian truth, anticipating that moment when, approaching the end-time, all Jews will see the light and convert, Jewish conversion also calls to mind, perhaps too keenly, the Jewish origin not just of the individual convert but of Christianity itself. Replicating the triumphal movement of Christian revelation, individual conversion also calls up the specters of Jewish identity that, declared dead, nonetheless continue to haunt Christian self-definitions, as excluded from but still necessary to them. Dramatizing the movement from Judaism to Christianity, the figure of the convert nonetheless also calls forth anxiety about the possibility of the reverse movement, a "relapse" to Judaism that was, in fact, forbidden, sometimes on pain of death, to converts.[54]

APPARITIONALITY AND IDENTITY

> Upon waking next morning about daylight,
> I found Queequeg's arm thrown over me in
> the most loving and affectionate manner.
> You had almost thought I had been his wife.
> —Herman Melville, *Moby Dick*, 32

My discussion of spectrality here has focused on questions of religious identity, but I want, in conclusion, to suggest that a similar sort of analysis might be useful for thinking about other medieval identity categories and how these intersect with religious self-definition. (I turn to a fuller consideration of identity and "intersectionality" in chapter 3 below.) The Freudian theory, with its emphasis on lost "sexual objects," is of course most directly pertinent to thinking about the development of gender and sexuality. Recently, indeed, Judith Butler has explored the ways in which Freud's work on mourning and melancholia might be used to develop a model of "gender as a kind of melancholy, or as one of melancholy's effects."[55] Moreover, in a treatment that does not make use of Derrida's analysis of specters but that in many ways complements that analysis (and that is itself indebted to Freud), Terry Castle has identified a tradition, stretching from the eighteenth century to the present, of "apparitional" representations of lesbians. In Castle's reading, lesbian "apparitionality" displays an ambivalence much like that of Derridean spectrality:

> [T]he apparitional figure seemed to obliterate, through a single vaporizing gesture, the disturbing carnality of lesbian love. It made of such love—literally—a phantasm: an ineffable anticoupling between "women" who weren't there.
>   —Or did it? As I have tried to intimate, the case could be made that the metaphor meant to derealize lesbian desire in fact did just the opposite. Indeed, strictly for repressive purposes, one could hardly think of a *worse* metaphor. For embedded in the ghostly figure, as even its first proponents seemed at times to realize, was inevitably a notion of reembodiment: of uncanny return to the flesh.... To become an apparition was also to become endlessly capable of "appearing." And once there, the specter, like a living being, was not so easily gotten rid of.[56]

Recognizing Castle's insistence that this specific tradition of lesbian representation be treated as important on its own and not dissolved into "queer" or "gay male" constructions, one might still argue that this tradition takes its place alongside other traditions of representing "otherness" to which notions of spectrality or apparitionality are central.

In a later period than the medieval, it is clear that spectral figures might condense several different aspects of identity—gender, sexuality, race, religion—focusing attention particularly on their ambivalences and instabilities. In "The Counterpane" chapter of *Moby Dick* when Ishmael awakens to find "Queequeg's arm thrown over" him, questions about gender, sexual, and racial identity are all in play. Queequeg, after all, has just been identified as a "cannibal," if a "clean, comely looking" one,[57] and the situation in which Ishmael finds himself leads him to express anxieties about gender and sexual identity, expostulating "upon the unbecomingness of [Queequeg's] hugging a fellow male in that matrimonial sort of style" (33–34). Strikingly, Ishmael's position here evokes for him "a somewhat similar" childhood "circumstance" that seems, if in largely undefined ways, crucial to Ishmael's sense of self. Sent to bed early by his stepmother as a punishment, he slips into "a troubled nightmare of a doze," and then,

> slowly waking from it—half steeped in dreams—I opened my eyes, and the before sunlit room was now wrapped in outer darkness. Instantly I felt a shock running through all my frame; nothing was to be seen, and nothing was to be heard; but a supernatural hand seemed placed in mine. My arm hung over the counterpane, and the nameless, unimaginable, silent form or phantom, to which the hand belonged, seemed closely seated by my bedside. For what seemed ages piled on ages, I lay there, frozen with the most awful fears, not daring to drag away my hand; yet ever thinking that if I could but stir it one single inch, the horrid spell would be broken. I knew not how this consciousness at last glided away from me; but waking in the morning, I shudderingly remembered it all, and for days and weeks and months afterwards I lost myself in confounding attempts to explain the mystery. Nay, to this very hour, I often puzzle myself with it. (33)

The encounter with a racial other who also threatens the self's sense of masculinity and heterosexuality recalls, significantly, a spectral figure that the "I" still feels as "mysteriously" significant, somehow crucially relevant to the moment of gender, sexual, and racial crisis in which it finds itself. Having suggested, in this chapter, that a similar spectral figure is crucial to the definition of Judaism in its relation to medieval Christianity, I wish to suggest, in closing (and in anticipation especially of the work of chapter 3 below), that that figure might also be significant for the investigation of medieval anxieties about gender and sexuality, and in particular for thinking about how those anxieties intersect with the concerns of Christian self-definition. As I will argue below, it is clear that a medieval sense of religious identity is crucially interimplicated with gender (note, for instance, the metaphorizing of interreligious debate, in the Peter Damian text discussed above, as a contest of masculinities), with sexuality (as the discussion of Guibert of Nogent's memoirs in the next chapter will make clear), and with a category like the modern one of race (that Jews are thought to be different from Christians in the very biology of their bodies suggests at least a quasi-racial definition of Jewishness). If Jewish identity is that which is excluded from the Christian self but also that which returns in the shape of the disavowed but inescapable specter, we might expect that a similar apparitional or spectral dynamic is at work in medieval constructions of hegemonic or "proper" gender, sexuality, and race as these categories operate on their own *and* in complex intertwinings with each other and with the category of religious identity.

2

Body Effects

Individual and Community Identity in the Long Twelfth Century

*We sell cattle to Christians, we have partner-
ships with Christians, we allow ourselves to be
alone with them, we give our children to
Christian wet-nurses, and we teach Torah to
Christians—for there are now many Christian
priests who can read Hebrew books.*
    —Rabbi Yeḥiel at the Paris Disputation,
        1240 (Maccoby, *Judaism on Trial*, 32)

*Sortiarii autem et sortiarie cum detecti fuerint,
maxime autem, qui Judeos consuluerint super
vita, vel actibus sorte discutiendum; ad
episcopum destinentur, pro sue discretionis
arbitrio, puniendi. . . .*
    *Prohibemus etiam, sub interminatione
anathematis, ne mulieres Christiane pueros
nutriant Judeorum, nec habeant Judei famulos
Christianos, in eorum hospitiis pernoctantes.*
    *Prohibemus etiam, ne Christiani recipiant
pecuniam Judeorum, quasi res proprias, ut
magis salvo custodiantur, in ecclesiis
deponendas.*

When men and women magicians shall be
found, and also such as consult Jews for the
purpose of finding out by magic about their life
or actions, they shall be brought before the
bishop to be punished in accordance with his
decision. . . .

Moreover, under threat of anathema, we
prohibit Christian women to nurse Jewish boys,
and Jews to have Christian servants lodging in
their quarters.

Moreover, we forbid Christians to receive
Jewish money as if it were their own, and to
deposit it in churches for greater safety.
                              —Synod of Worcester, July 26, 1240
                                (Grayzel, *Church*, 330–31)

PARADOXICAL RELATIONS

Recent work in cultural studies has strongly called into question any
easy division of "public" and "private," "political" and "psychic" realms,
importantly adopting and furthering a feminist critique of the unexam-
ined maintenance of a distinction between the "personal" and the "political." Thus, for instance, in continuing Foucault's excavation of the
complex and often self-contradictory ways in which large social entities—regimes of sexuality—are constituted, queer theory has insisted
on the importance of "psychic" process, bringing psychoanalytic thinkers
into the Foucauldian investigation and examining how individual identity formation is implicated with the operation of larger social and cultural forces.[1] The current chapter pursues a similar approach, situating
itself at a point of intersection between "psychology" and "politics" in
order to interrogate the mutual dependence of medieval constructs of the
"personal" and "social-political." Both a society's self-constitution and an
individual sense of "self" depend upon the casting out of "others," the
definition of areas of exclusion that secure realms of inclusion.[2] Here,
I am concerned with such processes as they operate in relation to medieval religious categories, and I explore the ways in which medieval
representations of difference work both to construct a religious hege-

mony crucial to Western European hierarchical (Christian, masculinist, heterosexist) society and to secure a "self" within that larger sociopolitical structure.[3]

At the same time that it emphasizes movements between "self" and "other" as crucial to the maintenance of both an individual "I" and a corporate "we," post-structuralist thinking also undermines the security of distinctions between "self" and "other," and of such related binary oppositions as internality/externality.[4] "Selves" are secured by means of disavowals that nonetheless depend for their stability upon the very "others" disavowed. Identifications necessarily involve *counter-* and/or *dis*identifications,[5] and they rest upon previous disavowals (the disavowal, for instance, of a figure with whom a prior identification has been made) without which the self might not cohere. What is externalized as "other" may thus nonetheless be particularly intimate to the self.

We may think the complications to such binary oppositions as self/other and inside/outside through the figure of the specter: radically other to the self that experiences spectral visitation, the specter nonetheless belongs to that self *as* its visiting other, as a figure that singles it out and speaks to it, making particular and "personal" demands. It is no mistake that we find, over and over again, the language of spectrality inhabiting the post-structuralist analytics of self and other. Thus, for one of many examples in Butler: "it is not, strictly speaking, that a subject disavows its identifications, but, rather, that certain exclusions and foreclosures institute the subject and persist as the permanent or constitutive spectre of its own destabilization."[6]

Such considerations—both the questioning of firm distinctions between psyche and politics and the undermining of strict oppositions between self and other, inside and outside—are perhaps particularly poignant for the period we might call the "long" twelfth century, ca. 1050–ca. 1200, a period that has been identified in much historical work with significant changes in the status of individuality or selfhood, on the one hand, and Christian Europe's corporate sense of self, on the other. Historians have marked the twelfth century as the moment when "the individual" is discovered; with that "discovery," ideas of self and psychological process change.[7] This period sees the development of a (romance) literature increasingly focused on "individuals," the birth of "courtly love," a new technical literature of the psyche (in, for instance, treatises *de anima* [concerning the soul]), new forms of spirituality whose center

is affective response, a humanization of Jesus, and an increasing emphasis on the human figure of Mary. The century has, indeed, been
associated with the beginnings of a Christian "humanism."[8]

At the same time that the status of the person is thus changing,
there are developments within Western European Christendom that
alter and help solidify its corporate identity. By the early eleventh century, missionary work had more or less fully succeeded in converting
Northern and Western European communities to Christianity: Iceland's
conversion in 1000, after a series of tenth-century Scandinavian conversions, left only segments of Eastern and Southern Europe (the Baltic,
Southern Italy, part of Iberia) as "pagan" territory.[9] (The succeeding centuries would see Europe seeking to eradicate these remnants of "non-
belief" in a series of crusades and reconquests.) But despite the successes
of Christian expansion, or perhaps precisely because Christianity had
extended itself so successfully through much of the territory of Europe,
the late eleventh century was marked by an increasing European awareness of threats to its hegemony. While Islam stood largely outside European Christianity, the fact of its "occupation" of Jerusalem, coupled with
the sense that it might easily violate—and had in fact (in Spain, Southern France, Italy, the East) violated—the borders of Christian Europe,
made for a vivid belief in Islam's dangerous proximity. Despite its successes, then, Christendom continued to look to its borders and beyond
to secure its territorial identity, pursuing a policy of further expansion. It
was of course in 1095 that Pope Urban II began to preach the First Crusade, which led to the capture of Jerusalem in 1099 and to centuries
of continuing (successful and unsuccessful) crusading activity in the
Middle East.[10]

At this very moment of territorial consolidation, outward-looking
anxiety, and continuing drive to expansion, Western European Christianity immersed itself too in movements of *internal* reform. This was
in part an unsurprising corollary to Christian success. Insofar as conversion operated locally, if under the loose control of a central (papal)
authority, variations in local religious practice developed; different, pre-
Christian traditions (religious, social, familial, political) were differentially incorporated into the practices of the newly Christianized. As it
solidified a trans-European *Christianitas*, the church recognized the
need to consolidate and standardize local practice. Furthermore, despite
Christianity's missionary success, there was an awareness within the

church of certain continuing, and perhaps proliferating, internal failures, a sense that the church that had been so successful in persuading
outsiders to join it was nonetheless somehow lacking, corrupt, in need
of reform from within. The Gregorian reform movement of the late
eleventh century involved attempts to settle doctrinal questions (e.g.,
about the nature of the Eucharistic miracle), to redefine the relationship
between secular and ecclesiastical authority (especially as that was called
into question in the Investiture Controversy), and to codify and control
structures within both Christian society and the church itself—marriage, clerical marriage and celibacy, practices of advancement in the
church hierarchy that came to be labeled as simoniacal.[11] And the
eleventh and twelfth centuries saw an efflorescence of new spiritual,
especially monastic, movements—Cluny, Cîteaux, Xanten[12]—that took
up the spirit of reform as reform simultaneously of Christian society
and of Christian self. That these movements of internal church reform
often operated through mechanisms closely related to those by which
Christendom distinguished itself from external enemies needs emphasis: the twelfth century marked not just a gentle, spiritual Christian
introspection but an often violent identification and casting out of errors
seen as having arisen within the body of the European church. This was
the moment at which the church strongly revived, from the Christianity
of Late Antiquity, the idea that internal heresies were to be vigorously
rooted out, and the foreign Crusades against Islam were matched by
domestic, inquisitorial actions, indeed crusades like the one waged, at
the opening of the thirteenth century, against the Albigensian heresy.[13]

These seemingly contradictory movements—centrifugal and expansive, on the one hand, and centripetal, introspective, and reformatory, on
the other—are ultimately complementary, part of a single larger movement necessitated by the historical shifts in the church's position that
were then being achieved. A formerly persecuted, minority institution
had become hegemonic. How was such hegemony to be justified given
the religion's continuing view of itself as historically persecuted, minori-
tarian? And at the same time, how was such hegemony to be maintained and solidified? The address to these questions took the form of
both a movement outward and one inward: the external threat of Islam
and its expansion simultaneously reemphasized the endangered status
of Christianity and necessitated movements (i.e., the Crusades) to shore
up and expand Christian hegemony; the internal threat of corruption,

dissension, a church rife with improper practices again called attention to the religion's precarious status and, at the same time, provided opportunities for insisting on greater uniformity of belief and practice and an increasingly centralized ecclesiastical authority.

Clearly, the movement of internal reform conflates the Christian individual and society: the reform of one rests on, and necessitates, the reform of the other. And the outwardly directed actions of Crusade and conquest are similarly both political and personal enterprises. "Taking the cross" means joining a mass religiopolitical movement, but at the same time it depends upon, and effects, a transformation of the crusading self. Crusaders join the cause both to support the corporate goals of their religion and to gain personal salvation; indeed, the first, corporate, benefit is thought to lead necessarily to the second, personal, one. In his sermon at Clermont in late November 1095, initiating the First Crusade, Pope Urban II—identified by Guibert of Nogent as "the first Frankish pope"[14]—emphasizes the endangered situation of Christianity in the East and then calls on his Frankish audience to take up arms to avenge Islamic attacks on Christian lands. In doing so, he evokes a corporate, Frankish history, "recalling the deeds of their ancestors, Charles the Great and his son Louis, who destroyed pagan kingdoms and expanded the boundaries of the church,"[15] but he also presents the Crusade as a pilgrimage intimately connected to individual salvation. As Guibert notes: "this most excellent man concluded his speech, and by the power of St. Peter he absolved all those who vowed that they would go, affirming this with the very benediction of the apostolate, and he instituted a quite appropriate sign of this so respectable profession, and ordered that something like a military belt or rather something carrying the stigma of the Lord's passion, the figure of the cross, be sewn out of cloth of whatever material onto the tunics, mantles, and cloaks of those going to serve as God's soldiers."[16]

Where do the complex twelfth-century positionings and negotiations of Christian identity leave *Jewish* communities? On the one hand, in their difference from Christianity, Jews were clearly allied with the external objects of Crusade; we need only remember that, in the First and Second Crusades, Jewish communities within Europe became the target of crusader violence to see how closely Jews and Muslims might be affiliated with each other as "infidels."[17] But Jews were also an enemy distinct from Muslims—proximate, indeed internal, to European society. Christian anxieties about Jews expressed themselves both in a discourse of foreignness and distance—Jews were, like Muslims, often depicted as beyond the pale of the human—and in one of proximity. The perceived need to identify Jews as different through clothing and "the badge,"[18] their isolation in particular quarters of towns and cities,[19] an economy of expulsions from and readmittances to Christian lands all express the strong desire to negate proximity, either by encapsulating the Jewish community and thus neutralizing its "power" or by excising it from the body of Christendom. Not only akin to Islam, Judaism, by inhabiting Christian Europe and yet not participating in Europe's Christianity, presents a challenge like that of the Christian heresies identified during this period as arising within Christian communities themselves. In terms of the geopolitical imaginary of Western Europe, then, we might read European Jewry as a sort of aporia, a place where inside and outside collapse into each other, and this was a problem recognized, sometimes explicitly, in the Middle Ages itself. Thus, for instance, Guy Terré, considering in his fourteenth-century *Summa de heresibus* whether the church had legal jurisdiction over Jews, notes: "The Jews are outside [the church] only when it comes to those things pertinent to the New Testament, nor concerning such things are they judged by the church; but concerning those things that pertain to the truth of the old Law, if the Jews err, the church judges and punishes them, since when it comes to this they are not outside."[20] Given the complex internal/external situation of the Jewish other, one might ask whether it is more a movement of internal reform or one of external crusade that, from the Christian perspective, would properly address the questions raised by the presence of Jewish communities within a recently expanded and solidified *Christianitas*.

This geopolitical situation is mirrored by, and itself mirrors, the historical relations of medieval religious difference. Despite the intimate, indeed genetic, historical tie between Judaism and Christianity, the great rupture of Christ's incarnation, and Jewish refusal of that event, necessitate an intense Christian disavowal of Jewish heritage. At the same time, as I have argued in the preceding chapter, Christianity maintains its relation to this disavowed heritage—if often only primarily via disavowal. Judaism is made into that which is definitively past, but this is also a past that (spectrally) inhabits the present. On the other hand, Islam haunts the borders of Latin Christian Europe as a feared and disavowed future: the structural relation of Christianity to Islam was often understood as exactly reversing that of Christianity to Judaism, with Muhammad depicted as at first a Christian and as founding his religion upon the "heretical" rejection of Christianity.[21] Here, instead of a new "truth" that fulfills and replaces an incomplete understanding of "truth," as in Christianity's narrative of its own birth from Judaism, Islam is presented as a monstrous, debased birth, a fall from Christian revelation into "heresy." Given such a historical account, medieval Christian disavowal of Islam, as of Judaism, is intense. The rejection of Christian doctrine by both Islam and Judaism, by Christianity's "descendent" as well as its "ancestor," holds special power because, in each case, it is understood to arise from a position of intimate relation, representing an *informed* refusal of the "truth" and thus a particularly strong "perversity." Not merely independent religious traditions, Judaism and Islam plot out two courses of spiritual understanding closely linked to the Christian, and thus, in the logic described by Jonathan Dollimore as the "paradoxical perverse," liable to be demonized in an especially anxious and hostile manner: "the shattering effect of perversion is somehow related to the fact that its 'error' originates internally to just those things it threatens."[22] To understand, then, how Christians and Christianity in this period position themselves in relation to Jews, we need also to think through how that positioning entails a relationship—in part of similarity, in part of significant difference—both to the perceived external threat of Islam and to the supposed internal danger of "heretical" deviations from orthodox Christianity with which Islam was in part conflated.

The complex relation of Christianity to its Jewish "parent" may help us to understand one of the central paradoxes in the history of medieval Jewish-Christian relations. The very period that scholars have identified with an intensification of anti-Judaism, and the beginning of a "true" anti-Semitism, in Western Christendom is also a moment when Jewish-Christian communication and collaboration appear to be especially intense.[23] That is, as Jews and Christians come together more intimately and cooperatively in this period, the disavowal of proximity and kinship becomes particularly keen. Though there is strong disagreement about precisely when, and why, an earlier medieval anti-Judaism began to become increasingly virulent, there is also a growing scholarly consensus

that this change began at some point in the long twelfth century and
strengthened across the century that followed, participating in the more
general "formation of a persecuting society."[24] Thus, the twelfth and
thirteenth centuries saw massacres like those in the Rhineland (1096,
1146) and England (1189–90), often associated with crusading activity;
the inquisition and burning of the Talmud and related Jewish books at
Paris (1239–48), echoed repeatedly in the decades that followed, with
Jewish books confiscated at Oxford in 1244, burned at Bourges in 1251,
disputed at Barcelona in 1263, and confiscated in Apulia in 1270;[25] waves
of local and national expulsion in the twelfth, thirteenth, and fourteenth
centuries; accusations of ritual murder (from ca. 1150) and host desecration (from at least 1290); and the rise of the blood libel (from 1235).[26]

During the same period, however, Jewish and Christian exegetes
were clearly consulting with each other in such centers of learning as
Paris.[27] The developing European vernacular literary traditions of trou-
badour poetry and romance narrative owe something, many scholars
believe, to the influence of Arabic traditions in Southern Europe, and
Arabic and Hebrew literary traditions in the South are themselves closely
linked; in turn, we might see Northern European Jewish narrative traditions responding to and incorporating elements of the new Christian literary forms.[28] The twelfth century saw a "reborn" learning dependent
upon the recovery and translation of ancient—philosophical, mathemat-
ical, medical—works mediated through Arabic and (to a lesser extent)
Hebrew learning, and this intellectual movement involved significant
and complex crossings of Islamic, Jewish, and Christian cultures.[29]

In the Hebrew account of the Paris disputation of 1240, the main
Jewish disputant, Rabbi Yeḥiel, can claim that Jews "sell cattle to Christians, . . . have partnerships with Christians, . . . allow ourselves to be alone
with them, . . . give our children to Christian wet-nurses, and . . . teach
Torah to Christians—for there are now many Christian priests who can
read Hebrew books."[30] Whether or not Yeḥiel's claims represent a common historical reality, they suggest the plausibility of such a vision of
interreligious interaction both for Yeḥiel's largely Christian audience at
the debate and for the readers of the Hebrew text recounting that debate.
Certainly Christian anxiety about too intimate relations with Jewish
communities was repeatedly expressed in twelfth- and thirteenth-century
legislation—against, for instance, Jews keeping Christian servants (and
specifically wet nurses). From the Third Lateran Council (1179): "Jews

and Saracens shall not be permitted to have Christian slaves in their homes; neither for the purpose of nursing their children, nor for domestic service, nor for any other purpose."[31] And several times documents suggest that such decrees were ignored and hence needed reiteration. Thus, a papal bull of 1205, addressed to the king of France, notes that, despite the legislation of Lateran III, Jews "do not hesitate to have Christian servants and nurses, with whom, at times, they work such abominations as are more fitting that you should punish than proper that we should specify"; a similar claim is made in a papal letter of 1244.[32] The particularly influential decrees of the Fourth Lateran Council (1215) concerning the Jews arise at least in part from a perception that Jewish and Christian communities have come into too close contact—through Jewish moneylending, interreligious sexual intercourse (necessitating the distinction of Jews and Saracens from the Christian population by the quality of their clothes), and Jews gaining "preferment in public office."[33]

One might attempt to explain the simultaneous rise in persecutory relations and flourishing of interreligious collaboration as separate movements occurring in separate social realms, and this is no doubt in part the case: popular violence against Jews often took place *despite* ecclesiastical or aristocratic wishes and commands. But it would be a distortion to assign persecution wholly to one social realm and interreligious collaboration wholly to another, or to argue that a purely popular animus against Jews expressed itself despite, or perhaps even because of, alliances between Jews and the nobility or ecclesiastical hierarchy.[34] The inverse of this situation at least sometimes pertains. Thus, church-authored legislation—frequently reiterated in secular legislation promulgated by the nobility—sometimes proscribes everyday, secular Jewish-Christian interaction, and this suggests that Jewish-Christian collaborations might be identified with the everyday and the "popular" and their proscription with the ecclesiastical hierarchy and nobility.[35]

Important to our understanding of this intersection between the persecutory and the collaborative are the Christian ideas of temporality discussed above in chapter 1, intended as these are to stabilize (and hence neutralize the power of) the older, parental religion. If Judaism is a fossilized system of belief, caught—because of the original Jewish refusal to acknowledge Christ as the Messiah—in a way of thinking once divinely sanctioned but no longer applicable to the postincarnational world, it should remain static, and that this was not the case must quickly have become clear to those Christians involved in the intellectual work of the twelfth-century "renaissance" and the Aristotelian revival that followed. Christian scholars like Andrew of St. Victor who studied Jewish exegesis intensely enough to be themselves accused of "Judaizing" must have recognized the vital and changing qualities of Jewish intellectual work.[36] Not the literal-minded and plodding (mis)understanding of scripture constructed by anti-Jewish polemic, Jewish exegetical work, while emphasizing the literal and historical, could involve as complex moves to allegorize and spiritualize the text as did Christian exegesis. Moreover, involvement in interreligious debate and polemic pushed Jewish scholars to rethink, refine, and alter their positions under the pressure of Christian argument; such revisions must have been striking to Christian opponents used to identifying Jewishness with a pure resistance to change. Thus, for instance, Jewish polemical literature shows Jews becoming quite practiced in responding to Christian charges that they read the Bible only literally and hence with only partial understanding. Joseph Kimhi, in his twelfth-century *Book of the Covenant* [*Sefer ha-Brith*], turns the charge of literal-mindedness back against Christian exegetes. Though the Christian unbeliever, the *min,* in Kimhi's dialogic *Book,* accuses his Jewish interlocutor, the *ma'amin* (believer), of "understand[ing] most of the Torah literally while we understand it figuratively," the *ma'amin* advances essentially the same charge against Christian reading practices: "Here [Genesis 1:26] image and likeness are not to be taken literally but metaphorically. Image is dominion and likeness is rulership, not a physical image. What is the matter with you? On the basis of one obscure passage, you deny His unity and expound it as [proof] of a plurality."[37] Rabbi Meir ben Simeon, in mid-thirteenth-century Narbonne, reports a disputation he had "on the subject of moneylending on interest" with a Christian in which Meir, like Kimhi, calls into question Christian approaches to reading the biblical text: "Why do you not interpret the law on interest figuratively like the other prohibitions and thus allow (following your own exegesis) the lending on interest even to your own people?"[38] Whether Christians commonly attended to such Jewish self-defense and polemic—Kimhi's text, for instance, was probably *not* widely available[39]—those directly in dialogue with Jewish scholars and polemicists would have been pushed to recognize that medieval Jewish exegesis did not simply reflect, as Christian polemic would have it, an obtuse, unchanging (mis)understanding of scripture. That Jewish thinkers like the great rabbi, philosopher, exegete, and physician Maimonides (1135–1204) also played prominent roles in bringing Aristotelian thought to Western Europe placed them (like their Muslim counterparts) at the "cutting edge" of European philosophy, strongly influencing thirteenth-century Christian thinking. When a scholastic philosopher-theologian like Thomas Aquinas incorporated Jewish philosophical work into his own thinking, as he did, he must have recognized that "new" knowledge was emerging from the "old," supposedly static, religion.[40]

The recognition that may have arisen through interreligious intellectual collaboration, that contemporary European Judaism did not fit the Christian notion of a religion wholly consigned to the past, and hence one valuable and worthy of survival only as it told the story of what led to the Christian present, must have disturbed Christianity's sense of its own unrivaled position in revealing an ongoing divine history. That persecutory actions followed is perhaps unsurprising: attacks and massacres violently attempted to put Jewish specters to rest; mass expulsions moved to purify the ground of Christendom of polluting presences; accusations of murder, poisoning, desecration allowed for the juridical elimination of local communities of Jews transformed through these fantastic accusations into inhuman, demonic presences bent on destroying Christian innocence; attempts to control Jewish doctrine and reading practices—by disallowing postbiblical (especially Talmudic) traditions, or by insisting that contemporary European Jews made an unacceptable use of these—reasserted (as we shall see in chapter 5) the strict identification of Judaism with the ancient, unchanging religion superseded (as Christian doctrine would have it) at the moment of the incarnation.

Jeremy Cohen notes (citing Jaroslav Pelikan) that "the twelfth century gave rise to more treatises of Christian anti-Jewish polemic than any prior medieval century, perhaps as many as the entire medieval period before the Crusades,"[41] and this literature is clearly enmeshed in the rethinking of Christian selfhood and Christian community that characterized the twelfth-century "renaissance." Indeed, many, perhaps most, of the figures who played important roles in the elaboration of new Christian models of theology, community, and self gave significant attention to the relationship of Christianity to Judaism and to such other religious "others" as Islam and "heresy." As we have seen in the preceding chapter, Peter Damian, among the notable voices of Christian reform in the eleventh century, devoted significant attention to anti-Jewish polemic. The extent of Anselm of Canterbury's engagement with Judaism (toward the end of the eleventh century) is controversial—with some seeing Jewish (and Islamic) positions as crucial to the formation of Anselm's own (counter)positions and others largely denying their importance[42]—but it is clear that late eleventh- and early twelfth-century adherents of the new Anselmian theology concerned themselves extensively with placing Judaism, Christianity, and Islam in relation to one another. One of Anselm's students was Guibert of Nogent, whose writings on Jews and Muslims are discussed at length later in this chapter.[43] Another was Gilbert Crispin, whose *Disputatio Iudei et Christiani* [*Disputation of a Jew and a Christian*] and its companion piece, the *Disputatio Christiani cum Gentili* [*Disputation of a Christian with a Gentile*] (where the "Gentile" is associable, at least in certain ways, with Islam) both bear the indelible marks of Anselm's new theology of salvation.[44] Odo of Cambrai [Tournai]'s *Disputatio contra Iudaeum Leonem nomine de adventu Christi filii Dei* [*A Disputation with the Jew, Leo, Concerning the Advent of Christ, the Son of God*] also seems to have been significantly influenced by Anselm's ideas.[45] Later twelfth-century figures of reform and theological and spiritual innovation—Rupert of Deutz, Peter Abelard, Bernard of Clairvaux, Peter the Venerable—all take Jews and Jewishness as significant topics of interest. As we have noted above, Rupert engages Jews in public debate, and, alongside his theological writings, he authors a dialogue that tests Jewish and Christian positions against each other.[46] Peter Abelard writes a three-way debate among a Christian, a Jew, and a "philosopher" whom many would take as a representative of Islam, "albeit one who voices the doctrine of classical philosophy more than that of Islam"; this *Dialogue* is closely connected to Abelard's elaboration of a new, rational ethics.[47] Peter the Venerable recurs repeatedly in his writings (including calls for the Second Crusade) to the discussion of Jews, Muslims, and "heresy," and we can see in his powerful rhetoric a move toward the more virulent anti-Judaism of the later Middle Ages.[48] And Jews appear in significant roles as Bernard of Clairvaux elaborates his reading of the Song of Songs and as he, like Peter, writes and speaks on behalf of the Second Crusade. On the one hand, Bernard's position toward Jews is gentler than Peter's, and he is credited by Hebrew chroniclers with having worked during the Second Crusade to prevent violent anti-Jewish outbreaks like those that characterized the First; on the other hand, his writings contain much standard anti-Jewish thought.[49] Even the innovative poet-philosopher Alain de Lille, whose work is strongly identified with the Neoplatonism of the twelfth-century "renaissance," turns, in his *De fide catholica* [*On the Catholic Faith*] to consider the nature of a "true" Christianity; in doing so, as the fuller title of the work, *Contra haereticos, Waldenses, Iudaeos, et paganos*, suggests, Alain positions *Christianitas* against the full panoply of its religious others—"heretics, Waldensians, Jews, and pagans," where *paganos* probably suggests Muslims.[50]

The new and revived literary forms of the twelfth century also often stand in a significant relationship to questions of religious difference. This is a period of crucial change in historical consciousness and historiographical writing,[51] with accounts of the Crusades, for instance, importantly different—less piecemeal, more narrative, more contemporarily focused—than earlier medieval chronicle. The Crusades accounts of course take up questions about the political and religious differences between Christendom and Islam, but they also often concern themselves with thinking about Judaism, Eastern vs. Western Christianity, and Christian "heresy." And the new Latin historiographic traditions are paralleled by the development of new sorts of Hebrew historical writing, again especially connected to the religious conflicts associated with Christian crusading.[52] Romance, with its emphasis on individual choice and development, is a counterpart to this new historiography, focused more fully on individual exploits than on larger sociopolitical movements.[53] Insofar as it shows cultures in conflict—as, for instance, in the matter of Troy or Thebes or Rome—it raises questions similar to those central to the Crusades narratives. (In doing so, it also continues in many ways the thematics of the earlier epic genres like *chanson de geste*.) Insofar as it focuses on the education, growth, and potential change of individual knights, it involves, too, a process that parallels in some significant ways the plot of religious conversion. Often, indeed, the romance takes on themes—the conflict of Christian and non-Christian knights, religious intermarriage, travel in non-Christian lands, religious conversion itself—that put questions of religious difference explicitly into play.[54] The incipient genre of autobiography, represented for instance by Peter Abelard's *Historia Calamitatum* and Guibert of Nogent's *De vita sua* (discussed below), draws heavily on the late antique example of Augustine's *Confessions* and tends to structure itself around the experience of conversion—in the case of an Abelard or Guibert, the conversion, within Christianity,

from one mode of life to another.[55] But significantly, early in its medieval history, the genre is also turned to the exploration of conversion
from one religion to another—notably, in Hermann of Cologne's detailed account of his conversion to Christianity.[56] And at least fragmentary evidence survives of autobiographical texts depicting conversion
from Christianity to Judaism.[57]

As these new or revived literary genres centrally take up interreligious questions, older, established genres commonly involved in treating religious themes are also subject to significant change. As suggested
above, biblical exegesis—as practiced, for instance, by the Victorines—
develops in ways influenced by interactions with Jewish scholars and
exegetes.[58] The older, ultimately patristic, *Adversus Iudaeos* and Jewish-
Christian debate traditions are actively taken up and transformed by
twelfth-century writers.[59] These polemical genres continue to focus on
certain ancient themes—especially concerning the interpretation of
particular Hebrew biblical passages read by Christian exegetes as pre-
dictions of Christ's coming—but we can also see them changing in line
with more general twelfth-century movements. Debate texts like Gilbert
Crispin's tend to emphasize the personal experience of the debaters. Gilbert introduces his *Disputatio Iudei et Christiani* by recalling with some
specificity the social situation of interreligious encounter: "this little
book I have lately written, committing to the page what a certain Jew
once brought forward about his law, disputing against our faith, and
what I responded for our faith to his charges. I do not know where he
was born, but he was educated in letters at Mainz, and he was very
knowledgeable in the law and also in our letters, and trained in scripture, and he had a genius for disputing against us."[60] The debate literature may thus reflect significant new social contacts between Jews and
Christians, or at least between Jewish and Christian intellectuals. Such
changes in the genre are also responses to the twelfth century's increasing attention to and respect for the individual and for individual religious
and spiritual experience. In the era of the "discovery of the individual," it
is perhaps no surprise that we see less of the earlier allegorical debate
between Ecclesia and Synagoga (though, as the discussion of the living
cross above makes clear, the two figures do continue often to be represented in conflict with each other, especially in the visual media) and
much more of debates in which the Christian author claims to recount
his personal encounter with a singular, historically specific Jew.[61]

The Christian literature of Jewishness in the eleventh and twelfth centuries is largely a literature of anxiety. It anxiously conjures up Jews and their religious difference in order to put these to rest, to conjure them away, and by so doing to reconfirm a sense of Christian identity and of an unchallenged, unchallengeable Christian society. The Christian historiography of the First Crusade focuses our attention (unsurprisingly) on Christian successes. A conversion autobiography like Hermann's emphasizes, quite literally, the disappearance of a Jew and the creation of a new Christian. As we have seen above in Peter Damian's letter to Honestus, the polemical debate literature presents Jewish voices and positions in large part to discredit them. Still, such anxious conjurings away are also conjurings up, bringing into the present a Judaism Christianity would consign to the past. Such a movement, while it does the performative work of laying Judaism to rest, also holds a certain potential for new valuations of Jewishness, ones that do not simply (wishfully) position Judaism and Jews as forever superseded. Christian "Judaizing"—an attention to Jewish truths that might challenge Christian orthodoxy—was often identified in the twelfth century as one of the characteristics of "heresy." While of course disavowed by the church, "heretical" attention to Judaism (insofar as the accusation of "Judaizing" represents real interests of the "heretical" movements and not just an orthodox attempt to discredit them) suggests that certain elements of European Christendom took seriously the possibility of reassessing the relations between Christianity and its ancestor religion.[62] Moreover, though the Christian literature of Christian-Jewish debate served more to close than open dialogue between the two religions, at least some Jews took that literature as providing the opportunity for serious response; alongside the Christian debate literature, a Jewish counterpart, which often directly took on Christian arguments, flourished.[63] The phenomenon of actual debates between Jews and Christians that we know characterized this and the later medieval period is again ambivalent—orchestrated by a Christian orthodoxy to put Jewish arguments aside, to reconfirm for a Christian populace the "truths" of their own religion, but also providing an opportunity for a Jewish public presence and voice that might not otherwise have been possible and potentially for the serious consideration of Jewish arguments. That interreligious debate was seen as potentially dangerous by Christian authorities is confirmed by the fact that it was sometimes explicitly outlawed.[64]

While in all of this there is of course no Jewish "victory" in Western Europe, no way in which Jews escaped their subordinated and precarious position, there are clear signs that Christians of the long twelfth century did not respond uniformly to what they knew of Jews and Judaism. Indeed, alongside accounts like Hermann of Cologne's of Jews who converted to Christianity, we have evidence that some Christians were moved enough by something about Judaism to take the risky step of converting.[65] Thus, in 1102, a Norman living in Italy converted to Judaism, changing his name to Obadyah.[66] L. Rabinowitz suggests that, in Northern France and England, "the number of such converts [from Christianity to Judaism] was considerable."[67] Despite the significant pressure for English Jews to convert to Christianity during the twelfth and thirteenth centuries, we have evidence, in the same period, of English Christians who chose to convert to Judaism.[68] Christian hegemony of course prevailed—Obadyah, for instance, was forced to leave Christian Europe for the Middle East—but, in this period of significant change within Christendom, it is clear that Christian identity was renegotiated in significant ways in relation to the specters of Judaism.

BODY AND THE CONSTRUCTION OF CHRISTIAN SELF: THE CASE OF GUIBERT OF NOGENT

I turn now to a fuller discussion of the work of one late eleventh-/early twelfth-century author, Guibert of Nogent (ca. 1060–ca. 1125).[69] My goal here is to consider how Guibert's representations of Jews in a variety of different kinds of work take their place within the larger project of defining both a Christian self and Christian society.[70] That larger project involves, too, the consideration not just of Judaism but also of other religious positions challenging to Latin Christendom—Islam, Greek (Eastern) Christianity, and local, Western European "heresies." Indeed, Guibert's work as a whole gives a particularly full account of how at least one informed and thoughtful twelfth-century writer attempted to define the Christian against its various religious others.

Guibert's writing is revealing, too, in its consideration of the simultaneously "public" and "private" significance of religious experience and identity. Jews figure, first of all, in Guibert's *De vita sua, sive monodiarum libri*—his *Memoirs* or *Monodies*—perhaps the earliest of the twelfth-century autobiographies that revive a tradition going back to Augustine's *Confessions*. The *Memoirs*, like other works in this tradition, concerns the construction of a "moral" self appropriate to the doctrines of Christianity and the political demands of Christian society.[71] At the same time, Guibert's corpus contains much writing concerned with more "public" matters; such works participate in traditions of historical and theological writing in which the medieval Christian West sought to constitute itself as a religiously and, at least to some extent, racially unified culture, a project made material in Guibert's day by the First Crusade, which Guibert chronicled in the *Gesta Dei per Francos*. Here, Muslims take center stage, and we can see Guibert's depiction of "infidels" within a grand Christian historical narrative.[72] And in the realm of polemical theology, Guibert directed his *Tractatus de incarnatione* "against the Jews" [contra Judaeos]; this last text gives us the chance to examine how Guibert's theological construction of Jews might shape, depend on, or diverge from his historical-autobiographical depiction of them in the *Memoirs*.[73]

Not only do these three works come from the pen of the same author, but Guibert himself marks their interconnection. The introduction to the *Tractatus* recounts a dream that is later retold in the *Memoirs* (1.17; 87–88); in both places, the dream provides a partial explanation of Guibert's decision to write "pious works."[74] In the *Memoirs*, Guibert refers twice to the composition of the *Tractatus*, indicating once that he sent a copy of the work to a converted Jew at the monastery of Fly "[t]o increase the strength of his unbroken faith" (2.5; 136), and twice claiming that the work was directed "against the count of Soissons, a Judaizer and a heretic" (2.5; 136).[75] Elsewhere in the *Memoirs*, he refers to the composition of the *Gesta Dei per Francos*, which he calls "a book on the crusade to Jerusalem" (3.11; 188).[76] John F. Benton suggests that these three works were written within a period of about seven years, with the *Gesta* dated ca. 1108, the *Tractatus* ca. 1111, and the *Memoirs* ca. 1115.[77] The references to the first two works in the last make it clear that these were fresh in mind while Guibert was at work on his autobiography.

In these texts, the construction of the Christian—Christian society as well as Christian self—depends upon a certain obsessive writing, and rejection, of Muslim and Jewish bodies. The corporealized figures of Muslim and Jew function both to further a sense of Christian cultural, social, and political unity and to project a vision of the (whole, rational, moral) Christian individual over against the (fragmented, irrational, immoral) religious "other."

As Benton and others have suggested, in both his *Memoirs* and his work on relics (the *De pignoribus sanctorum* [*On the Relics of the Saints*]), Guibert expresses a general revulsion at the body, and particularly at its involvement in sex.[78] In Guibert, however, repugnance clings especially strongly to the bodies of Jews and Muslims. This is not surprising given the widespread importance of the body as a locus for the expression of medieval anti-Semitic ideas and sentiments. As I have argued elsewhere, "Jews were often seen as the possessors of diseased and debased bodies,"[79] and one need look no further than Dante's *Inferno* 28, with its grotesque depiction of Muhammad ("cleft from the chin to the part that breaks wind") and his son-in-law Ali ("cleft in the face from chin to forelock"), to see the powerful potential of the (fragmented) human body for the representation of Islam as both a schismatic departure from Christianity and itself a religion rent by schism.[80]

In Guibert's *Memoirs,* Jews appear several times in a significant relationship to the loss of bodily integrity, though the focus of attention in these episodes is not the Jewish body itself—which Guibert keeps at some distance—but the failures of Christian bodies as these come under a seductive and profanatory Jewish influence. This makes clear that the concern with Jewish bodiliness is, in large part at least, not so much about the "other" as it is about feared encroachments on the privileged space of the Christian self, necessarily attached to a corporeal body even as Christian thinking emphasizes the importance of spirit and the potential dangers and debasements of body. In one especially striking instance, special Jewish expertise in the realm of body begins a chain of events that involves the progressive immersion of one Christian in simultaneous bodily and spiritual debasements. Upon "f[a]ll[ing] ill of a disease," a certain monk consults "a Jew skilled in medicine" (1.26; 115).[81] Consultation quickly becomes "intimacy," and Jewish medical "skill" quickly shades into illicit and dangerous manipulation of the natural world: "Gathering boldness from their intimacy, they began to reveal their secrets to one another. Being curious about the black arts and aware that the Jew understood magic, the monk pressed him hard" (1.26; 115).[82] Led on by his "curiosity," the monk ultimately falls into demonic

practices, enabled by his Jewish acquaintance, who "consent[s] and promise[s] to be [the monk's] mediator with the Devil" (1.26; 115).[83] When the
monk asks the Devil (through the Jew) for "a share in [his] teaching," the
Devil demands that the monk "den[y] his Christianity," make a "sacrifice,"
a "libation," of his sperm, and "taste it first as a celebrant ought to do"
(1.26; 115).[84] Guibert comments: "What a crime! What a shameful act!
And he of whom this was demanded was a priest!" (1.26; 115).[85]

The sequence of events here is revealing: while the Jewish doctor,
through his "skill," may effect a cure of bodily illness, "intimacy" with
him leads the monk into a much more dangerous bodily and spiritual
position. Pledged to the service of God, he ends up instead serving God's
"ancient enemy" (1.26; 115).[86] The demonic pact is sealed by pollution of
the priestly body, a sexualized parody of the sacrifice of the Mass, where
the priest's consumption of his own semen substitutes for the Eucharistic "libation." In the process, not only the priest's own spiritual health
but also the integrity of the corporate Christian body and the Eucharistic
body that grounds that integrity—"Thy priesthood and Thy Blessed Host"
(1.26; 115)—are threatened.[87] It is of course not insignificant that the
protagonist of this anecdote, contained in Guibert the monk's autobiography, is himself a monk: Guibert thus contrasts the bodily corruptions
undergone by the unnamed monk with his own overcoming and avoidance of such corruptions, but he also warns himself—and his fellow
monks (Guibert wrote the De vita sua while abbot and hence spiritual
leader of the monks at Nogent)—of the dangers one might encounter
through the body and through association with a bodily figure like the
medically knowledgeable Jew.

Other sexual sins and further challenges to bodily purity follow upon
the monk's pact with the devil. Guibert goes on to present to his readers
but "one instance of the magic which [the monk] learned by this accursed
bargain" (1.26; 115),[88] and significantly, he chooses an incident of sexually illicit behavior. The monk's "habit of having intercourse with a certain nun from a well-known family" (1.26; 115)[89] is about to be detected
by a fellow monk when, "with an incantation which he had learned," the
"novice sorcerer" turns the nun "into a monstrous dog" (1.26; 116), and
thus conceals her presence.[90] (Though the nun escapes through this
ruse, it is never made clear that she regains human form; she last appears in the narrative as a dog.) Here, the sexual transgressions facilitated

by Jewish proximity are revealed for what, in Guibert's view, they are—inhuman, both "monstrous" and animal. The end of the monk's story indeed suggests that he has fallen so far from the realm of the Christian (or even the realm of the human) as to be irrecoverable. Under the influence of another "severe illness," the monk "confesse[s]" his crimes. But the confession occurs "against his will," and though he is "cast . . . out from administering" the "divine mysteries" of which he is a "most filthy profaner," the monk never wholly returns from the realm of demonic illusion, continuing to expect his own ecclesiastical preferment: "He had no doubt taken this hope [of being made a bishop] from the demons, who are liars in all things and in this, too, since when he died a few years later, he was not only not a bishop but an unfrocked priest forever" (1.26; 116).[91]

Guibert's fullest treatment in the *Memoirs* of Jewish agency in the betrayal of Christianity, in the (often violent) debasement of Christian body, and in sexual crimes occurs in his account of the "Judaizing" and "heretical" Jean, count of Soissons.[92] Jean's own corruption is presented as part of the history of a deeply corrupt family. Guibert quotes Ezekiel 16:3—"Thy father was an Amorrhite and thy mother a Cethite" (3.16; 210)[93]—to describe Jean's parents; the biblical allusion tends to *racialize* Jean, to emphasize that his wickedness is not only genetic but *national* or *ethnic* in nature. He is not a true Israelite (and hence Christian), nor presumably a true Frenchman. Guibert notes that "the wickedness of his father and his grandfather was always exerted for the ruin of Mother Church" (3.16; 209),[94] and he devotes particular energy to a description of the crimes of Jean's mother, thus associating Jean especially with feminine corruptions or corruptions of the feminine. (We might here again note a contrast but also a parallel to Guibert's own biography as recounted in the *Memoirs:* his own corrupt father died before Guibert was a year old, and his most powerful bond was with his mother. But Guibert's mother is much different from Jean's: she leads him not into a life of wrongdoing but into the life of the spirit. After his mother takes up life as an eremite outside the monastery at Saint-Germer de Fly, Guibert emulates the example of her spiritual conversion and joins that same monastery.[95]) The countess of Soissons "poisoned her own brother through greed for his country," and accomplished this murder "with the help of a certain Jew" (3.16; 209).[96] This attack on a human body—and

not the only one (Jean's mother also "caused the tongue of a deacon to
be cut out of his throat and his eyes to be put out" [3.16; 209])[97] — leads
ultimately to just retribution against the perpetrators:

> [T]he Jew was burned. As for herself, after dining exceedingly
> well on the first day of Lent, she was stricken with paralysis in
> the beginning of the night when she went to sleep. She lost the
> use of her tongue and became infirm throughout her body, and,
> what was worst of all, after that she had no understanding of
> the things of God and lived the life of a pig. By the just judgment
> of God, her tongue was almost cut out in an attempt to cure
> her. So she remained from the beginning of Lent to the week
> after Easter, when she died. (3.16; 209–10)[98]

Bodily attacks are here turned back on the attackers.[99] The Jew is quickly
removed from the picture, his body consumed by fire, while the criminal female body undergoes a more complex punishment that emphasizes how it has been debased, at least partly because of its association
with Jewishness: "paralyzed," "infirm," mutilated in a manner that echoes
its crimes (specifically, the excision of the deacon's tongue), the body of
Jean's mother becomes just body, uninformed by "understanding" and
thus animal rather than human.

According to Guibert, Jean "not only became as bad as his parents,
but did things much worse" (3.16; 210).[100] Again, Christian crimes are
here introduced with an emphasis on their close association to Jewishness: "He practiced the perfidy of the Jews and heretics to such an extent
that he said blasphemous things about the Saviour, which through fear
of the faithful the Jews did not dare to do. . . . Although he supported the
Jews, the Jews considered him insane, since he approved of their religion in word and publicly practiced ours" (3.16; 210).[101] Jean's "heretical"
behavior is particularly expressed in the sexual realm. Even what appears
on the surface to be devoted Christian action ultimately reveals itself as
blasphemous, and motivated by sexual desire. Jean keeps vigil "[o]n the
eve of Easter," but only in order to await "with pleasure . . . the beautiful
women" whom he expects to arrive for their own vigil (3.16; 210).[102]

Furthermore, Jean's sexual desires, as Guibert presents them, are
decidedly "perverse," and facilitated by Jewish connections: "Although
he had a pretty young wife, he scorned her and was in love with a wrinkled old woman. He had a bed in the house of a certain Jew and often

had it laid out for him, but he could never be restricted to a bed and, in his raging lust, thrust himself and that filthy woman into any foul corner, or, at any rate, some closet" (3.16; 210–11).[103] And not content with being an adulterer himself, Jean tries to trick his wife into adultery: "[H]e ordered a certain parasite to go and lie with his own wife after the lamps had been put out at night, pretending to be himself, so that he could fasten a charge of adultery on her" (3.16; 211).[104] This plan would in turn facilitate Jean's own adulterous behavior by allowing him to charge his wife with that crime and thus be rid of her.[105] Jean's plan is, however, foiled by the revealing physical debasement of his own body: "she perceived it was not the count through the difference in bodies (for the count was disgustingly scabby) and hardily felled the rascal by her own efforts and with the help of her attendants" (3.16; 211).[106] Jean even directly attacks the church in his sexual behavior, "not except[ing] nuns or holy women from his abuse" (3.16; 211),[107] and he explicitly challenges Christian sexual laws in a clearly "heretical" formulation: "I have learned from many wiser persons than you that all women ought to be in common and that this sin [of lustful acts] is of no consequence" (3.16; 211).[108] All of this adds up to a quite monstrous depiction; as Jan M. Ziolkowski concludes:

> Jean undergoes at the hands of Guibert the same Franken-steinification as the Muslims do in *chansons de geste* contemporary with him: his human elements are detached, distorted, and reassembled in inhuman dimensions. It is very revealing that in his *Tractatus de incarnatione contra Judaeos* Guibert places Jean in a category neither male nor female, neither masculine nor feminine: for wavering between Christianity and Judaism, Jean becomes *Neutericum*.[109] From Guibert's perspective, Jean's Judaizing puts him in a no-man's-land and makes him close to the lepers, both moral and real, who inhabited such spaces.[110]

Like his mother, Jean is ultimately punished for his bodily abuses and transgressions in an appropriately bodily manner—indeed, in a manner that incorporates his own "perverse" attraction to the "wrinkled old woman" into the scene of punishment: "When the Virgin Mother, Queen of all, could no longer endure the blasphemies of this corrupt man, a great band of his brothers, the devils, appeared to him as he was returning from a royal expedition and approaching the city.[111] Coming home with his hair disordered and out of his wits, he repulsed his wife that night and lay with that old woman. That night he fell ill of a mortal disease" (3.16; 211).[112] The action of sleeping with the old woman ("concubuit") here clearly parallels the fall into fatal illness ("decubuit").

"[C]onsult[ing]" a cleric "for an examination of his urine," Jean is confronted with "reproache[s]" for "his lustful acts" and the demand that he examine his sinful behavior (3.16; 211).[113] But he blasphemously refuses and, like his mother, falls into a state of irrationality: "[A]ll that he said or did afterward was in delirium" (3.16; 211).[114] His bodily illness threatens to extend beyond himself, into a violence against others — "In trying to drive his wife away with a kick, he inflicted such a blow on a soldier as to knock him over" — and like the devils associated with his disease or like an animal, he must be restrained "so that he would not tear himself and his people to pieces" (3.16; 211).[115]

Significantly, Jean's story leads Guibert into a broader discussion of the "heresy" he sees as "spread[ing] secretly" near Soissons (3.17; 212).[116] Central to this "heresy" are again bodily corruptions — the burning alive of an infant and the consumption of its ashes "as a sacrament" (3.17; 213)[117] — and sexual "perversions": "[Y]ou may see men living with women without the name of husband and wife in such fashion that one man does not stay with one woman, each to each, but men are known to lie with men and women with women, for with them it is impious for men to go to women" (3.17; 212).[118] The story of the individual "Judaizer" and "heretic" Jean thus gives way to the recognition of a more widespread *social* problem. Where we might have seen Jean's transgressions as characteristic of just one eccentric nobleman, Guibert now makes clear that Jean's actions are widely echoed within the supposedly Christian landscape around Soissons. Though the focus here is on Christian heresy, and no explicit mention is made of alliances between the heretics and local Jewish communities, given the clear association of Jean with *both* heretics and Jews, we now have a picture of a local Christian scene that is troubled, in a variety of ways, by religious deviation.

In the episodes of the *Memoirs* that involve Jews, we can see Guibert developing a complex definition of the "righteous" Christian self. What must be excluded from that self — "heretical," "blasphemous," and "Judaizing" tendencies associated not with God but with the devil; an involvement in physicality that expresses itself in violence and in a strong, often "perverse," sexuality; the loss of bodily integrity that follows such self-dedication to the physical; an abandonment of rationality; the descent into an animal realm particularly associated with women's bodies—is revealed especially strongly in those instances where Christians give in to the influence of Jews, abandoning the Christian self to construct themselves "otherwise."[119] Of course, all of this takes place within Guibert's autobiography, a work that opens with the (Augustinian) confession of Guibert's own corporeal sins. While such sins—"my ingrained love of crookedness, which still lives on in the sluggishness of my worn body, . . . my persistence in unclean things" (1.1; 35)[120]—may be associated with those of the monk and Jean, Guibert here also emphasizes his withdrawal from sin, his distinction from those irremediably given over to bodily transgression: "I sin, it is true, but when reason returns, I repent that I yielded to the lust of my heart and that my soul, with unwilling heaviness, bedded itself in baskets of dung" (1.1; 36).[121]

On the one hand, those Christians who give in to Jewish influence and to sin represent Guibert's fears about the possible end of his own, or any Christian's, erring ways, fears offset, at least in Guibert's self-consideration, by the belief in a gracious God who "direct[s]" the wanderer "back . . . to the bosom of . . . Mercy" (1.1; 35).[122] On the other hand, however, the episodes of Jewish seduction occur in a realm from which Guibert strongly dissociates himself, a realm unrepresented in the depiction of his own moral struggles—that is, the realm in which one might actually come into contact with Jews. Though Jay Rubenstein, in his recent work on Guibert, has concluded, especially from Guibert's close engagement with Jewish arguments in the *Tractatus de incarnatione,* that "Guibert almost certainly engaged the Jews of Soissons in face-to-face debates,"[123] in the *Memoirs,* Guibert consistently distances himself from the tinge of Jewish interaction, even as his self-confessed errors echo those of "Judaizing" Christians like the monk and Jean. In Guibert's account of his own life, Jews in fact impinge directly on Guibert's immediate social world only after they are no longer Jewish, only after their conversion to Christianity; thus, Guibert depicts two converted monks whom he knew at the monastery of Fly (1.23; 109; and 2.5; 134–37), but he never suggests that he encountered Jews who were still Jewish.

While we look with some clarity at the violent behavior and "disgusting" bodies of Jean, his mother, and the monk, thus defining the boundaries of properly Christian behavior and body, the Jews who are the accomplices of these sinful Christians remain largely unrepresented, shadowy figures on the margins of Guibert's account. One Jew acts as demonic mediator for the monk, but it is that monk who is Guibert's main concern. Jews again play auxiliary roles in the accounts of Jean and Jean's mother. If Christians who fall under Jewish influence represent, in their "perverse" behavior, what is imaginable, even tempting, but disallowed in the struggle to shape a proper Christian self, the Jewish figures who lead Christians away from such a self occupy a certain "beyond" that Guibert chooses never really to represent. If, as it seems, to be in contact with unconverted Jews is already somehow to have stepped outside the Christian community, to have moved toward the "underground vaults" and "unfrequented cellars" of heretical activity (3.17; 212),[124] what it means actually to *be* a Jew is never imagined in the *Memoirs*.

Thus, while Guibert associates Jews with the most dangerous attacks on Christian bodies—fratricide, adultery, demonic sacrifice—Jewish bodies themselves are never the clear focus of his attention. While they sometimes suffer corporal punishment for their acts (thus, the Jew acting as accessory to murder is burned), Jews in Guibert's autobiography are never independent agents, instead remaining shadowy presences on the margins of the action, seducing Christians and facilitating the contamination of Christian bodies, but hardly embodied themselves. In other words, Jews here function spectrally, as presences not really present, possessing bodies but not bodies easily seen, dangerous precisely because they do not occupy definable social spaces, but lurk on the borders of Christian society, presenting to susceptible Christians alternative ways of being that, to Guibert's mind, must be strongly disavowed but that, to the erring Christians within the narrative, bear a strong attraction. Guibert brings Jews into his account in order to demonstrate their dangerousness—he conjures them up to conjure them away—but the effects of their textual presence are never completely controllable, no matter how strongly the author voices his disapproval and dismay; there always remains the possibility of a "perverse" reader, like Jean of Soissons, his mother, or the unnamed monk, drawn to rather than repelled from the spaces occupied by shadowy Jews.

The representation of Christians seduced by Jewish proximity, the recognition that Christians might indeed choose to approach Jewishness, leads to a certain destabilization of Christian identity. But the decision not to represent Jewish individuals in any detail—not to make them recognizable, particularized human beings on a continuum of humanness with both morally upright and morally suspect Christians—allows for the creation of an identity position fully outside the Christian, and against which Christian identity may be restabilized and reunified. While Christians are susceptible to Jewish temptations, and while Jews may convert and become Christians, nonetheless, in Guibert's *Memoirs,* even the most debased, "heretical," "Judaizing" Christians do not become Jews. Guibert thus attempts to maintain Christian identity in this text as somehow *essentially* different from Jewishness.

Guibert also accomplishes the restabilization of Christian self through a certain geopolitical erasure of Jewish communities. Despite the real dangers that Jewish contacts are shown to pose for individual Christians, and despite Guibert's willingness vividly to depict erring *Christian* communities (in the community of heretics outside Soissons or, later, in the account of the Laon commune's revolt), in the *Memoirs* Guibert never represents Jewish communities as having real power or even presence. (This stands in contrast to other medieval anti-Jewish depictions—for instance, those associated with ritual murder or blood libel accusations—in which the community of Jews is presented as a conspiratorial whole dedicated to attacks on Christians and Christendom.) Rather, as in the account of Jean of Soissons, Jews in the *Memoirs* are shown to be afraid "of the faithful" (3.16; 210) and easily contained or eliminated by Christian force. Briefly recounting the attacks on Jews that accompanied the First Crusade, Guibert depicts the power of the Christian attackers as overwhelming: "seizing their weapons, they herded the Jews into a certain place of worship, rounding them up by either force or guile, and without distinction of sex or age put them to the sword" (2.5; 135).[125] Though Guibert does not directly endorse such violence, in representing it he nonetheless asserts the power of a Western European Christian hegemony that exists despite the presence of Jews in its midst and that is consolidated in the very movement to suppress or eliminate that presence.

ON THE BORDERS OF LATIN CHRISTENDOM

The double move of the *Memoirs* is thus to construct a Jewish threat to Christian selfhood, through accounts of Christians seduced by Jews, and at the same time to neutralize that threat by making it fully marginal—

maintaining individual Jews as shadowy (if still dangerous) figures and emphasizing the easy containment of Jewish communities. Other, but similarly complex, strategies operate in Guibert's depiction of Muslims in the *Gesta Dei per Francos*.

Here, the explicit issue is not, as in the autobiography, the formation of the individual Christian "self," but rather the larger construction of Western European Christendom, the consolidation, in grand geopolitical terms, of the Christian over against its Islamic "other."[126] We might expect, in moving to this "other" more distant than the Jews of Northern France, that Guibert's sense of physical threat and revulsion would also become more distant, less distinct. Instead, Guibert offers an account of Islam and its supposed physical debasements more detailed and grotesque than anything revealed in the *Memoirs* about Jewish lives and bodies. Indeed, perhaps it is *because* Islam is more distant than local Jewish communities, evoking a different sort of anxiety than these more proximate "others," that it can be described more fully and luridly. With the distinction between the Christian and the Muslim secured by geographic distance, an obscure, unfamiliar Islam can be brought into clear focus to represent what is to be ruled out of communal Western European identity.

The movement here, however, is not unambivalent. While its distance may allow Islam to be represented more fully than Judaism, that full representation in turn intensifies the danger Islam is thought to pose for Christianity. The Muslim "other" is conceived not, like the Jews of the *Memoirs*, as a scattered presence within a Christian hegemony, but as a hegemony of its own, a massive, uncontained, perhaps uncontainable "nefarious custom, . . . covering over the Christian name" with its "darkness" and "obliterating [it] through almost all of the Orient, Africa, Egypt, Ethiopia, Libya, and, approaching us, the most distant coasts of Spain."[127] The last phrase in this description of Islam's geographical range—"juxta nos Hispaniae remotissimos sinus"—suggests some of the ambivalence Guibert feels in relation to the (distant but pressing) Muslim threat.

The sense of Islam as a vast, "nefaria institutio" threatening to breach the boundaries separating it from the West necessitates a reassertion of secure distance between the Christian and the Muslim. In part this is accomplished, toward the beginning of the *Gesta*, through displacements of attention from the current moment to the moment of Islam's origin and from the widespread geopolitical entity that Islam becomes to the single human being, Muhammad, from whom it springs. While Guibert will, in later parts of the *Gesta*, depict Islam in some geographical and political detail, this move to identify the religion with its founder, and particularly with his diseased, fragmented corporeality, serves both to define Islam as "other" and to contain its "otherness" in a single, frail and frangible, body.

Though Guibert's account of Muhammad's life echoes, in its focus on the body and bodily debility, the stories involving Jews in the *Memoirs*, it makes the Muslim "other" much more directly its topic, looking separately and intensely at Muhammad, his body and its corruptions, without drawing any immediate connection to the lives of Western Christians.[128] In this account, Muhammad is clearly identified with (hetero)-sexual desire and a strong materialism. He marries a rich widow, and, as we discover through his wife, who is "terrified by his turned up gazes, wasted face, foaming lips, and the gnashing of his teeth," Muhammad is diseased, suffering from epilepsy, a condition itself associated in Guibert's text with the sexual activity of the marriage bed.[129] Guibert goes on to show how Muhammad's wife is persuaded that her husband's illness is not an illness—that it is, in fact, quite the opposite, a spiritual gift, God's "glid[ing] into the minds of the prophets" so that "the whole mass of the human body is shaken, because the infirmity of flesh is not strong enough to stand it when divine majesty attaches itself to [the flesh]."[130] Despite her initial revulsion, she comes to judge "all that which she before reckoned filthy and contemptible . . . to be not only tolerable but even sacrosanct and remarkable."[131]

The deception here is one that may be taken as emblematic of Islam more generally: "filthy and contemptible" matters, bodily degenerations, masquerade as holy, spiritual experience. Where the central Christian mystery is a divine taking on of body that leads ultimately through the corporeal abasement of the crucifixion to the rebirth and apotheosis of dead flesh in the resurrection and ascension of Christ, Guibert's account shows Muhammad's body and the Muslim body more generally only illegitimately claiming the indwelling of spirit. Indeed, the prophet's physical infirmity, his epilepsy, is fulfilled in the death Guibert ascribes to him, a death made to contrast starkly with the miraculous overcoming of death at the heart of Christianity:[132]

But it must be said what exit this so great and so wondrous law-giver took from the public eye. Since the epilepsy, with which we said above he suffered, often fell with a sudden blow, it happened once, when he was walking alone, that, struck by that same illness, he fell; and while he was tormented by that suffering, [he was] found by pigs [and] was so far dismembered that no relics of him except for the ankle bones were found.[133] Behold the greatest lawgiver—while he toils to resuscitate, indeed absolutely resuscitates, the Epicurean pig, which the true Stoics (that is, the worshippers of Christ) had killed[134]—a pig himself is laid open to be devoured by pigs, so that the magistracy of obscenity, as is proper, may conclude in a most obscene end. He rightly leaves behind [his] ankle bones since he fixed the footprints of perfidy and infamy within miserably deceived souls.... But if these things [claimed by] the sect of the Manichees concerning purgation are true—that in everything eaten a certain part remains profane to God; and that that same part may be purged for God by the chewing of the teeth and the stomach's digestion, and that that purged part may now be converted into angels, who may be said to come from the belchings and windiness expelled from us—how many angels do we believe that the sows fed on the flesh of this man produced and sent forth from here to there in their great farts? But, putting such joking aside that is spoken in derision of those who follow [him], this should be insinuated: that they do not believe him [to be] God, as some judge, but rather a just man, and also a patron, through whom divine laws might be passed down.[135] They add that he was assumed into heaven, and [his] ankle bones alone left behind as a monument for his faithful, which [bones] they still revisit with infinite veneration; truly, for a wholly just reason they contemn the eating of pigs, which consumed with bites their lord.[136]

Here, as in the deceptive transformation of Muhammad's epilepsy into divine visitation, the bodily debasement of Islam is falsely transferred by its believers to a spiritual realm—Muhammad's assumption into heaven—when, in Guibert's view, the only metamorphosis Muhammad can be said to have undergone is from living flesh to "flatus" and to those dead bodily "vestigia" that continue to lead his followers astray.

While Guibert thus effects, in the identification of Islam with the history of its originator, a denial of any legitimate Islamic claim to spiritual "truth" or temporal power, the containment or neutralization of Islam in the *Gesta* is never complete. After all, Islam is not only an ideological figure against which Guibert consolidates Christianity but a real historical presence: the motivation for depicting the origin of Islam is to justify the First Crusade, and at every point, even in the temporally distanced account of Muhammad, the Muslim "other" is felt somehow to touch on Christianity. Thus, the history of Islam is, as Guibert emphasizes, also a history of Christian error, with Muhammad's "dogmata" discussed alongside the errors of the Eastern church and the Christian heresies.[137] Islam arises, in this account, out of a power struggle within the "Alexandrine" church that follows the death of its "patriarch" and that involves a heretical position similar to Arianism.[138]

The "heresies" with which Islam is thus associated are ones that involve crucial departures from the "orthodox" Christian theology of body, and Islam itself is depicted as deeply implicated in such corporeal "errors." Presenting the explicit motivation for crusading as Muslim oppression of Eastern Christianity, Guibert appeals to a letter supposedly sent by the Greek emperor to Robert of Flanders but probably forged in the West shortly before the First Crusade.[139] Requesting help against the "infidel," the letter presents the danger of Islam in strongly physical terms, with the body of Islam displacing Christian communities and with dangerous Muslim bodies, like Muhammad's own, directly and violently threatening Christians:

"This complaint is concerning the churches, which indeed, with Christianity overturned, the Gentiles [i.e., Muslims] held, [and] in which they constructed stables for horses, mules, and other animals. Which was so far true that they even established their holy places, which they call 'Mathomarias,'[140] in the churches, and practiced intercourse[141] of an infinite turpitude [therein], so that these now became not basilicas but brothels and theaters. Further, I would treat in vain the murder of catholics, since, for those dying in the faith, the reward of eternal life would seem to follow; those surviving under the wretched yoke of slavery led a life, as I judge, more bitter than those very deaths. Truly, when virgins of the faithful were seized, they were taught to become public harlots, since on no occasion was marriage offered for the sake of honor and honesty. Mothers seized within sight of their daughters were harassed many times by sex acts repeated by diverse men, while their daughters, standing by, were forced to sing abominable songs while dancing in the midst of such things. Immediately after, this same passion—as indeed it is both a sorrow and a shame to be spoken—was brought around to the daughters, which obscene foulness was again adorned by the songs of the unhappy mothers. In short, the reverence of the whole Christian name was handed over to the brothel. And while the feminine sex is not spared—which nevertheless might be excused by virtue of its agreement with nature—they proceed to the masculine, transgressing animality and breaking the laws of humanity." From which point, so that that wantonness—to be execrated by each and, in the greatness of its shameful crime, almost intolerable to hearing—which raged against the ordinary and the worst [of men], might spread, he says that they killed a certain bishop by means of sodomitical abuse. "And how might [this] appetite—headlong and standing out completely from all other madnesses, which, always fleeing counsel and modesty, is driven by a perpetual impetus, and by however much it is more frequently extinguished, by that much repeatedly is its flame more briskly kindled—[how might this appetite] temper itself toward human affairs, which is dirty with sexual minglings unheard of for brute animals and forbidden to the Christian mouth? And although it is allowed the wretches, in their own opinion, to have many women, this is accounted little by them unless dignity is also sullied in the pigsty of such filth with men. Nor is it surprising that God has impatiently borne their evil, dissolute and dragged into disrepute, and that the land has vomited forth, in the ancient manner, such execrations against its deadly inhabitants."[142]

The attack of Islam on Christianity in such a passage is much more violent, concerted, and overwhelming than the Jewish seduction of

Christians in Guibert's *Memoirs;* the whole of Christianity, not just isolated individuals led to make the wrong moral choices, is here seen to be
at risk. And where the "Judaizers" of the *Memoirs choose* to behave as
they do, here Christianity is positioned as *victim* of Islam's powerful
"perversions." Christian susceptibility to Muslim attack undermines any
firm sense of separation between the two religious forces that geographical or historical distance might seem to secure. Moreover, Guibert presents Christianity (particularly Greek Christianity) as not *simply* the victim of Muslim violence. Eastern Christianity, the spawning ground of
heresies, is seen, in Guibert, as susceptible to Muslim attack because in
many ways it is already like Islam in its "perversity." Having quoted the
Greek emperor's letter about Muslim abuses at length, Guibert goes on,
in his own voice, to suggest that the emperor's own mind was "perverse."[143] Guibert recalls that the emperor "by a famous decree" ordered
"daughters to be prostituted" and "sons to be made eunuchs," in order
to profit "his own treasury,"[144] and Guibert depicts the castration of men
as a particularly debasing and dangerous Eastern practice: "[H]e rendered the bodies of [such] men, their masculine powers taken away,
powerless and effeminate, which now do not have qualities fit for the
practice of warfare; indeed, as the finishing touch to the damage done,
future offspring were cut off in them, by whose increase [the Greeks]
might have been able to hope for aid against their enemies."[145] As the
home of such corrupt bodily practices, it is no wonder that the realm of
Eastern Christianity was both subject to foreign corruption and in need
of the virile crusaders of France, whose knightly virtue is particularly
connected to a "spurning" of worldly "honors" and a rejection of corporeal blandishments: "they thought [their] most beautiful wives mean, as
though something decaying; the sight of tokens of the promiscuous sex,
once more pleasing than any gem, became loathsome [to them]."[146] Here,
over against the corruptions of the East, Guibert posits an individual
Western Christian identity—the purified crusader—as guarantor of the
corporate virtue of Western European Christianity.

As Guibert's text shows Christian bodies subject to Muslim physical
violence, it also, and more disturbingly, shows the possible implication
of a (debased, Eastern) Christianity in an economy of body like that of
Islam. While in one sense all of this serves to confirm the purity of Latin,
Western Christianity over against its "others"—a purity reemphasized
in Guibert's attempt to remove the crusaders from any implication in a

sexualized corporeality[147]—the distinction between Western Christian and "other" is still undermined via the middle term of Greek Christianity.

THEOLOGY AND POLITICS OF THE BODY

Appeals to the body's debility in the construction of otherness operate powerfully in the Western tradition, speaking to the consistent (metaphysical) desire to distinguish humanness from animality via an assertion of mind or spirit and a suppression of body. Such appeals attempt to institute differences among human beings at the level of "the natural," claiming that these are not arbitrary or serendipitous but inscribed in the flesh, there for "anyone" to see and feel. An author like Guibert, disgustedly describing the corporeal debasements associated with Islam and Judaism, assumes, as the only possible "natural" reaction to his accounts, an answering disgust in his readers.[148] But such an appeal to disgust is always, at least in part, implicated in a corporeality subject to disturbance and degeneration: at the sight of others' bodily corruptions, *this* body too becomes ill, "revolts," signaling its own susceptibility to disease and debility, even as it rejects these. The body is a particularly evocative site for the projection of the disavowed qualities of the "other," in part because we all have bodies; but, precisely because we all have bodies, such disavowal carries with it a strong danger of self-implication.

Christian attacks on the body of the "other" are especially vexed, given the ways in which Christian theology, history, and ritual are themselves embedded in embodiment—Christ's incarnation, the physicality of the Eucharist, the power of relics. Though, as we have seen, Guibert often expressed a revulsion at bodiliness and its improper uses, as a Christian writer he nonetheless had to grapple with the ways in which his own religious tradition put body at its center. Sometimes in Guibert's grappling he continued to develop a position that repudiated body. Thus, his most famous work, the *De pignoribus sanctorum,* questioned the claims built up around relics; his argument here, while often hailed as a surprisingly "modern" rejection of "medieval" superstition, was guaranteed to disturb his contemporaries, especially those associated with institutions whose relics Guibert explicitly called into question.[149] And in fact Guibert never wholly rejected the institution of relics, recognizing that saintly bodies might indeed have special power, special access to a realm of spirit. Furthermore, in writing about a bodily institution like the Eucharist, central to Christian belief, Guibert, as a good Christian, displayed no impulse to reject the crucial claim that the consecrated host actually becomes Christ's body; though, as Jay Rubenstein has recently shown, in several of his works (including the *De pignoribus*) Guibert became embroiled in debates over the theology of the Eucharist, still unsettled in the early twelfth century, developing (and then retracting) arguments that seem to have verged on the heretical, his positions never questioned the crucial role of this corporeal institution for Christian practice.[150]

As medieval Jews quickly learned, while Christian attacks on Judaism often emphasized Jews' excessive physicality, Christianity itself, centered as it was in an incarnational theology, was vulnerable to similar charges. Listen for a moment to the twelfth-century Jewish polemicist Joseph Kimhi on the Christian incarnation: "[H]ow shall I believe that th[e] great inaccessible *Deus absconditus* needlessly entered the womb of a woman, the filthy, foul bowels of a female, compelling the living God to be born of a woman, a child without knowledge or understanding, senseless, unable to distinguish between his right hand and his left, defecating and urinating, sucking his mother's breasts from hunger and thirst, crying when he is thirsty so that his mother will have compassion on him."[151] The attack on Jewish or Muslim body, so easily available and so attractive to a writer like Guibert, necessarily bore the risk of Christian self-implication.

Strikingly, when Guibert comes to write a theological treatise against the count of Soissons, attacked in such visceral terms in the *Memoirs*, he writes both "de incarnatione" [concerning the incarnation] and "contra Judaeos" [against the Jews]. Guibert's revulsion at the flesh, and particularly its sexual involvements, at times surfaces here, anticipating the language Guibert will use against Jean in the *Memoirs*: "Why should I not be made wild with vehement zeal when I see those who desert a most beautiful and honest wife even attending to old women instead of their spouses, and now paying court to most wrinkled women?"[152] And as Anna Sapir Abulafia notes, Guibert here particularly associates Jews with material crimes—"theft and usury."[153] Furthermore, Guibert characterizes the Jew whom he constructs as his interlocutor in the *Tractatus* as "most stinking and worthless,"[154] and thus begins to deploy against him the charge of a corporeal debasement that we have seen variously directed against Muslims, Jews, Judaizers, heretics, and Greek Christians in the *Gesta* and *Memoirs*. But the charge here goes largely undeveloped. After all, the main purpose of the treatise, *De incarnatione*, is to *defend* body as the appropriate locus for Jesus's divinity. So, when Guibert quotes a Jewish attack on the incarnation similar to the position we have seen Kimḥi (at a later date) articulating—"[The Jews] say that no one, except someone foolish, believes that God would have wished to send himself forth into the meanness of the female womb"[155]—Guibert cannot simply dismiss the attack as a reflection of the Jew's own immersion in carnality. Although the Jew's questions are, Guibert makes clear, demeaning to the honor of Jesus and of Christianity, they nonetheless suggest what is indisputable in Christian theology—that, with Christ, the divine fully enters human embodiment. When the Jew provocatively calls attention to the specific bodily functions that must have characterized Jesus's human life, Guibert must respond not with a denial of these bodily facts but instead with an argument that defends body. God made all creatures good,[156] and therefore bodies, in the absence of sin, are "sancta" [sacred]:

> The Son of God coming into the flesh, if he had limbs suitable to his body, the composition of those limbs could do no harm. And let one not be wrongly ashamed for that which caused him no shame. And what would have shamed him where there was nothing that was not sacred! If anything is, it is good, except where sin is; the limbs which are good per se, when there is no sin, are sacred. Our limbs minister to our weakness, and since [our] ears, mouths, or nostrils serve [us] in expelling the superfluities of the head, what evil do the rest [of the organs] do, which, lower down, cast out the burden of the intestines?[157]

While Guibert may here still express some squeamishness in his embrace of body—he after all refers to the "lower" bodily organs and functions euphemistically—he does not fail to fight that squeamishness and, directly addressing those Jews who would ridicule the idea of the incarnate Christ, launch a spirited defense of body. Responding to the taunting Jewish questions about Christ's physicality—"whether he spit, whether he wiped his nose, whether he drew out the phlegm of his eyes and ears with his fingers"[158]—Guibert declares:

understand that, since he performed these higher [actions] with such honor, he also thus carried through the remainder [of bodily functions]. But tell me: in what belly did your God, who appeared to Abraham, deposit those things that he ate? also, how, and if this happened, what was the logical consequence [of eating]? I tremble violently when I dispute such things; but you, sons of the devil, drive me to it. May God, who knows with what feeling I act, drive [him] out of you. In short, accept that God humbly took on all human things and feared nothing human except sins.[159]

In this passage we see Guibert stirred by but squelching an impulse to attack the "stinking" and "worthless" body of the "other" who would wrongly read Christ's association with spit and snot and phlegm as a debasement of his body; any visceral attack on Jewish disbelief must be cut short because Guibert's project here is to mount a general defense of human body in the context of Christ's incarnation. This "body-positive" view stands in strong contrast to the deep revulsion at bodies that, in the *Memoirs* and *Gesta*, clusters especially around Jewish and Muslim bodies, but in the *De pignoribus sanctorum* and elsewhere also clings to the bodies of Christians and the (supposed) bodily remains of saints. While, in a certain theological context, an anti-Jewish or anti-Muslim position demands the defense of human body, elsewhere it evokes a violent attack on physicality. This incoherence presents a central problem not only in Guibert's writing but in medieval anti-Semitic literature more generally. It ultimately reflects a deep ambivalence within Christianity about the viscerally powerful and disturbing embodiments at the heart of the Christian mystery itself, an ambivalence worked out not only through Christians' own bodily celebrations and asceticisms but also upon others' bodies in acts of violence both symbolic and real.

TALKING BACK AND ACTING UP WITH THE BODY

As I suggest above, Guibert's treatment of contemporary Jews in Northern France is notable for its lack of attention to any real communal or social life. We get a strong sense of a thriving Jewish community only in Guibert's brief account of the massacres associated with the First

Crusade, that is, only as that community is threatened with annihilation. Significantly, this account occurs in Guibert's *Memoirs* rather than in his history of the Crusade itself, and we might read it as reemphasizing, in its depiction of a community destroyed, the strong tendency of the *Memoirs* to spectralize Jewish presence. Indeed, in the *Gesta*, which makes no reference to the massacres accompanying the Crusade, the French landscape is cleansed of threatening religious presences: neither heretics, Judaizers, nor Jews (all of these active players in the *Memoirs*) appear. In their place, of course, we find the powerful, consolidated threat of Islam, but that threat remains geographically distant, and consequently, in the *Gesta*, France itself can become, in Guibert's depiction, a pure land of Christian uprightness.

Unlike Guibert in the *Gesta*, some other Latin chroniclers do turn their attention to the attacks on Jewish communities that accompanied the First Crusade in Northern Europe, and particularly the Rhineland. Albert of Aix, for one, treats these events in some detail: "Whence, I do not know whether by God's judgment or by a certain error of mind, they [the crusaders] arose against the people of the Jews, dispersed through certain cities, and exercised against them a most cruel slaughter, and principally in the kingdom of Lorraine, asserting this to be the beginning of their expedition and their duty against the enemies of the Christian faith. This massacre of Jews was first committed in the city of Cologne by its citizens, who suddenly rushing upon a small band of them [Jews], mutilated many with grave wounds; they overthrew their homes and synagogues, dividing among themselves much of their [the Jews'] money."[160] But even such a more detailed and graphic account focuses attention primarily on Christians—Christian motives, Christian actions, a judgment of the Christian rightness or wrongness of those actions. Jews remain largely unrepresented.

When, however, we turn to the several Hebrew chronicles of these same events—*The Chronicle of Solomon bar Simson, The Chronicle of Rabbi Eliezer bar Nathan,* and *The Narrative of the Old Persecutions* (or *Mainz Anonymous*)—we find a very different perspective, as we would expect seeing events now from a Jewish point of view.[161] But even more striking, in contrast to the Latin accounts, is the Hebrew chronicles' extraordinary, unrelenting emphasis on *body*. While accounts like Albert of Aix's foreground some of the gruesomeness of the Jews' deaths in their

confrontations with the crusaders, these accounts pale beside the corporeally rich, bloody Hebrew accounts. Detailing the threat posed to Jewish communities in the Rhineland by gathering groups of crusaders,
who present Jews with the untenable "choice" of conversion or death;
those communities' largely failed attempts to find shelter or aid from
sympathetic Christians, to escape, and to fight back; and a series of violent confrontations that end most frequently with Jewish communal
suicide, death chosen at the hands of one's own community members
in place of the death threatened by the crusaders—detailing all this, the
Hebrew chronicles repeatedly place Jewish body at the center of attention, and both individual bodies and the corporate bodies of towns and
communities. Individuals are named and thus memorialized, their
sacrificed bodies unsparingly displayed: "There was a pious man there
of ripe old age by the name of Rabbi Samuel, son of Yeḥiel. He had an
only son, a handsome young man, whose appearance was like Lebanon.
They fled together into the water, and the youth stretched out his neck to
his father for slaughter as they stood in the waters.... Behold, all ye
mortals, the great valor of the son who, though not bound, submitted
himself to slaughter, and how great was the fortitude of the father, who
was not softened by pity for so pleasant and handsome a youth. Who
will hear and not weep?"[162] Such detailed examples pile up to suggest a
unanimity of action; other passages indeed emphasize the communal
nature of the martyrdom, as in the following striking example from
Solomon bar Simson:

> The women girded their loins with strength and slew their own
> sons and daughters, and then themselves. Many men also mus-
> tered their strength and slaughtered their wives and children
> and infants. The most gentle and tender of women slaughtered
> the child of her delight. They all arose, man and woman alike,
> and slew one another.... [E]ach first sacrificed the other and
> then in turn yielded to be sacrificed, until the streams of blood
> touched and mingled, and the blood of husbands joined with
> that of wives, the blood of fathers with that of their sons, the
> blood of brothers with that of their sisters, the blood of teachers
> with that of their pupils, the blood of bridegrooms with that of
> their brides, the blood of community deacons with that of their

scribes, the blood of babes and sucklings with that of their mothers—all killed and slaughtered in witness to the Oneness of the Venerated and Awesome Name.[163]

Such a passage presents us with thriving, socially complex Jewish communities—husbands and wives, brothers and sisters, deacons and scribes—whose existence we would never guess at from texts like Guibert's (or indeed from most other Christian texts of the period). And the relentless focus on the threatened, bloodied, sacrificed, and mutilated bodies of those communities and their individual members provides a strong counterdiscourse to writing like Guibert's that tends to make Jews, even when they are at the center of attention, either spectral or simply and basely corporeal, "most stinking and worthless."[164] This is a counterdiscourse different from, even contradictory to, that noted above in Kimḥi's *Book of the Covenant*—where the charge of excessive Jewish corporeality is turned back against Christians. Here, the Jewish authors embrace their associations with body, but now—as in Guibert's depiction of the purified knights of the Crusade or his defense of the incarnated figure at the center of Christianity—these are bodies heroized, exalted, purified, made holy in being sacrificed for the sake of the divine name.[165]

What the Hebrew chronicles represent is of course not just a discourse but also a series of actions that claim historical status; whether these have been exaggerated and other, less resistant responses to the crusaders downplayed or erased, the chroniclers mean us to see the violent, bloody, bodily self-sacrifice of the Rhineland Jewries as having really occurred. They present whole families, whole communities submitting voluntarily to death in a unanimity of action that had strong effects not just on the Hebrew chroniclers but also on Christian witnesses to these events. Thus, the one time that Albert of Aix turns his attention unambiguously to Jewish motive and action is to depict Jewish self-immolation: "Truly, the Jews, seeing that the Christian enemies rose up against them and their little ones, and that they spared no age, themselves also rushed upon each other and their confreres, and children, wives, mothers, and sisters, and killed each other in mutual carnage. As it is horrible to say, mothers cut the throats of nursing children with the sword, and they stabbed others, thus wishing rather to die by their own hands than to be extinguished by the arms of the uncircumcised."[166] But the Hebrew chronicles and chroniclers themselves provide evidence that the actions taken in 1096 were *not* so unanimous. They note explicitly that some Jews in fact converted under pressure, and, while they tend to de-emphasize this choice in favor of the more dramatic embrace of martyr-dom, they also refuse to condemn it, indeed emphasizing that the action of forced converts might itself be heroic resistance:

> It is now fitting to recount the praises of those who were forcibly converted. They risked their lives even in matters pertaining to food and drink. They slaughtered the animals they ate in accordance with Jewish ritual, extracted the forbidden fat, and inspected the meat in accordance with Rabbinic law. They did not drink prohibited wine and rarely attended church, and whenever they did go, it was under great coercion and fear, and they went with aggrieved spirits. . . . In the eyes of the Gentiles they observed the Gentile Sabbath properly; but they observed God's Torah clandestinely. He who speaks evil of them, it is as though he spoke thus of the Divine Countenance.[167]

Implicitly, too, the chronicles testify to the incompleteness of Jewish martyrdom: after all, the chronicles themselves are necessarily written by survivors, or the descendents of survivors, and whatever the specific histories of that survival, the chroniclers and those who might have provided them with eyewitness accounts of 1096 clearly do not belong to the martyrs heroized by their accounts. Why then is it the actions of the martyrs, not the survivors, that come to occupy the center of these accounts? Why, for the most part, do the chronicles turn our attention away from the *various* ways, more and less resistant, in which individual Jews and the communities they comprised responded to the crusaders' onslaught in 1096? Why, while recognizing a certain powerful and understandable impulse to self-preservation, do the chroniclers nonethe-less present self-immolation, the brave, unflinching embrace of bodily death, as an ideal? What purpose do these accounts and their emphatic memorializing of one particular response to 1096 serve for the survivors, at a moment when any sense of easy, peaceful, prosperous coexistence with Christian neighbors must have been shattered and when surviving Jews must nonetheless have been searching for ways to reconfigure and continue their lives in the wake of tragedy—a continuation that, given

the conditions of those lives, must have included ongoing, daily, interactions with Christians?

The insistence on remembering the martyrs, and not just on remembering them but on making their experience the quintessential Jewish
experience of 1096, serves (paradoxically) to resolidify the lives and
communities of precisely those who did not undergo that experience, of
those who survived. What the actions of the martyrs performed for the
martyrs themselves, a definitive rejection of Christian attempts to eliminate Jewish presence in Europe through either coerced conversion or
massacre, the discourse of martyrdom that the chroniclers develop performs, though of course in a quite different register, for the chroniclers
and their Jewish audience. That is, the emphasis on the willing embrace
of bloody death to the exclusion of other, less extreme sorts of response
attempts to make clear discursively an unambiguous separation between
Jewish and Christian communities. Those who have survived—whether
through the aid of Christian neighbors, luck, their own decision (however insincerely) to accept baptism—reconstruct their *proper* position as
standing necessarily *against* a Christianity that led to the crusaders' actions
and *with* a Jewishness wholly separable from its Christian surround.

The counterdiscourse that the Hebrew chronicles develop runs several strong risks. By emphasizing Jewish body, and by showing Jews
vividly involved in attacks on their own bodies—if only in response to
strong Christian threats of bodily harm—these accounts potentially
reconfirm Christian stereotypes of Jewishness as both excessively corporeal and violent. A Christian like Albert of Aix, while expressing no
sympathy for their Christian attackers, exclaims over the "horrible" or
"unspeakable" [*nefas*] nature of the Jews' actions.[168] After all, a strong
part of Jewish identity is associated, for medieval Christianity, with the
corporeal attacks that lead up to and include the crucifixion and that, in
both medieval written and visual sources, are largely attributed to Jews.[169]
Indeed, a recent scholar like Israel Yuval has argued strongly and con-
troversially that the association of Jews with a violent corporeality in the
mass suicides of 1096 was (at least partly) responsible for the development of Christian ideas of Jewish ritual murder: if Jews were capable of
executing their families and themselves, what would stop them from
exacting revenge on vulnerable Christians with similarly horrific attacks?[170]
The actions of 1096—the refusal at all costs to convert to Christianity—
also might be seen to reconfirm Christian ideas about Jewish stubborn-

ness: if medieval Christians see Jews as unable to recognize Christian truth and as therefore unwilling to leave behind their own, now superseded past, their resistance to conversion, so strong as to make death preferable to Christian life, would only go to show Christian witnesses how fully contemporary Jews remain a people of the past. Most risky of all, the valorizing of Jewish communal martyrdom responds to a threat to Jewish survival—whether through the forced abandonment of the religion or through the threatened massacre of those who might resist conversion—by embracing annihilation. The "choice" of conversion or death leaves no space for a specifically *Jewish* survival, but of course neither does communal suicide. Or, rather, communal suicide enables a separate Jewishness to "survive," but only in the realm of ideas, without actual Jewish survivors. That there were in fact survivors means that the ideal of mass suicide was *not* unanimously embraced, but the retrospective presentation of this as an ideal might pose future risks. Are future threats to Jewish survival to be met, over and over again, by embracing death?

The assertive Jewish actions of 1096 and the historical counterdiscourse that develops about those actions were nonetheless clearly seen to have been worth these risks. Both the Jewish insistence on self-determination, even if this means death, and the discursive reemphasis of that insistence present strong self-assertions. They insist on a vastly different understanding of the workings of divinity in the world than that expressed by Western European Christendom in the enterprise of Crusade. The fact and discourse of martyrdom serve strongly to consolidate both individual and corporate Jewish identity. If the Crusade claims (as in Guibert) that Christian bodies directed against the foes of Christendom are God's warriors, guaranteed everlasting life, the Hebrew chronicles insist in return that Jewish bodily resistance to the crusaders leads to a true martyrdom, a salvation guaranteed by the sacrifice of Jewish bodies to "the sanctification of the Name." The Christian crusader is the real perpetrator of ungodly violence; the Jew who resists, though a participant in violence, truly furthers God's plan. The crusaders may attempt to eliminate Jewish communities from Christendom, but the assertion of Jewish inassimilability makes the strong argument that this will never occur in the way Christians might imagine. Rather than self-destruct through a compliance with Christian demands for conversion, Jewish communities will remain Jewish even if, paradoxically, this means willfully embracing self-destruction.

Such a strong assertion of Jewish separateness and inassimilability belies certain historical facts: there is much evidence that, after 1096 as before, Jews and Christians in the Rhineland, and in Northern Europe (Ashkenaz) more generally, continued to live closely intertwined lives; Jewish and Christian communities may have been separate in terms of religious belief and practice, but they were not separable in terms of many of the features of daily life. There is, too, much evidence of the continued interaction of Jewish and Christian cultures. As we will see in the next chapter, too, conversion from Judaism to Christianity was not universally rejected by Jews in the Rhineland, or elsewhere. But the discursive emphasis on separateness, in the wake of 1096, and the memory of how one religious community, pushed toward the point of nonexistence, insisted on its own, separate identity nonetheless operated powerfully for Northern European Jewish communities. The events of 1096 represented a turning point not just in Christian-Jewish relations but also in the development of Jewish communities themselves. The Hebrew chronicle accounts themselves represent a new literary genre for medieval Jews, a new cultural way of marking historical events. And both the events they commemorate and the discourses they help develop inflect further cultural developments within Ashkenaz. Thus, for instance, Elliot Wolfson sees the growth of new (twelfth-century) Jewish mystical ("pietist") traditions that link martyrdom, eroticism, and asceticism as a clear response to 1096 and its discourses.[171] Such new cultural developments are of course complex. They do not occur within a Judaism that has wholly isolated itself from its Christian neighbor, and we may in fact link these same new Jewish traditions to similar developments within Christianity. The two religious cultures continue to interact and to influence each other. But we may note at the same time the growing importance, post-1096, of a Jewish belief in its own separateness from the Christian culture that surrounds it.[172] If both the twelfth and thirteenth centuries bring intensified attempts to lead Jews to the "light" of Christian "truth"—to lead them, that is, to the point of conversion—the violent events of 1096 and the Jewish discourses that develop in their aftermath serve to reconfirm a sense of Jewish self, a sense that, even if it might mean their demise, Jewish identity and Jewish community have the resources to resist a Christian hegemony, to move in directions they themselves determine.

ing spice" in her Caribbean mother's kitchen, is particularly associated with an ethnic/racial identification with and disidentification from her mother.[8] Or, for one last contemporary example, the African American basketball star "Magic" Johnson's announcement in 1991 of his HIV-positive status—that is, of a change in the health of his body—led to significant rethinkings of his sexuality (was he gay? bi? promiscuously heterosexual?), gender (was an HIV-positive "Magic" Johnson still admirably "masculine"?), race (did Johnson still fit into a [stereotypical] category of hypermasculine African American athletes?), and the interrelations of all of these.[9]

Such experiences of identity crisis will be differently coded in different social, cultural, and historical contexts. We consider menstruation "natural" and developmental, if still often private, unspeakable, and dirty, while HIV infection is thought of as "unnatural" (and closely associated with so-called "unnatural acts") and antidevelopmental; indeed, HIV infection is explicitly thought as (sero)conversion, a radical change in self that is unexpected and disruptive. Both kinds of experience—"normal" and "abnormal"—reveal something significant about what constitutes identity, what alignments of sex, gender, sexuality, race, etc., constitute coherent, knowable selves.

Part of what is revealed when we look at such experiences of changing identity is that, in any given cultural-historical configuration, different attributes of identity are thought differentially in relation to the possibility of change. That is, moments of identity crisis explicitly foreground the possibility of, as well as the limits to, a movement between different identity positions and between potentially opposed areas of cultural inclusion and exclusion (masculine/feminine, Jewish/Christian, hetero-/homosexual, etc.), and they therefore provide a particularly useful ground for testing the complex ways in which gendered, sexual, racial, and religious "normality" and "queerness" might interact, reinforcing but also diverging from one another. If, for instance, we consider how late twentieth-century Western constructions of race, religion, gender, and sexuality are related to the idea that identity might be converted or convertible, we begin to see important differences among these categories despite their shared capacity for generating excluded or abjected identity positions.

At the current moment, religion and race stand largely opposed to each other when it comes to their imagined susceptibility to conversion.

Indeed, conversion experience is thought of primarily *as* religious change, while racial "otherness" (in the American context, most often "Blackness") is biologized and geneticized, and hence defined as stable, unchangeable.[10] This is made particularly clear in ideas about the phenomenon of "passing," where the person who can "pass" as "white" is thought of not as having achieved a racial conversion but rather as concealing his or her "true (racial) self." Certain fantasies of racial convertibility—gathering, for instance, around the popular cultural figure of Michael Jackson—are powerful, but these remain largely confined to a phantasmatic realm and perhaps operate most strikingly to reconfirm the "proper" boundaries of racial distinctiveness.[11] Jackson's changes in skin color and facial features, for instance, are most often depicted as "perverse," "artificial" attempts to transform the self; they represent a conversion that exceeds what is "natural" and that is significantly linked to a suspect, "perverse" sexuality, itself understood as transgressive and "unnatural." But while contemporary views of religion and race are strongly differentiated by their differing relations to the experience of conversion, the two continue to be conflated in many ways—for instance, in the mixing of ethnic/racial and religious identifications in the construction of "Bosnian Muslims."[12] Most striking in the twentieth century was the Nazi racialization of Judaism and the concomitant denial of religious conversion as enabling a "true" conversion of identity. Religious conversion may provide a route toward assimilation into a dominant culture; but insofar as race remains intractable to conversion, and insofar as a "stable" racial identity is made to override religious "choice" in definitions of "true" identity—with race understood as a biological category more determinate of the "essential" self than is a culturally determined religious identity—religious conversion does not finally guarantee a full transformation of self.

The categories of sex, gender, and sexuality, in this same period, are made to stand somewhere between race and religion in their convertibility. While biological sex is still most often conceived of as essential and unchangeable—determined by chromosomes and/or genital configuration and/or secondary sexual characteristics—the theoretical distinction between sex and gender, foundational to second-wave feminism, introduces significant play into the essentialism of sexual difference.[13] As a socially constructed category, gender may or may not align with biological sex, and (in a further feminist move) the social constructedness of gender may even suggest ways in which the biologically based category of sex is itself a social/cultural construction.[14] Questioning the essential status of sex or gender does not, of course, mean that, once established, these attributes of identity are easily changeable; indeed, some of those who have been most insistent on the constructedness of these categories have also insisted that that constructedness does not at all imply that sex/gender identity is any the less firmly established.[15] But it is not insignificant that, in the same period when our understanding of the bases of sex/gender identity has been recast, the recognition of intersexed (nonmale, nonfemale) categories has been heightened,[16] and descriptions and technologies of transgender/transsexual experience have been extensively developed. These themselves play ambivalently between a sense of the self as fixed and determined in its sex/gender (note the frequent claim that the transgender or transsexual self is the "true" one) and a sense that transgender/transsexuality is particularly defined by the experience of change or transition.[17]

At the same time, sexuality—conceived, simultaneously and contradictorily, as biological difference, as social construction, as (unconscious) psychological effect, and as (conscious) choice—is, as Eve Kosofsky Sedgwick has suggested, caught between "minoritizing" models that posit distinct and relatively stable subpopulations of lesbians and gay men and "universalizing" models that envision homosexuality as a possibility for anyone.[18] Even with the current strong tendency to biologize (homo)sexuality, as in the work of Simon LeVay and Dean H. Hamer,[19] the possibility of radical sexual conversion maintains a powerful hold on contemporary thinking. Homophobic discourses emphasize, on the one hand, the feared possibility of "straight" subjects being "recruited" to gayness and, on the other, the hoped-for possibility of "curing" lesbians and gay men (sometimes, indeed, by means of an actual religious conversion).[20] While gay men and lesbians ourselves most often deny both these homophobic fantasies, we still maintain certain ideas of sexual convertibility—the belief, for instance, that "straight"-identified women and men may discover at some point in their lives a homosexual identity "buried" inside. The heterosexually married person who "comes out" relatively late in life is, in fact, a common and important figure in lesbian and gay communities, though often, retrospectively, that person constructs her/his own heterosexual experience as a deviation from a true, homosexual self that has always existed.[21] And in the realm of sexual fantasy, an equally central figure is the "straight" person who gives in to an irresistible homosexual desire.[22]

In sum, while Blackness, Jewishness, female masculinity or male femininity, and sexual queerness are all, in the contemporary American context, relegated to a certain realm of exclusion, the strong *differences* in construction of such categories can be at least partly recognized through a consideration of how susceptible they are thought to be to the phenomenon of a radical change or conversion.

A first glance at various possible attributes of medieval identity suggests that, for the Middle Ages, sex/gender, sexuality, (quasi) race, and religion are all constructed at least partly in moral terms, as choices that might be changed, and partly as biological difference, as attached to a more determinate and unchangeable (sexed/gendered, sexual, [quasi-]racial, or religious) "nature." Sex/gender might seem the most intractable of these attributes since there are extensive medieval medical discourses explaining the in utero determination of the difference between the sexes.[23] But it is also the case that the influential one-sex model—the idea that male and female are not opposed states of being but rather different points of development on a single continuum of sex—allows for the (rare) physical conversion of sex, for a woman to become literally a man and for a man to become physically and biologically more like a woman.[24] More commonly, Christian discourses consider spiritual reform itself in terms of a transformation of gender. Whether biologically male or female, one may become, on the one hand, the "virile" warrior of Christ; on the other, one gives up worldly, masculine power in dedicating oneself to a truly spiritual, Christian life.[25]

Insofar as homosexual behavior is conflated, for the Middle Ages, with hermaphroditism and eunuchry, as much of the material uncovered by John Boswell suggests, medieval sexuality would seem to be inextricably intertwined with "natural" sex/gender and hence constructed as irreducible biological difference.[26] But of course "sodomy" is also importantly seen as a reversible moral choice, a vice or crime that might be avoided or abandoned. Its complex nature—susceptible, but also resistant, to change—is captured, for instance, in the address to Pope Leo IX with which Peter Damian opens his *Liber Gomorrhianus*. Here, homosexual acts are constructed both as a vice demanding moral attention and as physical plague:

Alas! it is a disgrace to speak, it is a disgrace to intimate such a foul crime to the holy ears [of the pope]; but if the doctor dreads the poison of plagues [or wounds], who will attend to applying the cauterizing brand? If the one who is to attend to this is nauseated, who can lead sick breasts back to a state of safety? The vice against nature thus creeps as a cancer [or crab] so that it touches the order of holy men.[27]

Peter's biologizing of sexual "crime" bespeaks a strong sense of the deep intractability of the "vitium contra naturam," which, he predicts, may not be able to be stopped "from the impetus of its course"; he also, however, recognizes the possibility of intervention (cure) by "the vigor of the apostolic seat."[28]

A similar complexity marks medieval ideas of the convertibility of (quasi-)racial and religious identity. Depictions of "Saracens" as "dogs," or the distant "monstrous races" as only partly human, or Jews as having tails and horns, present ontological distinctions that would seem difficult to overcome through a process of conversion.[29] Still, there are accounts that depict even such biological differences as disappearing with moral change. In the king of Tars romances, when a Saracen sultan who has married a Christian princess converts and is baptized, "he changes color from black to white."[30] And in some Eastern versions of the Saint Christopher story, in which Christopher is depicted as originally from a "dog-headed" race, his conversion to Christianity also effects a transformation of physical form.[31] Such examples of striking (quasi-)racial conversion, however, are relatively rare, and Jews and Saracens, thought of as both religiously and racially different and as possessing bodies somehow essentially other than Christian bodies, are often depicted as strongly resistant to conversion, with Jewish "stubbornness" becoming a platitude in medieval Christian depictions of Jews.[32] More abstractly, at least in a certain strain of Christian thinking about the Jews as a people or race rather than as individual moral agents, strong arguments are presented for why the *gens Judaica* has not been, and should not be, wholly converted (or destroyed). The reasoning here is pointedly incoherent, maintaining the importance of individual conversion at the same time that it perpetuates the idea of a perverse race largely intractable to conversion. The Jewish people must survive in order to continue to be punished and to continue as an example of "infidelity," but also, in the words of the Jewish convert to Christianity Peter Alfonsi, "God did not wish to destroy the Jewish people" because "he saw truly that some of [their] seed at some time would believe in him and be saved, and, therefore, for them he did not wish totally to ruin [their] stock."[33]

Given the general duplicity or ambiguity of each of these medieval attributes of identity, the question remains, to what extent, and how intractably, are differences of gender or sexuality linked to differences of (quasi) race or religion. If, for instance, Jews or Muslims are thought to be somehow sexually queer, what happens if and when a Jew or Muslim becomes a Christian? Does each other attribute of the self change seamlessly along with religion, or are there ways in which conversion (like the modern identity crises sketched above) reveals rifts in the self, ways in which religious, (quasi-)racial, gender, and sexual attributes of identity are differentiable, disarticulable?

Thinking about medieval identity in relation to conversion experience should be particularly productive. Christianity is, after all, a religion founded in conversion, and the missionary posture of Christianity vis-à-vis both Judaism and Islam is an important component of interreligious relations throughout the Middle Ages.[34] European Judaism's resistance to conversion, as suggested in the preceding chapter, defines one of its important ways of relating to the Christian culture that surrounds it. Moreover, the idea of conversion remains always crucial to the individual Christian's self-definition, to a consideration of his/her own experiences in the world. Baptism may set the stage for the individual's salvation, but it by no means guarantees it. As various kinds of Christian moral texts emphasize, the individual must choose to lead the right kind of life: sometimes this involves simply making moral choices as one matures;[35] sometimes it entails a full change in way of life, as in the embracing of life in a religious order or institution. In either case, the experience of choice and change is likely to be understood via the idea of conversion. When medieval writers like Abelard and Guibert begin, in the twelfth century, to write autobiographically, they often frame their life histories as conversionary, and this continues to be true in later medieval autobiographical writing like that of Margery Kempe or Julian of Norwich.[36]

Of course, the original model for thinking the individual Christian's life change as conversion is the depiction in the New Testament (particularly the Gospels and Acts of the Apostles) of the conversion from Judaism to Christianity of the earliest of Jesus's followers as they embraced and then promulgated his new teachings. When a medieval Christian writer talks about his/her own conversion experience, then, even when this does not explicitly involve Jews or Judaism, the superseded, repudiated figure of the Jewish self is always, at least spectrally, present. The bodily self, the perverse self, the stubborn, unbelieving self put off in favor of a reformed, spiritual self—these evoke a bodily, perverse, stubborn, unbelieving, *Jewish* predecessor. The basis for a Christian theology of self-transformation is, after all, the Pauline idea of putting off the old Adam for the new, where the old and new (like the two biblical Testaments) are coded as Jewish and Christian respectively. And it is significant that Paul himself embodies a Jewish self transformed into a Christian.[37] The account in Acts of his conversion from the Jew Saul to the Christian Paul is more extended and dramatic than that concerning any of the other early apostles:

> But Saul, still breathing threats and slaughter against the disciples of the Lord, approached the high priest, and asked from him letters to the synagogues in Damascus, so that if he found any men or women of the [Christian] Way, he might lead them fettered to Jerusalem. And while he made his journey, it happened that he approached Damascus, and suddenly a light from the sky flashed around him. And falling to the ground, he heard a voice saying to him, "Saul, Saul, why do you persecute me?" And Saul said, "Who are you, Lord?" And he said, "I am Jesus whom you persecute, but arise and go into the city, and what you should do will be told to you." But those men who accompanied him stood stupefied, hearing a certain voice but seeing no one. But Saul arose from the ground, and with his eyes open saw nothing; but leading him by the hand they brought him into Damascus. And he was three days without seeing, and he neither ate nor drank.... And Ananias went and entered into the house, and laying his hands on [Saul], he said, "Saul, brother, the Lord Jesus, who appeared to you in the way by which

you came, has sent me so that you may see and be filled with
the Holy Spirit." And immediately something like scales fell
from his eyes, and he received sight. And arising, he was baptized, and when he took food, he was strengthened. And he was
with the disciples who were in Damascus for several days, and
immediately preached Jesus in the synagogues, since this one
is the Son of God.[38]

This is an account that continues influentially to shape a medieval sense
of what it means to convert, whether from one kind of Christian self to
another or actually from Judaism or Islam to Christianity.

Hovering in the background of medieval Christian conversion accounts is the figure of the hardened, persecutory Jew, who must, like
Paul, be chastened. Significantly, it is not the moment of Paul's definitive
embracing of Christianity that is most frequently evoked in medieval
illustrations of his conversion but rather the earlier moment when the
Jew Saul is confronted by a blinding light and falls from his horse in
astonishment (see Figure 3).[39] Emphasizing this moment makes clear
that the action of conversion entails not just a rational, moral consideration of one religious tradition against another; it involves the full body,
with its attributes of gender and sexuality. The martial figure of Saul,
opulently dressed, riding confidently forward, suggests a powerful, worldly,
masculine, virile, and Jewish position appropriate to the man responsible for pursuing and persecuting the early Christian "heretics" to Judaism.
But, in the moment of the fall, that position is revealed instead as weakness, paling in comparison to the spiritual power of "the light from the
sky." Saul's physically able body is humiliated through its tumble into
debility, and his inability to see the truth is literalized in a blindness
that is simultaneously a punishment from above and his own stubborn
refusal to recognize the meaning of the revelation presented to him. His
armed companions, able to hear but not see (or, in the account of Acts
22:9, to see but not hear), look on helplessly. The worldly masculinity of
the persecutory Jew—whose powerful, but here abased, steed would
often, for the Middle Ages, personify knightly prowess as well as sexual
energy and virility[40]—is here overturned, brought low by the incorpo-
real but immense force of divine illumination. And what is implied for
the Jewish, masculine, warrior self is the need to assume a new mas-

fact
lup
loft
næ
tis,
pla
fe qu
&
nun
pul
pun

debitatem indicatie dia
p universum ortem toto

Figure 3. The conversion of St. Paul on the road to Damascus: historiated initial "C." Detail from
Bodleian Library, Lat. liturg. e.39, fol. 15r (first quarter of the fourteenth century, 1307 or later).
Reproduced with permission from The Bodleian Library, University of Oxford.

culinity, a different embodiment, stimulated by the humiliation of the
flesh (blindness, illness) and eventuating in the embrace of a wholly new
way of approaching the world—spirit in place of body and worldly desire.

Recognizing the centrality of conversion to medieval Christian identity, as well as its crucial role in Christianity's relations to its religious
others, and especially Judaism, I ask, in the remainder of this chapter,
what conversion experience and its representation in medieval texts
might tell us about the construction of medieval identity, the imbrica-
tion of body, gender, sexuality, religion, and (quasi) race in the formation

of a self. First, I sketch as fully as possible the ways in which dominant Christian constructions tend to align religion with gender, sexuality, and embodiment; then, I ask how religious conversion tests and realigns such constructions.

THE GENDER TROUBLE OF RELIGIOUS DIFFERENCE

Gender was crucial to medieval Christian constructions of religious otherness. "Heretical" movements that challenged orthodox Christianity from within were often depicted as appealing particularly to women. John of Salisbury claimed, for instance, that Arnold of Brescia "built up a faction known as the heretical sect of the Lombards . . . [who] found their chief supporters among pious women."[41] A women's religious movement like the beguines was particularly likely to be viewed as heterodox,[42] and accusations against women perceived as leading "heretical" religious lives often arose from concern over a suspected subversion of gender hierarchy. Thus, in *The Book of Margery Kempe*, Kempe's suspected "heresy" and her violation of "properly" gendered behavior clearly depend upon each other. At the same time that Kempe is being examined on the articles of the faith, the Mayor of Leicester charges her with wanting "'to lure away our wives from us, and lead them off with you.'" Later, certain women more domestically inclined—that is, more properly "feminine"—than Kempe come "running out of their houses with their distaffs, crying to the people, 'Burn this false heretic.'" Some men call her a Lollard, and others instruct her to "'give up this life that you lead, and go and spin, and card wool, as other women do.'"[43]

As we have begun to see above, both Islam and Judaism were strongly affiliated with "heresy" in medieval Christian imaginations, with Islam often considered a Christian "heresy" and Judaism often linked to "heretical" conspiracies; moreover, Islam and Judaism were conflated with each other.[44] And from a Christian perspective, both these alternative religious traditions involved, like "heresy," a certain disturbance of gender. Western European Christian discourses tended to construct Muslim and Jewish men as failing to live up to "masculine" ideals in the public realm, and specifically in the realm of warfare—failures that Christian legislation (e.g., repeatedly barring non-Christians from holding public office) indeed helped to produce.[45] Louise Mirrer concludes that, in Castilian epic and ballad, Muslim men were depicted as "defeated, docile, and often 'unmanly'" and "Jewish men...frequently accorded the sexual and status identity of the powerless."[46] Marco Polo comments that "Christians are far more valiant than Saracens."[47] And Jews were rarely associated with martial prowess, in large part because they were often legally prohibited from bearing arms.[48]

The gender difference of Jewish and Muslim men was often tied, in Christian thinking, to the practice of circumcision, which was thought to mark a lack of masculinity on their bodies.[49] Classical Roman law associated circumcision with castration,[50] and some early Christians saw circumcision, not always disapprovingly, as occasioning a loss of virile sexual energy; thus, for Origen, the prophets' "acceptance of circumcision showed...that [they] accepted the discipline of sexual restraint, since circumcision signified a commitment to cut off the lusts of the flesh."[51] While "devirilization" might in some ways be a Christian desideratum, as Origen's own taking on of castration clearly suggests,[52] in medieval Christian depictions of contemporary Muslim and Jewish men (and not the biblical prophets), it most often served the purposes of stigmatization. The association of eunuchry with "the East"—not just Islam but also the "schismatic" Christianity of Byzantium—performed a certain hopeful (performative) emasculation of threatening forces on the borders of Western Europe, while at the same time a focus on disordered Eastern bodies and their uncontrolled desires expressed precisely the fears this performative emasculation tried to put to rest.[53] As we saw in the preceding chapter, in reporting that the Greek emperor had commanded each family in his realm to make one of its daughters a prostitute and one of its sons a eunuch, Guibert of Nogent made clear his view that castration enervated and devirilized not just the individual but the nation and necessitated the virile, martial, and more properly Christian intervention of the Frankish crusaders.[54] In this same moment, the Muslim threat to Christians and Christianity is particularly associated with circumcision: the circumcised Muslims themselves force circumcision on "Christian boys and youths." Their actions here are, moreover, associated with a disordered and violent sexuality, a failure of "proper" masculinity to bridle its forceful desire: the Muslim enemies rape "noble women and their daughters" and "sodomiz[e]...men of every age and rank—boys, adolescents, young men, old men, nobles, servants, and, what is worse and more wicked, clerics and monks, and even... bishops!"[55]

From such a conflation of Muslim circumcision, forced circumcision of Christians by Muslims, Muslim rape and forcible sodomy, it is clear that, while circumcision was felt to mark a deficient masculinity, and while Muslim men were indeed sometimes clearly depicted as "effeminate," their masculinity was not *simply* constructed as debility or "effeminate" powerlessness. Indeed, the deformation of the masculine body that circumcision performed was likely to operate not to discipline masculine libido (as in Origen's formulation) but to release that energy in uncontrolled, unpredictable, and dangerous ways. In Christian depictions of medieval European Jews, the construction of circumcision as a lack of Jewish "virility" tends to be conflated with a deep threat to Christian "masculinity."[56] In the 1494 confession forced from the Jews of Tyrnau, "the wound of circumcision" entails, on the one hand, a lack in Jewish gender and sexuality and, on the other, a compensatory violence directed against the unwounded bodies of Christians; supposed Jewish blood crimes are connected in a richly suggestive way to circumcision, menstruation, and unbridled sexual desire:

> Firstly, they were convinced by the judgment of their ancestors that the blood of a Christian was a good remedy for the alleviation of the wound of circumcision. Secondly, they were of [the] opinion that this blood, put into food, is very efficacious for the awakening of mutual love. Thirdly, they had discovered, as men and women among them suffered equally from menstruation, that the blood of a Christian is a specific medicine for it, when drunk. Fourthly, they had an ancient but secret ordinance by which they are under obligation to shed Christian blood in honor of God in daily sacrifices in some spot or other; they said it had happened in this way that the lot for the present year had fallen on the Tyrnau Jews.[57]

That circumcision made Jewish men less sexually attractive to women, a circumstance that would make necessary the artificial "awakening of mutual love," was expressed, for instance, by Peter Abelard, ventriloquizing the voice of a male Jew in his *Dialogue of a Philosopher with a Jew, and a Christian*: "the sign of circumcision seems so abhorrent to the

Gentiles that if we [Jews] were to seek their women, the women would in no way give their consent, believing that the truncating of this member is the height of foulness, and detesting the divine sign of holiness as an idolatry."[58] Further, that Jewish men experienced a "bloody flux," in Caesarius of Heisterbach associated with their crucifixion of Christ and clearly affiliated with menstruation, was a commonplace at least as far back as the thirteenth century.[59] The association of a "feminizing" deficiency in Jewish men's bodies with the originary moment of Jewish violence against Christ was part of a complex economy that bound the "degenerate" body of the Jewish man to attacks on Christian bodies, both the supposed murder of Christians for their blood and the desecrations of the host that represented a continued attack on Christ's own body.[60] Jewish violence was in particular imagined as threatening Christian "masculinity." Thus, as James Shapiro points out, ritual murder accusations, particularly in England, often sketched a "sequence of criminal acts beginning with abduction and circumcision and ending with crucifixion and cannibalism."[61] Jews at Norwich in the 1230s were prosecuted for kidnapping and circumcising (though not killing) a five-year-old boy who may have been the son of a converted Jew.[62] And D'Blossiers Tovey claims, in his eighteenth-century *Anglia Judaica*, that "the *first* Indictment that appears any where upon *Record*, against a *Jew*" was against "one *Bonefand* a *Jew* of *Bedford* ... not for *Circumcising*, but *totally* cutting off the Privy Member of one *Richard*, the Nephew of *Robert de Sutton*."[63]

The medieval Christian "feminization" of religious others operated in a variety of other ways as well. Jews were frequently associated with female prostitutes, with both sometimes similarly treated as polluting presences: "the Avignon municipality, for example, provided that, if a Jew touched fruit on a stand, he, like a prostitute, had to purchase it because he had defiled it."[64] Such ordinances in several Western European cities further associated both Jews and prostitutes with lepers, whose diseased bodies were objects of fear and segregation.[65] Brothels and "Jewries" were often located side-by-side; just as prostitutes satisfied certain disavowed sexual needs for Christian communities, Jews, in their assigned role as "usurers," satisfied certain disavowed economic needs.[66] Indeed, medieval economic accusations against Jews were importantly wrapped up with gender constructions. Commenting on the crime of coin-clipping, Matthew Paris notes that "it was said and discovered that the coins were being circumcised by circumcised people and infidel Jews who, because of the heavy royal taxes, were reduced to begging."[67] Those Christians who politically supported Jews, or those thought to be not vigilant enough in guarding against them, themselves became the object of gendered aspersions. Thus, Paris notes that "a certain most wicked and merciless Jew," acting in a royal investigation of Jewish economic crimes, "reproached without fail Christians who were grieving over and bewailing the sufferings of the Jews and called the royal bailiffs lukewarm and effeminate"; here, the Jewish enemy of Jews is also, complicatedly, cast as the "feminizing" attacker of Christians.[68] And the Jewish community as a whole might be "feminized." In Caesarius of Heisterbach, through the cleverness of a Christian clerk who has had sex with and impregnated a Jewish virgin, a Jewish community is led to expect the birth of its Messiah. The vanity of that wish, and of Jewish belief more generally, is demonstrated at the Messiah's birth: "The hour came in which the unhappy one should be delivered, and there ensued the usual pain, groans and cries. At last she brought forth an infant, not indeed the Messiah, but a daughter."[69] The "feminized" people, Jews who passed up their chance to recognize the "true" Messiah, can here bring forth only a weak (female) parody of Christ.

Given the "feminization" of Jewish and Muslim men in Western European Christian discourses, we might expect to find a corresponding "masculinization" of Muslim and Jewish women, and in at least some texts this is the case.[70] In Chaucer's Man of Law's Tale, the sultaness is a "Virago," "Semyrame the secounde," "serpent under femynynytee," and "feyned womman."[71] There are at least some social historical indications that, in certain parts of Europe, Jewish women were more involved in public life than Christian women:[72] Christians may have seen this as indicating a subversion of gender distinctions, both a "masculinization" of properly "feminine" behavior and a "feminizing" arrogation of male authority to women. On the other hand, however, we also find Muslim and Jewish women depicted as particularly "feminine"—beautiful and seductive. Thus, in Boccaccio's story of Alatiel, the daughter of the sultan (Decameron 2.7)—a story that might be read as a parody of the type of tale recorded more seriously in Chaucer's Man of Law's Tale—Alatiel is "according to everybody who had set eyes on her, . . . the most beautiful woman to be found anywhere on earth"; she arouses lust in a long series of men, and she satisfies that lust.[73] When finally she is returned to the man originally meant to be her husband, "despite the fact that eight separate men had made love to her on thousands of different occasions, she entered his bed as a virgin and convinced him that it was really so."[74] Here, the religiously other woman is seen in particularly corporealized and sexualized terms, and this is also the case of Jewish women in two of Caesarius of Heisterbach's narratives (ii.23–24). These women are, "like many of [their] race, . . . very beautiful," and they attract the attention of "young [Christian] clerks" who fall in love with them and by whom they are seduced.[75] The sexualized depiction of Jewish and Muslim women is not inconsistent with the general "feminization" and corporealization of Judaism and Islam. In Caesarius, the Jewish women's desire for Christian men also reconfirms stereotypes about the sexual unattractiveness of (circumcised) Jewish men. But something beyond the "feminization" of Judaism is also happening in Caesarius: in the first of his stories, the Jewish woman comes to "be born again in the grace of baptism," marrying the Christian clerk, who thus "lose[s] all hope of ecclesiastical preferment"; ultimately, however, both take vows in the Cistercian order.[76] Further, in the two stories (ii.25–26) that directly follow his accounts of sexually attractive Jewish women, Caesarius depicts two other Jewish women who are chaste and who become, "by the providence of God, imbued with the Christian faith."[77] Here, Jewish women, unlike the obdurate men of their "race," seem particularly susceptible to Christianity's "truth" and hence conversion. Perhaps this too represents a sort of gender reversal: where in Christianity it is the "fathers" of the church who most strongly recognize and speak its truths, here it is daughters who, despite a certain carnality associated with their female-ness and Jewishness, come to recognize spiritual truth and break the yoke of "the infidel father."[78]

QUEER JEWISH BODIES

The construction of religious, and specifically Jewish, otherness parallels and sometimes directly evokes the medieval imputation of femininity to classes of men *within* Christianity. Men's failure to live up to certain masculine ideals, including especially ideals of courtliness, marriage, and familial responsibility that we might associate with the contemporary category of sexuality, are often misogynistically conflated with the feminine. Sodomy itself is strongly feminized and sodomy accusations almost invariably include an implication of unmanly, effeminate behavior; like the effeminacy of religious difference, too, the sodomitical is not just seen as weakness or deficiency but also as dangerously disordered, threatening familial and social stability.[79]

The "feminization" of male homosexuality is made explicit for instance in the twelfth-century Latin debate poem "Ganymede and Helen," where the central subject of debate is the relative worth of male-male and female-male sexual relationships. In just one of several possible examples, Helen charges Ganymede with "try[ing] to be smooth and hairless below / So that your temple there might be like that of a woman, / So that in defiance of nature you might become a girl."[80] A similar "feminization" also operates in a wide variety of narrative works. In the Icelandic sagas, the suggestion of a homosexual relation—and particularly the taking of the passive role in anal sex—consistently represents an insult to masculinity, as in the opening pages of *Gíslasaga:* "[Skeggi] told Ref to make wooden figures of Gisli and Kolbjorn—'and have one stand close behind the other; and the nastiness of that will always be there to shame them.'" Gisli responds with a clear assertion of martial masculinity: "'you can look here at a man who is not afraid to fight you.'"[81] In the very different tradition of French verse romance, we find in such works as the *Roman d'Eneas* and Marie de France's *Lanval* accusations that conflate the charge of sexual misconduct with that of inappropriate gender.[82] The famous passage from Marie (cited, for instance, by Havelock Ellis),[83] in which the queen, rejected by Lanval, accuses him of having "no interest in women" and of "enjoy[ing] [him]self" with "fine-looking boys,"[84] is particularly interesting for the complicated ways in which it intertwines misogyny, the hetero- and homoerotic, and the homosocial. The depiction of the queen's attempt at seduction depends on misogyny, as does Lanval's self-defense. This defense also counterposes male homosocial loyalty (Lanval's commitment to the king) and sexuality (his refusal of the queen), even as the queen's attack pits the homoerotic, conceived of as socially disruptive, against the properly homosocial—"my lord made a bad mistake when he let you stay with him."[85] Heterosexual desire leads to the queen's attempt at seduction; it also (though secretly) motivates Lanval's rejection of her approach. Lanval's (hidden) heterosexuality—the fact that he has been pledged to secrecy by his lover—is what leads the queen to accuse him of homosexuality, and in turn it is this accusation that forces Lanval rashly to reveal the existence of his beloved. Since, in the terms of the story, this revelation endangers the love affair, we here have the defense against homosexuality paradoxically and intriguingly threatening the continuation of the heterosexual affair. In any case, the queen's accusation against Lanval threatens to take away his knightly manhood, to turn him into a "base coward [and] lousy cripple."[86]

The "gender insubordination" associated with various sorts of sexual "queerness" might also, although more rarely, involve turning the "properly" female into the male, as in the "masculinizing" representations of lesbians noted by Susan Schibanoff:

> One of the few extant medieval medical discussions of female homosexuality, by William of Saliceto in 1285, characterizes the lesbian as a figure of anatomical excess: some women, William explains, experience a growth called *ragadia*, which begins in the uterus and can protrude beyond the vagina in the form of a penis. Thus, William concludes, woman may take man's place in sexual intercourse with another woman.[87]

Both religious and sexual others are thus associated, in medieval discourses, with an inappropriate gender, and the non-Christian and sodomitical parallel each other in a variety of additional ways. Thus, sexual, religious, and (quasi-)racial "others" were consistently constructed as marked by both bodily and intellectual degeneracy and perversity. The hyena, thought to change its sex annually and depicted as devouring corpses, came to be associated with both homosexuality and Jews.[88] Muslims were thought to distort the truth of revelation, "heretically" claiming spiritual status for what was merely corporeal. As we have seen, Guibert of Nogent depicts Islam as illegitimately claiming that Muhammad's (supposed) epilepsy was not a bodily weakness but rather a spiritual gift; Islamic tradition, in Guibert's account, also conceals the (again, invented) grotesque mode of Muhammad's death.[89] Jews were proverbially literal readers of scripture, unable to penetrate the spiritual truth of their own texts, and this literal bent was closely associated with a Jewish corporeality that involved both bodily exorbitances and disintegrations.[90] As noted above, Jews were connected with a variety of physically deforming diseases, especially those involving a loss of blood.[91] In a work like the Croxton *Play of the Sacrament,* we see Jewish bodily corruption literally enacted, with the arm of the main Jewish character severed from its body and boiled until flesh and bone separate. Revulsion at Jewish bodies further expresses itself through a close association of Jews with infection, dirt, and defecation. Disgust at Jewish bodiliness is clearly at work in the *Prioress's Tale,* Chaucer's story of Jewish violence centered in a privy. Indeed, accusations against Jews often include not simply accounts of Jewish violence against Christian bodies or holy objects but a strong association of that violence with the excremental.[92] Host desecration narratives, as Miri Rubin notes, often depict attempts "to dispose of the host (by burial, by throwing it into water or into a place of filth)."[93] And in Matthew Paris, "a certain quite rich Jew, Abraham" buys "a nicely carved and painted statue of the blessed Virgin, as usual nursing her son at her bosom": "This image the Jew set up in his latrine and, what is thoroughly dishonourable and ignominious to mention, as it were in blasphemy of the blessed Virgin, he inflicted a most filthy and unmentionable thing on it, daily and nightly, and ordered his wife to do the same."[94]

The construction of "sodomy" likewise depended upon an association with both intellectual and bodily corruption—particularly in the close linkage of homosexual behavior to a "heresy" understood not just as doctrinal error but as a corruption of the body inseparably linked to such error.[95] The bodies of "sodomites"—male bodies associated with not just the effeminate but also the hermaphroditic and animal-like—were the locus of disgust and fear, as Boswell makes clear in his citation of such writers as John Chrysostom, Peter Cantor, and Peter Damian.[96] Sodomy and an associated physical degeneracy were conceived of as broadly dangerous, threatening the health of the body politic and indeed of the whole natural world, as in Alain de Lille's *De Planctu Naturae.* Of course, a similar danger was perceived in Jews: because of their supposedly debased bodies and unnatural loss of blood, they were thought to need replenishment from other, more perfect (Christian) bodies, and they were thought to fulfill these needs in ways that were frighteningly well-organized, involving secret meetings and international conspiracies. In 1321, in what was far from an isolated occurrence, Jews and lepers were accused of having worked in concert to poison the wells of France.[97]

The means for constructing sexual difference and those for defining religious, (quasi-)racial otherness are thus often parallel and intertwined.

Indeed, the very naming of certain sexual acts and (perhaps) a loosely defined sexual identity after the "egregious cities"[98] of Sodom and Gomorrah suggests an attempt to make sexual difference ethnic or (quasi-)racial, to fortify the casting out of sexual "perversity" by conflation with a morally charged geopolitical differentiation. Conversely, as we have seen, religious divergence—schism, "heresy," the "infidelities" of Islam and Judaism—and (quasi-)racial or ethnic difference are often associated with sexual "crimes": adultery, rape, promiscuity, incest, sodomy, bestiality.[99]

Indeed, the medieval policing of a separation between Christian and Jewish communities often focused on the realm of the sexual—including, but not limited to, the institutions of marriage and family. Christianity had a long history of legislation against intermarriage and interfaith sex,[100] legislation that was importantly involved in the (never wholly successful) effort to maintain a strict segregation of Jewish, Christian, and Muslim communities. Thus, one rationale often given for insisting that Jews and "Saracens" wear distinctive clothing was a specifically sexual one; the Fourth Lateran Council (1215) decreed:

> Whereas in certain provinces of the Church the difference in their clothes sets the Jews and Saracens apart from the Christians, in certain other lands there has arisen such confusion that no differences are noticeable. Thus it sometimes happens that by mistake Christians have intercourse with Jewish or Saracen women, and Jews or Saracens with Christian women. Therefore, lest these people, under the cover of an error, find an excuse for the grave sin of such intercourse, we decree that these people (Jews and Saracens) of either sex, and in all Christian lands, and at all times, shall easily be distinguishable from the rest of the populations by the quality of their clothes; especially since such legislation is imposed upon them also by Moses.[101]

Similarly, the often renewed injunction against Jews owning Christian slaves or employing Christian servants—particularly women servants and wet nurses—had a clear sexual component, as is evident in a papal bull of 1205 addressed to the king of France:

> [A]lthough it was enacted in the [Third] Lateran Council that Jews are not permitted to have Christian servants in their homes

either under pretext of rearing their children, nor for domestic service, nor for any other reason whatever, but that those who presume to live with them shall be excommunicate, yet they do not hesitate to have Christian servants and nurses, with whom, at times, they work such abominations as are more fitting that you should punish than proper that we should specify.[102]

And a similar letter some forty years later (1244) declares: "they make Christian women nurses for their children, in insult to the Christian Faith, and with these women they commit many shameful actions."[103]

Although such measures were certainly directed toward "obviat[ing] the kind of contact that might result in untoward religious influence,"[104] they also reflected, as the language they employ—"abominationes," "turpia"—suggests, a certain visceral repugnance at the bodies that they sought to rope off from Christendom. Intermarriage was classed as a sexual crime equivalent to adultery and hence subject to capital punishment, and sex that transgressed the lines of religious distinction was directly associated with both "bestiality" and "sodomy."[105] Thus, Joshua Trachtenberg notes that "in 1222 a deacon, after standing trial before Archbishop Langton, was burned at Oxford on a charge of bestiality: he had embraced Judaism in order to marry a Jewess."[106] In a postmedieval case, Jean Alard, "who kept a Jewess in his house in Paris and had several children by her, . . . was convicted of sodomy on account of this relation and burned, together with his paramour, 'since coition with a Jewess is precisely the same as if a man should copulate with a dog.'"[107]

SODOMY AND JEWISHNESS IN PETER DAMIAN

The linkages between sexual transgression and Jewishness just sketched in bold outline might be discerned already rather fully developed at the beginning of the period with which we are concerned, in the influential eleventh-century work of Peter Damian.[108] As Mark Jordan has shown, Peter's *Liber Gomorrhianus* represents a crucial development in the Western discourse on "sodomy,"[109] and the letter Peter focuses on the problem of Jews in Christendom, discussed above in chapter 1, is itself deeply influential, often cited in Christian polemical works about Judaism in the centuries that follow.[110] While Peter takes up the two topics—sodomy and Jewishness—in two separate treatises, the terms in which he discusses both suggest certain important convergences between his understanding of sexual behavior and his approach to religious/(quasi-)racial identity.

The *Liber Gomorrhianus* focuses its attention on behavior that Damian claims to be current and ongoing in the church, and like much of Peter's other work it thus insists on its *local* applicability. But of course at the same time Peter evokes the distant Gomorrah and Sodom to describe that "certain abominable and most shameful vice" that he claims "has developed" "[i]n our region."[111] In making the title of his work on sodomy the *Liber Gomorrhianus* and in repeatedly referring to the biblical story of Sodom and Gomorrah as he defines a fourfold taxonomy of "criminal" male sexual behavior, Peter, like the broader Western tradition that comes to call such behavior "sodomy," links particular sex acts—here, masturbation, mutual masturbation, interfemoral intercourse, and anal intercourse[112]—to geopolitical/ethnic (and of course biblical/historical) entities. Despite Damian's insistent focusing of attention on gomorran acts in their local contexts ("in our region"), the depiction of those acts depends upon a category of foreignness, evoked not just in the reference to Sodom and Gomorrah but in many of the other details used to define the gomorran "crime." In a wide range of medieval texts, "the egregious cities,"[113] in all their foreignness and Easternness, stand starkly posed against places of redemption like Jerusalem; indeed, they are understood to have fallen out of the natural world through the behavior of their inhabitants.[114] And in one of the reversals of Jewish understandings that typifies medieval Christian exegetical practice, (a new) Jerusalem commonly becomes the city of Christian redemption, and Sodom and Gomorrah specifically *Jewish* locales.[115] Underpinning Damian's treatment of sexual behavior, then, is a sense that religious, ethnic, (quasi-)racial difference inheres in sodomy. The subject of this "vice" is not simply a sinner who, by reversing his behavior, might reenter the Christian community; rather that subject falls into proximity with the ethnically, (quasi-)racially, and religiously different in such a way that a full return into Christian community becomes difficult to imagine.

Peter Damian's first letter, "to Honestus," was probably written about nine years before the *Liber Gomorrhianus;* as a refutation of Jewish positions, it is atypical in the corpus of Peter's work, which tends to focus on intrachurch issues.[116] Indeed, as we have seen above in chapter 1, Peter is at first reluctant to take up the topic urged on him by his correspondent, suggesting that Christians should attend to the individual battle against sin rather than a debate against Judaism. Soon reversing himself, however, Peter suggests that working out questions about Jewishness might be a good way to approach the more crucial questions of Christian morality. Peter thus agrees to take up the question of Jewish difference as part of the project of defining "the same" of proper Christianity. Conjuring up to conjure away the specter of Judaism, Peter hopes to resolidify "the faith," "the foundation of all virtues": "when the foundation is shaken, the whole structure of the building threatens to fall into ruin."[117]

Peter Damian's letter against the Jews and his *Liber Gomorrhianus* thus pursue two separate but complementary projects: the first defines Christianness against an other completely separate from it—indeed, it defines one nation or people against another—while the second, also concerned with a "proper" Christianity, makes distinctions based on moral choices and behavior among those who are within the Christian community from the start. Furthermore, these two projects are not only complementary but also intertwined: integral to Peter's depiction of Christians fallen into gomorran acts is a sense of their ethnic and religious difference, their full movement out of Christianness. And, conversely, for Peter, the Jew, although standing outside the realm of Christianity, shares in the characteristics of sodomitical behavior attached, in the *Liber Gomorrhianus*, to Christians, indeed to Christians in religious orders who should stand at the very heart of Christian spiritual life.

In the rhetoric of Peter's anti-Jewish and antisodomitical texts, we see religious/(quasi-)racial difference and sexual difference constructed in reciprocal ways, with each dependent on the other for its full definition. In both texts, we see difference—whether Jewishness or sodomy—defined as sin or crime,[118] and, moreover, as the worst of possible crimes: Jewish error "exceeds every kind of infamy, surpasses in barbarity every sort of crime,"[119] while "this shameful deed" that is sodomy is "not without cause . . . considered to be the worst of crimes."[120] The crime, in each case, involves "perversity,"[121] shamelessness or impudence,[122] and a certain trickiness or subtlety, which threatens to draw others into the "snares" of sin, and which is indeed, again in both cases, more or less

explicitly associated with diabolical action.[123] Beyond these qualities—
which might be thought to be under the control of the individual making
moral choices—the crimes of Jewishness and of sodomy both involve a
certain loss of control, a "madness" that seems beyond the power of
volition.[124] Indeed, complementing characterizations of Jewishness and
sodomy that would make these moral failings are descriptions that suggest rather that they are diseases, wounds, plagues—that is, "natural"
(physical) phenomena that attack the individual in the body against his
will (even though, at the same time, they are thought to result from acts
of the will). Judaism is marked by an "*incurable* crime," the crucifixion
of Christ.[125] Sodomy is a "wound" or "lesion,"[126] "poison" or "infection,"[127]
a "plague,"[128] "pestilence,"[129] "leprosy."[130] Jewishness and sodomy make
a difference not just in the individual's moral faculty but in the body
itself. Threatening masculinity, both Jewishness and the sodomitical
demand of "the knight of Christ"[131] masculine accoutrements, armor
and arrows,[132] as a defense against the subtle, diabolical, and feminine.
And both Jewishness and sodomy are closely allied, in Peter, to the monstrous and the bestial, and to a bestiality again particularly evocative
of the diabolical. Addressing the Jew, Peter insists, "Do not, as is your
custom, by using subtle dodges, turn yourself, as it were, into varying
types of monster, like a slippery snake when captured, try[ing] to escape
my hands,"[133] and this formulation is echoed in his depiction of the
"utterly diseased queen of Sodom"[134] as a "poisonous serpent,"[135] a
"four-headed" "serpent" that "we have sought to crush with the cudgel of
our disputation."[136]

The depiction of Jewishness and sodomy thus makes each a moral
failing at the same time that each is affiliated to an actual physical change
or difference in the body that threatens the ontological status of the
human being, drawing the male close to the female and out of the boundaries of the human into the monstrous and bestial. As Peter makes explicit in the *Liber Gomorrhianus*, sodomy "[w]ithout fail . . . brings death to
the body and destruction to the soul. It pollutes the flesh, extinguishes
the light of the mind, expels the Holy Spirit from the temple of the
human heart, and gives entrance to the devil, the stimulator of lust."[137]
Further, both Jewishness and sodomy are presented not just as individual
failings but as corporate, indeed national, entities. This is unsurprising
for Judaism, which Damian shows being corporately punished for its
disbelief;[138] it is more unexpected, however, to see sodomy so presented—

though of course the term *sodomy* itself facilitates the presentation. Like the Jews in rejecting Christ and Christianity, those practicing the vice of sodomy are seen as giving up "citizenship" in one city—"the heavenly Jerusalem"—to become "heir[s] of infernal Babylon."[139] An "outcast from his heavenly home,"[140] the sodomite finds himself, like the exiled Jew, "reduced to slavery at the feet of all mankind,"[141] "enslaved" and bound.[142]

We see, in these two texts, two discourses mutually constituting each other. The sexually disavowed is constructed on the model of that which is both ethnically or racially foreign and religiously misguided and erroneous; the Jew, on the other hand, takes on the qualities of gender disruption, shamelessness, perversity, bodily exorbitance imagined as integral to the gomorran. Associating Jews with sodomites operates to distance them further from the Christian, even as it works to fortify the casting out of sodomites from *Christianitas,* but it also, paradoxically, brings Jewish bodies *close,* since *any* body, including especially the endangered monastic body of Peter's *Liber Gomorrhianus* (standing in the very place from which the polemicist himself speaks), might become sodomitical and hence also like the Jewish body so strongly othered in Peter's letter to Honestus concerning the Jews.[143]

A trope that serves as a particularly rich site of overlap between religious/(quasi-)racial and sexual discourses in Damian's writing, and in medieval culture more generally, is that of blindness, which brings together many of the elements so far enumerated. Blindness is of course consistently associated with Jews in medieval texts, and it becomes, in treatments of Jewishness, an especially complex place for defining Jewish difference.[144] (It echoes, too, the account of Saul's conversion to Paul, fundamental to Christian understandings of how the Christian dispensation supersedes Judaism and of what must be given up in the move from Jewishness to Christianity.) Blindness evokes moral error and intellectual dimness, suggesting a Jewish inability to perceive truth through a "veil of ignorance,"[145] an inability particularly linked to the carnality of Jewish understanding, a clinging to the literal meaning of things that should rather be read spiritually: "Obviously, for anyone who still needs evidence after such enlightening testimony, it remains for him to request a lighted lamp to view the radiant sun at noontime. With the vision of so many heavenly stars sparkling before you, Jew, I marvel how such deep shades of blindness can hold sway, even in eyes that are totally without sight."[146] At the same time, the trope of Jewish blindness physicalizes both the moral and intellectual errors of the Jews, associating these with a bodily weakness and strangeness that makes Jews not just erroneous in belief or thought but wrong somehow in their embodied nature. Appropriately for a people thought to be unable to move from the corporeal to the spiritual, Jewish bodiliness is conceived of as particularly heavy and obtuse, plunged into a "darkness" insusceptible to enlightenment.[147]

Blindness, too, is central in medieval depictions of sodomy. Crucial in the biblical account of Sodom and Gomorrah, and there closely affiliated with the Sodomites' attempted sexual transgression (Genesis 19:11), blindness (along with mute animality) is indeed often presented as integral to the sodomitical: Jerome's etymology, "Sodoma . . . beast, silent, or blindness, or the similitude of these,"[148] is taken up by such medieval exegetes as Guibert.[149] "Luxuria," explicitly including sodomitical behavior, is seen by pseudo-Alcuin as leading to "blindness of mind,"[150] and blindness is also associated, in medieval physiological discourses, with sexually excessive and improper behavior: "Coitus destroys the eyesight and dries up the body."[151] It is not, then, surprising that Peter frequently evokes blindness in his depiction of the sodomitical.[152] Like Jews, sodomites are affiliated to darkness rather than light,[153] to carnality rather than the spirit,[154] and to a carnality that is dense, gross, and weighted down, sunk into "the filth of impurity":[155] "For him it will be 'a heaven of iron and an earth of bronze' [see Leviticus 26:19]. Burdened with the weight of his crime, he is unable to ascend to heaven."[156] Like Jews, sodomites have "lost their interior eyes,"[157] the ability to perceive realities beyond the purely physical. As in the depiction of Jews, then, the trope of blindness here allows for sodomitical vice to be connected to moral and intellectual error at the same time that it is biologized.

The call for Jewish conversion with which Peter closes the address to a Jew that constitutes a large portion of his letter to Honestus evokes in particular the trope of blindness: "Abandon the errors of Jewish blindness and follow the path to the truth of evangelical grace."[158] But this trope—in the depiction both of Jews and of sodomites—participates in the construction of a religious/(quasi-)racial and a sexual difference that would seem intractable to volitional change. Jewishness is, in Peter's depiction, an error that is bodily, intellectual, and moral all at once, an "*incurable* crime" entailing a "punishment *beyond all remedy*"[159]—to cite the terms in which Peter describes Jewish error just before he calls for Jewish conversion. Peter also prays for the conversion of sodomites: "Rouse yourself, I tell you, arise and be awake, you who were overcome by the sleep of pathetic pleasure; come alive at last, you who fell before the deadly sword of your enemies."[160] But such a "rousing," while it may allow the sinner to "receive full forgiveness of his guilt," leaves him still marked by the sodomitical, outside what might be permitted him had he never inhabited the terrain of Gomorrah: "even though he enjoys a good reputation, is zealous in promoting psalmody, is preeminent for his love of prayer, and is held in high esteem for his holy life, . . . nowise can he be permitted to aspire to ecclesiastical orders."[161]

Peter thus manages to construct both the difference of Jewishness and that of sodomy as, at least in part, irremediable—"beyonds" from which the individual can never fully return. Gathering the qualities of sexual difference into his depiction of a religious/(quasi-)racial other, and reciprocally showing the ways in which sexual difference might be thought in the terms of Jewishness, Peter constructs identity positions that cannot be fully abandoned when the individual changes his beliefs or behavior. Though I do not mean to suggest that there are "modern" concepts of subjectivity and identity at play in Damian's treatment of Gomorrah or of Jewishness, I do think that Jewish and gomorran identities, as these are constructed by Peter, are not merely "accidental," dependent upon acts or ideas the rejection of which would lead the individual straightforwardly into the (re)assumption of "normal" (Christian) identity. Rather, these disallowed identities are, at least partly, stabilized, kept separate and distant from a "normality" that is thus (wishfully) protected from the feared incursions of the perverse.

CONVERSION AND THE STUBBORN BODY

To investigate further the ways in which religious, (quasi-)racial, gendered, and sexualized identities might be (perhaps differentially) stabilized and destabilized, we need to return, in a frame larger than that provided by Peter Damian's texts, to the question of conversion or convertibility that we have seen Peter himself taking up in his treatment of both sodomy and Jewishness. Here, we might pose a rather general question and think through what the surviving medieval evidence suggests as a possible answer or answers. Given that non-Christian—Muslim and Jewish—men are generally depicted as not just religiously, doctrinally or spiritually, different from Christian men, but as different in their gendered and sexualized bodies, what happens when those men convert, when they *become* Christian men? Medieval Christian ideas of Jewishness or Muslimness involve more than what, in the strictest sense, we in the twenty-first century would call *religious* difference; in focusing attention on qualities thought to be based in biology, in the "nature" of bodies, medieval notions of religious difference move into a realm that, in terms of modern identity categories, we would call *racial,* a difference generally thought, at least in the modern West, to be intractable to change. As James Shapiro suggests, in relation to the early modern belief that upon conversion Jews lost their "natural" foul smell (the *foetor judaicus*),

> It was one thing to claim that Jews were, as John Foxe and others put it, aromatized by their conversion; it was quite another to figure out what happened to their racial otherness when they converted and entered, or tried to enter, a Christian commonwealth. The complications raised by conversion disturbed English commentators, some of whom offered vague theories of racial assimilation to explain away the problem. Richard Baxter, for example, proposed that once converted, the Jews "would be no Jews immediately in a religious sense nor within sixty to eighty years in a natural sense."[162]

To state my own question more pointedly, when Jewish or Muslim men converted to Christianity, what was thought to happen to their gendered and sexualized bodies? Insofar as conversion experience was conceived as effecting a complete reorganization of the self—that is, insofar as Jewishness or Muslimness was fully effaced in the convert—that experience should have entailed not just a religious realignment but processes of "masculinization" and "heterosexualization," a loss of "abnormal" gender and sexual features, a regendering and resexualizing simultaneous with the realignment of belief and of moral stance. Can we find such gender/sexual conversion in medieval texts that depict religious conversion? How susceptible to transformation are those embodied traits that, for medieval Christians, seem integral to the differentiation between "true believers" and "infidels" as that religious distinction is wrapped up in such distinctions as those between "men" and "women," "sodomites" and "nonsodomites"?

It is not unlikely that such a transformation of the gendered and sexualized body would have been thought at least possible in the Middle Ages. As noted above, the "one-sex model" of the sexed/gendered body provided at least one available understanding of the physiological relation between maleness and femaleness; Thomas Laqueur cites various medieval and Renaissance accounts in which "Bodies actually seem to slip from their sexual anchorage."[163] And insofar as sexual transgression—"sodomy"—had not yet become sexual *identity* in a modern sense (even if we might sometimes see medieval texts recognizing "sodomites" as somehow, even "essentially," different from others), it tends to be treated as a "vitium" [vice] that might, if with difficulty, be left behind.[164] But the idea that the Jewish or Muslim convert should and might, upon conversion, become more truly masculine and more properly sexual is complicated by Christian models of conversion that date back to the early church—models in which conversion entails *not* bodily "masculinization" or "heterosexualization" but the renunciation of worldly power, family ties, and sexuality. As in Chaucer's *Second Nun's Tale*, traditional Christian conversion is most often conceived of as a "demasculinizing" and "deheterosexualizing" movement out of the world. Valerian and his brother Tiburce, in converting to Christianity, submit themselves to Cecilia's superior spiritual authority; the gender hierarchy of Cecilia and Valerian's marriage is reversed, and that marriage is reconceived in sexual terms as chaste or spiritual rather than sexual and physically procreative.[165] And in an imagined world where the church has yet to gain political power, the move into Christianity also involves a forfeiture of public, "masculine" authority and a movement that we might simultaneously think of in terms of a loss of class privilege: Valerian and Tiburce, rightfully part of the Roman aristocracy, become, as converts, subject to legal action, "torment," and martyrdom.[166]

Though such a model of conversion remains central within Christianity (see, for instance, the Franciscan conversion accounts included in Ugolino's *Little Flowers of St. Francis*), by the high and late Middle Ages the social reality around conversion had changed significantly. The Western church was no longer a persecuted, powerless agent, and while converts like the early Franciscans who moved, *within* Christianity, from secular, and perhaps socially powerful, positions to embrace a spiritual life might still be understood through the model of conversion developed in the early church, the situation was significantly different for converts from *outside* Christianity who, in embracing the hegemonic religion of the West, potentially empowered themselves, moving out of positions of social and political marginality. Indeed, as the history of the Franciscan order shows, too vigorous an embracing of poverty, too stark a renunciation of worldly power, too strong a movement out of the realm of "masculine" authority, could come to be viewed with suspicion, even as "heretical," because potentially critical of the church and its real, secular power.[167]

A medieval Jewish or Muslim man converting to Christianity thus necessarily found himself in a vexed position in relation to gender and sexuality, and their social (including their religious) meanings. Conversion for the "feminized" and "sodomitical" Jew or Muslim seems to call for "masculinization" and "heterosexualization," a loss of those gendered and sexualized qualities used, in Christian constructions, to denigrate religious others, to keep them other. But the most common Christian models of conversion entail quite a different sort of movement, away from "masculine" roles and power and away from traditional kin and family forms based in heterosexual relations.[168] Indeed, while homo- and heterosexual acts *are* opposed to each other in the Middle Ages, medieval sexuality is not constructed primarily around a homo/hetero divide; both the hetero- and the homosexual are opposed to the "higher" state of chastity. Movements from a not fully heterosexual position toward heterosexuality, while reflecting a sense of what is accepted and normative in the sexual realm, do not necessarily participate in the "moral" reform of the individual. Insofar as such movements may represent an increasing awareness of and dedication to the corporeal, they may indeed be suspect from a Christian "moral" perspective. Thus, for instance, the conversion of Marie de France's Guigemar from a state of sexual indifference, defined explicitly as an error of nature, to heterosexual and courtly love involves a movement into adultery that runs counter to Christian precepts as well as to the social structures of vassalage, knighthood, marriage, and family (although all of these are ultimately recuperated in the *lai*). In Chaucer's *Clerk's Tale*, Walter's acquiescence to a married state allows for his family to continue as rulers of his people—it conforms to a particular sociopolitical agenda—and it represents a movement toward containing and reordering Walter's desires (his "lust present" [IV.80]), but at the same time it releases a certain perverse and violent energy.

The medieval privileging of chastity over either hetero- or homosexual commitments (at the same time that a hierarchy of "straight" and "queer" sexualities nonetheless existed) might have been enabling for some marginalized members of Christian society—for instance, giving some women a way out of some kinds of subjugation to men. As Dyan Elliott suggests, in the practice of "spiritual marriage," there might be "a collapse in the husband's authority and . . . a relative suspension of the gender hierarchy" that enabled women at least "a limited and situationally defined . . . agency."[169] And religious communities may have provided at least some women and men, whose affective attachments were somehow "queer," a place to escape compulsory heterosexuality. The same sexual system that might thus have "liberated" (however partially) certain individuals from certain kinds of oppression could, however, be deeply constrictive for others, including the new convert to Christianity. For him or her, the construction of ideal sexuality as chastity meant that religious conversion, conceived as moral transformation, was likely to entail not integration into Christian family and kinship structures but rather a movement into a delimited space beyond both "straight" and "queer" sexual expression. It is not, then, surprising that what we most often find in medieval accounts of conversion is not a straightforward rectification of gender and sexuality but their further problematizing: conversion most often entails a "gender trouble" and a "queerness" that continue to circulate around the figure of the convert even after religious conversion has been fully achieved.

Think, for instance, of the ways in which the two situations of conversion depicted in Chaucer's *Man of Law's Tale* are intimately, complicatedly, and perhaps contradictorily tied up with questions of gender and sexuality.[170] In each instance, a non-Christian ruler—the Muslim sultan, the pagan King Alla—converts to Christianity, and in each case the conversion is closely linked to his marrying the Roman Christian Constance, that is, to his entrance into Christian (and Roman imperial) kin structures (II.225–26, II.683–93). The association of marriage with conversion here might be read in a variety of ways: as "feminizing" the sultan, who surrenders his own religious tradition not out of any conviction of Christianity's superiority but in order to facilitate his marriage

(Alla on the other hand converts before there is any indication that he plans to marry Constance); as "masculinizing" the sultan, who through conversion and marriage becomes the son-in-law of the Roman emperor, forging an important male homosocial alliance with Europe; as "feminizing" Alla, who chooses not only to submit himself to a foreign religious tradition but to ally himself with a destitute woman who (seemingly) has no important family or political connections or social class standing. Significantly, in each case, the conversion and marriage are strongly opposed by the male ruler's *mother;* the defense of Islam and of paganism, as these are abandoned by men, falls to women, and in each case a woman who is both distinctly "mannysh" (II.782) and apparently unmarried, probably widowed, in any case no longer part of an appropriate male-female sexual and familial structure, not subject to the masculine control of a husband.[171] This situation is itself readable in (at least) two contradictory ways. On the one hand, perhaps the "masculine" authority that the sultaness and Donegild display reveals a gender and social/sexual disorder inherent to Islam and paganism, traditions where power is revealed as resting, inappropriately, from the perspective of the Christian text, with matriarchs rather than patriarchs.[172] Or perhaps the disruption of gender, marriage, and family is to be thought of not as inherent to these religious traditions but rather as consequential on the movement of conversion: the decision to abandon the native religious tradition undermines gender hierarchy and marriage- or family-based social order. I think that both these possibilities function in Chaucer's tale: non-Christian religions are always already sites of gender and sexual disruption but so too are the movements of conversion in which those religions are left behind for Christianity.

For the sultan, certainly, conversion, rather than providing the opportunity to escape a "feminized" religion, leads to the loss of "masculine" power and (despite the promise of a marriage that would cement an advantageous familial and political alliance) the violent and total loss of his political position. He, all the "converted" "Surryen[s]" (II.435), and all the "Cristen folk" (II.416) accompanying Constance to the wedding feast (except Constance herself) are massacred, and they meet their deaths in a particularly unvaliant way—"al tohewe and stiked at the bord" (II.430), subjected to the power of "This olde Sowdanesse, cursed krone" (II.432). Of course, the sultaness, as representative of the old religion, and not the conversion itself, is "responsible" for what happens to the sultan and his men, but one might still read the intransigent *mother* here as figuring some inherent, genetic, Muslim intractability to full religious transformation. The sultan may want to become a Christian, but something in the "feminized," gender-disordered family, realm, and religious tradition that he tries to leave behind will not allow his departure.

Alla's movement into Christianity, despite his mother Donegild's resistance, is, by contrast, more successful. He responds to his mother's treacherous activities, her undermining of his authority, with a strong reconsolidation of power, violently eliminating Donegild and thus those aspects of his prior, pagan life that she may represent: "Th'effect is this: that Alla, out of drede, / His mooder slow—that may men pleynly rede— / For that she traitour was to hire ligeance. / Thus endeth olde Donegild, with meschance!" (II.893–96). But though the narrator's final exclamation here indicates approval of Alla's violence, the movement of conversion does not end with the violent reassertion of "masculine" power. In terms of the traditional model of Christian conversion as a movement away from the world, into humility, Alla's entrance into Christianity is problematic, and the "masculine" violence he directs against his mother and his mother's religion is not a satisfactory endpoint for his entrance into the new religion. A countermovement of "repentance" and pilgrimage (II.988–94), in which he submits to the higher authority of the church—he "putte hym in the Popes ordinance / In heigh and logh, and Jhesu Crist bisoghte / Foryeve his wikked werkes that he wroghte" (II.992–94)—is necessary before he can be reunited with Constance and his son Maurice, and before he can return to England as a true Christian monarch. His arrival in Rome is furthermore marked by an unknowing submission to his lost wife Constance. She knows who he is, while he has no idea that she has survived. She manipulates him in order to re-present herself and her son to him in precisely the way she wants. She is, in sum, in the marriage relation, in control—acting as the "head" that, in the Pauline formulation, *should* be the husband.[173] Throughout the last sections of the *Man of Law's Tale,* Alla remains a problematic figure, even after his Christian repentance and his happy reunion with his family. Although returned to his position of political power in England, he quickly dies, and Constance herself returns to Rome, to "hir fader" (II.1152) the emperor, to the heart of a patriarchal Christianity left behind in her (missionary) journeys into Islam and paganism but finally fully reentered. And Alla and Constance's son

Maurice—unlike his father, born into Christianity; raised alone by the unambiguously Christian, even saintly, Constance—is destined to be made "Emperour... by the Pope" (II.1121–22). Unlike his father, he can "lyve[] cristenly" (II.1122) with little difficulty.

The *Man of Law's Tale* represents a whole body of texts—both fictional and historiographical[174]—in which a conversion is facilitated by marriage. Indeed, it is a much repeated historical pattern for marital alliances (usually with a Christian woman) to stimulate the conversion of whole political realms to Christianity.[175] But texts like the *Man of Law's Tale* also often consider the ways in which marriage's implication in sexuality complicates, and sometimes undermines, the movement of conversion. As noted above, Christian anxieties about Jewish and Muslim bodies—their impurity and imperfection, the tinges of animality clinging to them in Christian fantasies—often expressed themselves in legislation prohibiting Jewish-Christian sexual activity or marriage. These efforts at keeping religious communities segregated of course did not apply directly to those who had converted to Christianity; converts indeed sometimes married and entered into the social life of Christian communities. The early church Council of Chalcedon declared that "even clerics and their sons could marry converted Jewesses."[176] Innocent III ruled in 1199 that if a married person converted to Christianity but his or her spouse did not, the new Christian could remarry.[177] A Jewish woman who had converted to Christianity along with her husband petitioned Pope Martin V to allow her to marry a Christian after her first husband reverted to Judaism; the pope granted the petition in 1427.[178]

It is equally clear, however, that the anxious establishment of boundaries between religious communities that partly expressed itself in the condemnation of interfaith sexual contacts and marriage extended into uncertainty about the licitness of sexual and family relations with new converts to Christianity. The differences between Jewish and Christian rules concerning legitimate marriages—with Jews both accepting marriages that fell within the prohibited degrees of relationship for Christian marriage and legislating levirate marriages unacceptable to Christianity—raised the problem for Christianity of whether Jewish marriages that would have been disallowed to Christians could continue after a married couple's conversion. Innocent III's ruling that those marriages could indeed continue on the one hand displayed tolerance toward converts.[179] On the other hand, however, it reinscribed the Christian belief in the "perversity" of Jewish sexual mores that permitted "incest" and furthered inbreeding, and it suggested that Jewish converts, despite having embraced Christianity, might not be able to move out of such suspect practices. Furthermore, in an action that less ambiguously expressed a distrust of incorporating converts into the Christian community, Pope Clement IV in 1268 rebuked Alfonso III of Portugal for allowing marriages of Christian men to women of Saracen and Jewish *origin*—"those who have *taken their origin* from the Saracens or the Jews."[180] In at least one instance, in late fourteenth-century Aragon, "the death penalty for all sex relations between Jews and Christians" was reiterated in such a way as to "include[e] new converts."[181] And in 1459, Pope Pius II granted the annulment of the unconsummated marriage between a Christian man and a woman of Jewish heritage who was accused of "Judaizing" and "heretical" behavior. The pope's treatment of the connection between the woman's unorthodox behavior, her ancestry, and the possible Jewishness of her future progeny expresses a strong suspicion of the insincerity and incompleteness of Jewish conversion and some sense of a hereditary aspect of Judaism that might not easily be overcome—perhaps especially when female converts are involved:

> Surely, on the part of [our] beloved son Petrus dela Cavalleria, a minor in age, of the city of Saragossa, a petition presented to us not long ago included [the following claims]: That some time ago he himself in the legitimate verbal form of the present contracted marriage with Blancha Palau, of the city of Valencia, who was held and reputed a Christian, [but] a carnal joining [of the two] did not at all follow. Truly, since he manifestly detected that the said Blancha is a heretic in [participating in] the rites and ceremonies of Jewish insanity and of the Jews, and lives heretically, and [since] it was thus brought forward in the account of trustworthy men that the mother of this same Blancha, coming from the people of the Jews [and] toiling in this same heretical depravity, instructed and initiated the said Blancha herself— [because of all this] the aforesaid Petrus, a true Catholic, [is] prepared to submit to <the breaking out of>[182] perpetual imprisonment and every peril of death rather than be willing to consummate a marriage of this sort, lest perhaps his offspring that would be begotten might follow the insanity of the mother,

and a Jew would [thus] be created out of a Christian. On the part of the said Petrus it was to us humbly besought, that the marriage itself should be declared to have been and to be nothing, even if it could perhaps be called a marriage, [and] that we should consider it worthy, out of [our] apostolic benignity, both to dissolve that [marriage] for the preceding causes and to grant the aforesaid Petrus that he be able to wed another, and fitly to provide otherwise for himself and for his situation.[183]

Distrust of converts was not limited to the realm of sexuality. The Fourth Toledan Council (633) forbade the appointment to public office of the baptized second generation of Jewish converts.[184] In the dispute over the papacy between Innocent II and the "antipope" Anacletus II (1130–38), the great-grandson of a converted Jew, Anacletus's heredity became an issue, with Bernard of Clairvaux remarking that "it is well known that Jewish offspring now occupies the see of St. Peter to the injury of Christ."[185] Converted Jews in Catalonia and Valencia in 1437 had to petition the pope for relief against discrimination practiced by the established Christian community.[186] While conversion to Christianity was repeatedly encouraged, and indeed often coerced, converts clearly occupied an uncomfortable position in relation to both their old and their new religions, and perhaps particularly when it came to the possibility of being integrated into Christian sexual and familial structures.

Consider the fictional instance of Sir Palomides the Saracen in Sir Thomas Malory's "Book of Sir Tristram de Lyones." In this romance, Palomides hovers consistently on the edge of Christendom and on the edge of Tristram's court, his love for Isode simultaneously pulling him into the main action of the book and threatening his full alienation from knightly society as he becomes Tristram's rival.[187] At one point, his alienation is expressed as a marking of the body that suggests (quasi-) racial difference: "in the watir he sawe his owne vysayge, how he was discolowred and defaded, a nothynge lyke as he was. / 'Lorde Jesu, what may this meane?' seyde sir Palomydes. And thus he seyde to hymselff: 'A, Palomydes, Palomydes! Why arte thou thus defaded, and ever was wonte to be called one of the fayrest knyghtes of [the] worlde?' "[188] Of course, that Palomides sees his "discoloration" here as a *change* in his identity suggests—at least to a modern understanding of racial characteristics as unchangeable—that something other than racial marking is here at work. But, recalling medieval accounts in which something like modern race (indicated by skin color and other physical characteristics) is depicted as changing quite radically, perhaps we should consider whether this depiction and others like it (Arcite's physical changes in Chaucer's *Knight's Tale,* Orfeo's becoming "lene, rowe, and blac" in *Sir Orfeo*)[189] might suggest that a transformation of a loosely conceived (quasi-)racial identity can accompany a radical change in romantic and sexual status. In Malory, might the point be that Palomides can over-come a certain (quasi-)racial difference in attaining true knightly prowess but that, as he falls into the realm of sexual desire, such difference reasserts itself?

In any case, the action of the story suggests that Palomides's desire for Isode must be "conquered" if he is to move fully into the Christian world: in the story's final sequence, Palomides and Tristram engage in a battle that simultaneously enables Palomides's conversion (508) and leads him to abandon any claim to Isode's love (510). Baptized, with Tristram and another knight as "godfadyrs" (510), Palomides enters Christianity, but only as he abandons any hope of fulfilling his love. And while the story concludes with Tristram returning to "Joyus Garde" and Isode, it shows Palomides, although Christianized, still relegated to a place of marginality: he takes up again his never-ending search for "the questynge beste," a search that largely keeps him outside stable social structures (510).

The closing off to the convert of certain sexual possibilities that are accepted and even legislated for nonclerical Christians is one way to maintain the queerness of even the converted Saracen or Jewish body. The convert remains somehow different, still of an other people, *gens,* race than the Christian society to which he is assimilated. The naming of former Jews in medieval texts—Petrus Alphonsi "ex Judeo Chris-tiani,"[190] "Hermannus quondam Judaeus,"[191] Pablo Christiani[192]—asserts simultaneously the saliency of their conversion and their Jewish origin. Larger groups of Jews converting to Christianity (often under duress) were themselves often given separate names and social status. Visig-othic legislation referred to "Jews, baptized and non-baptized,"[193] sug-gesting that baptism did not truly transform a Jewish to a Christian iden-tity. In other locations and at other historical moments, converts formed a class of "New Christians" or conversos that continued to be distin-guished from the more established Christian community; even in legislation intended to argue for equal treatment of "New Christians," use of such a distinguishing designation suggests the real obstacles to achieving equal treatment.[194] While the move to convert represented a certain impulse toward amalgamation on the part of both Jewish converts and the Christian communities that encouraged or forced their conversion, such an impulse was often not allowed to reach fruition. The consistent Christian anxiety that converted Jews would "relapse" to their original religion—the fear that converts had not "truly" become Christian, that they were always on the verge of reverting to a prior state—suggests how fully problematic was their integration into Christendom.[195]

As Jeremy Cohen suggests, "Spurned by their former coreligionists, never fully assimilated into the rank and file of the European laity, and often deprived of their property by secular princes, many [Jewish apostates] must have remained on the margins of medieval society, frequently finding their only secure haven in the ranks of the Christian clergy, or hovering indecisively between two hostile religious communities."[196] Hermann of Cologne, after his conversion, became a priest in the Premonstratensian order. Pablo Christiani ended up a Dominican preacher dedicated to attacking Judaism in Spain, Provence, and France. Peter Alfonsi, whose intellectual and medical career seems to have continued relatively uninterrupted by his conversion, positioned himself, in his *Dialogi,* as quite distant from sexual expression.[197] Religious conversions—at least those that gain prominence in texts intended for a Christian audience—are likely to be accompanied not by an embracing of normative heterosexuality, but rather by a movement from uncontrolled "luxury" into a more chaste and "ordered" state.

In texts by Jewish men who converted to Christianity, the "femininity" and sexual disorderliness of the Jewish body is (unsurprisingly) less evident than it is in traditions of anti-Semitic Christian writing. Jewish male converts may not have experienced their own gender and sexuality as particularly labile; they may have felt themselves to be equally "masculine" and sexually "normal" (or not) before and after their religious transformation. Given, however, that the sense of Jewish gender and sexual difference was so strong in the Christian culture that converts entered, gender, sexuality, and the question of bodily difference must have been important issues, and points of anxiety, for new converts. Indeed, we might suppose that a certain *avoidance* of the body in the texts of converts was itself a response to anxiety about gender and the gendered and sexualized body. As we have seen, from Paul's epistles on, Jewishness was identified with carnality and, in the realm of interpretation, with a literalizing (mis)reading of texts; Christianity, in contrast, was spiritualized, and allegorical reading, a recognition of the "real" truths of texts, identified as a peculiarly Christian process.[198] Further, as Carolyn Dinshaw has shown in her discussion of medieval "sexual poetics," the same opposition was gendered: the "Pauline model of reading would mean to discard altogether the mode of woman as central, naked truth of the text, to rigorously pass through the text's female body on the way to its spirit—its male spirit, as Ambrose and others suggest."[199] Not to talk overmuch about body was perhaps one means by which the convert could demonstrate that he had overcome Jewish carnality, literality, and "femininity."

As I have argued elsewhere about Hermann of Cologne, one of the major movements in his conversion involves learning to read allegorically, learning to leave behind a literalizing, "Jewish" understanding of texts for a spiritualizing, Christian one.[200] The dream that opens his conversion account—a dream of being honored by the emperor with a feast and lush material gifts (a horse, a bag of gold coins)—is at first misunderstood by Hermann and his Jewish family and community as suggesting worldly success. (Hermann's family engages in moneylending, and his first intimate contact with Christian communities comes through the loan Hermann himself makes to Bishop Ekbert of Munster.) A sign of Hermann's successful conversion is the full reinterpretation of the dream with which the *Opusculum* ends, where all the dream's material symbols are shown to portend not material but spiritual success—that is, the grace of Hermann's own conversion. Such a process of learning to read spiritually is, as Dinshaw's work suggests, always also gendered: as Hermann enters into Christian reading practices, he also learns to read in a "masculine" fashion. Proper reading is also sexualized, at least in the realm of metaphor: the movement from Jewish misunderstanding to Christian enlightenment in a writer like Hermann is a movement from sterility to fecundity.[201] Indeed, in Hermann's autobiographical account, one of the main impediments to conversion, one of the Jewish "seductions" that makes him hesitate in embracing Christianity, is a carnal and female one. As he prepares to make the leap from Judaism to Christianity, he is held back from his growing understanding of Christian "truth" by "concupiscence," "pleasure," and "delight of the flesh."[202] The devil and the Jewish community orchestrate a (hetero)sexual temptation intended to prevent his becoming Christian: "he himself [the devil] sexually united a woman to me in matrimony to my ruin."[203] Hermann's Christian "familiars," who had previously brought him to the brink of conversion, lament this marriage as a fall back into the carnality of Judaism, a retreat from the spiritual (Christian) position he had earlier begun to approach: "We often gave to you prophecies of salvation, to which we hoped you would at some time assent and believe in Christ the author of our salvation; and behold against our hope you have chosen rather to follow your concupiscence and have surrendered yourself completely to perdition, without hope of salvation."[204] For a postconversion Hermann reflecting on his former life, as for these Christian friends, giving in to sexual pleasure is closely linked to the retreat from Christianity: "I began with the greatest pleasure of the flesh to lie there where before I had feared that I would fall";[205] "because of the limited delight of the flesh I had fallen into so great an abyss of perdition."[206] To convert, Hermann must overcome the allurements of a secular "femininity" and a Jewish materiality—here represented most strongly by the enticement of a married, family life within his childhood community. Ultimately Hermann regains his desire for spiritual truth—that is, in the terms of his account, he resumes his interest in Christian teaching—and he is converted in part through the prayers of two religious women: "by the merits and prayers of those same women, so great a brightness of Christian faith suddenly shone into my heart that it completely drove away from [my heart] the shadows of all previous doubt and ignorance—with this alteration truly appropriate, that they lifted up one who had fallen through a woman with the prayers of a woman."[207] As Hermann makes explicit, the "fall" back into hereditary Judaism, identified with a "fall" into heterosexual "concupiscence," is compensated for by a chaste spiritual involvement with women. As Christianity replaces Judaism, prayer replaces sex.

4

MERCHANTS, CONVERTS, JEWS

INTERRELIGIOUS DEBATE AND
THE TROUBLING OF CHRISTIAN IDENTITY

*There might seem to be a contradiction
between the work of transsexual narrative—
to document change: to say how I became a
woman—and the transsexual's claim to
already (truly) be a woman. Yet within the
genre of autobiography this play between
transformation and the continuity of the self,
between conversion and identity, is not a
disruptive paradox but a founding dynamic:
a dynamic that in turn, as transsexuality is
reliant on the autobiographical form, founds
transsexuality. Conversion—along with the
confession, thoroughly embedded in autobiography's generic origins—is, we might
say, autobiography's story of identity. For if
the narrative of autobiography documents
change . . . , the autos of autobiography
presumes identity, the continuity of the self,
an "I" across time. Autobiography not only
masters these splits between conversion and
identity into a generic form; it necessitates
them. Likewise transsexuality: its subject sex*

> *change of course, transsexuality is an*
> *archetypal conversion story; yet in*
> *conversion and change (transition) lies the*
> *key to transsexual identity.*
> —Jay Prosser, *Second Skins: The Body*
> *Narratives of Transsexuality,* 119

CONVERSION IDENTITY: PETER ALFONSI'S *DIALOGI CONTRA IUDAEOS*

Texts like Hermann of Cologne's that describe Jewish conversions, even as they suggest a unidirectional movement out of Jewish "darkness" into Christian "light," from "caecitas" [blindness] to lucid vision, often also preserve the dark point of origin from which the convert emerges. Hermann's *Opusculum de conversione sua* operates circularly to return us, in its conclusion, to a moment that precedes Hermann's conscious interest in Christianity, to the adolescent dream of imperial reward with which his autobiography began. This conclusion, in reinterpreting the dream in spiritual (Christian) rather than material (Jewish) terms, reiterates the truth of Christianity and thus brings the conversion narrative to a suitable close. At the same time, however, it makes us reconsider the whole complex route by which Hermann reaches his final, Christian position, plunging us back into his initial Jewishness and its materially implicated errors. The circular conversion narrative follows, one might say, a *spectral* logic: the prior, Jewish self must be conjured up so that that self may be made to disappear; but, even at the moment of its disappearance, the specter is, if liminally, present—as that whose disappearance is necessary for the emergence of the new, Christian self. Paradoxically, that new self could not emerge *as* new if the discarded self were simply forgotten or completely, successfully superseded; its aura must be maintained even as its disappearance is confidently proclaimed.

The identity of the convert *as* convert always stands in relation to some such paradox. While the convert's new religious identity depends upon its distance from an initial, "erroneous" identity, that defining distance can only be measured if the initial identity is kept in sight and in play, its relation to the new self visualized and revisualized. The reiteration of Hermann's dream enables an explicit recognition of the distance traversed in the course of the convert's enlightenment; at the same time, this reiteration reemphasizes that Hermann does not simply inhabit a Christian identity. His is a *convert*'s identity, an identity necessarily non-self-identical because dependent upon a narrative of change, the conversionary movement from one position to its polar opposite. Or, in a quite different staging of this paradox, the visual representations of Saul/Paul's conversion discussed above show us not an accomplished new identity but that liminal moment when the Jewish self falls toward its new Christian being. We see the old self abased, and, in this moment, we can imagine the (re)construction of a self on a new, very different basis. But the representations keep us frozen in that moment between identities, with Jewish identity no longer on a stable footing and Christian identity not yet fully established. It is the experience of change, of flux between identities—what we might call *conversion identity*—that these illustrations most insistently put before us.[1]

The simultaneous survival and repudiation of the Jewish self is an even more salient feature in the early twelfth-century *Dialogi* between a Jew and a Christian written by the Spanish convert Peter Alfonsi (sometime after 1106, the date of Peter's conversion to Christianity).[2] Rather than focus on the liminal moment between identities, as do the illustrations of Saul/Paul's conversion, and rather than tell a sequential narrative of conversion that nonetheless circularly brings its Jewish starting point back into play, as does Hermann, Peter constructs an interreligious, Jewish-Christian dispute for which the fact of his own conversion plays a foundational role. Here, Peter personalizes the Jewish interlocutor in a way unusual in the literature of religious debate, conjuring up the Jew whom Peter once was in a most striking way. The opening scene of the *Dialogi* proper is dramatic and literally spectral, presenting Peter with a figure from and of his past:[3]

> Therefore from the tender age of boyhood a certain most perfect friend named Moses attached himself to me, who from that earliest age was my companion and co-student. When the word came to this one that I had chosen the Christian faith, having left behind the paternal law, he came hurrying to me, having left behind the place of his abode, bearing in his very coming a certain face of an indignant man and, speaking angrily, greeted me in the manner not of a friend but of a stranger, and thus he

began: "Alas, Peter Alfonsi, much time has passed during which I have been anxious to come to you to see you to speak and linger with you, but my desire lacked effect, until now when I see you with a happy face, by the grace of God. Now I ask that you make clear to me your intention and show me the reason why you deserted the ancient or chose the new law."[4]

Here, both Jewish and Christian interlocutors are explicitly named, and their names, strikingly, identify each with the work's author: Peter, in his prologue, has revealed that the names chosen for the interlocutors of his dialogue are autobiographically significant: "For the Christian arguments that are to be defended, I have put forward the name that I now have as a Christian, but for the adversary's arguments to be confuted, the name that I had before baptism, that is Moses."[5] The work thus opens with the apparition to the convert Peter of Peter's former Jewish self, his "most perfect friend," fully personified as an individual distinct from Peter. Recreating his former Jewish self, the self cast off through conversion, Peter thus opens the dialogue with a confrontation between pre- and postconversion selves, dramatizing the different ways in which the unconverted Jew and the Christian convert understand scripture, the spirit, God, and the world. The dialogue can indeed be read as a long internal debate between the now-Christian Peter and his former, spectral, Jewish self.

Moses/Peter's conversion has resulted in a certain mutual alienation of current and former selves that Peter chooses not to cover over—he does not act as though the old Moses were irretrievably thrown out—but rather to dramatize, posing the old self, angry at Peter's self-desertion, against the new one, confident in its new positioning. The staging and structure of the *Dialogi* depend upon this conflict between old and new, with the main movement of the text enacting a complex dialectic between Christian and Jewish selves. Moses comes to Peter to bring him back to Judaism. At the same time, the action of his "advent," "le[aving] behind the place of his abode," echoes the terms in which Peter describes the movement of his conversion, "le[aving] behind the paternal law." Thus, paradoxically, Moses's coming to Peter to chastise him for converting seems to portend Moses's own relinquishing of (Jewish) "abode." And indeed the dialogue itself operates for the most part to transform Moses's angry movement against Peter into an abandonment of Jewish

positions. Moses is conjured up in order to conjure him, and the Jewishness he represents, away. Still, as we will see, Peter's text never fully
overcomes the splitting of self dramatized in its opening scene.

The paradoxical movements of this rich opening scene are intensified
by its resonant evocation of multiple literary genres. A literature of imagined interreligious debate stretches back to the very early years of Christianity and is central in both Christian polemics against Judaism and
Jewish polemics against Christianity.[6] We have already seen the genre
deployed several times in the polemical texts of the long twelfth century:
Guibert's *Tractatus de incarnatione contra judaeos* (ca. 1111), rather than
presenting a monologic defense of Christian doctrine or attack on Jewish belief, incorporates into its text the voices of Jewish figures speaking
for Judaism, as does the latter part of Peter Damian's letter to Honestus
(ca. 1040–41). Later in the twelfth century, in his *Dialogue of a Philosopher with a Jew, and a Christian* (ca. 1136–39), Peter Abelard develops a
fuller, more complex debate among three distinct religious traditions.
Hebrew polemicists respond in kind: Joseph Kimhi's *Book of the Covenant* stages a debate between a Jewish believer and a nonbeliever; Judah
ha-Levi's *Kitab al-Khazari*, like Abelard's *Dialogue*, presents a three-way
religious dispute. While Peter Alfonsi's *Dialogi* clearly participates in
this literary tradition of religious debate, his text also stands apart from
the main line of the tradition. In debates like those contained in Guibert
and Peter Damian, the Jewish figure whom the Christian author conjures up and confronts is clearly separate from, indeed diametrically
opposed to, the Christian self. And unlike his Christian opponent, often
identified as the (named) author of the work, the Jewish disputant most
often is unnamed, an unparticularized figure who clearly stands for *all*
Jews, operating essentially as a personification of Jewishness. In voicing
Jewish positions, the Christian narrator takes certain risks: presenting
Jewish voices and figures involves an embodying of the Jew, conjuring
up Jewish presences "to speak for themselves," and this potentially reinforces, despite the intention of the Christian polemicist, the opposition's arguments just by stating them. Nevertheless, of course, the Jewish
"spokesmen" in such works speak as their Christian authors determine,
and their embodiment usually remains sketchy and their voices weak.
Guibert or Damian clearly intends to conjure up Jewish voices only in
order to put them to rest. Even in a work like Abelard's, where Jewish
positions are expounded more fully and fairly, the real debate occurs

between the Christian and the pagan philosopher; the Jew disappears from the work halfway through, his arguments having been largely refuted (and not even by the Christian but by the philosopher). Most often, surely, the Jewish disputant is a fantasy figure—an imagination of what Jews might say to defend their disbelief—and that figure is, not surprisingly, easily defeated on the field of debate.

Sometimes, nevertheless, these literary debates bear a clearer relation to real-life interactions between Christians and Jews: as noted earlier, Rupert of Deutz in the twelfth century composed a literary debate, but we also know from Hermann of Cologne's autobiography that Rupert participated in a public debate with the preconversion Hermann/Judah.[7] Often, too, the Christian debate texts attempt to "realize" themselves, claiming, whether reliably or not, to be based on their authors' actual encounters with Jewish opponents; this is true for the texts of Gilbert Crispin, Peter of Cornwall, the Majorca and Ceuta disputations discussed below, to give just a few examples.[8] The arguments remembered from an actual debate and reproduced (at least in part) in the literary debate text may be less in the control of their author than those of a fully fictional text; insofar as he tries actually to report the events of a dispute, the author may grant the Jewish disputant some autonomy and self-authority. Still (and maybe even more powerfully than the "purely" literary debates), these debate texts continue to insist on a strong, unbridgeable distinction between Jewish and Christian speakers. The Jew is an opponent encountered directly and in the flesh, the text claims, and an opponent firmly defeated by the time the debate ends.

Peter Alfonsi's *Dialogi* of course also starkly poses Moses and Peter against each other as religious opponents. At the same time, however, quite unlike the typical Jewish-Christian debate text, the *Dialogi* insists on making the Jewish and Christian figures part of the same person, representing, as they do here, two distinct stages in the history of a single self. Such a situation may have no direct precursor in the tradition of medieval Jewish-Christian debate,[9] but there is nonetheless an influential late antique and medieval dialogue genre that provides Alfonsi a predecessor. This is the genre that arises in the wake of Boethius's enormously influential *Consolation of Philosophy*. Here, an essentially internal debate is externalized through the use of personification: the grieving, imprisoned figure of Boethius confronts the (forgotten) philosophical training of his youth, learning not for the first time the lessons of Lady

Philosophy, which are indeed presented as having earlier properly guided his life. In its medieval incarnations, the Boethian dialogue is often more or less explicitly presented as self-confrontation.[10] The narrator of Alain de Lille's *De Planctu Naturae* (ca. 1160–65) confronts a Nature who is both a universal force and his "kinswoman" and "foster-mother"— that is, a force intimately connected to his individual nature.[11] The narrator of Guillaume de Lorris and Jean de Meun's thirteenth-century *Roman de la Rose* encounters, among a variety of other kinds of figure, a Reason who stands for the quality of mind he himself should possess. The anonymous fourteenth-century *Parlement of the Thre Ages* poses against each other three figures—Youthe, Medill Elde, and Elde—who might (like Moses and Peter) be one and the same person at different stages in life. Peter's *Dialogi,* like other texts of this genre, begins with the appearance of a familiar figure, an "old friend," whose angry approach typically signifies that the central figure in the scene—the self, the speaker of the first-person text—is in need of correction or cure. In the *Consolation,* of course, it is Lady Philosophy—in the speaker's words, "nutricem meam" [my nurse or foster-mother][12]—who appears by the distraught narrator's bedside to drive the emotionally involved, antiphilosophical muses away and to set the narrator on the course of a properly rational, philosophical cure. Lady Philosophy, "cuius ab adulescentia laribus obuersatus fueram" [whose household deities or hearth I had tended since my youth],[13] has a long-standing, if recently ruptured, relationship with the speaker of the dialogue text, as of course does Moses, "qui a primaeva aetate meus consocius fuerat et condiscipulus" [who from that earliest age was my companion and co-student], with Peter. Lady Philosophy of course takes on a position of clear authority vis-à-vis Boethius, while Moses stands in a more equal relationship to Peter as "*con*socius" and "*con*discipulus." Still, the closeness of the relationship gives Moses a certain authority to speak directly, intimately, strongly to Peter, to come to him insisting on a hearing. And the affect that Moses brings to the encounter—angry and self-righteous, "in ipso adventu quemdam vultum ferens hominis indignantis" [bearing in his very coming a certain face of an indignant man], like the affect of Lady Philosophy, "mulier reuerendi admodum uultus, oculis ardentibus" [a woman of exceedingly reverent mien, with burning eyes],[14] driving away the muses who have seduced Boethius—reflects the impulse of the close friend (or nurse) moved to correct a major error of intellectual and emotional orientation in the other.

Though it quickly becomes apparent that it will be Peter who enlightens Moses, and not vice versa, the evocation of a genre that would lead us to expect the reverse puts Moses in a certain position of authority, if only momentarily. Indeed, one of the ironies of the *Dialogi* is that much of the knowledge it incorporates in fact comes from the productive interchange of Arabic, Hebrew, and Latin knowledge within which Moses, as a Jew growing up and educated in Muslim Spain, would have been immersed.[15] Peter expropriates the knowledge that he owes to his former self Moses—and presumably to a series of Jewish and Muslim as well as Christian teachers—and then re-presents that knowledge to Moses in order to defeat him and the Jewish tradition he represents. But while the dialogue thus tries to insist on a rigorous separation of the two central disputants in terms of the crucial question of knowledge and understanding, it also recognizes explicitly that any such separation cannot definitively hold. Moses and Peter, as old "consocii" and "condiscipuli," share a set of experiences and knowledges that it is precisely the business of the dialogue to put into play even as it denies, drawing upon Moses's history even as it insists that the new self completely supersede the old.

The staging of Jewish-Christian debate as an internal dialogue between two figures of the same self revisits many of the concerns that we have seen (in chapter 3) circulating around the experience of conversion and the figure of the convert—including notions about the gender and sexual identity of Jews and Christians. Despite the commonality of their origin and education, Moses and Peter are presented as radically different, understanding the world in dramatically opposed ways that are aligned with gender and sexual difference. Thus, as in Hermann's *Opusculum* (and many other texts), their differences are particularly affiliated with the strongly gendered opposition between the literal and the allegorical. Peter describes his own conversion as allowing a new kind of sight, removing an obfuscating "veil" described in terms that evoke medieval theories of allegoresis: "The omnipotent one inspired us with his Spirit, and directed me into the straight path, removing first the thin white film covering the eyes and afterwards the heavy veil of the corrupt soul."[16]

Moses, and Jews more generally, err particularly in how they read the biblical law, an error that the Christian Peter himself can now "see" and must demonstrate to Moses: "I see that they [Jews] attend to only the surface of the law and expound the letter not spiritually but carnally, whence they have been deceived by the greatest error."[17] Indeed, the first, and longest, chapter of the *Dialogi* is devoted to showing that "the Jews understand the words of the prophets carnally and expound them falsely,"[18] and the (Pauline) opposition between literal/Jewish and spiritual/Christian reading repeatedly recurs.[19]

As we have seen, this opposition is a firmly gendered one, and the debate structure of the *Dialogi* reemphasizes the traditional medieval gendering of Jewish and Christian positionings. Peter sets up the debate as a "masculine" contest, explicitly metaphorizing it as a battle between two armed opponents.[20] Moses eagerly participates in this contest; indeed, it is Moses who first proposes that "each of us run about on the *battlefield* of dialogic reason."[21] Soon after, setting the terms for using Hebrew scripture in the argument, Peter expresses his strong desire "to strike you [Moses] down with your own sword."[22] It quickly becomes clear, however, that only one of the two "combatants" has a truly "masculine" understanding of things, that the "sword" of reason and wisdom ("ratione et sapientia")—qualities that, in the opening prayer of the *Dialogi,* Peter sees as distinguishing man ("homo") from the animals[23]—belongs only to the Christian.

Moses's part on the debate's field of battle is consistently that of the defeated. In the "Prologue" to the text, as we have seen, Peter makes clear that Christian arguments are to be proven in Peter's own voice, Jewish ones refuted in Moses's,[24] and the course of the debate thus anticipated never wavers. Moses easily accepts most of Peter's arguments, giving in repeatedly to Peter's superior skill in reasoning. This means that the main trajectory of the debate (like the very different, *narrative* trajectory of a text like Hermann's) is one of enlightenment, with Moses admitting over and over again the truth of Peter's positions. This process of enlightenment explicitly evokes the gendered terms of allegorical reading, and in so doing it echoes Peter's description of the process that led to his own conversion: "You have poured out the light of truth most clearly, drawing forth the veil of great blindness from my breast; for which, may a worthy payment be weighed out to you by God."[25]

Moses indeed ultimately accedes to all of Peter's positions, and he concludes quite early in the dialogue, at the beginning of *titulus* v, "how empty and inconstant in all things the faith of the Jewish people has hitherto been," admitting "in how great an error I [myself] have hitherto persisted."[26]

But even this early and rather full accession, on Moses's part, to the proposition that his own "Judaic" belief is empty and erroneous is used initially to demonstrate not Moses's capacity for intellectual and religious reform but instead his continuing Jewish pertinacity. Even as he admits the errors of Jewish faith, Moses shows himself obtuse, expressing surprise that, given Peter's own recognition of Jewish error, he has chosen to embrace Christianity rather than *Islam*. Here, in what must have provided a certain shock to Christian readers, Moses introduces a third religious option into the dialogue and suggests that that third tradition, more familiar to an Iberian Jew like Moses than Christianity, provides the most attractive alternative to Judaism: "But I am amazed at why, when you left behind the paternal faith, you should choose the faith of the Christians and not rather that of the Saracens, with whom you have always lived and [by whom] you have been nourished."[27] That the Saracen faith has "nourished" *both* Peter and Moses suggests again the ways in which the vast and varied knowledge that Peter presents in the *Dialogi* as his own and as Christian is in fact the product of an Iberian syncretic intellectual community that the text, in bringing Moses and Peter together, both reveals and denies. But while the turn toward Islam here *might* have spoken to the ways in which Peter's Iberian Jewish/ Islamic personal history informs and enriches his now-Christian intellectual capital, it is instead used in the *Dialogi* to demonstrate, on Moses's part, and from Peter's perspective, a continuing Jewish materialism, a remaining inability to grasp spiritual truth.

Moses's error in turning toward Islam rather than Christianity shows him, in the terms of the text, to be still immersed in Jewish corporeal, and specifically "feminine," misreading and misunderstanding, and it provides Peter the opportunity to demonstrate that Islam is even more debased—more corporeal, "feminized," and sexually suspect—than Judaism.[28] Moses is clearly attracted to Islam because it is a religion of bodily (and particularly sexual) pleasures—multiple wives and concubines, easy divorce, incestuous alliances:

It is permitted ... to them to have, at the same time, four legitimate wives, and if one is repudiated [divorced] another always
can be taken, as long as they never go beyond the number of
four. ... However many bought or captive women one wishes to
have will be legal. ... Furthermore they are permitted to have
wives from their own kin, so that the offspring of their blood may
increase, and the bond of friendship among them be vigorous.[29]

Where Moses sees real attractions, however, the already Christianized
Peter identifies dangers and perversions:

Certainly, that which you have said concerning wives, that it is
allowed to take four and, when any of them has been repudiated [divorced], [it is allowed] to marry another, this indeed is
commanded by no reason, nor truly except for the cause of begetting sons was it commanded to take a wife. That moreover they
are able to have however many purchased wives and captives,
this certainly, as far as you are concerned, is adultery, since
oftentimes a father buys a woman defiled by his son, and conversely a son or brother one corrupted by his father or by his
brother.[30]

Peter comments on how Islam emphasizes "extrinsic" rather than "in-
trinsic" purity, and he makes clear that the "extrinsic" is to be associated
with the "feminine." Commenting on Muslim codes of purity, he argues
that "The purity of washing one's limbs, however, belonged to the worshippers of the star, Venus, who, wishing to pray to her, conformed themselves to the manner of women, dying their mouths and eyes."[31] (He
thus also directly connects Islamic ritual to paganism.) And, like other
twelfth-century Christian polemicists against Islam (for instance, Guibert), Peter ties the corporeal emphases and errors of Islam back to the
personal perversions of Islam's founder, Muhammad, suggesting that
Islamic practices arise not out of a systematic religious law but rather
from Muhammad's personal expression of inordinate sexual desire:
"Muhammad very much loved women, and was far too lustful; as he himself acknowledged, the strength of lust in him was that of forty men."[32]

At the center of Peter's *Dialogi*, then, is a movement that suggests
that the Jew, even after having been persuaded of the errors of Judaism,
is impelled (naturally?) toward the even more debased religious alterna-

tive of Islam. Attracted to the bodiliness of Islam instead of the spirituality of Christianity, Moses, even as he recognizes the errors of Jewish corporeality, is still a Jew, and Peter can—even toward the end of the debate, when Moses has approached most closely to a Christian positioning—repeatedly berate him, and his people, for stupidity: "Most foolish of all, O Moses," "There is not a nation in the whole world more obtuse than you."[33] The Jewish arguments advanced on the field of intellectual battle belong not to the "masculine" realm of the "campus" nor to the "human" realm of true reason and wisdom but to an infantilized and "feminized" realm: "they [your doctors] brought forth such statements concerning him [i.e., God], that these seemed not other than the words of boys jesting in the schools, or of women spinning in the streets."[34] This is not just a momentary comparison, but is later reiterated verbatim, and self-consciously recognized as a reiteration: "And thus this is as I said to you above: that the words of your doctors seem not other than the words of boys jesting in the schools, or of women spinning in the streets."[35]

The disparagement of Jewish positions as "feminine" and irrational, and hence perhaps not fully "human," presents a certain danger for Peter himself. It is, after all, a former Jew who writes the *Dialogi,* and who argues with, and creates, a Jewish interlocutor who is also himself. Of course, Peter anxiously positions his postconversion self in such a way as to "masculinize" it. The Peter of the debate is identified with spiritual (masculine/Christian) reading. He is in control of the dialogue, repeatedly defeating Moses on the field of battle. He is hyperrational and hyperintellectual, introducing into the text a variety of abstruse philosophical and scientific topics—the geography of the earth (15–23; 543–48), the physiology of "ira" and of crying (24–25; 549–50), philosophical proofs for the existence of God the Creator (31–33; 554–55)—uncommon in religious polemic, and clearly intended to impress the reader with the extent of Peter's intellectual capital and to contrast with the silly, often Talmudic, Jewish positions that he simultaneously refutes. It is, I would suggest, the feared remnants of Jewishness—including perhaps especially the remnants of Jewish gender difference—that necessitate such demonstrations of intellectual prowess. But, as I have suggested above, even (or perhaps especially) the most impressive intellectual material Peter brings forward in his own, Christian voice is potentially tainted by its derivation from a non-Christian, religiously complex, Iberian milieu. Indeed, the most abstruse Christian theological material Peter presents—his proof of the Trinity—depends upon his specifically Jewish knowledge of Hebrew and the secrets of the Tetragrammaton.[36] On the one hand, of course, Peter here takes Jewish knowledge away from Judaism, using the Hebrew of Judaism's sacred texts in a way that would outrage Jews—to prove specifically Christian truth. On the other hand, in doing so, Peter also shows himself still intimately connected to his Jewish past—and to Moses, whose continued presence (if fictional or psychological rather than actual or material) is the motivating force behind the *Dialogi*. Once a Jew, Peter is of course now able to stand opposed to his former self. He can defeat that self on the field of reasoned battle, and Moses's last words in the debate do perform a surrender that has been anticipated in his many earlier deferrals to Peter's Christian authority: "Certainly, God gave you much of his wisdom, and illuminated you with great reason, which I am unable to defeat; on the contrary, you have silenced my objections with reason."[37] Still, Moses is never brought to the point of conversion. (His words here have nonetheless been read as performing a conversion; quoting this same passage, John Tolan notes that "The *Dialogi contra Iudaeos* concludes, as do almost all works of medieval religious polemic, with the conversion of the adversary."[38]) But Moses here in fact only suggests that he has no more arguments to bring forward against Peter, and Peter himself would not seem to recognize, in Moses's surrender, an actual conversion. After all, Peter ends the debate with a prayer that urges Moses toward the illumination and conversion that Peter himself has undergone:[39]

> This is the gift of the Holy Spirit, without doubt, which we receive in baptism and which also illuminates our hearts so that we do not presume to believe anything false. And if you yourself also believed that which we believe and had yourself baptized, you would have the same illumination of the Holy Spirit, so that you would recognize those things that are true and reject those that are false. Now, moreover, since I have compassion for you, I implore God's mercy that he enlighten you with the fullness of his Spirit, and show to you an end better than your beginning. Amen.[40]

The *Dialogi* thus never takes the final step of remerging Peter and Moses. Peter's former self never disappears, is never transformed;

Moses remains present throughout—"stolid," making the arguments of women—a reminder of Peter's Jewishness that, at least in this text, is never effaced. Despite Moses's final concessions, and despite what we know about the real-life conversion of Peter, the text continues to enact a perverse Jewish countermovement to the (proper) movement of conversion. Moses's transformation through the spirit remains wished for rather than completed; as the text draws to its close, the preconversion Jew still stands alongside his postconversion self. A residue of Jewish identity is thus ineffaceably inscribed within Peter's celebration of his own embracing of Christianity. That residue, with its stubborn attachment to the flesh, remains resistant to full incorporation into the body of Christian society. It is a certain queer residue that maintains the converted Jew as still (in terms of gender, [quasi] race, and sexuality as well as religion) different from those whom he has joined through conversion.

The Jewish opponent—that is, in this case, the repudiated Jewish component of the self—is defeated, but it also survives as something that must be repeatedly grappled with. Or, to adopt a more explicitly Freudian reading, the Jewish identification that is laid aside is yet somehow necessary to the new Christian self, called forth in order to testify to the truth of that new self and thus, paradoxically, still available to that self, even still somehow a part of it. At the conclusion of the text, we thus see the paradox of conversion identity restaged. On the one hand, Peter's conversion is a fait accompli at the beginning of, and in fact throughout, the debate; this text, celebrating Christian superiority, would not exist were it not for the victory of Christian "truth" in the individual case of Moses/Peter, the victory embodied in the very fact that there *is* a Peter to compose the debate. But as the *Dialogi* draws to its close, Moses remains; the preconversion self in some way (intellectually? psychically? spectrally?) survives, despite the already effected conversion. Peter has definitively left Moses and "the paternal law" behind,[41] and yet his relinquishing of a Jewish past depends upon what has been relinquished; Moses has disappeared into Peter yet still dwells with him as Moses.

We might see the persistence of the figure of Moses in Peter Alfonsi's *Dialogi* as signaling some doubt regarding the full supersession of Judaism by Christianity—in the microcosmic instance of Peter's own autobiography and, by implication, in the macrocosmic realm of Christian history that the debate takes up as one of its central subjects. At the same time, however, Moses's reanimation and his persistence even past the end of Peter's text might be read as reconfirming Christian stereotypes of Jewish stubbornness and inconvertibility that themselves depend upon a supersessionist ideology (performatively) relegating Judaism to the past. Peter repeatedly shows Moses the Christian "truth," and Moses repeatedly acknowledges Peter's claims; nonetheless, Moses also turns in "perverse" directions (as in his interim movement toward Islam) and never, within the text, ceases to be Jewish. This "staying Jewish," while it may undermine Christian claims to having superseded its ancestor, at the same time reinforces notions of a stiff-necked, stubborn Judaism that will refuse to see the truth even when that has been clearly demonstrated. And it is the figure not only of Moses but also of Peter that participates in such paradoxes: by virtue of his status as convert, Peter of course shows Judaism being effectively superseded by Christianity, but because of that very potential for change, he also calls into question strongly held Christian notions of Jewishness as ossified, dead, unable to respond appropriately to "the truth."

This complex ambivalence in Peter Alfonsi's text, seen especially in its unusual treatment of its "two" disputants—a Jew turned Christian and the cast-off self conjured back into Jewish existence—may be related in significant ways to the remarkable popularity of the *Dialogi*, which was, in Tolan's judgment, "the most influential and widely read of all medieval anti-Jewish tracts."[42] Staging at one and the same time a clear Christian victory over Judaism (both in the person of the convert-author and in the content of the debate, where Jewish and Islamic beliefs and practices are considered and ultimately rejected in favor of the Christian) and a "staying Jewish" that perversely defies that victory, the *Dialogi* gives voice both to a discourse of Christian superiority and to the anxieties that inhabit (and perhaps in part motivate) such a discourse in an era when Islam in fact poses significant threats to European Christian hegemony, and Judaism itself, no matter how diminished or historically "humiliated," persists as a presence within Europe.

Judging by the surviving manuscript evidence, from the moment of its composition in the early twelfth century through the fifteenth century, Peter Alfonsi's *Dialogi* enjoyed an unusually broad diffusion. At least seventy-nine (complete and partial) manuscripts survive—twenty-one from the twelfth century, twenty-four from the thirteenth, fourteen from the fourteenth, eighteen from the fifteenth, and two from the sixteenth.[43] (There were also three sixteenth- and seventeenth-century printed editions of the text.)[44] As Tolan shows, the geographical distribution of the text was wide, with twenty-seven manuscript copies from France (two-thirds of these from the twelfth and thirteenth centuries), sixteen from Central and Eastern Europe (almost two-thirds from the fourteenth and fifteenth centuries), twelve from England (seven from the twelfth and thirteenth centuries, and five from the fifteenth), and one from Italy.[45] Tolan also shows that the manuscripts were produced and owned by a wide range of medieval institutions, especially Benedictine and Cistercian monasteries, but also universities, cathedrals, and the abbeys of Augustinian and Premonstratensian canons.[46] Extensive portions of the text were used in later writers' work,[47] and the encyclopedist Vincent de Beauvais incorporated a shortened version of the *Dialogi*'s first five *tituli* into his thirteenth-century *Speculum historiale*, itself immensely popular.[48] We find Peter's Latin text also translated into Catalan (probably in the fourteenth century).[49]

Of course, the reasons for this popularity must have been various. As noted above, the debate genre deployed by the text was a popular one, long established both specifically in the realm of Jewish-Christian polemic and more generally in Western European letters. If the "splitting" of its author into two opposed disputants was unique within interreligious dialogue itself, it would nonetheless have echoed familiar Boethian traditions. The compendiousness of Peter Alfonsi's text would also have appealed to audiences, especially scholarly ones. Like other twelfth-century works—for example, Abelard's and Judah ha-Levi's dialogue texts—it takes up not just a debate between Jewish and Christian positions but also assesses Islam's relation to these, presenting a particularly full "comparative" treatment of the three religious traditions. Not surprisingly, we see later readers and writers using the *Dialogi* for the information it presents on Islamic and Jewish traditions and practices little known or attended to previously in Christian texts.[50] Thus, *titulus* v (on Islam) is excerpted in several manuscripts where the main concern seems to be arriving at an authoritative account of Islamic practices.[51] The Talmudic material Peter incorporates especially in *titulus* i was mined extensively by later writers, including Peter the Venerable.[52] Furthermore, the *Dialogi* arose out of the "new learning" of the "twelfth-century renaissance," and it participated in the scrutiny of such popular "new" topics as cosmography, natural history, and emotion. For readers and compilers at St. Victor, one of the centers of the "renaissance," the *Dialogi* clearly figured as a text of the "new learning": it appears in a Victorine manuscript alongside such other innovative twelfth-century texts as Honorius of Autun's *Imago mundi* and Bernard Silvester's *Cosmographia*.[53] In an early thirteenth-century manuscript from Salisbury Cathedral, the *Dialogi* appears immediately after Guillaume de Conches's *Moralium dogma philosophorum*.[54]

Even such relatively straightforward reasons for the work's popularity are wrapped up in complex ways with the text's foregrounding of religious and cultural difference. As I have suggested above, not only the information pertaining to Judaism and Islam but also the "new" learning Peter Alfonsi brings forward in the text, even if largely presented in the voice of the Christian disputant, depends upon the text's emergence from a "contact zone," a place where Christian, Jewish, and Islamic religious cultures meet—dramatized in the text as the space negotiated by the two disputants, or (what may amount to the same thing) *within* the convert who evokes both his current stance as the Christian Peter and his complex prehistory as the Jewish Moses. This complexity of course was something the *Dialogi* itself treated ambivalently: if the very situation of the debate calls attention to the split identity of Moses/Peter, the text's consistent and confident assignment of knowledge, reason, successful argumentation to Peter rather than Moses pastes over that split. Later writers who engaged with Alfonsi's work sometimes went further toward erasing the text's complexity of voice: two recensions—Vincent de Beauvais's and what Tolan calls the "Schäftlarn recension"[55]—make the dialogue into a monologue; that is, they make the text speak with a more consistent (if still never *completely* consistent) Christian voice. Most commonly, however, the text was received and reproduced as a dialogue, and the text's doublevoicedness enabled uses of it that were themselves quite disparate, even opposed. Thus, we see in the traces of the text's reception that are suggested by the manuscript contexts in which the *Dialogi* was reproduced or excerpted something of the ambivalence with which the text itself presents us when it revivifies a Jewish presence in order ultimately to put that presence once and for all to rest.

On the one hand, medieval copiers and readers clearly saw the *Dialogi* as furthering knowledge of a Judaism that was the object, in and of itself, of intense interest and engagement. As the text of a convert who explicitly recalls the beliefs, positions, and voice of his preconversion, Jewish self, Peter's *Dialogi* seems to have been read as providing a particular and particularly strong sort of evidence about Judaism. In a number of manuscripts—for instance, BL Harley 3861 and BN lat. 10722—the text is reproduced alone, the sole object of attention, testifying to the interest it held, on its own, for readers. The text's presentation of Judaism, too, at times serves to further a kind of world historical knowledge, with Peter's treatment of Judaism (and Islam) serving to fill in a knowledge of the world and its history. This can be seen in a manuscript like the Victorine one mentioned above (BN lat. 15009) or BN lat. 5080, where Rufinus's Latin translation of Eusebius's *Historia ecclesiastica* precedes Peter's *Dialogi*.[56] Other manuscripts gather the *Dialogi* together with works like Gilbert Crispin's *Disputatio Iudei cum Christiano,* Odo of Cambrai's *Disputatio contra Iudaeum,* and Guibert of Nogent's *Tractatus de incarnatione contra judaeos* whose primary focus is Judaism and its relation to Christianity.[57]

Such manuscript configurations, of course, suggest not only a Christian desire to understand more about Judaism but also an impulse polemically to refute Jewish claims. Placing the *Dialogi* among other world-historical texts, for instance, clearly can support a supersessionist, Christian history. And manuscripts that include the *Dialogi* among texts like Gilbert's, Odo's, and Guibert's evince no neutral interest in Judaism. All of these dialogic texts, Peter's included, provide polemical attacks on and refutations of Jewish positions. Such manuscripts help reconsolidate Christian self-understandings of superiority vis-à-vis Judaism. When Peter's *Dialogi* appears along with a text entitled *De apparatu et armis et munimento militum Christi* [*On the equipment and arms and fortification of the soldiers of Christ*], we can easily imagine it as part of a Christian missionary project.[58] The same is true when manuscripts juxtapose the *Dialogi* to texts that depict the Crusades[59] or ones that attack Christian heresy.[60] One manuscript strikingly connects contemporary Judaism, as represented in Peter's *Dialogi,* to the early enemies of Christ; here, St. Bonaventure's *Lignum vitae* (meditations of the life of Christ) precedes a life of Judas, a life of Pilate, and finally the *Dialogi*.[61]

The complex ambivalence thus suggested by the manuscript contexts of the *Dialogi* reproduces itself at various particular moments in the text itself—most strikingly when specifically Jewish knowledge is used to support Christian ends. This occurs in both negative and positive modes. On the one hand, Jewish knowledge is presented as ridiculous and hence as demonstrating the ridiculousness of Judaism itself. This is especially true in Peter's presentation of Talmudic material in *titulus* i of the *Dialogi*, where Talmudic *aggadah* (narrative and homiletic material) is extensively cited and contemptuously dismissed. Peter notes, for instance, the Talmud's anthropomorphizing of God—"you contend that God has a head, arms, and the complete form of the body"[62]—in order to emphasize Judaism's strong misunderstanding of the deity. On the other hand, however, Judaism is sometimes depicted as having real if unacknowledged or actively denied knowledge of the (Christian) truth. Thus, as noted above, one of the foci of Jewish religious, mystical, and intellectual interest, the "name" of God as represented in the Tetragrammaton, is used by Peter to prove the doctrine of the Trinity:

> Indeed, the Trinity is something subtle and ineffable and difficult to explain, concerning which the prophets spoke only in occult ways and veiledly, until Christ came, who, one of the three persons, revealed it [the Trinity] to the minds of the faithful according to their capacity. If nonetheless you also pay attention carefully and inspect that name of God, which you find explained in "The Secrets of Secrets"—I say, the name, composed of three letters although with four figures, since one of those, twinned, is written twice—if, I say, you inspect that, you will see, since the same name is both one and three. But that it is one concerns the unity of substance, and truly that it is three concerns the trinity of persons. Moreover, that name consists of these four figures, "i" ["yod"] and "e" ["he"] and "v" ["vav"] and "e" ["he"], of which if you will join the first only with the second— that is, "i" ["yod"] and "e" ["he"]—to be sure, it will be one name. Likewise, if the second and the third—that is, "e" ["he"] and "v" ["vav"]—now you will have a second. Similarly, if you will connect the third only with the fourth—that is, "v" ["vav"] and "e" ["he"]—you will also find a third. Again, if you will bind all together in order, there will be nothing other than a single name, as is clear in the following geometric figure.[63]

The figure that follows represents in diagrammatic form the triune nature of the Tetragrammaton that Peter has just explained.

In this section of his argument, Peter obviously puts his own knowledge of Hebrew to use, but the more general unfamiliarity of the Hebrew language for medieval Christian readers and copyists—even at the basic level of the alphabet—meant that the Hebrew terms of Peter's argument needed to be translated (literally, transliterated) into more familiar, Latin terms. Unsurprisingly, then, in most of the surviving manuscripts, it is the Roman letters "i – e – v – e" that stand in for the Hebrew "yod – he – vav – he."[64] Significantly, however, in a minority of manuscripts, Hebrew letters are used, and used properly (see Figure 4).[65] Representations of Hebrew lettering abound in the medieval visual arts, but, as Ruth Mellinkoff has shown, these are most often inaccurate and exoticizing representations of the Hebrew alphabet.[66] In this copy of the *Dialogi* in the Victorine manuscript BN lat. 15009, however, the scribe incorporates Hebrew letters into the text—and uses them in the diagram—in a careful, precise manner.[67]

This particular textual moment—in which the truth of the Trinity is miraculously demonstrated even in the most intimate, secret knowledge of those who disbelieve—functions, too, as a moment when Jewish knowledge (at least the knowledge of the Hebrew alphabet) might become an object of Christian interest in itself. Indeed, in BN lat. 15009, we also see the scribe(s) focusing attention on Hebrew *outside* the context of Peter Alfonsi's Christian argument. On a folio toward the end of the manuscript, two folios after the text of the *Dialogi* concludes,[68] the scribe has written, upside down but without error, the whole of the Hebrew alphabet, and not just the three letters that constitute the Tetragrammaton and that are all that are necessary to make the text's earlier point about the Trinity (Figure 5). It is no mere coincidence, I think, that this manuscript is one produced at St. Victor, the place where, in the twelfth century, we have the strongest evidence of scholarly (particularly exegetical) interest in Jewish learning, especially the *literal* reading of the biblical text—an interest of course that was disconcerting enough to some to lead them to accuse the Victorines of "Judaizing."

INTELLECTUAL CROSSINGS, MISSIONARY ZEAL

What we see in the deployment of a text of conversion like Peter Alfonsi's echoes the broader tendency of twelfth-century Christianity to engage

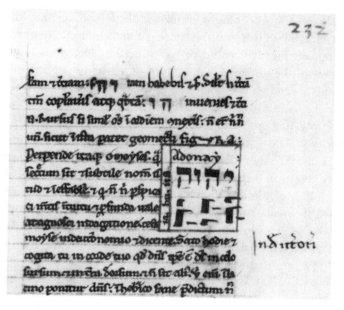

Figure 4. Proof of the Trinity using the Tetragrammaton. Petrus Alfonsi, *Dialogi*, BN lat. 15009, fol. 232r (late twelfth or early thirteenth century). Reproduced with permission of Bibliothèque nationale de France, Paris.

with Judaism in a simultaneously interested and hostile or aversive manner. The "renaissance" of the long twelfth century made intellectual advances dependent on the crossings of various linguistic, cultural, and religious traditions. Greek, Arabic, and Hebrew texts and ideas made their way into Latin; ancient (pagan), Islamic, and Jewish philosophies encountered, influenced, and were absorbed into Christian thought. More specifically in relation to Jewish and Hebrew traditions, there seems to have been an increasingly vivid sense that a deeper knowledge of Judaism might reveal something important about Christianity. Following on but also exceeding the Augustinian idea of Judaism as a *witness* to Christian revelation, Christian scholars and writers turned increasingly to the study of Judaism, looking to Hebrew for what it might reveal about the literal sense of scripture but also asking for a more detailed sense of Jewish (dis)belief and its relationship to Christian faith than seems to have been desired by most Christians of the earlier Middle Ages.[69] If such inquiries often sought primarily to reconfirm what was already "known"—the inferiority or insidiousness of Jewish belief—they

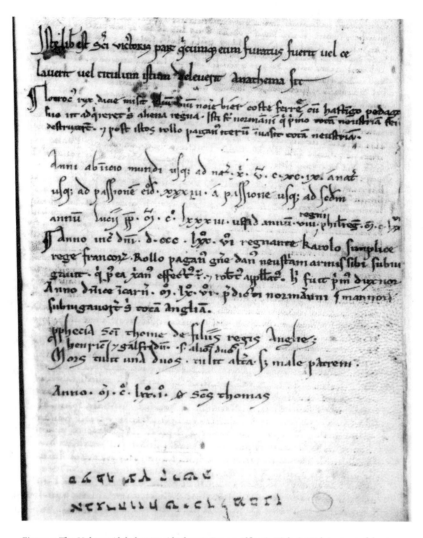

Figure 5. The Hebrew Alphabet (upside down). Petrus Alfonsi, *Dialogi*, BN lat. 15009, fol. 257r (late twelfth or early thirteenth century). Reproduced with permission of Bibliothèque nationale de France, Paris.

also potentially held surprises for those undertaking them. Indeed, medieval accusations of "Judaizing" imagined that the pursuit of knowledge about Judaism contained profound dangers for Christians. And, as we have noted above, there is evidence, though often fragmentary, that some European Christians responded to their contacts with Judaism by giving up the immense privilege of their Christianity and converting to the minority religion.[70] If Christian texts of interaction between Judaism and Christianity most often imagined that the consequence of Christians' learning more about Judaism would be a heightened facility in bringing disbelieving Jews to a proper Christian belief (that is, in bringing them to conversion), an often unacknowledged accompanying fear was that the opening of intellectual dialogue between the two religions might enable precisely the reverse. This fear led sometimes to the explicit banning of dialogue between ordinary Christians and Jews,[71] and yet the idea of such dialogue seems to have remained compelling for medieval Christians: it continues to be frequently imagined in texts like Peter Alfonsi's and the disputations of Ceuta and Majorca (which in fact claim to depict actual debates).

A danger inherent in any text that imagines conversion from one position to its "opposite" is the (most often unstated) possibility that the reverse conversion might just as easily occur. For Christianity as a religion of conversion the problem is especially poignant: since Christian identity is defined by its radical difference from an originary Judaism, it is important for Christians to envision that point of origin and to define precisely their difference from it. But, in doing so, might they discover that the move away from the origin is itself a deviation instead of the perfect route? Medieval ecclesiastical legislation intensively concerned itself with the problem of "relapse," of Jewish converts returning to Judaism, and we might read the intensity of this interest as reflecting as much a concern about the stability of Christian identity per se as it did a concern about those cases where Jewish conversion and relapse were in fact at issue.[72] One of the specters that haunts a text like Peter Alfonsi's *Dialogi* is the (acknowledged) possibility that confronting the Jewish interlocutor will lead not to his defeat but to his victory, that is, to a reversal of the conversion that makes Peter's Christian identity possible. (As we will see in the Majorca disputation, such a fear of relapse easily shades over into anxiety about whether a "born" Christian might turn Jewish.) In the *Dialogi,* Moses, after all, exists as the convert Peter's mental projection of a "relapsed" self: the text makes explicit that Moses comes to Peter to lead him back to Judaism. Of course, Moses fails in this mission, but the possibility of the reversal of Christian conversion still inhabits the text as a countermovement to the (more successful but still never fully accomplished) impulse to bring Moses to Christianity.

Much of the Christian engagement with Judaism, even when it represents a real, serious, interested engagement with Jewish ideas and beliefs, works to guard against the possibility that the Jewish origin might reassert itself in a too persuasive or potent fashion.

Christian interest in Judaism is thus consistently shadowed by the fear that such interest might lead in "Judaizing" directions, and we should therefore not be surprised that moments of interreligious interest and collaboration also often entail interreligious hostility. Even as, in the long twelfth century, connections and crossings arose among different religious traditions, and precisely because such connections and crossings became salient, influential, formative for high medieval European culture, they had to be aversively denied, the purity as well as the superiority of Christian tradition asserted. As we have seen in the *Dialogi*, what were clearly the intellectual fruits of interreligious collaboration could come to be claimed as specifically Christian knowledge, and, in an even bolder move, specifically non-Christian materials (as in Peter's treatment of the Tetragrammaton) could be reinterpreted as testifying to Christian truth. Such claimings of intellectual territory supplemented the attempt to convert people to Christianity. As the Christian West came to know Judaism better, came to immerse itself more and more fully in Jewish knowledge, it also moved increasingly to deny Judaism its own intellectual traditions, and concomitantly to deny Judaism to Jews. Of course, one might equally well reverse the suggestion of causality here: as Christianity adopted more and more hostile stances toward Judaism, reconsolidating its own hegemonic position in Western Europe, it moved more and more to know about its historical ancestor and its contemporary enemy. Rather than think of an impulse toward interreligious collaboration, tolerance, and rapprochement coexisting tensely with a separate and opposed impulse toward hegemony and domination, we might think of these two movements as part of a single if ambivalent set of relations wherein, as religious others became more familiar, they were also felt to be more threatening, and more actively to be guarded against and attacked.

This is not to suggest that there was no division, at this moment of intensifying collaborative and aversive relations between Judaism and Christianity, between those who stood more on the side of either collaboration or hostility. As scholars of the twelfth century have recognized, we can point to two contemporaneous theologians like Bernard of Clairvaux and Peter the Venerable for clearly differing (if also overlapping) attitudes toward Jews and Judaism.[73] But the larger dynamic of creative and hostile contact seems not to have been so clearly polarized, and positive and negative interreligious encounters are not easily relegated to different individuals, groups, or social spheres. If Bernard of Clairvaux acted, for instance, to prevent anti-Jewish violence during the Second Crusade, his theology was (as Jeremy Cohen has recently noted) in many ways in agreement with Peter the Venerable's in the anti-Jewish positions it took. The difficulty of distinguishing a hostile from a more benign engagement with Judaism is clear, too, in texts of the long twelfth century like Abelard's and Alfonsi's dialogues, where there is both a significant interest in and active hostility toward Judaism. As we move into the thirteenth century, the simultaneous attraction and aversion to Judaism becomes even more striking. Thus, for instance, the fraternal orders that arose in the early thirteenth century took up and significantly accelerated the incorporation of Arabic, Greek, and Hebrew texts and ideas into Latin Christian traditions. But they simultaneously contributed to an active, intellectually vibrant, and strongly anti-Jewish missionary movement.[74]

It might be useful to think about what is happening here in Foucauldian terms. In a very different context (the discussion of the "deployment of sexuality" in the first volume of *The History of Sexuality*), Foucault calls our attention to the intimate relationship between power and knowledge: "If sexuality was constituted as an area of investigation, this was only because relations of power had established it as a possible object; and conversely, if power was able to take it as a target, this was because techniques of knowledge and procedures of discourse were capable of investing it. Between techniques of knowledge and strategies of power there is no exteriority."[75] Power and knowledge, attempts to gain forcible or intellectual purchase on a "subject," are not fully separate or separable from each other. A shift in knowledge enables changes in force relations; power shifts mean that different things can become known about those involved in the relations of power—both those in a position of relative control and those whose agential possibilities might be more fully circumscribed. The "renaissance" of the twelfth century, following as it did on the heightening of Christianity's hostile relations with its religious others in the period of the First Crusade, was involved in a complex set of shifts in power/knowledge between Judaism and Christianity. As I will suggest more fully in the following chapter, especially crucial in these shifts was the recognition of the fact that Judaism was not a static, unchanging religion—that, like Christianity, it had changed and grown across the centuries and that it continued to do so. If Judaism was not a reliably stable (if also an uncomprehending and blind) witness to Christian truth, it presented itself as potentially more dangerous to Christian stability. It also presented Christianity with a whole new set of objects of inquiry: postbiblical Jewish legal and interpretive texts, especially the Talmud, came under Christian scrutiny (here, Peter Alfonsi's treatment of the Talmud was influential for later investigators), as did contemporary Jewish ritual and everyday practices. And as more came to be known about contemporary Judaism, additional points of Christian intervention and control could be identified. Should Jews be given free rein in biblical or Talmudic exegesis, or should such intellectual work be restrained by what Christianity knew about itself and therefore about "proper" Jewish interpretation and "witnessing"? Might intra-Jewish intellectual or sociopolitical disagreements need to be settled by Christian intervention? Shouldn't Christians put a stop to what were "clearly" questionable and reprehensible Jewish practices like "usury"?

Whereas earlier medieval disputation and missionizing contented themselves with a fairly standard and stable set of anti-Jewish arguments that corresponded in general and rather inaccurate ways to Jewish beliefs and practices, thirteenth-century missionizing began to emphasize the need to learn about current Jewish practices. Thirteenth-century polemicists began to engage, too, with Hebrew in an unprecedented way, emphasizing the need both to understand (most often untranslated) Jewish texts and to communicate Christian understandings more fully to Jews. The fraternal orders set up schools of Hebrew and Arabic,[76] and the study of these languages and the texts written in them meant that Christians began to gain access to previously unfamiliar Jewish and Islamic ideas. But of course the founding of such schools was not motivated by some "pure" intellectual curiosity: rather, it took its place in a concerted program of fraternal missionizing explicitly intended to bring non-Christian souls more effectively into the Christian fold. In the thirteenth century, too, Christian scholars rapidly gained an understanding of the Talmud that built on the writings of such twelfth-century figures as Alfonsi and Peter the Venerable but that moved far beyond these. Thus, in the 1240s in Paris, in a project directed by the papal legate Eudes de

Châteauroux, which involved also the Dominican Thibaut de Sézanne and the participation of several converts from Judaism to Christianity, a large and detailed compendium of *Extractiones de Talmut* was compiled.[77] The compilation served a clear political purpose, supporting at this place and time strong attacks on Jewish practice that involved especially the attempt to suppress the Talmud. Knowledge of the Hebrew text is useful here not in promoting some "objective" intellectual project of interreligious understanding but in providing evidence of Jewish perversion and perfidy; the Parisian manuscript compiles a detailed "case" against Judaism and Jewish practice.

If we compare a text like Raymond Martini's *Pugio Fidei* [*Dagger of Faith*] to even the strongest twelfth-century anti-Jewish polemic, we find a marked increase both in anti-Jewish (and anti-Muslim) sentiment and in the level of engagement with Jewish (and Muslim) texts.[78] If the incorporation of some Hebrew into some of the manuscripts of Peter Alfonsi's *Dialogi* suggests the increased possibility of medieval Christian engagement with Jewish learning that accompanied the twelfth-century "renaissance," the proliferation of Hebrew within Martini's text signals a massive leap into that engagement. When, in the fourth chapter of the third "distinction" of the third part of the *Pugio*, "De adventu Messiae ad salvandum Adam, & filios eius: & quod ipse est Deus a Deo ad hoc missus, & nomine Dei vocatus" [Concerning the advent of the Messiah for the salvation of Adam and his sons, and that he himself is God sent by God for this purpose, and called by the name of God], Martini discusses the significance of the Tetragrammaton, he turns to the Hebrew knowledge Peter Alfonsi had previously brought forward (though he presents this in a somewhat different manner):

As says Master Peter Alfonsi, who was in Spain before he became a Christian a great Rabbi among the Jews: the first three letters of this name, that is, "yod – he – vav," indicate that in God called by this name there are three "midot" [the Hebrew "mem – dalet – vav – tav"], that is, three properties differing among themselves in their diversity, which they have as much in figure as in name. . . . There is one of those letters, however, which repeats, and is placed at the end of the name, which is "he," and this is the first letter in this name "havayah" [the

Hebrew "he – vav – yod – he"], "Essence." This indicates that, of the three "midot," that is, properties or persons, there is a unity of Essence.[79]

Already we see that Martini works Hebrew more intimately into his discussion than did Peter Alfonsi. In the sentence that follows, Martini goes on to gloss the Latin "qvatuor literarum" [four letters] with the Greek "tetragrammaton" and Hebrew "shel arba otiyot" (using Greek and Hebrew characters respectively). And from this point on in the passage, Hebrew proliferates: Martini cites, in Hebrew with Latin translation, extensive passages from the Talmud and from "Moseh filius Maimon" [Maimonides], ultimately concluding that such Hebrew lore conforms to Christian truth: "it is manifestly shown that 'this is the name above every name,' as says the Apostle Paul to the Philippians 2:9."[80] Martini thus engages in remarkable ways with the Hebrew language and with Jewish texts, but, as the passage also makes clear, this engagement is not innocent or academically "objective": the incorporation of Hebrew texts into the *Pugio Fidei* forms an integral part of that work's program of combating, with the "dagger of faith," Christianity's religious enemies. After all, the three concluding chapters of Martini's work are "Concerning the reprobation of the Jews," "Again concerning the reprobation, and certain of their crimes, and concerning the stench of their doctrine, and concerning the iniquity of their laws," and "Concerning the state of the Jews from the ascent of Christ until the end of the world, and concerning the conversion of their remnant."[81]

Thirteenth-century intellectual engagements with Judaism are based on a broader and more intensive encounter with Jewish texts, ideas, beliefs, and practices than are those of the earlier Middle Ages, but this is not to say that a thirteenth-century understanding of Judaism is any more accurate or unbiased than earlier understandings.[82] Christian knowledge of Judaism might indeed be increasingly based in the reading of important, previously inaccessible Jewish texts or in the observation of actual Jewish practices, but it might equally be fabricated or fantasized: one need only think here of the strongly anti-Semitic accusations (of ritual murder, host desecration, blood-related crimes) that arose and intensified in this period and that presented themselves as firmly grounded in "insider" knowledge of Jewish ritual practice and communal animosity toward Christians and Christianity. Of course not all Christian students or observers of Judaism equally held the full range of Christian beliefs and "knowledges" about Judaism—from the more carefully observed and "neutral" to the more clearly fabricated and hostile. Some of these (i.e., accusations of Jewish crime and violence) were strongly contested from within the Christian establishment.[83] Still, the overall picture here is one in which Christian discourses of knowingness about Judaism grew and fed on each other, and where "advances" in knowledge frequently suggested the need to exert Christian (state and ecclesiastical) power over the Jews—through legislation (e.g., that of the Fourth Lateran Council), expulsion, local violence. Such exercises of power, themselves enabled by certain kinds of learning, often promoted interreligious contacts (hostile and otherwise) that led to further remappings of the field of knowledge. Ritual murder accusations, for instance, led to interrogations of Jews about beliefs and daily life that must have meant an increasingly intimate knowledge (at least among Christian authorities) of the details of Jewish private life.[84]

Inextricably involved in these thirteenth-century dynamics of power/ knowledge were converts from Judaism to Christianity. As converts entered Christian communities, whether willingly or not, special kinds of knowledge entered with them. The issue here is again not one primarily of the reliability of such knowledge, though some of what converts like Hermann or Alfonsi taught their new communities about Judaism was demonstrably accurate. Still, whether out of sincere belief or impulses of self-preservation or a more hostile stance toward the community that they had rejected and that had consequently also rejected them, converts at least sometimes also handed over knowledge tailor-made to feed anti-Semitic fantasies. Thus, in the twelfth-century ritual murder accusation at Norwich, a convert, Theobald, provided especially damning testimony about the Jews.[85] The knowledge these native informants brought forward had clear social effects—stark ones in cases where a convert's testimony supported inquisition and execution, more indirect ones in cases where converts provided information about Jewish beliefs and practices that bolstered efforts to control or suppress Jewish communities. As we will see in the next chapter, a convert, Nicholas Donin, was at the center of events that led to the condemnation of the Talmud at Paris in the mid-thirteenth century. And later in the century, one of the most active Dominican missionaries was the convert Pablo

Christiani. The large public disputations he helped stage were important sites for the reconfiguration of power/knowledge: as we will see,
they posed Jewish versus Christian knowledge, elaborating specifically
Christian understandings of Jewish practices and texts, particularly the
Talmud, even as they asserted Christian power, a power especially intent
on "leading" Jews—through argumentation that is at once "academic"
and coercive—to abandon Judaism (as, of course, had the converts themselves). The means of confronting Jewish communities with the Jewish
knowledge carried by converts elaborated by such thirteenth-century
figures as Nicholas Donin and Pablo Christiani proved to be a durable
tool in Christian missionizing, deployed as late as the fifteenth century
in spectacular fashion at the disputation of Tortosa (again, discussed
more fully in the next chapter).

JEWISH IDENTITY, MERCHANT IDENTITY

Texts like Peter Alfonsi's *Dialogi* and the disputations that will be examined in chapter 5 clearly concern themselves with the nature of Jewish
difference from Christianity, and at least a large part of their thrust is to
redefine Jewishness in ways that make it untenable for Jewish subjects,
in ways that militate for their conversion. But it is clear, at the same
time, that such texts are about Christian identity, attempting to define
and stabilize what it means to be a Christian. While most of the texts we
have so far looked at define the differences between Christian and Jewish identity in quite bald terms, suggesting that there is a single Jewish
identity against which a single Christian identity might be posed, some
medieval texts of Jewish-Christian encounter recognize the complexities of Christian identity and use an examination of Jewish-Christian
difference to ask and address questions about identity differences *within*
Christianity. This is true in a text like Peter Alfonsi's, which considers, if
largely implicitly, the differences between a convert identity and Christian identity tout court: a nonconvert could never take the place of Peter
in the interreligious debate of the *Dialogi*. In many other sorts of Christian text, representations of Jews and Jewishness are used to foreground
and critique variations in Christian behavior that are, in the author's
view, to be disallowed. That is, their focus is not only a Jewish other who
must be guarded against and defeated but also Christians and the possible

failures of "proper" Christian identity. We might see this, for instance, in Guibert's concern with Jean of Soissons as "Judaizer" and more generally in the way heretical positions are associated, in "orthodox" discourses, with both Judaism and Islam.[86] And we see representations of Jews used to comment on Christian transgressions especially frequently in contexts (like postexpulsion England) in which Jewish communities are not significant social presences. Thus, John Gower in the fourteenth century criticizes Christians for working on the Sabbath although "the Jew preserves the sacred Sabbath of the Lord, neither buying nor selling nor seeking for gain!"[87] Chaucer's Pardoner (in a comparison that works in an opposite direction) associates the Christian use of oaths with the paradigmatic Jewish attack on the Christian body, the crucifixion: "Oure blissed Lordes body they totore— / Hem thoughte that Jewes rente hym noght ynogh."[88] In the fifteenth century, Margery Kempe compares the way she is mistreated by her contemporaries to the Jews' treatment of Jesus: "sche wist wel þat þe Iewys seyd meche wers of hys owyn persone þan men dede of hir" [she knew very well that the Jews said much worse of his own person than people did of her].[89] Conversely, Margery's own contemporaries express their suspicion of her by asking "whedyr sche wer a Cristen woman er a Iewe" [whether she were a Christian woman or a Jew].[90] We could multiply examples in which medieval authors deploy a comparison to a disallowed (or more rarely, as in Gower, admirable) Jewish behavior or position in order to emphasize specific Christian transgressions.

Not only particular Christian actions but also more agglomerated sets of behavior that might be taken to constitute separate *identities* within Christendom come to be negatively associated with Jewishness and strongly critiqued or even disallowed at least partly on the basis of such an association. Religious identity is so central to medieval conceptions of persons that social changes we (in the early twenty-first century) might think quite separate from religious belief, especially those perceived as changing in significant ways fundamental societal arrangements, tend in the Middle Ages to be viewed through a religious lens. That is, perceived challenges to an orderly society are likely to be seen, too, as challenges to *Christianitas* and, perhaps, as incursions of heretical, pagan, Muslim, or Jewish beliefs and practices, or some dangerous admixture of these. Beginning with the long twelfth century, Christian Europe experienced especially pervasive and far-reaching socioeconomic changes involving extensive urbanization; an economy increasingly dependent on monetary exchange; the reformulation of a tripartite social structure of clergy, warrior-aristocrats, and peasant-workers to include, more or less uneasily, a variety of middle social strata; and the increasing investment of the church hierarchy in secular power.[91] Such changes were intimately wrapped up with what ascetic Christian thought would consider an inappropriate materiality, and this was consistently associated, as we have seen, with both Jewishness and femininity/effeminacy. It is therefore not surprising to see such changes often understood, especially in more socially conservative discourses, as expressions of both religious difference (i.e., a failure of Christian identity) and gender deviance.

Insofar as the church, in gaining secular power and involving itself in worldly matters, was seen from within as deviating from its proper spiritual route, it might itself be depicted in reforming discourses as betraying properly Christian principles, as falling into an association with the non-Christian. But while we might expect the use of discourses of religious accusation in the context of explicitly religious critique and reform, similar accusations also came to be attached to changes that we tend to think of as inhering in more purely secular social and economic processes. Of course, associating such changes with Judaism was enabled by the discursive availability of anti-Jewish stereotypes and by a Christian theology and exegesis that consistently associated Jewishness with the material. But it was not only in the realms of discourse and ideology that Jews and Jewishness were susceptible to such an association. Indeed, the very processes of European socioeconomic change that led to anxieties about proper Christian behavior and identity involved real changes in the status of Jewish communities that strongly reinforced the ideological bringing together of Jews and materiality. Jews associated with royal families were often positioned as (unpopular) tax collectors. They were also the first group in Europe's growing money economy to be allowed and encouraged to participate in moneylending,[92] and, more broadly, with many occupations not allowed to Jews, professions involving monetary exchange, particularly the mercantile, became crucial to the survival of Jewish communities. Such social positioning of Jews built on preexisting discourses associating Jews with materiality; it also allowed those discourses to be strengthened and realized (that is, literally made real). Jews in Western Europe came increasingly both ideologically and experientially to be associated with the monied interests of those noble families they served, with tax collection, with lending money at interest, with mercantile practices critiqued repeatedly from a Christian perspective as improper. Such real associations, propped up, as they were, by theological and exegetical traditions, easily slipped into more fantastic charges of a Jewish materialist criminality. After all, "usury" was already defined by the church as a crime, though one allowed to Jewish communities by Christian authorities.[93] That Jews then came to be associated with the debasement of the currency and with coin-clipping is a small step.[94] A larger slippage occurs when Christian thinking moves from a consideration of Jewish economic "crimes" to fantasies of Jewish violence against both Christian bodies and Christian religious sanctity— well poisoning, ritual murder, host desecration.

As the European money economy grew, of course, it became less and less possible to claim that questionable materialist practices were confined to Jewish communities. As Lester Little suggests,

> It was both inaccurate and unfair to regard commercial activity, especially moneylending, as the exclusive preserve of Jews, for the Jews always formed a tiny minority of the people so engaged. And yet the main function of the Jews in the Commercial Revolution was to bear the burden of Christian guilt for participation in activities not yet deemed morally worthy of Christians. Christians attacked in the Jews those things about themselves that they found inadmissible and that they therefore projected on to the Jews.[95]

The development of a licit Lombard moneylending and the rapid growth of Christian mercantilism made especially clear the implication of Christians in "Jewish" practices. Although we tend to think of such developments as characterizing especially the later Middle Ages and the early modern period, mercantilism and new social forms began to take hold— unevenly across Europe, in Italy and the Mediterranean, in new urban centers, in the Low Countries—as early as the twelfth century. These were readily associable with Jewishness, not least because Christian merchants and others intimately involved in the new money economy would be more likely to come into contact with Jews than were other groups within Christian society. A significant aspect of the stabilization of such new social forms became their defense not just on broadly social

but also on more narrowly religious grounds. If a presumed Jewish materialism must be spurned by Christians in favor of the spiritual, what
was to be made of Christianity's growing dependence upon the monetary and mercantile?

If we focus on merchants as one of the crucial emerging social
groups dependent upon new economic arrangements and struggling to
find a secure place within medieval society, we see developing, on the
one hand, a consistent association of the mercantile with the religiously
disallowed, particularly the Jewish, and, on the other, a growing counterdiscourse that defends merchants on religious (theological and doctrinal) grounds.[96] Critiques of merchants, like those of Jews, associate them
especially with excessive materiality. In Langland's *Piers Plowman*, the
pardon Truth grants to all members of Christian society includes merchants, but only "in þe margine": they belong and yet do not belong
fully or properly to Christian society, and their problematic status is
explicitly connected to the monetary—"couetyse of wynnynge."[97] The
problem of salvation, here posed in relation to a particular class of
Christians, is one Langland's poem also returns to repeatedly in regard
to non-Christians, and specifically Jews; merchants thus, implicitly, stand
close to those more fully outside Christendom whose elect status is all
the more problematic.[98] John Gower, in the *Mirour de l'Omme*, even as
he presents a defense of mercantile activity based in a God-centered politics, strongly affiliates merchants with fraud and usury; though here
he does not explicitly connect that usury to Jews, such an association
would have been readily available to his audience.[99] The merchant in
Chaucer's *Shipman's Tale* is a man who, rather than attend to his wife
and his guest (a monk), locks himself away with his money and then
leaves home to pursue a potentially lucrative business deal that involves
credit and perhaps "usury." His absence gives the monk and the wife
the opportunity to attain an intimate understanding that involves the
exchange of both money and sex, and, by the end of the tale, the marital
relation, sex, and monetary exchange have been thoroughly mixed up
with each other. An older set of social relations—between husband and
wife, host and guest, secular and clerical men—is disturbed and re-
configured in the face of new mercantile arrangements.[100] In what seems
to be a significant juxtaposition, the tale that follows immediately after
in Fragment VII of the *Canterbury Tales* is the *Prioress's*, where a Jewish
community explicitly identified with usury is first responsible for the

violent, gruesome death of a Christian innocent and is then punished by itself being violently humiliated.[101] The bringing together of Christian merchants and Jews is performed more directly in a work like the fifteenth-century Croxton *Play of the Sacrament,* where the powerful merchant Aristorius is explicitly paralleled to his Jewish counterpart Jonathas, and where the Christian merchant directly contributes to the crime of host desecration by means of a monetary exchange, selling the consecrated host to the Jews.[102] Such a strong association of Christian merchants with Jews is preserved in later, early modern texts—most famously in Christopher Marlowe's *Jew of Malta,* where it is difficult to distinguish Jewish abuses of power from Christian mercantilism and Machiavellian politics, and William Shakespeare's *Merchant of Venice,* where the intertwining of Christian mercantile and Jewish identities is intimately connected to the exploration of love and marriage, kin relations and inheritance, the law and social (dis)order.[103] As David Wallace has recently shown, Genoa, as a city of merchants—"Genuensis ergo mercator" [Genoese, therefore a merchant]—is shadowed, for centuries that span the medieval and early modern periods, by the "imaginative shadow" of the Jew; from James Howell's 1642 *Instructions for Forreine Travell:* "And when a *Jew* (and the *Jews* are held the most Mercuriall people in the World, by reason of their so often transmigrations, persecutions, and *Necessity,* which is the *Mother* of Wit) [I say when a Jew] meeteth with a *Genoway,* and is to negotiat with him, he puts his fingers in his eyes, fearing to be over-reached by him, and outmatched in his cunning."[104]

As we might expect, the association of mercantile identity with Jewishness and materiality also entails a certain gender trouble. Insofar as merchants may be (like Jews) usurious, inappropriately immersed in the material, unable to recognize the importance of the spiritual, they are also (like Jews) in danger of falling out of properly masculine positions. From socially conservative points of view, a classed identity like that of the merchant, emerging without any clear, preestablished place within Christian society and hence forcing a reorganization of that society, would be seen as lacking in relation to the demands of both a secular-aristocratic and a clerical masculinity. The merchant's failure to exert power in accepted noble or aristocratic modes, his distance from the field of battle, the skills of the warrior, and the seats of official power, was coupled with an economic power threatening to the aristocracy but—in its fluidity and disconnection from a stable social place, from the land and land-owning that traditionally conferred high status—felt to be illegitimate. From a clerical perspective, the merchant's immersion in materiality raised the question of whether he could ever be a good Christian. Certainly, merchants stood far from ascetic clerical ideals of masculinity, far from a sense of the sort of Christian virility that depended especially on the ability to distance oneself from bodily needs and to take on an "armor" spiritual rather than corporeal.

To establish and defend new Christian mercantile identities meant, then, constructing not only a new sense of what might be licit and proper for Christians as Christians but also a new gender identity that might enable merchants to present themselves as men worthy of honor and status. The increasing social and economic importance of the middle strata (including the merchant class) brought pressure to bear toward valorizing these strata in relation to both the aristocracy and the clerisy, and such moves of self-validation often worked through attempts to claim or repudiate or reshape clerical and aristocratic ideals of masculinity. Glenn Burger's recent book, *Chaucer's Queer Nation,* looks at the gender/sexual implications of this process in some detail, examining particularly the ways in which the identity of "husband" might represent a new "middle" ideal of masculinity different from either the aristocratic or the clerical.[105] This new masculinity is, from the start, challenged by its close and necessary association with the female and the domestic; it cannot claim for itself a wholly male space like that of the battlefield or cloister. In his professional life, however, the itinerant merchant might approach more closely to such an all-male world than those of other middle status. At the same time, if the emergent masculinity of his class depends upon the proper "husbanding" of a domestic realm from which the (itinerant) merchant necessarily strays, this new middle ideal might itself be difficult of attainment, might throw the merchant back into the search for a stable masculinity.

Two unusual high medieval Latin texts, the disputations of Ceuta and Majorca, take up the challenge of validating Christian mercantile identity by putting merchants into direct confrontation with Jews.[106] These texts present a scenario very unusual within the extensive medieval literature of Christian-Jewish debate, whether this is fictional or, as here, purports to represent actual, public encounters. In the larger tradition, the Christian disputants almost universally fall into one of two categories,

either theologically trained clerics (Gilbert Crispin or Guibert of Nogent
or Rupert of Deutz, speaking in their own persons) or Jewish converts to
Christianity, as in Peter Alfonsi's *Dialogi* or in the great public debates
held, in the thirteenth to fifteenth centuries, at Paris, Barcelona, and
Tortosa, where Nicholas Donin, Pablo Christiani, and Geronimo of Santa
Fe, converts all, speak for Christian doctrine. One must ask, then, what
work it accomplishes, in the two debate texts at hand, for the Christian
disputant to be neither a cleric with special, professional knowledge of
Christian doctrine nor a convert with privileged double access to Christian
and Jewish teaching, but instead a Genoese merchant. What is at issue,
in terms of the politics of identity, in the intellectual, disputational confrontation of a Christian merchant with Jewish men who are not themselves merchants but, as is common in the medieval debate literature,
notably learned men—at Ceuta, "that most wise Jew named Mo[ses]
Abram"; at Majorca, "most wise Jews and doctors in the Jewish synagogues," rabbis, a "magister" who is also a physician, and "a certain Jew,
who was a doctor in the synagogues, who himself was also most wise in
Hebrew and greatest in the skills of writing"?[107]

Both texts seem to have been produced in Genoa, and they claim
respectively that the debates they represent occurred at Ceuta in North
Africa in 1179 and at Majorca in 1286. That, in the twelfth and thirteenth
centuries, merchant identity would be a particularly salient issue in Italian texts when it might not be so prominent elsewhere in Europe is
no surprise: mercantilism and merchants became central to Christian
society more quickly in cities like Genoa and Venice than in most other
medieval European locales.[108] That religious identity and difference are
crucial to these texts also makes sense: complex interreligious contact
characterized the Mediterranean routes of Genoese trade as it characterizes the Mediterranean locales represented in the two disputations. In
1179, Ceuta, like Southern Spain (only thirteen miles away across the
straits of Gibraltar), was under Islamic Almohad (Muwaḥḥid) rule, and
both Jews and Christians would have been part of severely disadvan-
taged minority populations.[109] In 1286, Majorca had only recently been
"reconquered" by the Christian king Jaime I; he was aided in his campaign (1229–32) by Jewish interpreters, and he several times presented
"charters of privilege" to Majorcan Jews.[110] More generally, the Mediterranean (in the Middle East, North Africa, the Balkans, Sicily and Southern Italy, Southern France, Iberia) had long been and remained in the

twelfth and thirteenth centuries a primary location for the working out of Latin Christendom's relation to its religious others—Islam, of course, but also Eastern (Greek) Christianity, Christian "heresies," and Judaism.

The texts of the Ceuta and Majorca disputations clearly raised and addressed questions important to at least a certain medieval (and early modern) audience: though the Ceuta disputation is preserved only in a single manuscript of ca. 1200, the Majorca text survives in eighteen manuscripts, one of them a translation of the Latin into Italian.[111] All of the manuscript texts seem to have been produced in Italy—so, we may think of the issues raised about mercantilism and religious difference as having a certain local interest. At the same time, almost all of the manuscripts of the Majorca disputation date from after the mid-fourteenth century, with the large preponderance having been produced in the fifteenth. The text of Majorca was also printed several times—in 1524, at Venice, and in 1672 and 1677, again at Venice. Given this history of textual production, one might posit that at least some of the issues felt to be most striking in the Majorca debate resonated more fully in the later Middle Ages and early Renaissance than at the moment of the text's original redaction.

So, why might two authors of the late twelfth and late thirteenth centuries rewrite the traditional Christian-Jewish dispute as the confrontation between a Genoese merchant and Jewish intellectuals? One possible answer that the texts themselves put forward is that they "truthfully" represent a social reality, real discursive confrontations between Jews and Christian merchants that were enabled by an increasing trans-Mediterranean trade. But whatever the truth of the texts' claims to represent real encounters—and Ora Limor presents compelling evidence that the Genoese merchants named and represented in the text were historical figures involved in Mediterranean trade at the same time that she shows the *literariness* of at least the Majorca debate, which reproduces verbatim significant sections of the Ceuta text[112]—we are still left with the question of why authors would choose to represent these particular situations and not others, what they thought was especially significant about the encounters they preserved textually, and what might have most interested the (contemporary and later) audiences that read and reproduced the texts. One could think the purpose of these texts in purely interreligious terms: What might be more humiliating to Judaism and more strikingly prove Christian superiority than a debate in which the most learned of Jewish leaders fail to out-argue even a non–clerically trained Christian merchant? The two debates are largely traditional in the questions they take on, focusing especially on the differential Jewish and Christian reading of prophetic passages from the Hebrew Bible.[113] The Jews are concerned of course to show that the prophets cannot be used to prove either that the Messiah has already come or that the Messiah was Jesus; the Christian side, of course, argues the reverse. In all the debate literature produced from the Christian point of view, the Christian disputants easily vanquish their Jewish opponents, and the Ceuta and Majorca debates are no exception. But it is a striking spectacle to see the theologically and exegetically complex Christian argument handled deftly by the merchant disputants, who defeat their opponents as handily as any theologian. Certainly, this is humiliating to Judaism; still, the very choice of Christian merchant disputants means that it is difficult to read these texts simply as valorizing a unified, undifferentiated Christendom or Christian identity over against its Jewish other. The disputational victory, after all, belongs to a particular, merchant identity that, especially within twelfth- and thirteenth-century Europe but also well into the Renaissance, was suspect and marginal in relation to an idealized *Christianitas*.

These disputational texts, that is, represent not bald confrontations between generalized Christian and Jewish identities but instead encounters that give us insight into the long medieval and early modern movement to construct new, valorized, masculine identities for the middle strata and particularly for merchants. The disputational character of these texts is especially well suited to the exploration of masculinity: as we have seen above in such writers as Damian and Alfonsi, the space of disputation is a strongly gendered one. At Majorca, the Jewish and Christian disputants are explicitly presented as "fortified with good arms, so that each might defend his side manfully."[114] Victory (which belongs ultimately to the Christian disputant) situates the victor, at least symbolically, in the place of the successful warrior-aristocrat, the wielder of a secular power to which the merchant aspires but from which he is in many ways excluded. During the twelfth and thirteenth centuries, too, the *disputatio* is emerging as a dominant mode for proving one's intellectual worth—for instance, in the context of formal university instruction and examination.[115] Success in intellectual debate might thus also speak to one's clerical manliness. Metaphorized as virile battle, on the one hand, and providing an actual proving ground for intellectual prowess, on the other, the debates at Ceuta and Majorca thus present their merchant protagonists with perfect sites for the testing and elaboration of emergent social identities and the new forms of masculinity associated with these.

Indeed, as Limor has suggested, these two disputational texts clearly elaborate "the motif of the merchant as hero."[116] In each debate (but especially at Majorca), the Christian disputant is particularized in a way unusual in the larger disputational tradition; each disputant is named — Guilielmo Alphachino at Ceuta, Inghetto Contardo at Majorca — and given a name that we can identify with an actual Genoese merchant. In each text, too, the merchant's disputational ability is presented as unexpected and marvelous, and noteworthy particularly because of his merchant status. Though, at Ceuta, Guilielmo's merchant identity is largely implied rather than made explicit — he is named as Genoese at the beginning of the text ("Guilielmum Alphachinum Ianuensem"), is at "Septe" (Ceuta) presumably for reasons of trade, and (as we discover at the debate's conclusion) is associated with a Genoese ship ("navem Ianuensium") that leaves Ceuta for points east[117] — it is clear that his disputational prowess is a surprise because his social status differs from that of more usual Christian apologists. The Jewish disputant, ceding to Guilielmo's superior arguments, is ultimately moved to exclaim:

> Truly I testify to you that, if it were possible for all Christians to assemble together and for me to set against them all the arguments I've set against you, it does not seem to me that they would be able to respond as wisely as you, on your own, have responded.[118]

According to his learned Jewish opponent, this solitary Genoese figure, identified nowhere as having formal theological or exegetical training, can outargue the whole of Christendom.

At Majorca, the Christian heroism of the merchant is dramatized even more explicitly and vividly. The Genoese merchant Inghetto Contardo — identified as such, "Ingetum Contardum mercatorem Ianuensem," from the outset of the text[119] — promises to demonstrate to the

Jews "the day of the advent of the Messiah."[120] His Jewish opponents' response is confidently dismissive; they suggest that, since Inghetto is a mere merchant, he will not be able effectively or persuasively to address such a theological question:

> But if all the clerics and Dominican and Franciscan friars and doctors and wise men among the Christians came together, they could not do this. And you, who are a merchant, believe that you can? You deceive yourself![121]

They bolster their argument here with an explicit evocation of the 1263 Barcelona disputation between the convert Pablo Christiani and the great Jewish rabbi Naḥmanides,[122] strongly implying that, if a panoply of theologically trained figures failed to defeat Naḥmanides in religious disputation, the merchant Inghetto's chances of success are slim indeed:

> And we wish to say and assert to you, that in the time of Lord Jaime the good king of Aragon, who was the father of Lord Pedro and grandfather of that Lord Alfonso who now reigns, there were at Gerona Dominican and Franciscan friars, and friar Pablo who had been a Jew [i.e., the convert Pablo Christiani], and many other most expert Christians, and in addition how many doctors of the law, and they disputed against our Jews. What kind of end that had, ask those who were present, and you will know if the end was good for the Christians or not.[123]

The implication of course is that the end was *not* good for the Christians, that Jewish arguments won out, even against the best prepared of Christian polemicists, and that the merchant disputant is therefore bound to fail in the current confrontation. Later, however, having experienced Inghetto's skill in argumentation, his Jewish opponents are forced to retract their negative assessment, declaring that they find it hard to believe that Inghetto is not theologically trained:

> You would be a good preacher, since you know well how to put words together and to gild them. But, by god, tell us, if you have been a Franciscan or Dominican friar, or if you are a cleric, and whence come to you these things you have said and now say to us.[124]

Inghetto's "modest" answer, however, asserts his innocence of clerical training, emphasizing instead the ways in which his *merchant* experience is itself responsible for his religious knowledge and disputational skill, having enabled him to engage in interreligious debate all over the Mediterranean, from Provence to Alexandria.[125]

As we see here in the repeated comparison of Inghetto to clerical figures, the main route for heroizing the merchant is via the claiming of a position of clerical authority that implies, too, a clerical masculinity, and more specifically a newer model of clerical authority and masculinity that has emerged in the thirteenth century with the birth of the fraternal orders.[126] The merchant is most insistently and specifically compared to the Dominicans and Franciscans, orders whose ideals (for instance, of poverty) might seem strongly to clash with a mercantile life but which also provide some clear spaces of identification for a merchant like Inghetto. While Jewish disputants in the Ceuta and Majorca texts several times refer to their family life, Inghetto (whatever his "real" marital and family status) never speaks as a married man, as a father, or as tied to a biological family; instead, his social world is focused on his workplace, the Genoese *logia*, the company of merchants within which he works and travels. Here, as in a fraternal chapterhouse, the place of "home" is the all-male community, different though the goals of the mercantile and fraternal communities might be. Compared to an earlier cloistered, monastic asceticism, the life of the friars is furthermore notably engaged with the world; their itineracy mirrors that of the merchant, and their strong commitment to interdenominational missionizing (the use of their itineracy to further the spread of Christianity among the "infidel") is clearly taken up here by the merchant hero.

Inghetto himself is scrupulous in denying the Jews' assertion that he resembles the Dominicans and Franciscans, or that he must have had the rigorous intellectual training associated increasingly across the thirteenth century with the fraternal orders. He reemphasizes that whatever disputational success he might have comes from his own mercantile experience. But he also never denies that his intellectual arguments are as good as clerical ones; he tacitly accepts the Jewish suggestion that his disputational prowess rivals or even exceeds that of the friars. While there are of course clerics, and specifically friars, present in Majorca, whenever Inghetto is approached by Jews in search of religious argument or enlightenment about the beliefs of Christianity, he himself takes on the role of Christian spokesman, never sending the Jews to consult with the more authoritative, theologically trained clerics and never himself admitting a need to get clerical advice about sometimes quite abstruse questions of doctrine and exegesis.[127] Inghetto thus, de facto, sets himself up as an alternative religious authority. But his self-positioning here does not rely on a simple identification *against* a clerical other: Inghetto indeed resists opportunities for antifraternalism, expressed quite directly by the Jews, who identify both the Dominicans and Franciscans as false prophets "who preach to and seduce the peoples."[128] He does not, then, make his own Christian authority and masculinity dependent on the denigration of other, clerical, positions; he in fact defends the friars against Jewish attack,[129] and thus maintains the sense that there is a pure clerical ideal against which his own mercantile Christian position might be measured and found successful. We might read Inghetto's self-positioning, then, as a *dis*identification in José Muñoz's sense of the term—an ambivalent identification both with and against the established fraternal/clerical position. Such an identification clears space for a new sense of mercantile self even as it places that self into a significant relationship with an established, already secure identity. Thus, despite his confident taking on of the role of Christian spokesman, Inghetto ultimately does have to admit that, as a merchant, he is not fully competent to speak or act for official Christianity, that the clerisy still serves a necessary role. When Inghetto succeeds in persuading the Jewish "master" Astruch Ysayas to convert, he serves as religious instructor and baptismal sponsor; but he also brings Astruch to the Franciscans, asking them to "instruct him in the New Testament and in the catholic faith."[130]

While the validation of a merchant identity here thus positions the merchant mainly in relation to clerical authority and masculinity, the debates also, at least at moments, recuperate merchant identity vis-à-vis a more secular, aristocratic ideal. The merchant-disputants are not just smart, but (physically and politically) bold. The Ceuta disputation ends with its Jewish disputant Mo[ses] Abram professing himself ready to convert. The political-religious situation of Almohad Ceuta, however, leaves him reluctant to do so: "I would most willingly... [make and baptize myself a Christian] if I were not so afraid. Because these Muslims are so greatly evil, indeed the worst, and if they by chance were to know about this, both we and you would be in mortal peril; and for the whole world I would not want such a thing to happen because of me." He proposes that his conversion wait until "the lord Jesus Christ, who through his grace deigned to send the Holy Spirit by means of you, will himself allow that I be baptized in his own most sacred river, in which he himself was baptized." The idea that the baptism has to happen in the Holy Land, in the Jordan River, might be read skeptically as one final argumentative ploy, a Jewish feint intended to provide a way of escaping from an uncomfortable dispute by conceding defeat, but a defeat that will mean nothing in real terms: what are the chances, after all, that Mo[ses] Abram and his family can in fact be brought to the other end of the Mediterranean to convert? But of course, the Jew here is dealing with a Genoese merchant, one of the few who could in fact fulfill the Jew's expressed wish; and the text concludes with the merchant Guilielmo having succeeded not only in bringing the Jew to the point of conversion but also in removing him from the political situation that makes his conversion dangerous: "When these words were finished, with sons and brothers and sisters and relations [the Jew] boarded a Genoese ship and proceeded to Jerusalem, baptized himself in Christ's name in the Jordan River, with He Himself standing sponsor who with the Father and Holy Spirit lives and reigns God infinitely world without end. Amen."[131]

With this culminating action, the Ceuta text makes it clear that merchant heroism is a hybrid of clerical and aristocratic, religious and secular, skills and ideals. Having made strong intellectual arguments, arguments at least the equal of those a doctrinally sophisticated cleric might make, and thus having succeeded in bringing the Jewish opponent to the point of conversion, the merchant, enabled specifically by his mercantile position and skill—his ship, his mobility, his experience and knowledge of Mediterranean trade routes—is able, too, to effect the political situation necessary for the promised religious transformation to come about. Here, the European Christian merchant's very involvement in the world of trade, in the mercantile matrix that implicates him in a materiality threatening to his proper Christian identity while also (dangerously) bringing him into contact with non-Christian cultures, proves to be precisely what is necessary to the successful promulgation of Christianity. Mercantilism and *Christianitas* are here presented not as antitheses but as flipsides of the same European economic and cultural success—as will increasingly be the case in the later Middle Ages and Renaissance with the full-fledged development of merchant-missionary-explorer identities.

The conversion that occurs in the Majorca debate is also shown to be dependent on both the clerical and secular, intellectual and political, prowess of the merchant hero Inghetto. The conversion of the great Jewish "doctor" Astruch Ysayas, "most wise in Hebrew and greatest in the skills of writing,"[132] follows, as at Ceuta, on a series of persuasive theological arguments brought forward by the merchant disputant. But again there are political barriers to the conversion, in this case provided by the Jewish community of Majorca itself. The leaders of that community ("very many Jews from among the best and greatest who were in Majorca")[133] come to Astruch, pretending to know nothing of his discussions with Inghetto and claiming to have received letters from Catalonia urgently requiring his presence there—"since they stand in great need of your counsel."[134] Astruch Ysayas tries to delay his departure without revealing his intention to convert, claiming that the recent local activity of pirates ("cursariorum") makes the trip to Barcelona in the available ships too dangerous.[135] The Jews are ready with a counterargument, noting that a "great ship of the king's,"[136] sure to provide secure passage, is ready to depart, carrying other members of the Jewish community. Astruch Ysayas's further attempts at delay are unsuccessful, and he is forced to board the ship immediately, turned over by the Jewish leaders directly to the custody of the Jews on board ship.[137]

Here, however, a miracle intervenes. The ship is becalmed, and, while his Jewish captors sleep, Astruch Ysayas prays for rescue. The prayer receives an immediate response:

> And while he was saying this, suddenly there appeared near the ship a fishermen's boat. And when he saw the boat, he was very happy and he said to the mariners: "By God, hail that boat." And then the mariners hailed the boat, and they said to those in the boat: "For God's sake, bring this man to land," because if they had said "this Jew," the fishermen would then not have come. Therefore they came and picked him up and carried him to land. And when they approached land, he wanted to pay them what they might ask; but indeed they themselves wanted to accept nothing, saying to him: "Go in the name of the Lord! We might have done a greater service than this for you."[138]

While the merchant Inghetto plays no direct role in this miraculous scene, its insistently *maritime* quality—involving, all at once, pirates, mariners, and fishermen—reminds us of the mercantile emplacement of the conversion events. The conclusion of the rescue scene even directly invokes trade, when Astruch Ysayas offers to pay for his safe passage, even as (unexpectedly, miraculously) the fishermen refuse payment, refocusing attention on "the name of the Lord" instead of fair compensation.

Paired with this maritime miracle is a second miracle simultaneously emphasized in the text but now one that is wholly in the intellectual-spiritual rather than the political-material realm:

> Truly there was a second miracle at his baptism, because those who were his godparents along with Inghetto wanted to call his name John. And at the entrance of the church, when the priest said: "How is he called?" They responded: "He is called John." And he himself said: "No, my lord! If it please you, that my name be called Phillip!" And thus his name was called Phillip. And those events because of which he arrived at baptism had been begun on the feast of the blessed apostles Phillip and James.[139]

God's hand thus intervenes in Astruch Ysayas's conversion in both intellectual-spiritual and political-material ways, and, though Inghetto is not directly involved in the miracles, their double quality helps emphasize the merchant hero's double role as intellectual persuader and secular facilitator of the conversion. Inghetto's theological sophistication is complemented by his political savvy, and his bravery is repeatedly praised in the Majorca text. Indeed, his behavior is several times held up to specifically aristocratic standards: his Jewish opponents refer to him as "iste dominus" [that lord],[140] and his speech is recognized not just as the equal of preachers'—"you would be a good preacher"—but also as "curialis" [courtly].[141]

The disputations of Ceuta and Majorca thus work to valorize a new merchant status and identity in relation to both clerical and aristocratic ideals. At the same time, as we might expect, this valorization depends upon a more traditional denigration of Jewishness and specifically Jewish masculinity, and a denigration that involves placing Jews into the position of the merchant as he is conceived in conservative, antimercantile Christian discourses. As is typical in the Latin debate tradition, the Jews at Ceuta and Majorca are hard-hearted, stiff-necked, and blind.[142] They are also intellectually weak, lacking in reason, suffering from "dementia,"[143] all of these deficiencies suggesting (as we have seen earlier in other texts) a lack of a properly masculine, or even properly human, mind. Furthermore, throughout the disputations, Jews show themselves to be underhanded, unreliable, and cowardly. Several times, when especially challenged in the debate, they retreat from discussion to speak among themselves in Hebrew—"And the Jews drew back speaking Hebrew together, greatly confused, not knowing what to say"[144]—a move that suggests a certain conspiratorial stance commonly associated in medieval Christian texts with Jewish communities and their linguistic difference. Sometimes, too, the Jewish disputants retreat into silence, unable or unwilling to respond to the persuasive Christian arguments with which they are confronted.[145] Inghetto in fact suggests that such Jewish retreats and evasions reflect more than simply confusion; he accuses his opponents of knowing but perversely denying the (Christian) truth.[146] And he makes clear that their argumentative feints have crucial consequences for their spiritual life; he especially criticizes them when they (all except Astruch Ysayas, of course) show themselves unwilling to follow through, with action, on the promises that they have made, particularly on the promise to convert if defeated in debate.[147] While we can find most of these dishonest, intellectually bankrupt moves characterizing the Jewish participants in other debate texts, their location here, in texts that bring Christian *merchant* identity to the fore, calls forth resonances additional to those usually attached to the stereotypical figure of the uncomprehending, obstinate, dishonest Jew. Within a mercantile context, Jewish stances and actions also associate them with the stereotype of the treacherous merchant—dishonest in his business dealings, never intending to follow through on the promises he makes, concerned not with truth or honor but with profit.[148]

The same sort of association emerges in the texts' insistent, and wholly conventional, tying of Jewish arguments (particularly exegetical ones) to the material, rather than the spiritual or allegorical.[149] That, at several points in the text, one of the main Jewish disputants at Majorca is identified as both "magister" and physician reemphasizes the Jews' traditional association with the materiality of the body and its ills.[150] This materiality is reemphasized in a specifically mercantile setting when, toward the end of the text, Inghetto and the Jewish "magister"-physician enter an "apotheca" (apothecary or spice shop) to continue their debate; the shop owner ("dominus domus") comments, "Lord Inghetto, if you can make this man a convert, you will have a good physician."[151] Earlier, when asked to define "veritas," the Jews come up with a definition more mercantile than it is philosophical: "*Veritas*, truth, is that this piece of cloth is green, and that piece black, and that other piece red, and this one of yours blue, and that this house is built of stone and wood."[152] The Jewish sages who propose this definition must have their materialist view corrected by the merchant Inghetto, who scolds them: "This isn't truth but rather transitory humanity and that which is subject to change. Truth truly is not subject to change."[153] And when one Jewish master fails to convert, despite having conceded essentially all the theological points at issue in the disputation, Inghetto identifies the impediments to his conversion as strongly material (and feminized) ones: "The love of children and the cupidity of usury and that cursed sin."[154] Again, usury is often directly connected not just to Jews but to merchants.[155] Jews are associated too, in the Majorca debate, with the sexual sins of Sodom and Gomorrah and with the sterile destruction—the "nichil"—visited on those cities.[156] Reading Isaiah 1:9, Inghetto declares:

> [Y]ou live in hope that the Messiah will come, and this hope is vain just like a flower that flowers but produces no fruit, and in hoping you rejoice, and your rejoicing is nothing and has nothing of good, and it is just as the roof-thatch which withered before it was plucked [Psalm 128:6 (RSV 129:6)]. And truly fulfilled in you is that which the prophet says: "Unless the Lord had left behind for us a seed, we would have been like Sodom and we would be like unto Gomorrah" [Isaiah 1:9], because in truth you are properly Sodom and Gomorrah when it comes to power. But you who have remained, you exist for our witness, and concerning you no mention is made just as though you have not existed.[157]

If the merchant Inghetto comes to be identified as a powerful "lord" who speaks and behaves "curialiter," courteously, refiguring Christian merchant identity as both politically potent and religiously reliable, the Jews in these debates remain consistently in a very different classed and gendered location, a location in fact associable with the Christian merchant as conservatively and negatively conceived. Jews here, like the negative stereotype of the merchant, are treacherous, usurious, associated with the material, the feminine, and indeed the sodomitical.

Humiliated, "in captivity" [*captivi*], "slaves" [*servi*], the Jews of these texts are never again, as Jews, to have the possibility of ruling their own nation.[158] It is only when the Jew Astruch Ysayas converts that he can gain a politically potent masculinity. But this masculine position depends first and foremost on his religious transformation; he becomes, in Inghetto's words, "a new soldier of Christ."[159]

The Ceuta and Majorca disputations thus (as is common in the larger debate tradition) serve to valorize Christian identity, and specifically Christian masculinity, at the expense of the Jewish. But they do so in such a way as more specifically to valorize merchant status and project what might be troubling to conservative Christian thinkers about that status onto the Jewish adversary. While the clear strategy here is firmly to separate out Christian merchant and Jewish positions, that strategy is nonetheless perhaps not wholly successful. Just as, in a text like Alfonsi's, convert identity is haunted by its seemingly ineradicable Jewish past, so, here, the merchant identity even of a heroic figure like Inghetto Contardo remains wrapped up with the Jewishness onto which negatively associated merchant qualities are displaced. The two merchant disputations evince not just a confident Christian triumphalism but also the strong anxieties of Christian identity, and specifically merchant identity, vis-à-vis its religious others. The merchant-disputants stand in a different kind of relation to their Jewish opponents than is usually the case in the debate literature. In the large public Jewish-Christian disputations that we know occurred at Paris, Barcelona, and Tortosa, and in relation to which the Majorca debate (happening after Paris and Barcelona) explicitly places itself, the social-political situation is always heavily tilted toward the Christian, with the debates presided over (as we will see in chapter 5) by either Christian rulers or ecclesiastical authorities. These debates are filled with pomp and ceremony, occurring "on-stage" (as it were) and with the Christian disputants (in all three of these cases, Jewish converts to Christianity) clearly on the side of power. At Majorca, however, the "staging" of the disputation shifts dizzyingly back and forth among locales both Christian and Jewish—from the Genoese *logia*, to the house of the Jewish "master," to "a certain house of a certain great Jew in which there was a great multitude of books," to an unspecified site "outside the city," into the street and the storeroom of a spice-merchant (or apothecary), and finally into an empty house; Inghetto even recalls a discussion he has previously had with a learned Jew on board a ship.[160] Partly the shifting of location is motivated by the Jewish disputants' desire for secrecy, by their wish not to be seen by their co-religionists losing argument after argument. But the shifts in locale also emphasize Inghetto's merchant rootlessness, the lack of any institution-ally sanctioned site that centers his missionizing activity; even itinerant, missionizing friars, after all, have their chapterhouse awaiting them, and they have a firm place in the ecclesiastical hierarchy. Inghetto can return "home" to the Genoese *logia,* but of course this is far from home, and it is, in any case, a mercantile rather than a religious center.

Similarly, the Majorca debate is unusual in that it makes one of its early premises the idea that whoever loses the disputation, whether it be the Jew or the Christian, will convert. The Jew promises that, if defeated, he "will be made a Christian and be baptized"; in a strictly parallel for-mulation, Inghetto responds that, should he lose the argument, he "will be made a Jew and be circumcised."[161] This potential event—the Chris-tian becoming Jewish, rather than vice versa—hangs over the whole debate as one possible outcome, and in fact, late in the text, just as the Jew who will ultimately convert to Christianity (Astruch Ysayas) is intro-duced, we are explicitly reminded of the possibility of Christian conver-sion. Soon after Astruch's arrival in Majorca, his Jewish confreres inform him that "There is in this land a certain Genoese merchant whom we cannot resist in regard to the law, nor [can] our greatest *magister*"; rather than simply emphasize Inghetto's disputational superiority, however, the Jews also note, "And he himself says that, if we can show him that Jerusalem must be rebuilt by the Jews, he himself will be a Jew and accept circumcision."[162] This puts the disputants on a more equal footing than is usual in medieval interreligious disputes, and as his Jewish interlocu-tors recognize, it places Inghetto in real danger: early in the text, the Jew-ish *magister* counsels Inghetto not to make such a vow, "since he would be dead, nor should he dare to do this, for fear of death."[163] Inghetto responds fearlessly, manfully: "Do not worry about my death, since I say to you in certain truth and in good faith, that if you will be able to show me that the Messiah has not come, I will be a Jew. And if I had a thousand lives, I would lose all to save my soul, because I seek nothing other than the way of truth."[164] He even chooses a Jewish judge to decide who wins the argument.[165] How different this is from the situation at Paris, or Barcelona, or Tortosa, where it is the Christian monarch or pope who presides!

On the one hand, of course, the ways in which Inghetto is endangered in his encounters with the Jews serve to emphasize all the more strongly his confidence and courage, helping to solidify his heroized, masculine position. On the other hand, however, they serve to place him into dangerous proximity with his Jewish opponents: he travels the same roads with them, secreting himself in Jewish homes to talk about religion, and, like his opponents, Inghetto is subject to the possibility that he will have to change his religious identity in a radical way. Interestingly, the Majorca text concludes not with the miraculous conversion of Astruch Ysayas but instead, much more anticlimactically, with Inghetto trying to engage yet another Jew in controversial discussion, promising that they can retreat together to an "empty house that has been prepared . . . in which no one will enter except you with your fellows and I alone."[166] If here again we see Inghetto bravely willing to take on his opponents in a situation disadvantageous to him, we also see him as *alone,* separated from his own Christian fellows, a figure standing oddly if heroically between two religiously opposed social worlds.

All of this might suggest not just the reconsolidation of a strong split between a masculinized Christian identity (though here a newly emergent, mercantile one) and a repudiated, demasculinized Jewish identity, but also—alongside or within that reconsolidation—a sense, if largely buried and unacknowledged, that the at-risk identity of the merchant in fact stands closely allied with the Jew. It is clear from the beginning of the text that Inghetto has a long history of discussing religious questions with Jews.[167] When asked where he has gained his theological knowledge, Inghetto proudly admits that this has largely been through his encounters with learned Jews:

> I neither am now nor have been a cleric, nor ever was I a member of a religious order. On the contrary, I am a merchant. But those things which I know I have learned from Jews and by the grace of God and the Messiah our Lord Jesus Christ. And I rightly say to you that in my time I have entered into dispute with many Jews, especially in Provence and in Alexandria in Egypt with that Jewish angel[168] whom the Jews of Syria called the "king of Jerusalem," and similarly with Beloasem[169] of Babylon, who is, if he's still alive, the greatest doctor among the Jews.[170]

When the Jews mention the 1263 Barcelona disputation, of which
Inghetto has not previously heard, he evinces a strong interest, even
though, or perhaps precisely because, the Jews depict that disputation as
a Jewish victory; he eagerly asks his Jewish interlocutors, "whether they
have that disputation in writing," and urges that, if so, they "deliver a
copy of the text" to him, "since I desire with a great desire to have a
translation of it."[171] While Inghetto may strongly criticize Jewish argumentative strategies as dishonest and underhanded, the Jews respond in
kind, attempting to police his rhetorical strategies and accusing him of
just the sort of lies and evasions that the text largely identifies with Jewishness, *ambages* and *fabulis:*

> The Jews said: "Don't rush into winding ways [circumlocutions,
> ambiguities, obscurities]! Let us speak of that which we began
> to speak! Let us return to Isaiah."[172]

> The Jews said: "If you wish to respond to us, respond, or we will
> get up and go . . . these are the words of a man withdrawing him-
> self from truth and wishing to turn back to fables."[173]

If Inghetto becomes, in the Majorca text, a Christian hero, a great
merchant missionizer to the Jews, he also remains, at least in certain
ways, the merchant who stands a bit too close to the Jews, a Christian
who, because his profession brings him into frequent contact with the
non-Christian, lingers at the edge of Christendom. The debate text makes
a valiant effort to pull Inghetto to the Christian center, and to bolster the
merchant's *Christianitas* with the claims of masculinity. But the anxieties about merchant identity that make such an effort at centering necessary continue nonetheless to inhere in the text.

Though there are clear and significant differences between a disputational text like Alfonsi's *Dialogi* and the merchant debates of Ceuta and
Majorca, in the uncertainties these introduce about Christian (convert or
merchant) identity, the texts share a certain dynamic. In neither case,
despite insistent moves clearly to distinguish Jewish and Christian positions from each other, is that wished-for distinction ever fully, securely
attained. The identity of Christian convert necessarily depends upon
and conjures up the Jewish identity from which it emerges; as long as

the convert remains a *convert,* Jewishness will always contribute essentially to his sense of self. To valorize the merchant born a Christian might seem a simpler task. But insofar as mercantile qualities remain from an orthodox Christian perspective subject to suspicion, and a suspicion specifically related to traits traditionally associated with Jewish identities, the Christian merchant will always have difficulty (like the convert) shedding the remnants of a nonheroized, mercantile, materialistic self. In the Majorca text, after all, the explicit and self-conscious evocation of the 1263 Barcelona debate, and with it the larger tradition of real-life debate between Jews and Christian converts that began at Paris in 1240, clearly places the merchant Inghetto into the position of the Christian convert. In the chapter that follows, we turn to a fuller examination of this tradition and the place of "conversion identity" within it.

5

STAYING JEWISH?

PUBLIC DISPUTATION, CONVERSION, AND RESISTANCE

Hec ... corporeis oculis intuemur, dum in diversis mundi partibus, ex conversione iudeorum, fetu nove prolis Ecclesia fecundata, illos quos inimicos prius habuerat, in pacis filios letatur esse conversos.

We see this [Paul's prediction that all Israel would be saved (Romans 11:26)] with our bodily eyes when, in diverse parts of the world, the church is made fruitful with a new bearing of offspring arising from the conversion of Jews, and she rejoices that those whom she earlier held to be enemies have been converted into sons of peace.
    —Pope Benedict XIII, *Disputa*, 2:597

For sikerly, though thyn enemy be reconsiled and maketh thee chiere of humylitee, and lowteth to thee with his heed, ne trust him nevere.... And Peter Alfonce seith, "Make no felawshipe with thyne olde enemys, for if thou do hem bountee, they wol perverten it into wikkednesse."
    —Chaucer, *Tale of Melibee* VII.1187, 1189

At one point in the Majorca disputation, Inghetto Contardo ties historical and contemporary Christian identity in a particularly explicit and
strong way to the experience of conversion:

> I find that the impious and the iniquitous—that is, Samaritans,
> publicans, and sinners, and Gentiles—had converted in the time
> of Christ and also after the time of Christ up until now, since we
> Christians were born from the Gentiles, or [at least] the greater
> part of Christians.[1]

Here, the merchant who has come to stand in the place of the convert,
disputing the Jews, reminds us that Christian identity itself is intimately
related to a history of conversion. In the deeply influential Pauline view,
Christians are always somehow converts: "And there was a time when
you were dead in your crimes and sins, in which you once walked following the present age of this world, following the prince of the power
of the air. . . . But God, who is rich in mercy, because of the great love
with which he loved us, brought us to life in Christ even when we were
dead in sins; by his grace you are saved."[2]

One of the first things the new Christian self does as a Christian is
to turn back toward his former self to consider the ways in which he has
moved beyond it. We see this strikingly in Alfonsi's *Dialogi*, but much
earlier as well, in Paul's biblical theology, its grappling with the meaning
of Jewish beliefs and its rejection of Jewish practices like circumcision.
Indeed, Paul was recognized in the Middle Ages not only as a paradigmatic convert but also as a crucial founder of anti-Jewish polemic and
dispute. Thus, it is not only a Saul/Paul in the process of conversion that
we find represented in the medieval visual arts, but also Paul the disputant, as in a late twelfth-century English plaque (probably from a box
or casket) that depicts the saint immersed in intellectual argument (Figure 6). This representation makes clear the doubleness of Paul's polemical mission. He here confronts both the "Greeks," to whom he will devote
the bulk of his career as preacher and who represent the main future direction of the church as it moves into Europe, and the Jews, the people who
represent Paul's past and the past of Christianity. Paul himself holds a
scroll that quotes Acts 9:29, "disputabat cum Grecis" [he disputed with
the Greeks]; though this confrontation takes place at Jerusalem, soon after
Paul's conversion and his return from Damascus, and though "Grecis"
is typically read as referring to "Hellenists" or "Greek Jews," the illus-

Figure 6. St. Paul disputing with the Greeks and Jews. Copper gilt with champlevé enamel plaque (English, 1170–80). Victoria and Albert Museum, Z.1215, ref. no. 223–1874. Reproduced with permission of Victoria and Albert Museum Picture Library.

tration seems to understand the word more literally as referring to non-Jewish Gentiles, the shaven, hatless men who occupy the second tier of Paul's opponents and to whom the scroll in Paul's hand points. In front of them are positioned three men whose similar facial features, beards, clothing, and postures associate them with each other; indeed, the man furthest to the right grasps the shoulder of his fellow, and the two hold almost identical books. Both the figure on the left and the one in the middle gesture with their left hands argumentatively toward Paul; Paul responds with a similar gesture of his right hand. At least the two figures toward the left are clearly identified as Jews, by their conical hats,[3] and probably all three bearded figures are meant to evoke Jewish sages. The Jew furthest to the left, in place of a book, holds a scroll that reads, "et revincebat iud*eos*" [and he refuted the Jews], a reference to Acts 18:28.[4] While the illustration of course puts Paul directly into confrontation with those whose religion he has left behind, it also associates him much more closely with the Jews than with the Greeks: his gestures (both holding the scroll and pointing as he makes an argumentative point), his robe, his facial features, and his beard draw him close to his former coreligionists even as his nimbus replaces the Jewish hat to make clear that he is now in a very different position than he once occupied.

The position of the Christian convert-disputant is thus one established in early Christianity and one of which the Middle Ages remains cognizant. Although Peter Alfonsi's turning back toward his former Jewish self, his own superseded Jewishness, might be dangerous, threatening his position as a "real" Christian, it also positions him within a firmly established (ultimately Pauline) tradition. The availability of that tradition might also help explain the striking way in which, starting in the thirteenth century, Jewish converts to Christianity begin to take a more and more *public* role in the polemic against their former religion. While Alfonsi writes his own internal struggle with his former Jewishness, converts like Nicholas Donin, Pablo Christiani, and Geronimo of Santa Fe stand up openly to refute their Jewishness, debating Jewish spokesmen in dramatic, public confrontations.

Their claim is that, like Paul, they speak for Christianity, as quintessential Christians (that is, as converts to Christianity); the most polemically active of them, the Dominican Pablo Christiani, even takes on Paul's name at the time of his conversion. But the politics of conversion in an early Christian moment like Paul's differs significantly from that of the thirteenth century. Paul enters a religion only beginning to define its own identity, and a religion in which every member is new. The converts of the thirteenth and succeeding centuries enter an established, powerful religion, within which they must find their own way. As Inghetto makes clear to Astruch Ysayas when he first announces his intention to convert: "O, Jew, you do not know what you are saying! Because, if you accept baptism, you will be called 'dog son of a dog,' as much by Christians as by Jews. And you will be in poverty, and he who today will give you a halfpenny in one whole year will not give you another; and thus you will have great need and could perhaps fall quickly into despair."[5] There is indeed much evidence that Jewish converts to Christianity encountered many material boundaries to their successful incorporation into Christian society. Thus, for instance, thirteenth-century English converts often needed to avail themselves of the support offered by the "Domus Conversorum" [Converts' Home], and many never succeeded in leading lives outside the confines of the "Domus."[6] Material barriers to the success of converts were also buttressed by the very ideology that associated Christian identity with the experience of conversion. If the Christian is defined by his susceptibility to conversion, then his opposite—the Jew who has failed to embrace Christian revelation—is easily understood to be trapped in a single, unchanging and unchangeable, position. That is, as I have argued above in chapter 1, the Christian reorganization of history makes Judaism "archaic"—superseded, immovable, and obstinate. After the incarnation, Jews—unlike Christians, that is, unlike converted Jews and Gentiles, those revivified by "grace"—are "a stiff-necked people," "stained by obstinacy of heart."[7] In the words of the Spanish law code, *Las siete partidas*, of 1265, "The reason that the church, emperors, kings and princes, permitted the Jews to dwell among them and with Christians, is because they always lived, as it were, in captivity, as it was constantly [a token] in the minds of men that they were descended from those who crucified Our Lord Jesus Christ."[8]

A corollary to the identification of Christians as converts is the idea that the Jewish convert is really a contradiction in terms: from a stony, "stiff-necked," obstinate, blind, and deaf people, a Jew who chooses to become Christian is either a miracle, someone who must never *really* have been Jewish but instead had a Christian heart from the beginning, or a fraud, someone claiming conversion but still secretly, stubbornly, really Jewish. Of course, as we know, "the conversion of the Jews" is part of a Christian anticipation of the end-time. But occurring in apocalyptic time, at the end of history, this imagined millennial conversion identifies Jewishness with convertibility only at the moment when Judaism must disappear; (re)imagining Jews as susceptible to conversion makes them no longer Jews. All of this does not mean that medieval Christians did not attempt to convert Jews—they certainly did—but such attempts are wrapped up in a paradoxical thinking that has important consequences for both Jews who stay Jewish and those who don't.

Even as Benedict XIII imagines former enemies "converted into sons of peace," fructifying the church, he identifies the Jewish converts as "fetu nove prolis" [a new bearing of offspring], or quite literally "a new *fetus*" or "pregnancy," Christians in utero but not yet fully adult members of a community. And in the *Tale of Melibee*, a tale that is all about reconciling with one's enemies, Chaucer's Prudence cites the Jewish convert Peter Alfonsi to caution against trusting one's reconciled enemy (including, presumably, the Jew turned Christian).[9]

JEWISHNESS AND CHANGE

Within medieval Christian Europe, staying Jewish is always for Jews a problem, and not just because of Christian pressure on Jews to convert; that pressure of course exists, at various times and places more or less strongly, but there is also intense Christian ideological pressure, as we have just seen, to make Jewish conversion an impossibility, a contradiction in terms. As a consequence, staying Jewish, insisting on one's unchangeable Jewishness, is not only a positive self-assertion but also a reconfirmation of the anti-Semitic view that Jews are a people trapped by their own stubbornness in the past, a people incapable by their very nature of embracing change, the truth, the future. But of course staying Jewish is also the only possible route for medieval Jews *as Jews* to resist the pressures of a Christian anti-Semitism. This double bind has far-reaching consequences: if Jews are (stereotypically) incapable of change, and if they in fact confirm that stereotype by refusing "opportunities" for change, what alternative does Christianity as the religion of the present and the future have except expulsion or violence? That Jewish attempts to survive, to stay Jewish, simultaneously make survival in Christian contexts problematic is also seen in the shape of Jewish resistance to Christian attack. In 1096, how could Jews in the Rhineland, faced by Christian crusaders with the choice of conversion or death, respond productively?[10] Staying Jewish meant precisely choosing death—a choice that the Jewish chroniclers of these events make the majoritarian one. The chroniclers nonetheless make clear that some Jews did submit to a forced conversion, though most of the converts sought to return to Judaism once the imminent threat posed by the crusaders had passed. This return seems to have been supported by local ecclesiastical and secular authorities like Bishop Rupert of Bamberg and Emperor Henry IV; yet, although forced conversion was contrary to the bulk of church doctrine, Pope Clement III intervened in 1097 or 1098 to prevent a so-called Jewish "relapse."[11] The Hebrew chroniclers celebrate the faithfulness of both martyrs and forced converts, noting that the latter "observed God's Torah clandestinely,"[12] but to Christian eyes, both the Jewish embracing of death and the attempted reversion of converts reconfirm the stereotype of a stubborn, unchangeable Jewishness.

That stereotype is made all the more powerful in that it depends not only on an intellectual and moral distinction between Christian and Jew but also, as we have seen above in chapter 3, on a difference constructed in the body and emphasizing especially anomalies of gender and sexuality. Jewish bodies smell. Jewish women take the female body to an extreme of beauty and seductiveness. Jewish men, in part because they are circumcised, are not fully men. And their bodily difference derives not just from a self-inflicted "wound" but also from an essential, hereditary lack. Jews, then, seem especially unsusceptible to conversion, but this insusceptibility does not necessarily dampen Christian missionizing impulses. After all, Christianity's self-definition as a religion of conversion means that the drive to missionize is very strong, and perhaps especially toward those who, in the first instance, refused to embrace Christian revelation. What could be a more persuasive demonstration of the efficacy of the Christian dispensation than bringing the most adamant of Christianity's opponents to testify to its truth? And yet, as we have also seen in chapter 3, there is clear evidence that medieval Jewish converts to Christianity were often still seen as corporeally anomalous, not quite Christian and still in some ways Jewish in body if not in soul. In places like Iberia where there were a large number of both voluntary and coerced converts, their description as conversos or New Christians made evident their difference from other Christians.[13] And the taint of a former Jewishness could attach itself not just to first generation converts, as we see clearly in the 1459 papal annulment of an unconsummated marriage to a woman of Jewish heritage, Blancha Palau.[14] It is Blancha's mother, not Blancha herself, who is depicted as "coming from the people of the Jews" and "toiling in this same heretical depravity." She has "instructed and initiated" her daughter into the Judaizing heresy, and the document consequently depicts Blancha as a "heretic" who participates in "the rites and ceremonies of Jewish insanity and of the Jews." Jewish stubbornness, a refusal to forget the practices supposedly given up with conversion, is here handed down from mother to daughter. Moreover, the text expresses the fear of a *hereditary* corruption. The reasons for the desired annulment include not just Blancha's "heretical" behavior but also the possible consequences of "consummat[ing] a marriage of this sort," the "begetting" of "offspring" that might "follow the insanity of the mother," with "a Jew . . . [thus] be[ing] created [*crearetur*] out of a Christian." The verb "crearetur" here means equally "created" or "produced" and "begotten" or "born." A mother "from the people of the Jews" bears a daughter who herself will bear daughters and sons somehow tainted with Jewishness.

Most dangerous here is the potential reversal of the "proper" direction of conversion from Jew to Christian, a directionality celebrated by Benedict XIII ("the church is made fruitful with a new bearing of offspring arising from the conversion of Jews, and she rejoices") and associated by Christians with the very movement of a progressive, that is, a Christian history.

The maintenance of an idea of Christian progressiveness, however, depends upon a continuing vision of Jewishness—that which Christianity has left behind—as regressive, fossilized. Paradoxically, then, the very process that defines a Christian movement into the future—the conversion of former "enemies" into "sons of peace" (in Benedict's formulation)—is disallowed, or at least suspect. Judaism's stolidity, its obstinacy, is necessary to Christianity's view of itself as superseding the "old" law, the "old" dispensation. Indeed, Judaism's unchangeableness is written into Christian theology as the Augustinian doctrine of witness: Jewish survival is only allowed as a testimony to the ancient, superseded position over against which the Christian defines itself. Much as Christianity may push—in its expansive missionizing—toward an incorporation of new converts, its ideology and theology depend upon the idea of an unchanging, stable Jewishness, a Jewishness exempt from the "grace" that allows Christians to be born anew. At the same time that we see missionaries trying to convert individual Jews, then, we also see within Christian thinking an insistence that Judaism itself *not* be allowed to change, not be allowed to deviate from its essential, archaic, fossilized self.

The problem, however, is that medieval Judaism *has* changed from its ancient and late antique predecessors, and continues to do so. For the most part, in the earlier Middle Ages, Christians ignore Jewish change, preferring instead to maintain the idea of a monolithic, stony religion identified as the past of Christianity. But with the increasing interaction between Jews and Christians that characterizes the twelfth and thirteenth centuries—interaction that is, all at once, social, economic, intellectual, and religious—it would have been difficult for the idea of a static Judaism to survive intact and unchallenged. How to respond to the recognition of Jewish change? Acknowledging that Judaism as well as Christianity was a living, changing entity would mean rethinking not just Judaism but Christianity itself and Christianity's special claims to historical uniqueness.

In the thirteenth century, Christians began more urgently to express concern about contemporary (medieval) Judaism's "deviations" from its

past beliefs and practices, responding especially with attempts to reestab-
lish Judaism's essential relationship to an unchanging "Old Testament"
past. Thus, Dominican and Franciscan inquisitors at Montpellier in the
early 1230s made, in Jeremy Cohen's words, "an unprecedented intru-
sion into internal Jewish affairs," condemning and (perhaps) burning
the works of Maimonides.[15] The details of the affair are not wholly clear
from the historical documents that survive, but the condemnation seems
related to the broader early thirteenth-century backlash against Aris-
totelianism.[16] Unlike the challenges to Christian Averroism, however, the
actions at Montpellier are directed not toward Christian self-regulation
but toward the control of Jewish intellectual life, a control perhaps at
first welcomed by conservative intellectual forces within Judaism. In several Jewish accounts of the events leading up to the condemnation, conservative, anti-Maimonidean Jews are depicted as calling on Christian
inquisitors, "while you are exterminating the heretics among you, [to]
exterminate our heresies as well," and "to guard us from error in the exact
same way as yourselves."[17] It seems clear that the inquisitors here acted
to guard Judaism from internal "error," to keep it a pure witness to the
truth of Christianity (in Augustine's words, testifying "that we have not
fabricated the prophecies about Christ"), a witness unchanged since the
time of Christ.[18]

A similar, if more complex, movement can be seen in Christian
attacks on the Talmud in this same period. Beginning probably with Peter
Alfonsi, who in the *Dialogi* cites and ridicules Talmudic *aggadah* (non-
legal, narrative material), Christian anti-Jewish polemicists (Peter the Venerable, Raymond Martini, Nicholas of Lyra) began to pay increasing attention to the Talmud. Judah M. Rosenthal connects the increasing attention
to the Talmud specifically to the movement of Jewish converts into Christianity: "The number of learned converts in the thirteenth century who
put their knowledge of the Talmud and their zeal for conversion at the
disposal of the Church was steadily on the increase."[19] A text largely
ignored in earlier polemic, and yet a crucial text for medieval Judaism and
for Jewish self-understanding, the Talmud demonstrates in quite spectacular fashion the changing nature of Jewish law and interpretation. An
ancient set of texts incorporating oral rabbinic thought developed over
the course of many generations, and itself subject to continual interpretation and reinterpretation, the Talmud makes it obvious that the elaboration of Jewish thought never stopped. With its multiple layers of exegesis

and argument, its dialogical qualities, its inclusion of legal, narrative, and homiletic material, the Talmud represents a Judaism that is vital and changing, and that, much like Christianity, has spun out a significant body of texts questioning, interpreting, rethinking, and updating the "Old Testament" with which Christianity so firmly identifies its parent religion.

Where ridicule and refutation characterize the earliest Christian attacks on Talmudic learning, by the late 1230s, we witness more public and direct attempts to control the Jewish text and its uses. In 1239, Pope Gregory IX calls for the kings of France, England, Aragon, Castile, Leon, Navarre, and Portugal to "seize all the books belonging to the Jews of your Kingdom," intending by that order to challenge in particular the Talmud's place within Jewish communities. Most directly, Gregory accuses the Talmud of containing explicitly anti-Christian and immoral material, presenting "matter so abusive and so unspeakable that it arouses shame in those who mention it and horror in those who hear it."[20] Gregory's letter is a direct prelude to the "trial" of the Talmud in Paris in 1240 where, as Rosenthal has suggested, most of the charges are concerned with the Talmud's supposedly anti-Christian and "blasphemous" qualities: its "hostility towards Christians" (including commands to kill and deceive Christians, and the claim that Christians suffer in hell eternally while Jews do not), its "blasphemies against God" (including claims that even God has sinned, lied to Abraham, and commanded Samuel to lie; that he curses himself for having destroyed the Temple and enslaved Israel; that he studies the Talmud, was defeated in a legal debate by the Rabbis, and weeps three times each day), its "blasphemies against Jesus, Mary and Christianity" (including the use of obscene language to designate the pope and the church, and claims that Mary was an adulteress and that Jesus is boiled in excrement in hell), and the "stupidity of talmudic laws and stories" (including accounts of Adam having intercourse with all the animals and the serpent with Eve, Cham abusing his father Noah, and God wearing phylacteries).[21]

Serious as they are, however, these concerns about specific doctrinal claims and a more general Jewish-Talmudic hostility toward Christianity do not seem to represent the most basic Christian objection to the Talmud. In addition to, and overriding, the focus on doctrinal error is the strong polemical suggestion that the Talmud should never have been written, that its very existence violates divine order. Nine of the forty-three charges Rosenthal identifies as having been leveled against the Talmud in Paris concern "the authority of the Talmud and the Rabbis":

1. They claim that the Law which they call Talmud was given by God.
2. They say that the talmudic Law was transmitted by God orally.
3. They claim that the Oral Law was implanted in their minds (and not written).
4. They say that the Talmud was preserved without being written down until the day arrived when those whom they call scholars and scribes, in order that the talmudic Law should not be forgotten among the people, put it in writing, the product exceeding in length that of the Bible.
5. The Talmud contains among other absurdities the opinion that the above mentioned scholars and scribes are superior to the prophets.
6. These scholars are entitled to abrogate the words of the Law.
7. It is a duty to follow the scholars even when they say that the right is left and that the left is right.
8. One who does not observe what they [the sages] teach deserves the death penalty.
9. They prohibit children from studying the Bible because they prefer that they study the Talmud from which they voluntarily derive laws.[22]

All of these supposed Jewish claims are of course seen by the Christian accusers as false and dangerous, and largely because such claims suggest a postbiblical elaboration of Jewish religion and thought unacceptable to a Christian ideology that identifies Judaism firmly with the "Old Testament." To quote again from Pope Gregory IX's letter to the kings of Christendom, the terms of which clearly influenced the charges brought forward at Paris:

If what is said about the Jews of France and of the other lands is true, no punishment would be sufficiently great or sufficiently worthy of their crime. For they, so we have heard, are not content with the Old Law which God gave to Moses in writing: they even ignore it completely, and affirm that God gave another law which is called "Talmud," that is "Teaching," handed down to Moses orally. Falsely they allege that it was implanted within their minds and, unwritten, was there preserved until certain men came, whom they call "Sages" and "Scribes," who, fearing that this Law may be lost from the minds of men through forgetfulness, reduced it to writing, and the volume of this by far exceeds the text of the Bible.[23]

Here, as Cohen notes, medieval Jews are seen as "deliberately forsaking the literal biblical Judaism of their ancestors."[24] And as Joel E. Rembaum argues, from the papal point of view, "[t]he problem was not simply an internal Jewish matter" but "had a direct impact upon the Church":

> The Jews had abandoned the position and function assigned to them by Christian tradition. . . . Thus, the Jews had perpetrated a kind of "heresy." Christian law allowed them to keep their Bibles at a time when many Christians were prohibited from keeping copies of Scripture. But, with this privilege the Jews were *non contenti,* for they had elevated the Talmud to a level of importance above that of the Bible. The Jews were allowed to keep their Bibles; they were not to be allowed to keep their Talmuds.[25]

At Paris in 1240, the convert Nicholas Donin, who was the main Christian disputant, argued that the Talmud must be disallowed to Judaism altogether. As a "heretical" outgrowth of Judaism, it makes Judaism no longer itself; it must be cut off if not by Jews themselves then by the Christian guardians of Jewish truth. Through the accusations brought forward concerning the Talmud, Cohen suggests, "The Church . . . depicted the 'living' Judaism of its own day as a heresy and perversion, a pernicious oral tradition of religious law and doctrine, a gross deviation from the religion of the Old Testament,"[26] and it pursued, for a time at least, not just the censoring of individual Talmudic passages deemed offensive but the Talmud's full suppression, attempted spectacularly in its condemnation at Paris in 1240 and the burning there of "probably ten to twelve thousand volumes" in 1242.[27]

While Christianity thus "maintained that it was illegitimate for Jews as Jews to preserve the Talmud and live according to its teaching," what seems a contradictory approach also developed in Christian anti-Jewish polemic.[28] Here, the authority of the Talmud was acknowledged, but now presented both as revealing *Christian* truths and as needing to be read in particular ways known definitely to Christians but not to Jews. Christian disputants thus sometimes claimed, as the convert Pablo Christiani did in the Barcelona disputation of 1263, to "prove" the truth of Christian doctrine by Talmudic means: the Latin account of Barcelona claims that "it was proved to him [the Jewish disputant, Naḥmanides] both by the authority of the Law and the Prophets and by the Talmud, that Christ had in truth come, as Christians believe and preach. To this he was not able to reply."[29] Further, Christian disputants attempted to police acceptable modes of reading the Talmud. Thus, the kind of argument the great Jewish philosopher, scholar, and rabbi Naḥmanides presented at Barcelona, distinguishing between *halakhah* (as an authoritative explication of the commandments of Torah) and *aggadah* (as narrative material which, in Naḥmanides' words, "if anyone wants to believe in . . . well and good, but if someone does not believe in . . . there is no harm"),[30] was explicitly prohibited in the Tortosa disputation of a century and a half later. Here, the Christian convert Geronimo of Santa Fe could argue "that a Jew must necessarily believe the entire contents of the Talmud, whether they are explanations of the Law, or legal decisions, or ceremonies, or homiletic material, or edicts, commentaries, additions or novelle made about the said Talmud; nor may a Jew deny anything of it."[31] And he can accuse his Jewish interlocutors of having "committed or perpetrated a great crime when you denied the authoritative passages of your Talmud."[32]

Although very different from the active suppression of the Talmud, such regulation of Jewish thinking from outside nonetheless shares with it the impulse to fix Judaism in place and time: even as Christian polemicists are forced by the witness of the Talmud to admit that Judaism has changed during the Christian era, they deny current Jews any flexibility in the treatment of their own traditions and thus again confine Judaism to a static moment outside the dynamic present. The situation Jews found themselves in with regard to the Talmud is thus at one and the same time ambivalent—including both the condemnation of Talmudic writings and the doctrine of necessary belief in them—and, in a certain incoherent way, coherent, with each seemingly contradictory side of the Christian position reasserting the necessity of Jewish archaism, a Jewish temporality violently removed from the present.

JEWISH-CHRISTIAN DEBATE AND THE
CONSTRUCTION OF IDENTITY

At stake in Christian attacks on the Talmud, then, is the control of Jewish identity, and consequently of Christian identity as well. The very existence of the Talmud, the authority granted it, its treatment as a sacred text to be studied and interpreted—all suggest an ongoingness to Judaism that threatens Christianity's self-definition as the religion of the present, and the future. To treat Judaism as growing and changing rather than as a fossilized remnant of a past left definitively behind through the incarnation is essentially unthinkable for medieval Christianity; and such a thought, "forced" upon Christianity by an increasing knowledge of Judaism that in part results from closer contact between the two religions, challenges not just Christian conceptions of Jewishness but also Christian self-conceptions insofar as these depend on a relation of clear distinction from the Jewish.

The intimate connection between Christian concern over the Talmud and both Jewish and Christian identity is dramatized in one of the central means used to call Talmudic learning into question—the public disputation. As we have just begun to see, the series of notable disputations between Christians and Jews that began at Paris in 1240, continued at Barcelona in 1263, and reached a certain culmination at Tortosa in 1413–14 made one of its central concerns the Talmud and its suppression or, alternatively, its correction and control. There were other public debates as well: relatively small-scale and local affairs like that reported by Hermann of Cologne between his preconversion self and Rupert of Deutz;[33] a debate at Narbonne between Meir ben Simeon and an unnamed archbishop;[34] the Ceuta and Majorca disputations examined in the preceding chapter; a second dispute at Paris (ca. 1272) between Rabbi Abraham ben Samuel and the convert Pablo Christiani (the main Christian spokesman, too, in Barcelona).[35] In some, but not all, of these debates Talmudic teachings are also partly at issue. But the debates at Paris (1240), Barcelona, and Tortosa are particularly noteworthy.[36]

The 1240 Paris debate seems to have instigated a new genre of public disputation. While still arising in part out of local circumstances, all three of these disputations gather to themselves much broader attention from secular and ecclesiastical authorities, and from Christian and Jewish communities. Hebrew and Latin accounts of each of the three debates survive, suggesting that they were perceived, on both sides, as significant interreligious confrontations. Indeed, all three are sanctioned by the highest church authority, the pope, and presided over by either a royal or papal figure. In the case of Paris, Pope Gregory IX helps provide the impetus for the dispute, and the queen mother Blanche presides; in Barcelona, Raymond de Peñaforte, a Dominican with long-standing and close connections to the papacy, participates and King Jaime I of Aragon presides. In Tortosa, one of the three contending popes of the moment, Benedict XIII (Pedro de Luna), both convenes and presides over the dispute, with the support of King Ferdinand. All three disputations also have as their main Jewish disputant an extremely learned and prominent rabbi or group of rabbis. If the disputes are Christian "set-ups," as in many ways they are, they nonetheless bring forward spokesmen quite capable of defending Judaism. In Paris, a group of rabbis from Melun, Château Thierry, and Coucy is headed by Yeḥiel of Paris. In Barcelona, Naḥmanides, one of the greatest of medieval Jewish philosopher-theologians, speaks for Judaism, and his account of the debate, the *Vikuaḥ* [*Disputation*] comes to be widely disseminated among European Jews.[37] In Tortosa, the most prominent rabbis of Aragon and Catalonia are gathered together. All three debates also significantly bring forward as the main Christian spokesperson not the most learned or sophisticated of theologians present but a Jewish convert to Christianity: in Paris, Nicholas Donin, who seems before his conversion to have repeatedly expressed doubts about traditional Jewish teaching and who after his conversion became a Franciscan friar dedicated to attacking Talmudic, rabbinic Judaism;[38] in Barcelona, Pablo Christiani, who became a Dominican and one of the most active and anti-Jewish of thirteenth-century Christian missionaries in Aragon, Provence, and (it also seems) further north;[39] and in Tortosa, Geronimo of Santa Fe, born Joshua Lorki [Halorki], a learned Jew who upon his conversion became physician to Pope Benedict XIII and a preacher and missionizer.[40] Lastly, as I have already suggested, all three debates focus much of their attention on the Talmud, a focus that (as I hope to show) is particularly significant in relation to questions of religious identity and conversion, changeableness and stability.

As has been argued, none of these disputations—not even the Barcelona debate where, by his own account, Naḥmanides argues successfully a Jewish point of view—is a debate in the true sense of the word.

As Robert Chazan suggests, the disputations do not involve "intellectual confrontation on an equal footing."[41] The terms of discussion are set throughout by the Christian side, which after all convenes and presides over the debates, compelling the Jewish discussants to appear. Toward the start of the debate at Paris, Rabbi Yeḥiel addresses the queen mother, "Your Majesty, do not compel me to answer him [his opponent Nicholas Donin]."[42] Naḥmanides begins the *Vikuah*, "Our Lord the King commanded me to hold a Disputation with Fray Paul."[43] The Hebrew account of the proceedings at Tortosa similarly describes the genesis of the disputation as involving compulsion: "the leaders of Israel stood in trouble and distress before the pope at the request of Joshua Halorki, who, after his apostasy, was called among the Gentiles Maestre Geronimo de Santa Fe . . . for he asked the Pope that the scholars of Israel should come before him, and he would prove to them that the Messiah has come, and is Jesus, and he would prove this from their own Talmud."[44] Indeed, the proceedings have been read as inquisitorial or trial records rather than as debates, with Jewish speakers testifying as witnesses or defendants rather than as disputants in an evenhanded discussion.[45]

Still, these interreligious confrontations take the *form* of debate, and we might productively ask what is served by setting up the trial of the Talmud *as though* it involved an equal facing-off of Judaism and Christianity (rather than, for instance, a more monologic and one-sided Christian anti-Talmudic polemic). As we have seen in much of the discussion above, debates, whether real or fictional, serve as emblematic restagings of Jewish-Christian distinction and division. Posing Christian truth against Jewish error, the Christian debate literature attempts to rearticulate Christian identity by reconfronting the Jewish identity from which Christianity emerged and by resettling that identity as fully superseded. Conversely, the Jewish debate literature that responds to Christian polemic represents an attempt to take back control of the definition of what it means to be a Jew, and in so doing to unsettle a Christian sense of stability, truth, and chosenness. As the earlier discussion of texts like Alfonsi's *Dialogi* and the Ceuta and Majorca disputations would suggest, however, the resettling of identity that debate texts attempt is rarely fully and confidently achieved: the medieval literature of Jewish-Christian debate stands in an anxious relation to identity, striving to assure its stability, but at the same time—by bringing "truth" into the forum of debate; by reaffirming "truth" through the consideration of "false" positions; and thus by allowing, in no matter how incomplete, constrained, and confined a way, "false-hood" to speak for itself—serving to *de*stabilize identity. The fictional debate form, although usually firmly in its author's control, leading to a predetermined end, still may hold surprises along the way, momentary shocks when the opponent's reasoning, however temporarily, seems to make sense. Such effects of surprise might be even more salient in the real-life debate, even if—as was certainly the case at Paris, Barcelona, and Tortosa—the trajectory of discussion was carefully marked out so as seriously to disadvantage the Jewish side.

If the public debate format itself, posing the Christian against the Jewish, focuses our attention on questions of religious identity and dif-ference, the fact that the main Christian disputant in each of the three debates is a Jewish convert to Christianity reemphasizes the concern with questions of religious identity. Other converted Jews, too, were involved more peripherally in these public debates and the events surrounding them.[46] Though there are obvious pragmatic reasons why Jewish converts to Christianity might play a valuable role in these disputes over Talmudic knowledge—having fuller access to the Hebrew texts central to the de-bates than even the most highly educated of Christians—the promi-nence of converts perhaps also suggests something significant about precisely what is at stake for the Christian side in the disputations. That debate with Jews is perceived as dangerous to the faith of Christian dis-putants, even though such debates occur in political situations firmly controlled by Christianity, is clear, for instance, from Pope Gregory IX's decree of 1233 to the prelates of Germany, calling on them "to prohibit most stringently that [Jews] should at any time dare to dispute with Chris-tians about their faith or their rites, lest under pretext of such disputa-tion the simple-minded slide into a snare of error, which God forbid."[47] (In a mirror image of this, following the initial series of discussions with Inghetto Contardo at Majorca, the leaders of the Jewish community are depicted as forbidding their Jewish confreres from engaging Inghetto in debate—an injunction ignored by Jews like Astruch Ysayas.)[48] Chris-tians other than converts indeed participate in these disputations mainly in roles that keep them out of the debate proper, presiding over the pro-ceedings but only occasionally intervening in the actual discussion. This suggests a certain attempt to keep Christians "pure" of direct contact with Jewish intellectual positions, "safe" from the destabilizing effects that might follow upon a Jewish challenge to Christian positions.

Christian converts themselves were of course already in an "impure" position vis-à-vis Judaism, no matter how avid they were in the defense of the newly embraced faith (and Nicholas Donin, Pablo Christiani, and Geronimo de Santa Fe were avid Christians, and Christian polemicists, indeed). The very act of conversion, even as it is crucial to the establishment of a Christian self, also of course emphasizes changeability, the potential for moving from one identity to another, in this case from the Jewish identity against which Christian identity was resolutely defined to Christian identity itself. Indeed, as we have seen, though conversion of individual Jews to Christianity was the goal of much polemical missionary work, and sometimes the result of coercive action, it was not uncomplicatedly treated as a praiseworthy end. If Jews could, before their communal conversion, disagree among themselves, and if some Jews could move beyond their Jewish identities to embrace Christianity, what did this say about the notion that Jews were caught in a static past, that Jewish identity was a stubborn, obtuse, dead substance insensible by its very definition to the living spiritual force of Christian truth?[49] Moreover, the very possibility of a movement from Judaism to Christianity—demonstrating, as it did, that Jewish identity was neither stable nor static—might suggest, too, the instability of *Christian* identity, the possibility that, in an inverse movement, Christians could become Jewish. "New Christians" like Blancha Palau were seen as particularly susceptible to such an inverted conversion, and to guard against this possibility the church repeatedly legislated against the "relapse" or reversion of Christian converts to Judaism. From the Fourth Lateran Council, for instance, comes the following decree that clearly voices the anxiety that the "new" self of the convert might not be wholly cleansed of the "old":

We have heard that certain ones who had voluntarily approached the baptismal font, have not completely driven out the old self in order the more perfectly to bring in the new. Since they retain remnants of their former faith, they tarnish the beauty of the Christian Religion by such a mixture. For it is written "Cursed be he who walks the earth in two ways" [Ecclesiasticus 3:28], and even in wearing a garment one may not mix linen and wool [Leviticus 19:19, Deuteronomy 22:11]. We decree, therefore, that such people shall in every possible manner be restrained by the prelates of the churches, from observing their old rites, so that

those whom their free will brought to the Christian religion shall
be held to its observance by compulsion, that they may be saved.
For there is less evil in not recognizing the way of the Lord than
in backsliding after having recognized it.[50]

While the anxiety here is expressly concerned with the "relapse" of converts, insofar as Christian identity altogether is conceived in terms of
individual conversion (the Pauline experience of being "brought . . . to
life in Christ"), we may recognize, too, a broader concern about the
maintenance of a stable, "converted" Christian self.[51]

The prominence of converts in the disputations over the Talmud
thus richly complicates the involvement of questions of identity in the
dynamics of debate. On the one hand, as I have just suggested, this
prominence may point to a certain Christian reluctance to engage head-
on with Jewish interlocutors, a reluctance that may arise at least in part
from an anxiety about the destabilizing effects of debate on Christian
identity. Further, the converts themselves, though firmly identified *as*
Christians, speak out of necessarily complex and vexed identity positions.
All speak for a Christian orthodoxy, but at the same time—because of the
debates' Talmudic focus—all claim, as well, to speak the truth of Judaism
and Jewish texts. Though, on the one hand, this puts them in a position
of particular authority, it also potentially undermines their standing as
full members of the Christian community. Such a situation also means
that the *Jewish* disputants are arguing not simply against Christian positions but against positions their former coreligionists at least try to present as Jewish. The resulting dynamics of debate become extremely
complicated—and generally in ways that destabilize *both* Jewish and
Christian identity. Thus, even when the Jewish disputant gains the up-
per hand, the larger movement of the debate tends to call into question
Jews' competency to interpret their own texts and traditions. At the
same time, Christianity speaks in these disputations at least in part via
"Jewish" voices, and Jewish arguments do not leave Christian positions
and claims safely unquestioned.

Consider, as just one instance of the complex (de)stabilizations of
identity that occur in these debates, the following moment from the
Barcelona disputation (as presented in Naḥmanides' account), in which
a prominent rabbi, an anonymous Jew off the street, a former Jew, a Christian cleric, and a Christian king confront one another.[52] Arguing about

the time of the coming of the Messiah, in a discussion that depends upon close readings of both biblical and Talmudic passages, the convert—once Saul, now friar Pablo Christiani—argues that "There is no Jew in the world who will not agree that 'day', in Hebrew [yom], means literally 'day.'" He claims that his opponent Nahmanides "changes the meanings of words just as he likes." King Jaime of Aragon, presiding over the debate, has "the first Jew" that his men can find brought in. Asked, "What is the meaning of the Hebrew word yom?" the Jew answers, "Day," confirming Pablo Christiani's position. But Nahmanides responds: "My lord King, this Jew is certainly a better judge of the matter than Fray Paul, but not better than I. The word yom, in Scripture, sometimes means 'time'.... And in the plural yamim it can be used to mean 'years'.... But I am speaking on matters of wisdom to someone who does not know and does not understand, and it is fitting that fools should give judgment for him!" At this point, a second friar, Arnold of Segarra (the Dominican prior of Barcelona), intervenes: "See, Jerome has interpreted 'days' in this passage as meaning 'days of the people.'" In response, Nahmanides "rejoices," concluding that "You can see from Jerome's words that 'days' here are not to be taken in their literal sense as in other passages, and that is why he felt it necessary to give an interpretation."[53]

The Christian position here depends not just on the argument of the converted Jew Pablo but also on the testimony of a Jew brought in from the street. And the Christian position here suffers a setback, with one friar indeed supporting the Jewish argument by citing Jerome, the most venerable of patristic authorities on the literal meaning of scripture. But while Nahmanides scores a certain victory here, this comes only at the expense of the Jew brought in off the street and the former Jew, Pablo Christiani; the Jewish position is confirmed only at the cost of making fellow Jews play the "fool." Nahmanides' victory means, moreover, ceding interpretive authority both to the Christian friar Arnold and to the great Christian "author" of Jewish scripture, Jerome. Is this, then, truly a Jewish victory or rather a realignment of what it means to speak both for Christianity and for Judaism, with the alliances of the moment— Dominican convert and Jew off the street versus Jewish rabbi and Dominican prior—suggesting something other than a clear *opposition* of Christian and Jewish beliefs and identities? Though this is just a moment in the debate, it is surely a moment that dramatizes the slippery ground public disputation provided for both Jews and Christians.

Of course, the political stakes were by no means equal for the two sides: Christians controlled the terms and results of the debate. Though the Barcelona disputation has often been judged a victory for Naḥmanides,[54] he would be brought to trial by the Dominicans in 1265 for having published his account of the disputation. Jaime I of Aragon seems to have protected Naḥmanides against this prosecution, but Pope Clement IV demanded, in a letter to Jaime, that Naḥmanides be punished: "let a strict severity manifest itself and, by the example of that one, the audacity of others be restrained."[55] Naḥmanides left Europe for Palestine soon afterward (1267), as had Rabbi Yeḥiel two decades earlier in the wake of the Paris debate.[56] These events surely demonstrate how dangerous it was for Jews to speak Jewish belief publicly in Christian Europe—even when, like Naḥmanides, *compelled* to do so. But these events also suggest how threatening the statement of Jewish belief might be even within a Christian religious-political order firmly in control of its material circumstances. And if such statements of belief were felt to be threatening, how much more so must have been the fact that Jewish communities, in the face of active Christian missionizing, continued to live their lives within Europe, *staying* Jewish in the midst of Christian hegemony?

THE SPECTERS OF TORTOSA, 1413–1414

I will now focus attention on one late medieval moment—the disputation of Tortosa, 1413–14—when the problems of "staying Jewish" were particularly intense. In this disputation we see Jewish-Christian relations dramatized in a particularly extensive and intensive way: the disputation clearly grows out of and serves local late medieval Aragonese interests at the same time that it picks up on broader high and late medieval Western European concerns, concerns that it has been the project of this book to analyze. Especially striking at Tortosa are the ways in which the movements of becoming Christian and staying Jewish, the impulse toward conversion and an answering resistance, take center stage, given both local political-religious pressures and the longer history of ideas about Jewish and Christian (un)changeability. Akin to the public debates between Christians and Jews held at Paris and Barcelona in the thirteenth century, and making extensive textual use of earlier anti-Jewish polemic, including, for instance, Alfonsi's *Dialogi*,[57] the disputation at Tortosa, which was to last sixty-nine sessions and over twenty-one months, nonetheless stands out because of its extent (while the two surviving Hebrew accounts of the debate are incomplete, the Latin text, preserved in three manuscripts, runs to over six hundred printed pages) and because of the explicit and complex ways in which it participates in a Christian push for Jewish conversion.[58]

The Latin Christian account of the disputation opens:

> In the year one thousand four hundred and thirteen after the birth of the Lord, on the seventh day of the month of February, in the nineteenth year of the pontificate of the most holy father and lord in Christ, Lord Benedict the thirteenth, pope by divine providence, with the most illustrious and serene king of Aragon Lord Ferdinand ruling in the first year of his dominion, in the city of Tortosa of that same realm, by mandate of the aforesaid our lord pope, all the greatest doctors, or rabbis, who were found, in the regions of the said realm, among the congregations [aljamas] of the Jews, were gathered together so that they might be admonished . . . against the errors because of which they have hitherto deviated from the acts of the Messiah, themselves asserting especially that the Messiah has not come. And they were brought together in order to prove . . . that our Lord Jesus Christ the son of God, redeemer of all, is the true Messiah, promised by God and foretold by the prophets.[59]

This introduction makes it clear that the debate is not intended to provide an evenhanded consideration of the relative merits of Christianity and Judaism; Jewish belief is clearly identified as "erroneous," Christian belief as true. The opening statement of Pope Benedict XIII presented in one of the Hebrew accounts of the disputation corroborates the Latin text: "it is a known thing with me that my religion and faith is true, and that your Torah was once true but was abolished." And Benedict quickly narrows his attention to the (unexpected) way in which the Christian side will support its case: "Geronimo has said that he will prove from the Talmud of your Rabbis, who knew more than you do, that the Messiah has come."[60]

The paradoxical claim here, which (as we have seen above) Pablo Christiani began to elaborate in his thirteenth-century polemic, is that

Christianity's great, historical opponent, Judaism itself, testifies strongly
to Christian truth. If the Jewish participants in the disputation can be
brought to accept this claim, as they are repeatedly urged to do, they will
no longer be able to reject Christianity. In effect (and, again, paradoxically), coming to see the truth of Jewish writings, they will have to leave
Judaism behind. The disputation attempts to move the most prominent
of Aragonese and Catalan rabbis to admit an essential Christian claim
whose very acceptance would signal an abandonment of Judaism and an
embracing of Christianity, and it attempts this feat at least in large part
through turning the essential postbiblical Jewish text, the Talmud, against
Judaism. Making that text a "convert," really Christian in its intent, is
the strategy the Christian side adopts in order to bring the Jewish disputants themselves to convert. The author of one Hebrew account, Bonastruc Desmaestre, also one of the participants in the disputation, clearly
states his understanding of the impulse that underlies a discussion so
framed: Joshua Lorki, later Geronimo of Santa Fe, the Jewish convert
who acts as the main Christian spokesman in the debate, "said to the
Pope that when he proved this [from their own Talmud that the Messiah
had come], it would be fitting to force them [the Jews] to adopt the Christian religion."[61]

The Tortosa disputation occurs at a moment in Iberia, and more specifically in the Kingdom of Aragon, when, as is all too evident looking
backward from the decree of expulsion of 1492, the pressure toward
Jewish disappearance—whether via conversion, massacre, or expulsion—
was building. Of course, medieval Iberia had a long history of convivencia (living together) of Muslim, Jewish, and Christian communities and
kingdoms, and medieval Jews had often here been integrated into structures of power more fully than elsewhere in Europe.[62] The Jewish community of Tortosa itself was one of the oldest in Iberia.[63] The fourteenth
century, however, marked increasingly hostile relations among distinct
religious communities, with the longstanding anti-Muslim project of
Reconquista (reconquest)[64] paralleled by a series of actions directed toward
containing and eliminating Jewish communities within Christian Iberia,
usually by means of conversion. These movements culminated together
in 1492 with the defeat of Muslim Granada and the expulsion of the Jews.

The pressure for Jews to convert in the two centuries before 1492
was multifarious—sometimes direct, coercive, and violent, sometimes,

at least in form, gentler. Some individual Jews chose conversion more or less voluntarily, and some of these were prominent community leaders who went on to participate in efforts to convert others. Thus, Abner of Burgos ("one of the three leading [Jewish] communities of Castile") converted in the earlier fourteenth century, changed his name to Alfonso de Valladolid, and became an anti-Jewish polemicist.[65] Another native of Burgos and its chief rabbi, Shlomo (Solomon) ha-Levi, in part taking Abner as his exemplar, converted in 1390 or (more probably) 1391, along with his four sons, his daughter, three brothers, mother, and later his wife.[66] Changing his name to Paul, he studied theology in Paris, became a priest in 1394, bishop of Cartagena in 1403, and of Burgos in 1415. Paul of Burgos (also Paul de Santa María) directed missionary letters to prominent Jewish figures like Rabbi Joseph Orabueña, physician to Charles III of Navarre and chief rabbi of the Navarre Jewry. He also wrote a polemical work called the *Scrutinium scripturarum* that staged a dialogue "against the Jews" "between Saul and Paul."[67] From the early 1390s on, Paul of Burgos was closely connected to Cardinal Pedro de Luna, who became Pope Benedict XIII at Avignon in 1394,[68] and Paul was highly active in both ecclesiastical and secular politics, working especially to influence papal and royal policy on Jews and Jewish conversion.

One of Shlomo ha-Levi/Paul of Burgos's Jewish students from the period before his conversion was Joshua Lorki [Halorki], later Geronimo of Santa Fe, who emerged as the central Christian disputant at Tortosa. In the more than two decades between Shlomo's conversion and Lorki's, the two corresponded about theological questions, with Lorki arguing the Jewish side.[69] He nonetheless converted in 1412 and was quickly appointed the pope's personal physician;[70] he seems (perhaps along with Paul) to have pressed Benedict to set up the debate at Tortosa.[71] Indeed, soon after converting, Geronimo wrote a polemical work called *Contra perfidiam Judaeorum* [*Against the Perfidy of the Jews*], "to which he appended a special tract on the errors of the Jews according to the Talmud."[72] This clearly laid the ground for the main line of argument at Tortosa.

Simultaneous and intertwined with such individual conversions and their aftereffects was an active Christian missionary effort, particularly on the part of Dominican and Franciscan friars; this activity of course picked up on earlier fraternal missionizing, including that of the thirteenth-century Spanish convert Pablo Christiani. Most prominent among these fourteenth- and fifteenth-century fraternal missionaries in Spain was the Dominican Vincent Ferrer who lived from 1350 to 1419 and who was canonized as a saint in 1455.[73] Ferrer spent much of his career as a traveling preacher of penitence, and he attracted enormous crowds of enthusiastic Christian penitents and flagellants—crowds that may have acted as persuasively on potential Jewish converts as did Vincent's sermons. In 1413, the memory of the 1391 anti-Jewish riots in Aragon, with which Ferrer is associated by Jewish writers and from which he is dissociated by Catholic historians, was still fresh. Henri Ghéon, writing in the 1930s, claims that Ferrer "did all in his power to save Jews from the cruelties that threatened them."[74] Rabbi Joseph ben Joshua ben Meir, writing after 1492, claims on the contrary that "[Vincent] was unto [the Jews] a Satan [literally, Adversary] and stirred up against them all the inhabitants of the country, and they rose to swallow them alive, and slew many with the edge of the sword, and many were burned with fire."[75] In the midst of this violence, faced with the (familiar) choice of conversion or death, many Jews converted and many died, in Tortosa as elsewhere. Christian authorities soon showed themselves anxious about the sincerity of the conversions, as is suggested by a decree of August 1393 prohibiting Jews and conversos from living in the same quarter or eating or praying together.[76]

While the violence of 1391 did not recur on the same scale in the next several decades, and while Vincent Ferrer himself in the early fifteenth century seems to have eschewed coercive means to conversion, the threat of violence was strongly associated, for Jews, with Vincent's activities. And his preaching of conversion was highly effective. Vincent's first biographer attributes 25,000 converts to his mission, while a contemporary chronicle puts the number at 100,000. Modern estimates suggest that these numbers are not outlandish; Yitzhak Baer puts the number of Iberian Jewish converts at the time of the establishment of the Inquisition in the tens of thousands, while B. Netanyahu suggests a number in the hundreds of thousands.[77] Ferrer seems to have been influential in the conversion of both Shlomo ha-Levi/Paul of Burgos and Joshua Lorki/Geronimo of Santa Fe, and he worked with both converts to stimulate further conversion. In the early teens of the fifteenth century, he pursued his mission throughout Castile; in 1412, he was called by Pope Benedict to Aragon, where he continued his campaign; and in 1413, he was asked by King Ferdinand to work for the conversion of the Jews assembled at Tortosa for the disputation.[78] While he does not play a significant part in the disputation proper, his presence is indicated at least once in the Latin transcript, when Geronimo notes, on June 26, 1413, that "the very venerable and famous father and holy man, my lord, the most singular brother Vincent, of the order of Preachers, [is] here present."[79]

Simultaneous with Vincent's movements in 1412 and 1413 is the promulgation of new anti-Jewish legislation—associated with the activity of both Vincent and Paul of Burgos.[80] The laws of Catalina, put in place in Castile in January 1412, confined Jews to "special areas assigned by the authorities, in complete separation from the Christians," and ordered Jews to move to these locations within eight days or risk corporal punishment and the loss of all their possessions.[81] Jewish professional and economic life was more severely limited than by any prior legislation; Jews were forbidden to serve Christians as "smiths, carpenters, doublet-makers, tailors, clothmakers, shoemakers, butchers, carriers, or clothiers" and were barred from selling Christians anything edible and any article of clothing.[82] Where previous legislation had forbidden Jewish physicians, surgeons, and pharmacists from treating Christians, the new laws forbade them "to serve altogether in the medical professions."[83] As Netanyahu suggests, the laws were "part of a broader policy, whose aim was to effect a complete separation—and permanent isolation—of the Jews from the Christians."[84] But expulsion from Spain is here clearly not the goal: one of the new legal provisions is that "All Jews ... departing from my Kingdom ... and taken in the road ... shall lose whatever they have with them, and be my slaves forever."[85] Netanyahu concludes that, subjected to "economic strangulation" and cut off from emigration, the Jews of Spain were left with conversion as "the only open way for their survival";[86] Baer similarly concludes that "The legislators did not intend to bring about the physical destruction of the Jews, but merely to convert them to Christianity by means of servitude and oppression."[87]

At the very moment of the institution of these laws, the royal succession in the crown of Aragon was contested between Queen Catalina of Castile (daughter of the duke of Lancaster) and her infant son, Juan II, on the one hand, and Juan's uncle the regent Ferdinand, on the other. Pope Benedict's 1412 call for Ferrer to return to Aragon was partly an attempt to influence the decision regarding succession. Ferrer was appointed one of nine arbiters responsible for the selection of the king, and he strongly supported Ferdinand; in 1412, the succession was decided in Ferdinand's favor. One of the new king's first acts was to bring forward "a modified version of the laws of Catalina for the part of Castile [still] controlled by his regency," and, a month after the start of the Tortosa disputation, in March 1413, "he published in Barcelona th[is] same version [of the laws] for Aragon."[88] The disputation is not just *temporally* tied up with the legislation intended to constrain Jewish communities and bring about conversion. In the final session of the disputation (actually held at San Mateo), in November 1414, Benedict promulgated his own extensive set of anti-Jewish ordinances, and these overlapped in significant ways with the laws of Catalina. They forbade Jews from listening to, reading, or teaching the Talmud; legislated the confiscation of copies of the Talmud and banned all Hebrew books contrary to Christian dogma; outlawed the building of new synagogues or the refurbishing of existing ones; required Jewish attendance at Christian sermons; obliged Jews to wear the badge; forbade Jews from binding Christian books or manufacturing Christian religious objects and from practicing the professions of physician, surgeon, pharmacist, midwife, business agent, trader, matchmaker, or moneylender (that is, many of the professions practiced by late medieval Iberian Jews).[89] Half a year later, on May 11, 1415, Benedict reiterated this legislation in a papal bull, appointing as the bull's executor the son of the convert Paul of Burgos, Gonzalo de Santa María. And in this same year Benedict made Paul himself bishop of Burgos.[90]

The presiding figure at the Tortosa disputation, Pope Benedict XIII, shared with his close associates Paul of Burgos, Geronimo of Santa Fe, and Vincent Ferrer an eagerness for Jewish conversion. In 1395, while still established in the papacy at Avignon, he confirmed a Jewish convert's authority to preach conversion in synagogues,[91] and he granted an indulgence to Christians supporting this missionary work.[92] In 1410, from Barcelona, Benedict authorized the abbot of Beata Maria de la Real, in the diocese of Majorca, to "impose suitable penance on" and grant absolution to "some Jewish converts... accused of judaizing."[93] And in 1415, the year after the Tortosa debate, he issued the following series of orders: to prohibit Jews visiting Alcañiz from staying for long periods of time, in order to prevent their contact with converts;[94] to convert several synagogues in Belchite, Barbastro, and Calatayud into churches or chapels;[95] to grant a convert income from the property of one of the synagogues in Maqueda, which was about to be closed;[96] twice, to allow Jewish converts to wed despite familial relations that would normally have precluded Christian marriage;[97] eleven times, to grant annual pensions to Jewish converts (which of course responded to the economic difficulties faced by Jews converting to Christianity);[98] several times, to grant Jewish converts in Tortosa public offices and church stipends.[99] These bulls, along with the legislation promulgated at Tortosa in 1414 and reiterated in 1415, constituted a concerted papal effort to pressure Jews to convert and to support converts once they had entered Christianity.

Clearly the anti-Jewish legislation that preceded and followed from Tortosa was in part wrapped up with the politics of Aragonese royal succession. As Netanyahu suggests, arguing that Paul of Burgos was instrumental to this legislation, Paul "was well aware . . . that both [Ferdinand] and Catalina aspired to win the monarchic prize of Aragon; he must have repeatedly pointed out to them that both the Pope and Ferrer would have a decisive voice in the selection of the King; and he must have stressed that the attitude of Castile's rulers toward the conversion of the Jews would go far in determining the Pope's and Ferrer's choice."[100] Jewish conversion also was part of the political program of the embattled Pope Benedict. At a moment when three rival popes commanded allegiance in different parts of Europe, with Benedict himself presiding only over Aragon, Castile, Navarre, and Scotland, the campaign to convert the Jews of Spain may have been intended, as some historians suggest, "to draw the Christian world to [Benedict's] side," or more limitedly, as others would have it, to solidify his base of power in Iberia.[101] Benedict himself, in the last session of the Tortosa debate, directs us to think of a successful push to convert Jews alongside an effort to reunify the church. Immediately following his claim that the church "rejoices" in "the conversion of Jews" (see the first epigraph to this chapter), Benedict notes:

> We therefore, [as] farmer of [the church's] vineyard, whom, although undeserving, one considered worthy to preside as guardian over these restless times, however much occupied by other great and arduous business concerning the union of the Blessed Mother Church, and the extirpation of pestilential schisms, which altogether endeavor to devastate her, insofar as it has been possible for us, with the Lord cooperating, have given effective labor to this work of grafting [Jews into Christianity].[102]

Benedict continues by claiming that his own actions, particularly in attacking the Talmud, "imitate" the "footsteps"[103] of a preschismatic line of papal authority, "our predecessors Gregory IX [1227–41] and Innocent IV [1243–54], who because of the errors and heresies contained in it ordered the aforesaid books of the Talmud burned."[104] That, in setting up the disputation at Tortosa, Benedict was thinking of the line of public disputations that began at Paris following Gregory IX's order to confiscate and investigate Jewish books seems clear.

Working toward the conversion of Jews seems, then, to have taken much of the pope's energy at this moment. And much energy, time, and money were given over specifically to the disputation at Tortosa. As Bonastruc's Hebrew account suggests, the more than twenty rabbis involved in the dispute were lodged and fed at papal expense, and the proceedings themselves were invested with due pomp: "all the great court [was] draped with embroidered cloths.... And there were seventy thrones there for the prelates who are called 'cardinals,' and 'bishops' and 'archbishops,' all of them dressed in golden garments; and all the dignitaries of Rome were there, and some of the burghers and noblemen, nearly 1,000 men, and so it was all the days of the Disputation."[105] The Latin text also shows the dispute occurring before a full papal court and with an audience—including Jews, Jews ready to convert, and converted Jews—sometimes numbered in the thousands.

Why was so much effort expended on the disputation at a moment when secular legislation and widespread, popular missionizing already presented strong challenges to the survival of Jewish communities? We might see Tortosa playing several different roles in the overall push toward Jewish conversion. Pragmatically, the dispute withdrew the most prominent Jewish religious leaders of Aragon and Catalonia from their communities at a moment of particular vulnerability, opening those communities more fully to the force of Christian missionizing for a period of almost two years. Perhaps as importantly, Tortosa provided the locus for an abstract, but nonetheless powerful, theological and ideological argument against staying Jewish. And it staged this argument in a highly *visible* form, providing a concrete focal point for a not wholly centralized (indeed, an often dispersed and diffuse) series of movements directed toward Jewish conversion. If the real work of conversion occurred at the level of individuals, families, and local communities—who embraced

Christianity whether out of a sincere conviction of its truth or because of
the strong economic, social, and political pressures of the moment or
from some combination of these—Tortosa provided a venue in which
Jewish existence and persistence could be both presented visibly and
corporately, in the body of the assembled rabbis "standing in for" their
communities, and at the same time challenged and undermined.

The more than twenty prominent rabbis, summoned from their
homes to speak for Judaism, to account for themselves and their beliefs,
were separated from any broad communal support, standing vulnerable
before secular and ecclesiastical authorities in the papal court. How to
be Jewish, how effectively to stand for Judaism in such circumstances?
On the one hand, their refutation of Christian arguments could easily
be read as an all-too-predictable Jewish obstinacy. On the other, any hesi-
tation, any incoherence, any concession on the rabbis' part made itself
available to the Christian opposition as evidence of Jewish weakness,
inconsistency, untenability. The double work of the debate—emphasizing both Jewish obstinacy and a (wished for) Jewish susceptibility to
Christian truth—is evident especially in the Latin text's focusing of attention not only on the rabbis actively involved in the dispute but also on
the large Jewish audience said to be in attendance, an audience whose
reported actions undermine Jewish stolidity and solidarity in dramatic
fashion. While, at least until the closing sessions of the disputation, the
rabbis consistently resisted Christian arguments for conversion, as early
as the twelfth session, only one month into the debate, Geronimo's
arguments led to another sort of action on the part of Jews not officially
involved in the proceedings:

> At the end of the said day, the divine grace that illumines each
> man coming into this world poured itself forth brilliantly, mer-
> cifully inspiring ten notable Jews—five, to be sure, from the
> *aljama* of the town of Monzón, two truly from the *aljama* of the
> place of Falset, one from the *aljama* of the place of Mora, and
> one famous talmudic scholar, from the *aljama* of the town of
> Alcañiz, who from the cradle in his paternal home and school
> had never departed from hearing the Talmud continually, and
> also a certain youth from the city of Calatayud.
>
> Who, all ten equally, with devotion and great humility, and
> bent knees, prostrate before the footstool of the most blessed

Lord our Pope Benedict XIII, confessed, saying unanimously: "In truth, we see evidently and understand clearly that the arguments of master Geronimo are true, and the responses of the Jewish rabbis are completely without strength. Therefore, with the greatest devotion and with the greatest humility, we entreat your Holiness, most blessed Father, and most clement Lord, and ask, insofar as your Holiness is most benignant, that you have us baptized, so that we may be able to gain the salvation of our souls."[106]

The pope complies: the ten are baptized "with honor and solemnity," and they in turn bring "[their] wives and families," numbering "thirty souls and more," to "the baptismal font" to be "cleansed of the Jewish leprosy."[107]

A similar scene occurs at the end of session fourteen, with the conversion of thirteen men and their families; at the end of session twenty-two, with the reported conversion of over 250 Aragonese Jews; and so forth until, at the end of the debate, the pope can claim that "more than three thousand men" have converted.[108] The disputation thus provides not only a stage upon which to dramatize a Christianity facing off against an unyielding Judaism but also the repeated spectacle of Jews abandoning that Judaism.

In the remainder of this chapter, I will look more closely at the dynamics of dispute in Tortosa, focusing principally on three features that reflect the complex relations among Jews, Christians, converts, and potential converts: first, the attention the debate gives to the Talmud; second, a movement between embodiment and disembodiment in the staging of Jewish presence in the disputation; and, third, the significance of Geronimo of Santa Fe's identity as a convert to the debate.

At Tortosa, the Talmud is treated complexly, even contradictorily. On the one hand, especially toward the end of the dispute, Geronimo condemns the Talmud as an immoral book containing "many vanities, sophistries, deceptions, heresies, disgraces, and innumerable errors," identifying "six species of abomination" found in it.[109] He depicts the Talmud's origin as an illegitimate and envious attempt on the part of pharisaical rabbis to "contradict the law of Jesus Christ."[110] Indeed, as we have seen, one end result of the Tortosa disputation was the removal of Talmudic books from Iberian Jewish communities. On the other hand, however, the debate itself is premised on Geronimo's and Benedict's claim that the truth of Christianity is revealed in the Talmud. In relation to such a claim, Geronimo tries to fix Judaism in place now not by throwing out the Talmud and identifying Judaism only with "legitimate," that is, "Old Testament," beliefs and practices, but by insisting on the Talmud's unchangeable centrality to Judaism and further on the testimony it provides for Christianity. This paradoxical or impossible positioning of the Talmud—as a perfidious and erroneous text that nonetheless somehow tells the truth—reflects a similar paradox or impossibility in medieval Christian conceptions of Jewishness. On the one hand, Jews, as historical witnesses to the incarnation who deny its truth, perfectly embody an evil—indeed, demonic—rejection of divinity; on the other hand, they *are* witnesses of divine grace, the descendents of a people who experienced Jesus's presence directly. It was a common medieval belief that, despite their denial of Christ's divinity, the Jews who betrayed and tormented Jesus knew the truth about him.[111] In any case, as custodians of the "Old Testament" and its messianic prophecies, Jews were seen as crucial witnesses to Christian truth. In Geronimo's presentation, the Talmud was the written product of those rabbis who witnessed Christ's life, denying and attempting to contradict his teaching even as they recognized its truth, and the text they produced similarly both denies the truth and bears witness to it.

In the course of the disputation, Geronimo repeatedly makes the claim that he, and not the rabbis, understands the true Jewish way of reading the Talmud. In a frequently reiterated movement, he first presents a particular Talmudic text as proof that the Messiah has come. The rabbis, then, drawing on the traditional distinction between *halakhic* (legal) and *aggadic* (narrative and homiletic) materials, respond that this particular passage is "aggadic" or "fabulistic" and hence not intended to be taken as necessary doctrine.[112] (The Jewish argumentative strategy here has a distinguished history, including especially Nahmanides' use of it at Barcelona.) Geronimo in turn responds that, since Jews believe in the Talmud as the oral law, they must adhere to it fully, crediting "aggadah" as much as "halakhah"; to do otherwise is "the destruction and downfall of the law" and "manifestly heresy."[113] (Again, this is an argument anticipated at Barcelona, by Pablo Christiani.) This policing of Jewish reading practices attempts to stabilize not just the meaning of

Jewish texts but Jewish identity itself. The former Jew here in essence insists that he understands more fully than do the Jews themselves what it means to be a Jew. The rabbis insist that there are multiple ways in which to understand traditional Jewish texts, and Geronimo responds by arguing that such a claim is itself the product of an essential Jewish perfidy: it avoids the truth of Judaism's own texts by means of a conscious and perverse obfuscation of that truth. For Geronimo, there is only one way to read the Talmud as there is only one way to understand Jewishness—as an erroneous and hardhearted blindness that conceals a true, but disavowed, understanding. If this means that Jews are morally more culpable than others who are not Christians—having witnessed the truth directly and refused it—it also means that there is something in their very Jewishness closely connected to Christian truth. On the one hand a people particularly recalcitrant to conversion, Jews nonetheless stand in such intimacy to Christianity as to seem its most "natural" converts. Indeed, the Talmud is, in Geronimo's presentation, as in the earlier formulations of Pablo Christiani, a paradoxical, convert text, a Jewish text that despite its errors and perversions comes to speak the Christian truth. In preserving Talmudic knowledge (along with the "Old Testament" and its prophecies), Jews, despite themselves and their obstinate, obfuscatory means of reading, serve a Christian project. It is the convert Geronimo's role to teach Jews, through their most precious and seemingly most anti-Christian text, the Talmud, their "true" relation to Christianity, to emphasize the ways in which Jews and Jewish texts, despite their explicit claims, are "really" about Christian truth. The convert-disputant thus tries to bring both the Talmud and Judaism with him into a convert position—that is, into the impossible place of a Judaism that changes. The convert is at one and the same time the Jew who has left Judaism firmly behind and the Jew who is somehow a truer Jew than those who claim to speak for Judaism, the Jew who understands the true (that is, the Christian) meaning of Judaism and its traditions. Geronimo and the other convert-disputants of the Talmud debates thus speak with special authority, but clearly the space they speak from is a paradoxical one and their position at least somewhat precarious: they speak for Christianity but also for Judaism, if a reconceived, converted Judaism. While the convert-disputant can associate himself with the Talmud as a text really testifying to Christianity's truth, he also stands in a dangerous relation to the continued Jewishness—the "obscenities" and "heresies"—of that text. For, after all, much as Geronimo may try to make Jews and their texts testify to that which they most resist and disbelieve, the debate itself depends upon the failure of this attempt. There would be no disputation without Jewish resistance. The Jewishness of Jews (and of the Talmud), their recalcitrance to Christian cooptation, is necessary for the shaping of Christian arguments against them and indeed for the shaping of Christian identity itself.

Jews thus stand at Tortosa both as resistant Jews and, despite themselves, in the Christian formulations to which they must respond, as testifiers to Christian truth, as the Christians they might become. Jews are brought to the center of our attention in the hope that they will disappear into a new, Christian identity. And we see such a paradoxical positioning of Jews—bodied forth and yet subject to a wished-for disappearance—not only in the complex treatment of the Talmud but dramatized throughout the Tortosa debate, and dramatized explicitly in the terms of Jewish embodiment (presence) and disembodiment (absence).

The pope insists first and foremost on a real, bodily Jewish presence at the disputation, gathering the rabbis together as representatives of their respective *aljamas*.[114] When, on June 23, 1413, seven of the assembled rabbis attempt to leave Tortosa, they are insistently called back by papal order.[115] The rabbis body forth a broader Iberian Jewish presence imagined, despite its recently straitened circumstances, as flourishing, powerful, and hence threatening to Christendom. Toward the end of the disputation, Geronimo conflates a "you" referring specifically to the rabbi-disputants with one referring to the communities they represent: "you have been very prosperous in temporal goods and fortune until now, as much living in delicacy and quiet, in luxurious positions, as also in having abundantly great lucre [gained] without labor, by means of usury, and also keeping sumptuous synagogues, even holding the persons and lives of Christians in your power through the office of medicine and surgery, and [holding] their money through the office of agent and other administrative positions."[116]

The impulse to realize Jewish presence at the debate, however, is the flipside of a quite opposed drive. The same passage that identifies the rabbi-disputants with thriving Jewish communities and a luxurious Jewish life calls for both them and their communities to disappear. The rabbis are told that, despite their denials, Geronimo has proven that the "Messiah has come" and that he came as "our Savior Jesus Christ";[117]

they should acknowledge these truths, and thus, in effect, abjure their Judaism. At the same time, the text here lays out a concerted ecclesiastical and secular campaign against Iberian Jewish communities altogether: "the most blessed Lord our pope and the most serene Prince our king are aroused. And seeing that to sustain this [Jewish prosperity] would be greatly unjust and irrational, and [would] manifestly work against divine duty, they unanimously will restrict [that prosperity] with a will both united and singular, and [bring you] into that order and rule by which you should live according to the condition and rule of captives."[118]

If one motivating impulse of the Tortosa disputation is having Jews actually present and in dialogue with Geronimo, from the outset their presence and voice are seen as dangerous and in need of containment. At first, the disputation provides the rabbis with a space in which they can develop strong, full, confidently voiced interpretations and counter-arguments to Geronimo's positions. These Jewish arguments, however, are never really given serious consideration by the Christian side. Indeed, the statements of the rabbis are often held up to ridicule by Geronimo, and the pope often intervenes to make clear his own dismissal of them. The intense intellectual engagement of the rabbis in the disputation is reflected, early on, in their tendency to debate issues not only with Geronimo but also with each other. Thus, at one point, the Latin transcript notes, "Master Salomon Ysach said that Rabbi Astruch had responded not well and insufficiently."[119] Rather than be taken as indicating intellectual vibrancy or a real Jewish interpretive dissent that might be further explored, intra-Jewish disagreement is simply read as laying Jewish arguments open to easier challenge. Here, for instance, Salomon Ysach goes on to present his alternative view, but this is quickly dismissed by Geronimo, and the session ends with a fall into silence: "the said master Salomon stopped speaking."[120] The disputation quickly begins to appear a set-up designed to humiliate the rabbis not just before a Christian court but before the Jews witnessing the disputation. The third session, held on February 9, 1413, ends with one of Jucef [Yosef] Albo's arguments dismissed first by the pope, then by Geronimo; the text concludes: "When the many unsuitable things in rabbi Jucef's words had been presented, and then followed up, and then called into question, the copious multitude of Jews standing by in that place, parting from the said gloss of rabbi Jucef as discordant, vain, and of no use, and deriding the said rabbi Jucef as vacillating as much as possible concerning this, in this matter

judged him to have been proven wrong."[121] And only nine sessions into
the debate, on February 20, 1413, Benedict insists on a change in procedure that serves to remake Jewish presence, to take the contentious and
varied voices of more than twenty rabbis and reduce these to a single
voice—or not even a voice but a text. As is common in the Christian debate literature, the pope identifies a Jewish argumentative instability, a
wish "shamelessly to negate that which they earlier conceded,"[122] that he
moves strongly to contain: "considering their variability [in argument],
and that that which they conceded one day, on the next they certainly denied, he not improperly devised an arrangement, commanding that the
arguments of each side be offered manifestly and publicly in writing so
that they could be in no way denied."[123] To stabilize the Jewish position,
to keep the Jewish disputants honest, the pope insists on a written
record in the Jews' own hand, additional to the transcript of oral arguments already being made by the "apostolic secretary."[124]

What begins as oral debate thus becomes an exchange of documents, *cedulae*, between the Jews and Geronimo, and in the process, the
varied voices of the rabbis are reduced to a single, and disembodied (or
at least only textually embodied), voice. Their position papers, as entered
into the record by the papal scribe, consistently begin: "Dixit . . . iudeus"
[The Jew said],[125] "Iudeus . . . respondet dicens" [the Jew responds, say-
ing],[126] and so forth. *Iudeus*, "the Jew," serves here almost as a personification that represents all Jews in a single, unified and abstract, identity
rather than through the individualized, embodied rabbis. The debate—
which, at first, in its noting of distinct Jewish disputants speaking sometimes unifiedly, sometimes not, stood apart from the more literary, clearly
fictional debate texts of the larger tradition—here moves formally to
approach these, echoing a text like Gilbert Crispin's *Disputatio Iudei et
Christiani*, where the narrator makes explicit his decision to leave unmen-
tioned the disputants' names, writing instead "in the *persona* of the Jew
disputing with the Christian concerning our faith."[127] The singular,
unnamed, unparticularized *Iudeus* speaks for his whole people, as the
representative "Jew" who stands in for any real, embodied, disparate,
living, changing community.

Such a move allays the Christian anxiety, repeatedly made explicit in
the Latin text of Tortosa, that the Jewish disputants are not to be trusted,
that their Jewishness conditions a slipperiness in debate that must be
arrested. Geronimo expands many times on the "variable," untrustworthy

qualities of Jewish speech, excoriating it as "pertinacious," "perfidious," "shameless."[128] Bonastruc's Hebrew account also recognizes explicitly that the Christian side is concerned to control Jewish argumentative strategies; early in the debate, the pope declares: "You are already acting as Jews do in arguments, for when they are asked about one thing, they shift to another."[129] The directive to shift from oral to written arguments clearly expresses (as, of course, does the treatment of the Talmud) an impulse to control Jewish reading practices, traditions of intellectual discourse, and voice. But it may also in part serve Jewish interests. In the Hebrew account, the rabbis agree, going into the debate, "that their procedure would not be in the style of the Jews taught in their academies, to interrupt each other and to abuse each other in disagreements, so that they would not be humiliated before the Pope."[130] The Jewish disputants are aware of the dangerousness of their position, of the ways in which internal disputes might be used against them, and their conscious attempt to achieve a unity of voice is ironically fulfilled by the Christian move to control their expression.

If the pope's decree that the Jews write out their arguments draws an explicit limit to how they might speak, the Jewish disputants recognize such a boundary even earlier. They expect to be misheard and, from the start, censor themselves. And they put no more trust in the written record of the debate than they do in their opponents' ability to listen. Following a particularly heated exchange, the Hebrew account comments: "we noticed that they were writing down all our words, and a strong fear fell into our hearts, for we thought that the intention was that the scribes would falsify our remarks, and later, the Pope would say, 'You spoke thus!' And the result would be that we would be convicted by our words, and we would not be able to call the scribe a falsifier, since he was a scribe well known to the Pope."[131] The self-censorship the rabbis impose moves more and more, as the debate proceeds, toward simple silence. As the disputation drags on for twenty-one months, sixty-nine sessions, over six hundred printed pages in the Latin transcript, and as Jewish attempts to put an end to the dispute or to escape from it are thwarted, the rabbis, over and over again, fall into silence. In the Hebrew text, immediately after they voice their fear about possible falsification of the written record, the Jewish disputants "agree[] to be guarded in our speech, and to keep silent as much as possible."[132] From the start of the Latin account, individual Jews fall into silence: "To this the said Rabbi

Mathatias responded not at all."[133] "Then indeed the said Rabbi publicly confessed that he knew nothing more with which to respond."[134] "To all of these things the said rabbi took silence as his response."[135] "Then however Rabbi Ferrer was silent."[136] Later, in the *cedulae* presented in the singular voice of "the Jew," we also see a consistent retreat from argument into silence. For one instance among many: "The Jew... responds that he adheres to the answers he gave above... saying that at present no other response occurs to him because of his insufficiency and infirmity of intellect and ignorance. And with this he puts a final end to his responses as one whose knowledge goes no further."[137] Such repeated descriptions of Jewish nonresponse in the Christian record of the disputation add up to a declaration of Christian triumph, and in such moments of self-silencing, we might read the rabbis as participating in their own erasure, in the moves to contain and reduce the Jewish embodiment put at center stage in the disputation.

But Jewish self-censorship and silence might also be read as resistance—a refusal, increasing as the debate proceeds, to participate in a process over which the rabbis have no control. That is, silence may be one strategy for staying Jewish—for the rabbis' maintaining an integrity as Jews—in a situation where doing so by presenting honestly the varying and sometimes discordant traditions of Jewish interpretation or by strongly proclaiming one's beliefs seems increasingly impossible. For whether their bodily presence is foregrounded or erased—whether they speak volubly or do not respond—Geronimo turns the moment to Christian advantage. The following sequence is typical: Geronimo answers one of the terse, nonresponsive Jewish *cedulae* by upbraiding Jewish silence: "they can attribute to themselves no ignorance in the present matter, since it is certain that they themselves are the wisest and greatest rabbis who exist at present in this whole realm. And given that they do not attain to the sufficiency of the ancients, nonetheless it cannot be denied that they well and sufficiently understand the sayings of the ancients, and see something over and above that. / It is for them as for a dwarf sitting or riding on the neck of a giant."[138] Later, however, when the Jewish disputants do present a more extended argument, they are now accused of a wordy evasiveness: "the response of the Jews is so long and so prolix concerning those things that deviate from the proper matter, and so succinct and so brief concerning the questions raised by the Jews themselves about this present matter, where the whole marrow of the proceeding is centered."[139] Whether speaking fully or tersely, the Jews cannot speak properly, and the voice of the Latin text becomes more and more the singular voice of Geronimo's arguments interrupted only by declarations of Jewish nonresponse.

Tortosa is often presented as an unambiguous failure for the Jewish side. Thus, Netanyahu concludes, "The Tortosa Disputation was the longest and most crucial of all the medieval debates of its kind. It was crucial because it served as an effective instrument of the conversion campaign as it developed at the time. It gave thousands of Jews, who had decided to convert for purely social and economic reasons, a convenient excuse to carry out their wish: they could argue that the debate at Tortosa had proven Christianity right."[140] Certainly, the debate ends on a dispirited note for the Jewish disputants, whose voices we last hear in the following statement:

> And I Astruch Levi, with due humility, subjection, and reverence for the most reverend paternity and lordship of the Lord Cardinal [pope], and the other reverend Fathers and Lords here present, respond saying: That although the talmudic authorities which have been adduced against the Talmud, as much by my reverend, charitable Lord as by the honorable master Geronimo, as they stand according to the letter have an ill meaning, in part because they seem heretical prima facie, in part because [they are] against good morals, in part because they are erroneous; and although according to the tradition of my masters I held that these had or could have another sense, I nevertheless confess that I don't know it. For that reason, I place no faith nor any sort of authority in the said authorities, neither do I believe them nor do I intend to defend them. And this my last response obviates whatever response was given by me earlier, which I revoke and hold as though it had not been spoken insofar as it contradicts this [present statement].[141]

The account then notes, "All the Jews and rabbis of the whole congregation of the Jewish communities present in that place, Rabbi Ferrer and Rabbi Jucef Albo at most excepted, clamored and said with a great voice: And we also to the said statement agree and adhere."[142] This is followed immediately, in the last two sessions of the debate, by the uninterrupted voice of the pope as he declares his "sentence against the said Talmud . . . along with certain constitutions or ordinances against the Jews."[143]

The Latin text of the debate here clearly points toward Jewish acquiescence. And in his long concluding statement, Pope Benedict claims that, associated with the public disputation at Tortosa, there have been "more than three thousand"[144] Jewish conversions: "As much by persistent debates as by repeated instruction, sometimes in our presence, sometimes *in absentia* through the insistence of those whom we deputized to this end, it has happened that, with God's inspiration, very many of them have received sacred baptism with a pure heart and devout mind, publicly confessing themselves convinced [or convicted] by their own books, recognizing that he whom their predecessors pierced, Jesus Christ of Nazareth, [was] true Messiah and their Savior and Lord."[145] And it is certain that at least some of the rabbis directly involved in the disputation did convert, most notably Vidal de la Caballería, the Jewish representative of Saragossa.[146] Nonetheless, might Astruch Levi's statement and the rabbis' final fall into silence at the end of the disputation be read (along with their earlier evasions and silences) not as a conversion but as a resistance, a refusal to participate further in a debate where their views, no matter how fully presented, have never really been heard?

Many Iberian Jews were indeed converting at this moment when so little space for staying Jewish seems available. But of course it is a hotly contested historical question whether and how often such conversions might have covered a staying Jewish that is precisely a resistant claiming of the dominant Christian suspicion that a Jew could and would never truly become a Christian.[147] Might we read Blancha Palau and her maternal family in this way, as embracing Christianity in coercive circumstances all the better to stay Jewish? We might recall here the strong words of the Hebrew chronicles of 1096 in regard to forced converts: "He who speaks evil of them, it is as though he spoke thus of the Divine Countenance."[148]

While the Christian fantasy motivating the debate at Tortosa is a spectacular conversion of rabbis that will bring the whole body of Iberian Jewry to follow suit, in the face of the rabbis' refusal to capitulate what is orchestrated instead is the reduction of Jewish presence and voice to a single thin text—the accumulated rabbinical *cedulae*—that, finally, refuses to speak any further. Even the last Jewish refusal of speech, however, more acquiescent than earlier nonresponses and finally read by the Christian side as a full concession of victory, expresses some resistance. Despite the concessions he makes, Astruch Levi does not, after all, abandon Judaism; he does not convert. And in this final *cedula,* as at the beginning of the disputation, the Jews do not speak with the unified voice of a singular *Iudeus:* Rabbis Ferrer and Jucef Albo defer from Astruch's retraction—though, in the Latin account, we do not learn how their positions differ from that expressed by Astruch and endorsed by the remaining rabbi-disputants. We do not know whether they speak or simply remain silent; the Latin text empties their position, presumably more resistant than Astruch's, of content.

The overall dynamics of the debate thus calls forth, indeed demands, Jewish presence while at the same time pushing presence toward absence—whether actual conversion or simply silence. At the same time, of course, the debate lays out not just starkly opposed Christian and Jewish positions but also a convert identity in the figure of Geronimo. In the Latin account, that identity is not especially foregrounded, though the oddness of Geronimo's choice as chief Christian spokesman, given the presence of more learned and authoritative Christians, is acknowledged at the outset: "although in the said curia of the aforesaid lord pope there be so many masters and doctors of sacred theology, shining forth with no mean wisdom, knowledge, and discernment, it has pleased the said lord our pope, concerning the abovementioned conclusions, that the discerning man and honorable master Geronimo of Santa Fe, physician of his own most blessed person, be specially appointed in order to inform the Jews."[149] Pragmatically, Geronimo is the appropriate Christian spokesman because he is "abundantly grounded in . . . the Bible of the Old Testament and its glosses, and also the Talmud and all the treatises of the Jews."[150] Geronimo's role as spokesman is also, however, emblematic. If the rabbis embody a Jewishness that stubbornly resists conversion, Geronimo impersonates a Jewishness subject to conversion, a Jewishness that speaks, as does the convert himself and the Talmud in Geronimo's reading of it, for Christianity.

But this is a delicate position for Geronimo to occupy. Though he consistently presents his positions with full confidence and unrelenting opposition to the rabbis, that confidence perhaps conceals and compensates for an anxiety about whether converted Jewish identity can in fact be orthodox Christian identity. The Hebrew text, which unlike the Latin foregrounds Geronimo's convert status, indeed suggests that Geronimo's motive for participating in the debate is "to show that he was a true Christian and faithful to his new religion."[151] Moreover, Geronimo's access to the Talmud and to Jewish means of argumentation make him associable with their duplicity. If Jews perversely conceal a knowledge of Christian truth and hence a potential for conversion, might Jewish converts like Geronimo conceal a potential for reversion, a residual, hidden Jewishness? Bonastruc's Hebrew account puts such a possibility explicitly into play. When the rabbis complain about Geronimo's hostile stance in the debate, the pope responds, "do not be surprised at this bad behaviour, for he is one of you!"[152] Later, the pope comments that Geronimo "has already lost the character of a Christian disputant and returned to being a Jewish disputant, running away to another side, when the first side has proved weak."[153]

If bringing Jews to silence does not work wholly to erase their presence or the possibility of a resistance to Christianity, the dynamics that circulate around Geronimo suggest that even bringing Jews to convert does not fully erase Jewishness. If this is not an idea made explicit in the Latin text, it was of course an anxiety repeatedly expressed in fifteenth-century Iberia, as more and more converts entered Christendom.

The Tortosa disputation makes clear the powerful ideological push directed against Jewishness at this point in time in Iberia. At the same time, its ambivalences—seeing Jews and Jewish texts as staunchly resistant to conversion and yet as necessary converts; bodying forth Jews and Jewish communities and yet wishfully, performatively, erasing Jewish presence and voice; making the convert at once the most vocal and visible figure of Christianity and yet a figure in whom Jewishness might continue to dwell—all these ambivalences, while they work to put Jews and Jewish converts alike in impossible situations, also present gaps in which Jews might find some space for survival as Jews. At the moment of Tortosa, however, there was also on the part of some of the rabbi-disputants, as with many other Jews, a more active resistance. Jucef Albo, one of the two rabbis at Tortosa who refused to sign on to Astruch's closing statement, went on to write *Sefer ha-Ikkarim* [*The Book of Principles*] in defense of Jewish belief.[154] And perhaps the last great Spanish Hebrew poet of the Middle Ages, Shlomo Bonafed, present at the Tortosa disputation,

continued to compose his polemical poetry on behalf of Judaism, including poems like the following, written in response to the conversion of
the Jewish scholar Vidal de la Caballería in the wake of Tortosa:

> Day and night I see the foes of my peace. What power can
>   I summon to succor me . . .
> Or how can my heart be at rest . . .
> When I see, as in a dream, Lavi [i.e., Vidal],
> Like a column of diamonds, pound day after day with his
>   demands upon my communal peers;
> And when I see how hearts and faces are transformed, and
>   how the learned wise speak those things which my Torah
>   condoneth not,
> Scholars who were precious beyond words, who girded
>   themselves with valor! My stars have changed and left me!
> Yea, I remember them their company, I recall them not in
>   parting, for ever since my heart and soul are lost!
> Their names are engraved on my forehead! How now, that
>   they are gone, shall I erase those pleasant names from
>   my doorposts?
> I cry for desolation and dispersion! I weep like the sea for my
>   redemption which exile postponeth!
> Yea, I cry, and they laugh.[155]

Bonafed here acknowledges, of course, the force of Christian polemic
like that presented at Tortosa, and the pressure from former Jews like
"Lavi" on their one-time "communal peers." The poem is a lament, and
its speaker ends in tears while those who have deserted him laugh. But
Bonafed also here constructs, via memory, a counterforce to the loss of
"heart and soul," and significantly, rather than recall the staying Jewish
of those who (like himself) have resisted conversion, he chooses to reimag-
ine the *converts* as they once were: "I remember them their company . . .
not in parting." Even while acknowledging the converts' betrayal of Judaism, Bonafed insists on their remaining presence, their inerasable
"engraving" in the heart of a Jewish community Bonafed mourns but
at the same time makes live on (in his own refusal to convert; in his insistence that the converts remain, despite themselves, part of Judaism;
in this poem).

We might see such an expression as the flipside of Christian anxiety about the completeness of Jewish conversion. Christians worry about whether a Jew can ever be truly Christian; Bonafed insists that renegade Jews like Vidal nonetheless somehow remain significant to Judaism, both as renegades and as Jews.

If the accounts of an event like the Tortosa disputation demonstrate a powerful impulse on the part of one group to eliminate another, they also speak to the ways in which such an impulse might generate not the purity of a wished-for hegemony but complex dynamics of oppression *and* resistance, disappearance *and* survival. The staying Jewish of Iberian communities in the years following Tortosa negotiates such complexities, with unconverted Jews standing in tense relationship to converts, with converts entering Christianity more or less "sincerely," holding a greater or weaker intention of retaining ties to the community and practices they leave behind. The decree of expulsion of 1492 is clearly intended to put a stop to such ambiguities: from henceforth, Spain will contain only true Christians. But, disruptive though it is to the Jews who are forced to leave behind their homes, the decree fails spectacularly, as is shown by the subsequent career of the Inquisition: whether because converts in fact remain secretly Jewish or because Christians are unable to believe that converts might really leave behind their Jewishness, post-1492 Iberia continues to be haunted by Jewish specters.

Of course, these specters are different from those of 1413–14 or those that inhabit texts of the long twelfth century like Peter Damian's, Guibert of Nogent's, and Peter Alfonsi's. But as I hope this book has shown, later medieval moments continue (of course, with differences) tropes and movements established earlier: a sense of Christian identity remains dependent upon a relationship, both of derivation and of opposition, to Jewishness; Jewish converts to Christianity both confirm and destabilize a sense of firm Christian identity; Christian polemic insists on the stubborn difference of Jewish bodies even as it tries to make them disappear. Because an unstable fluctuation between presence and absence defines such movements, these tend to operate whether "real" Jews are present, as in Spain in 1413–14, or absent, as after 1492 or in England after 1290: medieval attempts to define the Christian consistently depend upon a conjuration of the Jew. And though 1492 is a strong point of historical division, often thought to mark the beginning of modernity, the medieval dynamics of Jewish spectrality continue. To understand why a

Marlowe or a Shakespeare thought new Christian mercantile identities through the representation of strongly embodied Jewish figures; how explorers and colonists saw, in Native Americans, members of the ten lost tribes of Israel; how, in the mid-seventeenth century, the (never resolved) debate over whether Jews should be "readmitted" to England concerned the very nature of English Christianity, we must look not only forward to new modern constructions but also back to the medieval inheritance of modernity, the conjuring up of a spectral Jew that—no matter how often or forcefully it is declared dead—haunts the projects of Christian Europe.

Notes

Introduction

1. The fullest discussion of the living cross tradition remains Füglister's *Das Lebende Kreuz*, which examines thirty examples of the motif, dating from the first quarter of the fifteenth century to the late seventeenth century. My Figure 1, from Munich, Bayerische Staatsbibliothek, Codex Monacensis 23041, a Latin Gradual from the "Klarissinnenkloster [convent of the Order of Clair] auf dem Anger" in Munich, is reproduced as Füglister's Figure XII; Füglister dates it 1494–97 and discusses it extensively at 54–57, along with a second, smaller example of the living cross found in the same manuscript at fol. 181v. As Füglister notes, the initial "A" illuminated on fol. 3v is from the "Introitus des ersten Adventssonntages ('Ad te levavi animam meam . . .')" [Introitus for the first Sunday of Advent ("I have lifted up my soul to you . . .")] (54; my translation); the text is ultimately from Psalm 142:8 (in the Vulgate; 143:8 in the RSV). Recently, Timmermann has published an extensive treatment of the living cross tradition, reproducing ten examples of the living cross (but not the illustration at hand) and noting that about three dozen survive. He defines the tradition as flourishing in the late fourteenth, fifteenth, and sixteenth centuries "in a wide geographical arc defined by the northernmost Italian provinces, the Alpine countries, Bavaria, Slovakia, Silesia, and some areas of western Poland. Three isolated examples also survive from Denmark, Westphalia, and the lower Rhine" ("Avenging Crucifix," 143). Timmermann reads the tradition as having developed out of the secular allegory of *Iustitia* [Justice]; as inverting "contemporary narratives of Jewish abuse, especially stories of Eucharist desecration"; and as participating in a program of "anti-schismatic and anti-heretical propaganda, which often accused the Jews of collaborating with heretics" (143). For briefer discussions, see Seiferth, *Synagogue and Church*, 146–47 and Figure 59; Blumenkranz, *Juif médiéval*, 109 and Figure 124; Schreckenberg, *Jews in Christian Art*, 64–66, III.1d.4, and Plates 5–6; Rose, "Jewish Mother-in-Law," 12–13; Schiller, *Iconography of Christian Art*, 158–61 and Figures 527–31; Guldan, *Eva und Maria*, 137–39 and Figures 153–55. Füglister (*Das Lebende Kreuz*, Figure IX), Guldan (*Eva und Maria*, Figure 154), and Schiller (*Iconography of Christian Art*, Figure 529) all reproduce a Bavarian-Austrian woodcut dated ca. 1460–70 that is strikingly similar in composition to the two historiated initials in Codex Monacensis 23041; see Füglister, *Das Lebende Kreuz*, 57. On broader traditions of representing Synagoga, also see Mellinkoff, *Outcasts*, vol. 2, Figures II.32, 34–37; III.17, 18, 20, 57, 90, 91; XI.6, 7, discussed at 1:48–51, 64–65, 80–81, and 217–20.

2. Biblical references throughout are to the Latin Vulgate text. I have consulted both *Biblia Sacra Latina* and *Biblia Sacra iuxta Vulgatam Versionem*. Translations of the Latin are my own, but I have also consulted the Douai-Rheims translation: *Holy Bible*,

Translated from the Latin Vulgate. Though the RSV of Genesis 3:15 attaches the action of "bruis[ing]" the serpent's head to the woman's "seed" (*Holy Bible,* RSV), the Vulgate clearly indicates a female agent ("ipsa")—in this context, "the woman" ("mulierem").

3. This prophetic reading of Genesis 3:15 is extremely common. See, for an overview, the *Catholic Encyclopedia* article on "The Blessed Virgin Mary," which opens with a discussion of this verse.

4. Seiferth at first reads this figure as "Ecclesia, representing the church, with a crown and staff of the cross, spreading the folds of her mantle over her protégés," but he later notes that "This is an example of the equating of Ecclesia with Mary. The so-called Madonna in the Protective Mantle became a frequent and popular motif at just that time, near the end of the fifteenth century" (*Synagogue and Church,* 147). For another example of the "Schutzmantelmadonna" associated with the living cross, see Timmermann, "Avenging Crucifix," 146.

5. See Schiller, *Iconography of Christian Art,* 160, and Timmermann, "Avenging Crucifix," 146. And on the tradition of host and skull trees associated with the opposition between Mary and Eve, see Guldan, *Eva und Maria,* 140–43, 221–22, and Figures 156–59, and Füglister, *Das Lebende Kreuz,* 134–57.

6. For one striking vernacular example of this trope, see Geoffrey Chaucer's *Prologue to the Prioress's Tale:* "O mooder Mayde, O mayde Mooder free! / O bussh unbrent, brennynge in Moyses sighte" (*Riverside Chaucer,* VII.467–68). And on pictorial representations, see Harris, "Mary in the Burning Bush."

7. Several high medieval Jesse Trees can be viewed at the Getty Museum Web site: http://www.getty.edu/art/collections/objects/0112629.html, http://www.getty.edu/art/collections/objects/03506.html, and http://www.getty.edu/art/collections/objects/03551.html. A late medieval example by Jan Mostaert (1485) is available at the Rijksmuseum, Amsterdam, Web site: http://www.rijksmuseum.nl/images/aria/sk/z/sk-a-3901.z.

8. Isaiah 11:1: "et egredietur virga de radice Iesse et flos de radice eius ascendet."

9. The cross's *life* is stressed in a wide range of medieval depictions, visual and otherwise, and such depictions are not limited to late medieval culture. Thus, for instance, several Anglo-Saxon images emphasize the fecundity of the cross, as does an Old English poem like *The Dream of the Rood,* where the cross itself speaks the story of the crucifixion. On the images, see O'Reilly, "Rough-Hewn Cross," and Vaccaro, "Crux Christi/Cristes Rod."

10. Often in the living cross tradition, a hand grows from the top of the cross, holding a key with which it unlocks heaven; see Figures 527, 528, 530, and 531 in Schiller, *Iconography of Christian Art,* and most of the figures in Füglister, *Das Lebende Kreuz.*

11. See Füglister, *Das Lebende Kreuz,* 56. In most of the living cross images reproduced in Füglister, Schiller, *Iconography of Christian Art,* Guldan, *Eva und Maria,* and Blumenkranz, *Juif médiéval,* this bottom hand wields a hammer with which it strikes at hell or death (sometimes represented by a skull). That life emerges from the base of the cross directly reverses a pictorial convention in which the cross stands on a skull and/or bones (the crucifixion, after all, takes place at Golgotha, consistently interpreted in the Gospels as "Calvariae locus" or "the place of the skull" [Matthew 27:33, Mark 15:22, Luke 23:33, John 19:17]). See the twelfth-century example in Bynum, *Resurrection,* Plate 9, and the early sixteenth-century example in Steinberg, *Sexuality,* 301 (Fig. 284).

12. The scroll in the same position in the Bavarian-Austrian woodcut whose composition echoes that of the manuscript illustration (see n. 1 above) reads: "Sine gewalt ist dir geben / du pist das ewig leben" [His lordship is given to you / you are the deathless life] (Guldan, *Eva und Maria*, 220; my translation). For a full discussion of the various texts associated with the living cross tradition, see Füglister, *Das Lebende Kreuz*, 167–84.

13. Seiferth, *Synagogue and Church*, 146. Mellinkoff notes that "often [Synagoga] is shown riding on an ass" (*Outcasts*, 1:49).

14. Thus, for instance, goats are associated with both demonic practices and Old Testament sacrifice in the program of illustrations analyzed by Lipton, *Images of Intolerance*, 42–43, 52, 56, 58, 65, 118, 191–92 n. 34. Mellinkoff notes that Synagoga's "connection to lust was suggested by portrayals of her riding a goat or holding the animal's head in her hand" (*Outcasts*, 1:49), a reading supported by Blumenkranz, *Juif médiéval*, 109. The scroll that accompanies Synagoga on the living cross depiction in San Petronio Cathedral reads: "Hirco[rum] sanguis me decipit velut anguis / he[um] su[m] cecata [et] a regno dei separata" [The blood of goats has deceived me like the serpent / Alas, I am blind and separated from God's reign] (Timmermann, "Avenging Crucifix," 157 n. 19; Timmermann's translation 146), associating the goat with Temple sacrifice. (Compare the fresco by Thomas von Villach in Thörl [Kärnten], ca. 1470 [Figure X in Füglister, *Das Lebende Kreuz*], where the scroll reads "Heu sum cecata tradit [a?] a . . . a privata . . . Hircorum sanguis [?] me decepit velut a[n]guis [?]" [ibid., 47].) The contrasting scroll of Ecclesia in San Petronio Cathedral evokes the Eucharist: "Sanguine doctata su[m] xri sponsa vocata / ad coelu[m] scandit q[ui] mi[hi] selera pandit" [Born from the blood, I am called the Bride of Christ / He who confesses his sins to me will rise to heaven] (Timmermann, "Avenging Crucifix," 157 n. 18; Timmermann's translation 146). Also see Guldan, *Eva und Maria*, 137, and Füglister, *Das Lebende Kreuz*, 28, 168–74.

15. Rose, "Jewish Mother-in-Law," 12.

16. The influential theoretical work of Slavoj Žižek provides support for work that sees the figure of the Jew operating in primarily ideological and phantasmatic ways: "Jews are clearly a social symptom: the point at which the immanent social antagonism assumes a positive form, erupts on to the social surface, the point at which it becomes obvious that society 'doesn't work,' that the social mechanism 'creaks.' If we look at it through the frame of (corporatist) fantasy, the 'Jew' appears as an intruder who introduces from outside disorder, decomposition and corruption of the social edifice—it appears as an outward positive cause whose elimination would enable us to restore order, stability and identity. But in 'going through the fantasy' we must in the same move identify with the symptom: we must recognize in the properties attributed to the 'Jew' the necessary product of our very social system; we must recognize in the 'excesses' attributed to 'Jews' the truth about ourselves" (*Sublime Object*, 127–28). For one recent work that makes extensive and interesting use of Žižek, see Biberman, *Masculinity, Anti-Semitism*. To my mind, the central problem of Žižek's formulations about the Jew is that they look always at Jews from a non-Jewish, hegemonic, European perspective and hence do not enable us to conceive of a Jew who is an agent and not just a symptom. This is potentially a problem with all formulations that conceive of the Jew primarily as a Christian figure, including my own, and it is a problem that I am concerned to address in my deployment of the figure of "the spectral Jew" below.

17. Cohen, *Living Letters*, 2, 5. More recently, Cohen, "*Synagoga conversa*," has begun to describe a different medieval construction, which he calls the "eschatological Jew."

18. Cohen cites Dahan's "theological Jew" at *Living Letters*, 3 n. 3.

19. Dahan, *Intellectuels chrétiens*, 585: "On ne sera pas surpris non plus que chez certains—voire chez la plupart—des penseurs, cette bipolarité ait abouti à une vue en quelque sorte schizophrénique des juifs: au juif quotidien et réel, avec qui l'on discute volontiers de Bible ou de sciences, se superpose ce que nous avons appelé le 'juif théologique,' un juif irréel, en qui viennent se mêler, s'additionner divers stéréotypes—nés d'abord de la réflexion des théologiens." Compare Bauman's formulation of the "*abstract Jew*, the Jew as a concept located in a different discourse from the practical knowledge of 'empirical' Jews, and hence located at a secure distance from experience and immune to whatever information may be supplied by that experience and whatever emotions may be aroused by daily intercourse" ("Allosemitism," 148).

20. Lampert, *Gender and Jewish Difference*, 29. In developing the idea of the "hermeneutical Woman," Lampert depends especially on Dinshaw, *Chaucer's Sexual Poetics*. Cohen's "hermeneutical Jew" has also been taken up by Paula Fredriksen, "*Excaecati*," 321, and "Divine Justice," 52.

21. The phrase is used by Tomasch, "Postcolonial Chaucer," 243; repr. 69. Delany also uses the phrase ("Editor's Introduction," ix), attributing it to Cigman (ibid., xi n. 2).

22. I quote here from Cohen, *Medieval Identity Machines*, 185–87, and "Was Margery Kempe Jewish?"

23. Despres, "Protean Jew," 146, 160.

24. Narin van Court, "Socially Marginal," 325–26. What Bush calls "notional Jews" ("'You're Gonna Miss Me,'" 1264) continue to be significant in English culture well into the early modern period. Indeed, as Bush points out, although, during the fourteenth and fifteenth centuries, most English legal material ceased to refer to Jews, this was reversed in the sixteenth century, before any significant readmission of Jews to England: Jews came to be prominently "included in sixteenth- and early seventeenth-century legal expositions, despite the absence of circumstances in which the status of Jews would be directly relevant or even legally possible" (ibid., 1225).

25. Biddick, "Paper Jews," 594, 599 (revised and expanded, *Typological Imaginary*, Chapter 3). Also see Biddick's "ABC of Ptolemy" (revised, *Typological Imaginary*, Chapter 1).

26. Tomasch, "Postcolonial Chaucer," 253; repr. 78. See also Tomasch, "Judecca."

27. Bauman proposes that we think in terms of "allosemitism" rather than "antisemitism": "'allosemitism' refers to the practice of setting the Jews apart as people radically different from all the others, needing separate concepts to describe and comprehend them and special treatment in all or most social intercourse" ("Allosemitism," 143). "Allosemitism" would subsume both "anti-" and "philosemitism" and would express "a radically *ambivalent* attitude" resonating with "the endemic ambivalence of the other, the stranger—and consequently the Jew, as a most radical embodiment, the epitome, of the latter" (ibid., 143–44).

28. Dove, "Chaucer and the Translation," 102 n. 2, responding to Kruger, "Spectral Jew."

29. Lawton, "Sacrilege and Theatricality," 291. Lawton here oversimplifies Tomasch, who does claim that "Jewish absence is likely the best precondition for virtual presence," but continues, "*wherever* in Western culture actual Jews come to reside, they encounter the phantom that follows and precedes them" ("Postcolonial Chaucer," 253; repr. 78; my emphasis). It seems clear, then, that "virtuality" in Tomasch does not apply, as Lawton suggests, just to "absent Jews." The same, I hope, is true of "spectrality" as I use it in the essay to which Lawton refers (where my main examples in fact are not from times and places where Jews were absent) and as I elaborate it in the work at hand.

30. Derrida, *Specters*, 6. Derrida works out the phenomenality of the spectral body most fully in his discussion of Marx in Chapter 5.

31. Nirenberg, *Communities*, esp. 3–17; for use of the term "structuralist," see 5. In his recent plenary address at the International Congress on Medieval Studies, Nirenberg himself evoked the figure of the specter—calling his lecture "The Specter of Judaism in the Age of Mass Conversion: Spain 1391–1492."

32. Cohen, for one, in *Living Letters*, devotes much energy to plotting the ways in which the notion of the "hermeneutical Jew" changes with time, while still retaining certain crucial features.

33. One of the most important accomplishments of Nirenberg's *Communities* is its deconstruction of the binarism of tolerance/intolerance, "[t]he central dichotomy in modern studies of the treatment of medieval minorities" (9). Nirenberg argues that "The identification of a constructive relationship between conflict and coexistence suggests that such a dichotomy is untenable" (ibid., 9). For recent work that continues to emphasize "tolerance," see Nederman, *Worlds of Difference* and *Beyond the Persecuting Society*.

34. Foucault, *History of Sexuality*, 100–102.

35. Medieval shifts in anti-Jewish or anti-Semitic attitude and action are discussed in more detail below. The phrase "persecuting society" is from Moore, *Formation*.

36. See the fuller discussion in chapter 3 below.

37. Abelard, *Dialogus*; translated in *Dialogue* and *Ethical Writings*.

38. Several scholars have, however, rightly emphasized that an assumption of a *total* Jewish absence from England during this long period is unwarranted. See, for instance, Lawton, "Sacrilege and Theatricality," 293. But it is clear that there were no organized Jewish communities in England during the fourteenth and fifteenth centuries. Stacey, "Conversion," notes that the Domus Conversorum [House of Converts], "a kind of halfway house" for Jews who converted to Christianity, designed to ease their entry into Christian society, functioned until the mid-fourteenth century (274): "after 1290 the inmates of the Domus and their descendants would themselves remain as the only surviving representatives of Jewish culture in medieval England" (283). Shapiro notes that "From 1290 until the mid-sixteenth century there is no evidence of organized communities of Jews in England," but that "This changed after 1540," more than a century before the traditional date of "readmission" (*Shakespeare and the Jews*, 68).

39. For a fuller consideration of the historical shifts sketched here, see chapter 2 below.

40. Derrida, *Specters*, 40–48.

41. Castle, *Apparitional Lesbian*, 62–63.

42. For the Latin text of Rupert's dialogue, see Arduini, *Ruperto di Deutz*; the text is also contained in the *PL*, Rupert, *Dialogus*. For the reference to the debate with Rupert in Hermann's autobiography, see Hermann, *Opusculum*, 76–83; Morrison, *Conversion and Text*, 81–85.

1. THE SPECTRAL JEW

1. Augustine, *City of God* 22.30, 1091; *De civitate dei*, 866: "Post hanc tamquam in die septimo requiescet Deus, cum eundem diem septimum, quod nos erimus, in se ipso Deo faciet requiescere." The historical schema is also developed in Augustine's *De Genesi contra Manichaeos* I.23, 190–93. Boas provides a convenient summary and sketches the importance of Augustine's schema for other medieval conceptualizations of history (*Essays on Primitivism*, 177–80). For a discussion of Augustine's historical schema and its importance for Christian treatments of Judaism, see Cohen, *Living Letters*, 24–26, 52–55, and the bibliography provided there.

2. For an important body of work on medieval temporality, see Le Goff, *Time* and *Medieval Imagination*. And see the more recent work of Schmitt, *Corps*.

3. Patterson, *Chaucer*, 86.

4. Ibid., 89. See also Patterson, *Negotiating*, esp. the discussion of "medieval historicism," 157–230.

5. Emmerson and Herzman, *Apocalyptic Imagination*, 2; see esp. the discussion of Joachim of Fiore, 1–35. Le Goff, *Medieval Imagination*, emphasizes the importance of the thirteenth-century invention of "purgatorial time" (67–77); also see his *Birth of Purgatory*.

6. Such formulations shape Pauline thought rather generally. For some exemplary passages, see Romans 2–5, 7:6, 8:2–27; Galatians 2:14–21, 4:22–31, 5:16–25; Ephesians 2:8–9; 2 Corinthians 3:6–8. See Boyarin, *Radical Jew*, for a challenging reading of these formulations as arising out of Paul's "internal critic[ism] of Jewish culture" (12).

7. For foundational work on Christian exegesis, see Auerbach, "Figura"; Daniélou, *From Shadows to Reality*; de Lubac, *Exégèse médiévale*; and Smalley, *Study of the Bible*. For more recent work, see *Moyen Âge et la Bible*; Whitman, *Allegory*; and Dahan, *Exégèse chrétienne*, esp. 359–87. See Cohen, *Living Letters*, 44–51 and 59–60, on the significance of Augustine's exegetical procedures for his doctrine of Jewish witness. Central to Biddick's *Typological Imaginary* is a rethinking of Christian typology and supersessionism that has much in common with my own project here.

8. See, for instance, Galatians 3:28 and Romans 2:28–29 and 10:12. On Paul's "apparent about-face" in Romans 11, where he "endow[s] his Jewish coreligionists with a critical role in the divine economy of salvation," see Cohen, *Living Letters*, 7–9, at 7. And see Boyarin's reading, *Radical Jew*, of Paul's complex position as part of "an inner-discourse of Jewish culture": "Both the passionate commitment to Jewish difference and the equally passionate commitment to universal humanity are dialectically structural possibilities of Jewish culture as it is (always) in contact with and context of the rest of the world" (12).

9. This is an important move in Pauline theology, as when Sarah and Isaac become types of the Christian and Hagar and Ishmael types of the Jews; Galatians 4:21–31. For a

recent reading of this allegory, see Boyarin, *Radical Jew*, 32–36. On competing Jewish and Christian allegorizations of Jacob and Esau, see Boyarin, *Dying for God*, 2–6, 46–49, 53, 125–26. On the importance of this mode of allegorical reading in early Christian anti-Jewish polemic, see Simon, *Verus Israel*, 148–49, 170–71, 188.

10. Damian, *Letters 1–30*, 1:39 (Letter 1). Letter 1 is printed in the *PL* as two separate "opuscula," *Opusculum secundum* and *tertium;* the citation is at 42: "contra omnem Judaicae pravitatis insaniam, et eorum ventosa commenta." In the references to Letter 1 that follow, I first present volume and page numbers from the English translation, then column numbers from the *PL* edition. I have checked the *PL* text against the more recent and reliable MGH edition, *Briefe,* and I note any significant differences below.

11. Damian, Letter 1, 1:39; 42: "confligentem Judaeum."

12. Ibid., 1:51; 49: "De . . . Christi adventu . . . testimonium."

13. Ibid., 1:52; 49, citing Obadiah 18: "erit domus Jacob ignis, et domus Joseph flamma, et domus Esau stipula."

14. Ibid., 1:52; 49: "Quid enim per domum Jacob, et Joseph, nisi Ecclesia Christi? Quid per domum Esau debet intelligi, nisi infidelium populi?"

15. See Simon, *Verus Israel*, esp. 79–80, 169–73.

16. Recent work on early Christianity has indeed emphasized the ways in which the new religion developed in close connection to an also changing Judaism. Boyarin, *Dying for God,* for instance, describes (in at least the first three centuries after Christ) an unbroken continuum stretching from Judaism to Christianity through various intermediate Jewish-Christian and Christian-Jewish configurations. See also the extensive bibliography on the period provided by Boyarin.

17. Thus, for instance, the situation of Jews in Spain was materially different from that in the rest of Europe in part because of the powerful presence of Islam. For an impressively particularized consideration of the relations among Christians, Muslims, and Jews in Northern Iberia during the fourteenth century—and for a comparative consideration of parallel events in Southern France—see Nirenberg, *Communities*. Economic factors clearly played an important role both in the protection of Jews and in the animus expressed against them. For another finely developed analysis, see Mundill, *England's Jewish Solution,* on thirteenth-century England and the events there leading up to the 1290 expulsion of Jews.

18. Compare the suggestion in Chazan, *Daggers,* that there was "an inherent instability in the traditional and fragile Church position with regard to Jews," an "ambiguous combination of toleration and repudiation" (180). Also see Cohen, *Living Letters,* on ambiguity as central to medieval attitudes toward Jews and Judaism.

19. Augustine, *City of God* 18.46, 827–28; *De civitate dei,* 644: "Iudaei autem . . . per scripturas suas testimonio nobis sunt prophetias nos non finxisse de Christo. . . . Nobis quidem illae sufficiunt, quae de nostrorum inimicorum codicibus proferuntur, quos agnoscimus propter hoc testimonium, quod nobis inuiti perhibent eosdem codices habendo atque seruando, per omnes gentes etiam ipsos esse dispersos, quaqua uersum Christi ecclesia dilatatur." On Augustine's treatment of the Jews' continuing historical role, see Cohen, *Living Letters,* 19–65, as well as his earlier discussion in *Friars,* esp. 19–22; see also Chazan, *Daggers,* esp. 10–11. Blumenkranz's older studies of Augustine's relation to Jews

and Judaism remain useful—see *Judenpredigt* and "Augustin." For recent rethinking of Blumenkranz's conclusions, see Fredriksen, "*Excaecati*" and "Divine Justice."

20. Augustine, *City of God* 4.34, 178; *De civitate dei*, 127: "si non in eum peccassent, impia curiositate tamquam magicis artibus seducti ad alienos deos et ad idola defluendo, et postremo Christum occidendo: in eodem regno etsi non spatiosiore, tamen feliciore mansissent."

21. Ibid. 20.29, 957; 753: "conuerso corde."

22. For one important treatment of nineteenth- and twentieth-century racialized thinking about Jews, see Gilman, *Jew's Body*. In the post-Holocaust era, the Catholic Church has in some ways recognized the violent effects that a supersessionist view of Judaism has helped enable, and it has tried to distance itself from that view, if often not successfully. See the brief discussion in Biddick, *Typological Imaginary*, 7, and Kwalbrun, "Playing God's Chosen," 1–5, discussing Pontifical Biblical Commission, *Jewish People*.

23. Haftmann connects the *White Crucifixion* to the Mannerists, specifically El Greco, and "the characteristic qualities of the votive picture" (*Marc Chagall*, 118). Meyer, however, sees no "connection with the forms of the icons," noting that "If Chagall had any models they were sixteenth- and seventeenth-century works he had admired in museums" (*Marc Chagall*, 414). Alexander perceptively notes that "Unlike medieval crucifixions, which occur out of history and out of place (hence the gold ground), or Renaissance crucifixions, which occur in an optically real space, this one occurs in *history*, in twentieth-century history" (*Marc Chagall*, 316).

24. See Meyer's comments on how the *White Crucifixion* rewrites Christian understandings: "The scenes that frame the cross, twined round it like a crown of thorns—from the shattered village to the pillaged, burning synagogue—constitute an exemplary Jewish martyrology.... But, most important of all, this Christ's relation to the world differs entirely from that in all Christian representations of the Crucifixion. There it is not the world that suffers, except in grief for his death on the cross; all suffering is concentrated in Christ, transferred to him in order that he may overcome it by his sacrifice. Here instead, though all the suffering of the world is mirrored in the Crucifixion, suffering remains man's lasting fate and is not abolished by Christ's death. So Chagall's Christ figure lacks the Christian concept of salvation" (*Marc Chagall*, 414, 416). Most critics, however, read Chagall's turn to Christian imagery as expressing a "universalizing" impulse, a reading that finds some sanction in Chagall's own words: "If a painter is a Jew and paints life, how is he to keep Jewish elements out of his work! But if he is a good painter, his painting will contain a great deal more. The Jewish content will be there, of course, but his art will aim at universal relevance" (quoted in Walther and Metzger, *Marc Chagall*, 63). Walther and Metzger themselves conclude that "In the figure of Christ on the cross . . . Chagall located a universal emblem for the sufferings of this time" (ibid.). In a chapter on Chagall as a religious painter, Cassou suggests that the *White Crucifixion* shows "the catastrophe of Jewry, foreshadowing the universal catastrophe" (*Chagall*, 242); for Cassou, Chagall's religious art "goes beyond the differences between Judaism and Christianity, beyond the personalities and the doctrines of the two religions, and expresses rather what unites the two. Chagall takes no account of the differences and distinctions between them, but reduces all to the common denominator of human suffering" (ibid., 247). For a subtler reading, see Roskies,

who reads Chagall as "addressing a particularist message to a universal audience": "The primary purpose of Chagall's 'White Crucifixion' was to interpret the course of Jewish events in terms of an absent God and a powerless Son" (*Against the Apocalypse*, 286). My own reading, in its insistence on the Jewishness of the *White Crucifixion*, is out of sympathy with this tradition of universalizing readings.

The crucifixion was a consistent theme in Chagall's work, appearing as early as 1912 in *Golgotha* or *Calvary* (Museum of Modern Art; see the reproduction in Haftmann, *Marc Chagall*, colorplate 10), and continuing to appear in works later than the *White Crucifixion*. See especially the *Blue Crucifixion* of 1941, the *Yellow Crucifixion* of 1943, *The Martyr* of 1940, and *The Crucified* of 1944 (the latter two discussed in relation to the *White Crucifixion* by Roskies, *Against the Apocalypse*, 286–89); for related depictions, also see *Descent from the Cross* (1941) and *Flayed Ox* (1947).

25. The phrase is Meyer's (*Marc Chagall*, 416).

26. Haftmann proposes that these "lamenting figures" are "from the Old Testament" (*Marc Chagall*, 118), a view echoed by Walther and Metzger (*Marc Chagall*, 63). Meyer sees them as "elders" (*Marc Chagall*, 414), an assessment with which Alexander concurs (*Marc Chagall*, 316).

27. Ibid.

28. Alexander, however, suggests that "In this picture the Red Army certainly figures as a liberating power" (ibid.).

29. Derrida, *Specters*, 56. Subsequent page references are given parenthetically in my text.

30. For Derrida's earlier and fuller engagement with speech act theory, see *Limited Inc*.

31. For a similar recognition of the ambivalence of the ghost, see Brogan, *Cultural Haunting*: "As an embodiment of the continuity between the living and the dead, the ghost evades the finality of death. It represents a compromise, or an essentially antithetical act: a simultaneous acknowledgment of and denial of death.... Yet continuity with the past can be a source both of comfort and anxiety, at times even of terror" (20). Brogan here depends on specifically Freudian models (ibid., 177 nn. 43, 45). For a further recognition of the complex historical work ghosts might accomplish, this time in a medieval context, see Chism, *Alliterative Revivals*. And for an intriguing treatment of medieval ghosts and ghost stories, see Schmitt, *Ghosts*.

32. The ambivalence also works in reverse: "positive conjuration" of specters, "in order to call up and not to drive away," while it "seems welcoming and hospitable, since it calls forth the dead, makes or lets them come,... is never free of anxiety. And thus of a movement of repulsion or restriction" (Derrida, *Specters*, 108).

33. Douglas, *Purity and Danger*. Models of pollution tend mainly to emphasize spatiality—threats from the margins and interstices of a culture; the preservation of social boundaries and the integrity of social bodies—but it is clear that pollution involves temporal violations as well. In the contemporary moment of the AIDS crisis, for instance, while much energy has been expended in erecting and policing spatial barriers around so-called "risk groups," and in projecting HIV/AIDS *elsewhere* geopolitically, the "protective" distinctions of Third World/First World, gay/straight, minority/majority operate as well by means of a *temporal* logic. Thus, Africa is constructed in the West as the primal

scene of AIDS not just because it is distant but because it is thought to be archaic, some-how outside "modernity." A time not our own intrudes on the present, threatening to mark, or pollute, this moment with qualities and experiences—an encounter with a so-called "plague" constructed as both "primitive" and "medieval"—that we thought we had superseded. As I will suggest here, a similar temporal logic characterizes medieval Christian constructions of the relation to Jews and Jewishness, and it is as much the temporality of this relation as a spatial logic of proximity and distance that defines the dynamic of Jewish pollution. For a fuller treatment of the temporality of representations of HIV/AIDS, see Kruger, "Medieval/Post-Modern."

34. Butler, *Bodies*, 8.

35. See Kruger, "Bodies," and Abulafia, "Bodies."

36. I will examine some of the consequences of this paradox in chapter 2 below.

37. Damian, Letter 1, 1:66–72; 57–61.

38. Ibid., 1:38; 41: "aliquid . . . Judaeorum ora rationalibus argumentis obstruere." Damian, *Briefe,* reads "rationabilibus" for "rationalibus" (65).

39. Damian, Letter 1, 1:38; 41: "si Christi miles esse, et pro eo viriliter pugnare desideras, contra carnis vitia, contra diaboli machinas insignis bellator arma potius cor-ripe; hostes videlicet, qui nunquam moriuntur: quam contra Judaeos, qui jam de terra pene deleti sunt." Note here the strongly masculine, military, gendering of the Christian disputant; this gendering is discussed at greater length in chapter 3 below.

40. Ibid., 1:38; 41: "Inhonestum quippe est, ut ecclesiasticus vir his, qui foris sunt, calumniantibus, per ignorantiam conticescat: et Christianus de Christo reddere rationem nesciens, inimicis insultantibus victus et confusus abscedat. Huc accedit, quod saepe hujus rei noxia imperitia, et cavenda simplicitas non solum audaciam incredulis suggerit, sed etiam errorem et dubietatem in cordibus fidelium gignit. / Et cum haec scientia ad fidem certe tota pertineat, fides autem omnium virtutum sit proculdubio fundamentum; ubi fundamentum quatitur, tota mox aedificii fabrica praecipitium ruitura minatur."

41. Ibid., 1:39; 42: "pauca et apertiora prophetarum testimonia curamus apponere, quibus tamen contra omnem Judaicae pravitatis insaniam, et eorum ventosa commenta valeas cum Dei adjutorio obtinere victoriam. Et quia sagitta directius mittitur, si meta, cui infigi debeat, e diverso primitus opponatur, nos ipsum confligentem Judaeum hic intro-ducimus, ut verborum nostrorum spicula non in ventum effusa inaniter defluant, sed ad certam potius materiam jaculata pertingant."

42. This is Psalm 45:1 in the RSV.

43. I cite just one of many such moments of direct address in Peter's letter. Damian, Letter 1, 1:57–58; 52: "Quid ad haec, Judaee, jam tentabis [*Briefe:* temptabis (81)] objicere? Qua inverecundae mentis audacia tam claris, tam apertis, tam divinis poteris assertionibus obviare? Esto, quod blasphemantes dicitis, Christum de se potuisse mendacia fingere; nunquid, et antequam nasceretur, si Deus non esset, per aliorum ora semetipsum valuit prophetare? Illud etiam qualiter intelligas, audire delectat: 'Eructavit cor meum verbum bonum, dico ego opera mea regi' [Psalm 44:2]. Quis est ille rex, cui Deus opera sua dicat [*Briefe:* dicit (81)]. Dicis mihi fortasse: David; sed lege sextum [*Briefe:* textum (81)] psalmum per ordinem, et sensus intellige veritatem: descende paululum inferius, et interroga non me, sed ipsum Dominum, quis sit rex, cui ipse opera sua dicat. Audi quid praedicto regi Deus ipse loquatur."

44. Ibid., 1:65; 57: "Ecce qui post tam perspicuam exemplorum lucem adhuc testimoniis indiget, restat ut ad contemplandum radiantem in meridie solem lucernae lumen efflagitet. Nam cum tot astrorum coelestium radios coram te, Judaee, videas enitescere, miror, quae tam densae tenebrae caecitatis locum etiam in vacuis oculorum orbibus valeant obtinere."

45. Ibid., 1:66; 57: "Nunc autem de quibusdam caeremoniis, super quibus saepe scrupulosissime quaeritis, et garrulis ambagibus quaestionum lucem [*Briefe:* litem (88)] movetis, sub quodam inquisitionis, responsionisque dialogo brevis inter nos contexatur oratio, ut cum tibi fuerit ex omnibus satisfactum, aut compellaris manus dare convictus, aut cum ignominiosa tua recedas infidelitate confusus."

46. Ibid., 1:72; 61: "Sed jam post tantam testium nubem, Judaee, tibi epilogum faciam, et incipiens ab exordio humanitatis Christi per incrementa temporum usque ad consummationem, prophetica testimonia tibi, si habes, ante oculos ponam, ut quasi sub uno aspectu collecta breviter videas, quae me diffuse, et sparsim ponere superius attendebas."

47. Ibid., 1:79; 64: "ratiocinatione."

48. Ibid., 1:82; 66.

49. Ibid., 1:82–83; 67–68: "dum nuda pene tibi Scripturarum exempla proposui, velut sagittarum fasciculum in pharetram misi. Et quia ex verbis contrariis [*Briefe:* contrarii (102)] suggeritur copia respondendi, arma quidem praebui; quo vero te invictum [*Briefe:* inictum (102)] effundere debeas, quo clypeum circumvolvere, quia bella necdum imminent, ad plenum docere non potui. Habes igitur coram posita, quae ad hujusmodi conflictum sunt necessaria. Utere paratis, ut expedire decreveris."

50. Ibid., 1:83; 68: "Omnipotens Deus, dilectissime frater, ab invisibilium te insidiis hostium misericorditer protegat et immunem te de hujusmodi [*Briefe:* huius mundi (102)] certamine ad coelestia regna perducat. Amen."

51. Freud, *Ego*, 35–36. Freud here builds on his earlier "Mourning and Melancholia." (He also of course presents his own reading of the historical relations between Judaism and Christianity in *Moses and Monotheism*, esp. 109–17.)

52. For the framing dream, see Hermann, *Opusculum*, 70–72, 122–27; Morrison, *Conversion and Text*, 77–78, 110–13. On the significance of the dream for structuring Hermann's conversion account, see Kruger, *Dreaming*, 154–65. On Hermann's conversion, and for further bibliography, see Cohen, "Mentality," and *Living Letters*, 289–305; Morrison, *Understanding Conversion*, 50–57, and *Conversion and Text*, 39–75. There has been significant debate on the authenticity of Hermann's *Opusculum*; for the case against authenticity, see Saltman, "Hermann's *Opusculum*." I read the *Opusculum* as an authentic autobiography, but even if it is a Christian fabrication, it gives us significant insight into the meanings of conversion for its audience. See Schmitt, *Conversion*. For an extensive discussion of Jewish conversion to Christianity in a later period, see Carlebach, *Divided Souls*.

53. Hermann, *Opusculum*, 70: "peccator ego et indignus sacerdos Hermannus, Iudas quondam dictus, genere Israelita, tribu Levita, ex patre David et matre Sephora, in Coloniensi metropoli oriundus"; my translation (see also Morrison, *Conversion and Text*, 77).

54. For a papal statement of 1097–98 on the "relapse" of converts, see Simonsohn, *Apostolic See*, 1:42. Also see Baron, *Social and Religious History*, 3:39, 3:247, 4:5; and Rabinowitz, *Social Life of the Jews*, 107. On the case of the fourteenth-century "relapsed convert" Baruch the German, see Grayzel, "Confession."

55. Butler, "Melancholy Gender," 21. Also see Butler's *Gender Trouble*, esp. 57–65, and *Psychic Life*.

56. Castle, *Apparitional Lesbian*, 62–63. Edelman's formulation of what he calls "homographesis," which can be both "regulatory" and "deconstructive," emphasizes a similar ambivalence; see *Homographesis*, esp. Chapter 1.

57. Melville, *Moby Dick*, 31; I give subsequent page references parenthetically in my text.

2. BODY EFFECTS

1. See, for instance, the complex navigation of "psychological" and "political" questions in Sedgwick, *Between Men*, *Epistemology*, and *Tendencies*; Butler, *Gender Trouble*, *Bodies*, and *Psychic Life*; and Pellegrini, *Performance Anxieties*.

2. See, for instance, the (different) formulations developed by Butler, in the works cited above; Dollimore, *Sexual Dissidence*; and de Lauretis, *Practice of Love*.

3. I use a contemporary term like "heterosexist" advisedly, aware that the work of medievalists like Lochrie (*Heterosyncrasies*) and Burger (*Chaucer's Queer Nation*) calls into question the notion that medieval and modern "heterosexuality" are cognate constructions, or even that "heterosexuality" or "heteronormativity" existed in the Middle Ages. Still, we can certainly recognize as part of a medieval sexual system a privileging of what we would call "heterosexual" acts and relationships — alongside, of course, privileged sexual categories like virginity, celibacy, and chastity that have very different meanings and values in the Middle Ages and in (post)modernity.

4. For one cogent example, see Fuss's deconstruction of an internal/external binary in "Inside/Out"; also, more generally, see the work of the queer theorists cited above, nn. 1–2.

5. Muñoz usefully develops a three-part distinction based on the work of Michel Pêcheux: "Pêcheux built on [Althusser's] theory by describing the three modes in which a subject is constructed by ideological practices. In this schema, the first mode is understood as 'identification,' where a 'Good Subject' chooses the path of identification with discursive and ideological forms. 'Bad Subjects' resist and attempt to reject the images and identificatory sites offered by dominant ideology and proceed to rebel, to 'counteridentify' and turn against this symbolic system. . . . Disidentification is the third mode of dealing with dominant ideology, one that neither opts to assimilate within such a structure nor strictly opposes it; rather, disidentification is a strategy that works on and against dominant ideology" (*Disidentifications*, 11).

6. Butler, *Bodies*, 116.

7. See, for instance, Southern, *Making*, 219–57; Ullmann, *Individual and Society*; Dronke, *Poetic Individuality*; Morris, *Discovery*; Hanning, *Individual*; Benton, "Conscious-

ness of Self"; and, more recently, Gurevich, *Origins*. For a partly skeptical response to some of this work, see Bynum, *Jesus as Mother*, 82–109. For a recent discussion of "the discovery of the self" that directly treats Jewish-Christian relations, see Elukin, "Discovery."

8. For more on the "twelfth-century renaissance," see, in addition to the sources cited in the previous note, Haskins, *Renaissance*; Lewis, *Allegory of Love*; Chenu, *Nature, Man, and Society*; Leclercq, *Love of Learning*; Stock, *Myth and Science*; Wetherbee, *Platonism and Poetry*; *Renaissance and Renewal*; and Stiefel, *Intellectual Revolution*. For the fullest treatment of Jewish-Christian relations and the "twelfth-century renaissance," see Abulafia, *Christians and Jews in the Twelfth-Century Renaissance*.

9. For a fuller treatment of European expansion and Christian consolidation, see Bartlett, *Making*. For essays that treat various moments in the history of medieval conversion to Christianity, see *Varieties of Religious Conversion*.

10. For a fuller treatment of European crusading, see the essays collected in *History of the Crusades*.

11. On the Gregorian Reform, see Fliche, *Réforme grégorienne*, and Cowdrey, *Cluniacs*.

12. Cluny was founded in 910 and played an important role in eleventh- and twelfth-century reforms. Cîteaux and the Cistercian order were founded in 1098, in part in reaction against Cluny. Norbert of Xanten founded the Premonstratensian order in 1120, under the influence of the Cistercians. For an extensive treatment of Cluniac positions vis-à-vis non-Christians and "heretics," see Iogna-Prat, *Order and Exclusion*.

13. For one treatment of eleventh- and twelfth-century heretical movements and orthodox reaction to them, see Moore, *Origins*. On the Albigensian crusade, see Evans, "Albigensian Crusade."

14. Guibert, *Gesta*, in *Recueil*, 135: "papa primus ex Francis." I have consulted the *Gesta* in the *Recueil* edition, the *PL*, and the more recent Corpus Christianorum text. In my references, I will give page numbers from the *Recueil* edition followed by column numbers from the *PL*. Unless otherwise noted, I cite the text from the *Recueil*. Translations are my own, but I have also benefited from Levine's translation: Guibert, *Deeds of God*.

15. Cole, *Preaching*, 14, summarizing the account of Robert of Reims.

16. Guibert, *Gesta*, 140; 702: "Peroraverat vir excellentissimus, et omnes qui se ituros voverant, beati Petri potestate absolvit, eadem, ipsa apostolica benedictione firmavit, et signum satis conveniens hujus tam honestae professionis instituit, et veluti cingulum militiae, vel potius militaturis Deo passionis Dominicae stigma tradens, Crucis figuram, ex cujuslibet materiae panni, tunicis, palliis et byrris iturorum assui mandavit."

17. Cohen has argued, in *Living Letters*, that the twelfth century is the period in which we begin to see in Christian understandings a blurring of distinctions between Jews and other religious others like Muslims and heretics; the earlier medieval sense of a special status to be accorded to Judaism as Christianity's forerunner begins, Cohen believes, to fade—and along with this change, Christian positions begin to become more strongly anti-Jewish (see esp. 147–66; also see Cohen, "Muslim Connection"). Such a view is consonant with that of Moore, *Formation*; Moore sees Jews as one of several "others" in the period subjected to an increasingly persecutory Christian hegemony. While much evidence supports Cohen's and Moore's positions, however, it is also the case that Jews do not

simply dissolve into Muslims and heretics in the work of twelfth-century writers. As I hope my discussion in this chapter suggests, Judaism, Islam, and "heresy" function together, but *differentially*, in the way in which they serve to solidify and stabilize, by contrast, orthodox Christian identity.

18. See the repeated (re)institution of the badge by papal decree—for example, in the documents in Simonsohn, *Apostolic See*, 1:101, 103, 105, 111, 117, 118, 132, 141, 145, 174, 185, 199, 200, 209, 227, 268, 388, 431, 445, 460.

19. Although the development of official ghettos occurs later in the history of Europe, it is clear that Jewish homes were often segregated from Christian living quarters. See, for a general discussion, Dahan, *Intellectuels chrétiens*, 37–38, 176–79, and the bibliography given there. For one more specific case study, see Anchel, "Early History."

20. Quoted in Dahan, *Intellectuels chrétiens*, 106–7 n. 40, from the 1631 Cologne edition of Guy's *Summa* (5): "Iudaei foris sunt solum quantum ad pertinentia ad Novum Testamentum, nec quoad haec ab ecclesia iudicantur; quoad ea vero quae ad veritatem veteris Legis pertinent, si errent Iudaei, ecclesia de illis iudicat et punit, quia quantum ad hoc non sunt foris."

21. On the medieval Christian view of Islam as "heresy," see Daniel, *Islam*, esp. 209–13; Daniel, *Arabs*, 246, 249–52; Southern, *Western Views*, 38–39; and Tolan, *Saracens*, esp. 135–69. For the related view of Islam as "schism," see Daniel, *Islam*, 217–18. And for the alternative understanding of Islam as "paganism," see Daniel, *Islam*, 214, 391 n. 61; Daniel, *Arabs*, 33–34, 97–98, 238–41, 254, 260; and Tolan, *Saracens*, esp. 105–34. For a fine overview of "European approaches toward the Muslims" pre-1300, see Kedar, *Crusade*; on Christian attempts to convert Muslims, see Burns, "Christian-Islamic Confrontation."

22. Dollimore, *Sexual Dissidence*, 121.

23. On this paradox, see Cohen, "Scholarship": "It is instructive that in the period of the most intense Christian study of Judaica new polemics undermined the security of European Jewry. . . . In the high medieval academy, increased study of a minority viewpoint led not to greater toleration but to greater bifurcation between the circumscribed value of such an outlook and its despised protagonists" (612–13; repr. 330–31). Similarly, Funkenstein, "Basic Types," suggests: "Christian and Jewish polemics during that period are characterized by increase of knowledge of the antagonists' theological literatures and modes of thinking. It is true indeed that there was mutual influence and that many parallel movements may be found. Even in their polemics, Christians and Jews used a common theological language. Yet subjectively, the increase of mutual knowledge was accompanied by a growing awareness of, and stress upon, the gap. If there existed a mutual cultural language it served for contradictory assertions" (382). Dahan, *Intellectuels chrétiens*, identifies a related paradox in the period of the twelfth, thirteenth, and fourteenth centuries: "In a paradoxical enough manner, at the very moment when the West, by means of expeditions like those of Marco Polo or the Vivaldi brothers, by means of crusades and commercial exchanges, multiplies its contacts with the non-Christian world, it feels itself imperiled within its own boundaries and ends up seeing all those who do not conform to the model it has marked out for itself as potential or real enemies" [D'une manière assez paradoxale, au moment même où l'Occident, par le biais d'expéditions comme celle de Marco Polo ou celle des frères Vivaldi, des croisades et des échanges commerciaux, multiplie les contacts

avec le monde non chrétien, il se sent en péril dans ses propres frontières et finit par voir tous ceux qui ne se conforment pas au modèle qu'il s'est tracé, des ennemis potentiels ou réels] (34; my translation).

24. The phrase is from Moore, *Formation*. For influential suggestions about this historical shift, also see Funkenstein, "Changes" and "Basic Types"; Cohen, *Friars*; Chazan, *Daggers*, esp. 169–81; Langmuir, *History*, 275–305. Also see the linkage Boswell draws between a growing anti-Semitism and growing intolerance toward "gay people" (*Christianity*, esp. 271–75).

25. See Cohen, *Friars*, 78–85, on the implications of the 1240 inquisition of the Talmud in Paris. As Golb, *Jews*, points out, the pope's initial order for the confiscation of Jewish books involved not just the Talmud but "universos libros Judeorum vestre Provincie" [all the books of the Jews of your province] (427), and Golb argues that the attack on Jewish learning included, "*inter alia*, commentaries written by earlier French scholars such as Rashi, Jacob Tam, and Rashbam, and by Tosafists of the following generations" (428). The order to burn the Talmud was renewed by Louis IX in 1254 (Golb gives the date as 1253) and by his two successors, Philip III and Philip IV; see Cohen, *Friars*, 80, and Golb, *Jews*, 429. For a fuller discussion of the Talmud's role in thirteenth-century (and later) Jewish-Christian relations, see chapter 5 below.

26. I follow Langmuir's dating of ritual murder accusations and the blood libel; see *Toward a Definition*, esp. 266–68. On "the first fully documented case of a complete host desecration accusation" in Paris in 1290, and on the fuller history of such accusations, see Rubin, *Gentile Tales*, quotation at 40. On the later medieval and early modern history of ritual murder accusations, see Hsia, *Myth* and *Trent 1475*.

27. On the influence of Jewish scholarship on Christian biblical exegesis in this period, see Smalley, *Study of the Bible*, esp. the chapter on Andrew of St. Victor, 112–95. For further treatment of the interimplication of Jewish and Christian exegetical and intellectual practices during the twelfth and thirteenth centuries, see Graboïs, "*Hebraica Veritas*"; Grossman, "Jewish-Christian Polemic"; Timmer, "Biblical Exegesis"; Dahan, *Intellectuels chrétiens*, 229–336; Dahan, "Connaissance"; Dahan, *Exégèse chrétienne*, esp. 359–87; Signer, "God's Love for Israel"; and Van Engen, "Ralph of Flaix."

28. Thus, Einbinder, "Signs of Romance," suggests a significant influence of romance structures and tropes on the emerging Ashkenazic historiography of the twelfth century. For one influential treatment of how Arabic culture was transmitted to the medieval West, marking literary traditions, see Metlitzki, *Matter of Araby*.

29. For a convenient overview of the work of translation undertaken in Islamic, Jewish, and Christian centers during the twelfth century, see d'Alverny, "Translations." For a reading of medieval Jewish culture that suggests often close relations between Christian and Jewish communities, see Marcus, *Rituals*.

30. Maccoby, *Judaism on Trial*, 32; also see 160–61.

31. Grayzel, *Church*, 296–97: "Judei sive Sarraceni nec sub alendorum puerorum suorum obtentu, nec pro servitio, nec alia qualibet causa, Christiana mancipia in domibus suis permittantur habere."

32. Ibid., 106–7 ("ipsi et servos Christianos habere non dubitant, et nutrices, cum quibus eas interdum abominationes exercent, quas te potius punire convenit quam nos

deceat explicare"), 252–53. The latter letter also calls for the burning of the Talmud. The same documents are available in Simonsohn, *Apostolic See*, 1:82–83, 180–81.

33. Grayzel, *Church*, 306–13; quotation at 310–11: "ne Judei publicis officiis preferantur."

34. Relatedly, see France's critique of the common idea that, during the First Crusade, "the 'Crusade of the Poor' ... is sharply distinguished from that of the knights [and] is alone guilty of persecuting the Jews" ("Patronage," 7).

35. For an overview of the legal material, see Dahan, *Intellectuels chrétiens*, 63–91, 95–226. For one case in which everyday relations between Jewish and Christian neighbors seem clearly to have been largely cordial and respectful, see Shatzmiller, *Shylock Reconsidered*.

36. Smalley notes that Richard of St. Victor "rebukes" Andrew "for judaizing" (*Study of the Bible*, 110); see also 112–95.

37. Kimhi, *Book of the Covenant*, 46–47, 40–41.

38. Stein, "Disputation," 51. Stein translates a section of Meir ben Simeon's *Milḥemet Miẓvah*. Also see Chazan, *Daggers*, on the *Milḥemet* (39–44, 49–66).

39. The text of Kimhi's *Book* survives only in a very late form, in a compendium of polemical treatises, the *Milḥemet Ḥovah*, published in 1710 at Constantinople; see Talmage's introduction to Kimhi (*Book of the Covenant*, 18).

40. See the essays collected in *Studies in Maimonides and St. Thomas Aquinas*.

41. Cohen, "Mentality," 32; see also *Living Letters*, 154. Cohen refers here to Pelikan, *Christian Tradition*, 3:246.

42. For an overview of the different positions, see Cohen, *Living Letters*, 167–79. And for more specific work on Anselm's stance in relation to Judaism and Islam, see Gauss, "Anselm" and "Auseinandersetzung"; Abulafia, "St. Anselm," "Christians Disputing," and *Christians and Jews in the Twelfth-Century Renaissance*, esp. 39–46, 77–85.

43. On Guibert's relation to Anselm, see Pelikan, "First-Generation Anselmian"; and Abulafia, "Theology."

44. For the texts, see Crispin, *Works*. On Gilbert's work, his treatment of Judaism, and the relationship between the "Gentile" and Judaism, Islam, and pagan antiquity, see Blumenkranz, "*Disputatio*"; Berger, "Gilbert Crispin"; Abulafia, "*Ars disputandi*," "Gilbert Crispin's Disputations," "Attempt," and *Christians and Jews in the Twelfth-Century Renaissance*, 77–81, 97–100; and Cohen, *Living Letters*, 180–85.

45. For the Latin text, see Odo, *Disputatio*; for an English translation, Odo, *On Original Sin and A Disputation*. On Odo's work, see Abulafia, "Christian Imagery" and *Christians and Jews in the Twelfth-Century Renaissance*, 83–85; and Cohen, *Living Letters*, 186–92.

46. See Introduction, n. 42. For discussion of Rupert's treatment of Judaism, see Arduini, *Ruperto di Deutz*; Van Engen, *Rupert*, 241–48, 353–56; Abulafia, "Ideology" and *Christians and Jews in the Twelfth-Century Renaissance*, 118–21, 126–27, 131–34.

47. The quotation is from Cohen, *Living Letters*, 285; also see 285–86 n. 51 on the critical debate over the possible Muslim identity of Abelard's philosopher. On Abelard and Judaism, see Graboïs, "Chapitre de tolérance" and "Dialogue religieux"; Abulafia, "*Intentio*," "Twelfth-Century Renaissance Theology," and *Christians and Jews in the Twelfth-Century Renaissance*, 89–91; and Cohen, *Living Letters*, 275–89.

48. On Peter the Venerable and the Jews, see Langmuir, *Toward a Definition*, 197–208; Abulafia, *Christians and Jews in the Twelfth-Century Renaissance*, 87–88, 115–17, 128–33, and "Twelfth-Century Renaissance Theology"; Chazan, "Twelfth-Century Perceptions" and *Medieval Stereotypes*, 41–57; Cohen, *Living Letters*, 245–70; and Iogna-Prat, *Order and Exclusion*. For discussion of Peter's relation to Islam, see, again, Iogna-Prat, *Order and Exclusion*, and Kritzeck, *Peter the Venerable*.

49. On Bernard of Clairvaux and Judaism, see Berger, "Attitude"; Lotter, "Position of the Jews"; Chazan, "Twelfth-Century Perceptions" and *Medieval Stereotypes*, 41–57; and Cohen, *Living Letters*, 221–45.

50. Alain, *De fide catholica* and "Contra Paganos." See d'Alverny, "Alain de Lille"; Berger, "Gilbert Crispin"; and Cohen, *Living Letters*, 157–58, 305–12.

51. See, for instance, Chenu's essay "Theology and the New Awareness of History" (in *Nature, Man, and Society*).

52. For English translations of the Hebrew Crusades chronicles, see Eidelberg, *Jews and the Crusaders*, and Chazan, *European Jewry*. On the chronicles' distinctive historical and literary features, and on their relations to Latin historiography, see Yerushalmi, *Zakhor*, esp. 37–40; Marcus, "From Politics"; Chazan, *European Jewry*; Marcus, "Communauté"; Cohen, "'Persecutions of 1096'" and "Hebrew Chronicles"; Chazan, *God, History, and Humanity*; Cohen, "1096 Complex?"; Chazan, "From the First Crusade"; Einbinder, "Signs of Romance"; and Shepkaru, "To Die for God".

53. See Hanning, *Individual*.

54. For some of the rich recent work on the thematics of religious and racial difference in courtly romance, see Ingham, *Sovereign Fantasies*; Chism, *Alliterative Revivals*; Heng, *Empire of Magic*; McCracken, *Curse of Eve*; and Cohen, *Medieval Identity Machines*.

55. On the significance of the twelfth century for the history of autobiography, see Misch, *Geschichte der Autobiographie*.

56. See chapter 1, n. 52.

57. See, for instance, Prawer, "Autobiography of Obadyah," and Momigliano, "Medieval Jewish Autobiography." Prawer makes the claim that "As an instance of its literary genre, the autobiography [of Obadyah], written some time after 1121–22 (this being the last date which can be accurately fixed), is the earliest written by any Westerner in the Middle Ages, probably contemporary with that of Guibert of Nogent" (110).

58. See n. 27 above.

59. On the patristic *Adversus Iudaeos* tradition, see Ruether, "*Adversus Judaeos* Tradition." For wide-ranging surveys of the tradition, see Williams, *Adversus Judaeos*, and Schreckenberg, *Christlichen Adversus-Judaeos-Texte (1.–11. Jh.)*, *Christlichen Adversus-Judaeos-Texte (11.–13. Jh.)*, and *Christlichen Adversus-Judaeos-Texte (13.–20. Jh.)*. For one treatment of the high medieval transformation of this tradition, see Cohen, *Living Letters*.

60. Crispin, *Works*, 9: "libellum . . . nuper scripsi, pagine commendans que Iudeus quidam olim mecum disputans contra fidem nostrum de lege sua proferebat et que ego ad obiecta illius pro fide nostra respondebam. Nescio unde ortus, sed apud Maguntiam litteris educatus, legis et litterarum etiam nostrarum bene sciens erat, et exercitatum in scripturis atque disputationibus contra nos ingenium habebat."

61. On the confrontation between Ecclesia and Synagoga, see, in addition to the works cited above in the discussion of the living cross, Schlauch, "Allegory of Church and Synagogue." The disputation of Church and Synagogue does not disappear from the polemical literature of the high and late Middle Ages; see the brief history in Dahan, *Christian Polemic*, 69–70, and, for one example, *Disputatio Ecclesiae et Synagogae*.

62. On the medieval association of "heretics" with Jews, see further Moore, *Formation*, and the opening chapters of Ginzburg, *Ecstasies*.

63. See, for instance, such twelfth-century works as Kimḥi's *Book of the Covenant* and Judah ha-Levi's *Kuzari*. The latter has been connected to Abelard's *Dialogue*, to which it bears several striking resemblances; both, for instance, present themselves as dream visions. See Graboïs, "Chapitre de tolérance." For a compendium of many of the Jewish arguments used in such debates—in the words of its editor, "a virtual anthology of Ashkenazic polemic in the twelfth and thirteenth centuries" (17)—see Berger, *Jewish-Christian Debate*.

64. See the overview of such legislation in Dahan, *Intellectuels chrétiens*, 350–54. For the text of some of this legislation, see Grayzel, *Church*, 198–201, 300–301, 318–19, 324–25.

65. See Blumenkranz, "Jüdische und christliche Konvertiten," and Golb, "Notes."

66. See Prawer, "Autobiography of Obadyah," and Momigliano, "Medieval Jewish Autobiography."

67. Rabinowitz, *Social Life of the Jews*, 108.

68. On thirteenth-century Jewish conversion to Christianity in England, see Stacey, "Conversion." On English Christians becoming Jewish, see Stacey, "Jews and Christians," 344–45, and Mundill, *England's Jewish Solution*, 48–49, 275.

69. There is controversy about the dates both of Guibert's birth and of his death. I follow here the recent suggestions of Rubenstein, *Guibert of Nogent*, 17, 197.

70. Cohen, *Living Letters*, 192–201, treats Guibert as attaining "new levels of intolerance in the Jewish-Christian debate" (201). While this may be true, I am most interested here not in measuring intolerance but in considering how Guibert's representations of Jews and Jewishness function within an economy of Christian identification, counteridentification, and disidentification vis-à-vis a variety of religious "others."

71. Within the *Memoirs*, too, one might identify more "private" and more "public" moments; thus, while the opening section of the work is largely autobiographical, the later treatment of the revolt of the commune of Laon, while still concerning events intimate to Guibert, fits more into historiographical than autobiographical traditions. On Guibert as autobiographer and historian, see Blurton, "Guibert of Nogent." In my discussion of the *Memoirs*, I cite Benton's revision of Swinton Bland's translation of the *De vita sua*, providing, in my parenthetical references, book and chapter numbers (consistent for both English and Latin texts) and page numbers from Guibert, *Self and Society*. I have also consulted the more recent English translation by Archambault: Guibert, *Monk's Confession*. I have used both the *PL* edition (Guibert, *De vita sua*) and Labande's edition and translation (Guibert, *Autobiographie*). My citations of the Latin are from *Autobiographie*. On Guibert's place in medieval autobiographical traditions, see Misch, *Geschichte der Autobiographie*, 3.1:108–62, and Ferguson, "Autobiography as Therapy."

72. On the texts and translation of the *Gesta Dei per Francos*, see n. 14 above.

73. I cite Guibert, *Tractatus*, hereafter providing parenthetical references; translations are my own. I do not treat Guibert's exegesis—either the *Moralia Geneseos* or the *Tropologiae* on the Prophets—in any detail here; for a full and interesting discussion, see Rubenstein, *Guibert of Nogent*, esp. 31–37, 38–60 *(Moralia)*, 176–99 *(Tropologiae)*.

74. Guibert, *Tractatus*, 490: "piis . . . operibus." On this dream, see Kruger, *Dreaming*, 151–52, and Rubenstein, *Guibert of Nogent*, 20–21.

75. Guibert, *Autobiographie*, 252: "Ad hunc, ob augendum infractae fidei suae robur, libellum quendam direxi, quem contra Suessorum comitem, judaizantem pariter et haereticum, ante quadriennium ferme scripseram." See also 3.16; 210: "How evilly he [Jean of Soissons] 'set his mouth against heaven' [Psalm 72:9] may be understood from that little work which I wrote against him at the request of Bernard the dean" [Quam male autem in coelum posuerit os suum, intelligi potest ex meo illo libello quem contra ipsum, rogatu Bernardi decani, scripsi *(Autobiographie, 424)*].

76. Ibid., 372: "librum quendam de Hierosolymitana expeditione."

77. Guibert, *Self and Society*, 237. More recently, Rubenstein, *Guibert of Nogent*, presents a similar sense of Guibert's career, dating the *Gesta* 1107–8 (95–96), the *Tractatus* IIII (116 and 253–54 n. 25), and the *Monodies [Memoirs]* 1115 (101 and 253–54 n. 25).

78. See Benton's introduction to Guibert, *Self and Society*, 10, 13–16, 21–30, and Benton, "Consciousness of Self." On Guibert's attitudes toward the body and sex, also see Kantor, "Psychohistorical Source"; Duby, *Knight*, 139–59; and Stock, *Implications*, 499–510; on Guibert's fear of pollution and his social conservatism, see Moore, "Guibert." And for a discussion of the significance of the *De pignoribus sanctorum* in addressing a problem that Stock would place "[a]t the centre of the growth of religious intellectualism and of scientific naturalism"—"the status of a physical object having religious associations during an age of increasing literacy" (244)—see Stock, *Implications*, 244–52. Benton's and Kantor's approaches to Guibert are self-consciously "psychohistorical"; for a critique of their work, see Coupe, "Personality of Guibert." And for a recent overview and assessment of the various critical approaches in the reception of Guibert—including the psychohistorical—see Rubenstein, *Guibert of Nogent*, esp. 1–12.

79. Kruger, "Bodies," 303.

80. Dante, *Divine Comedy, Inferno* 28.22–36: "rotto dal mento infin dove si trulla . . . fesso nel volto dal mento al ciuffetto." On visual representations of Jews and "Saracens" as possessing monstrous bodies, see Strickland, *Saracens, Demons, and Jews*.

81. Guibert, *Autobiographie*, 202: "in morbum incidit, cujus causa cum Judaeo quodam, gnaro medicinae, loquendi malo suo occasionem sumpsit."

82. Ibid.: "Ex mutua ergo familiaritate sumentes audaciam, sua sibi incipiunt revelare mysteria. Sentiens ergo monachus, malarum artium curiosus, Judaeum maleficia nosse, multum ei institit."

83. Ibid.: "assentit Judaeus, et sequestrum ei apud diabolum se futurum pollicetur." On the close medieval association of Jews with the devil, see Trachtenberg, *Devil and the Jews*; Gregg, *Devils, Women, and Jews*; Strickland, *Saracens, Demons, and Jews*.

84. Guibert, *Autobiographie*, 202: "petit se doctrinae hujus eo fieri auctore participem.

Refert praeses ille nefandus neutiquam hoc fieri, nisi christianitate negate sibi sacrificium deferatur. Interrogat ille quod. 'Quod delectabilius est in homine.—Quid illud?—Sperma libabis,' ait, 'tuum, quod cum mihi profuderis, / inde quod sacrificantibus est debitum praegustabis.'"

85. Ibid.: "Proh scelus! Proh pudor! Et is a quo haec exigebantur erat presbyter!"

86. Ibid.: "antiquus hostis."

87. Ibid.: "tui ordinis et tuae benedictae hostiae." For brief discussions of this episode, see Trachtenberg, *Devil and the Jews*, 213 (and compare 66); Moore, *Formation*, 35; and Abulafia, "Theology," 26–27. On Guibert's Eucharistic theology, see Pelikan, "First-Generation Anselmian," and Rubenstein, *Guibert of Nogent*, 132–72.

88. Guibert, *Autobiographie*, 204: "Quas igitur artes execrabili hoc mercimonio compararit, facto notificemus in uno."

89. Ibid.: "Quandam cogniti generis monacham colloquio suo assueverat."

90. Ibid.: "novus incantator...praecantans ei quae didicerat, in canem eam convertit immanissimum." The story here echoes a more widespread folk narrative; see, e.g., the English *Dame Sirith*.

91. Guibert, *Autobiographie*, 204, 206: "Diu igitur sine Deo vivens, demum gravi morbo, Deo propitiante, percutitur et, velit nolit, quod gesserat confitetur.... [A]b omni divinorum mysteriorum ministerio eorum spurcissimus prophanator abicitur. In qua tamen abstentione positus, nunquam ab ejus animo obliterari / poterat, quin adhuc futurus esset episcopus. Quam spem indubie acceperat a daemonibus, semper quidem, et hic quoque mendacibus, quia ante paucos annos non modo haud pontifex, sed in aeternum expresbyter est defunctus."

92. For brief comments on Guibert's depiction of Jean, see Moore, *Formation*, 117; Duby, *Knight*, 155–56; and Rubenstein, *Guibert of Nogent*, 115–16. For a more extensive, recent discussion, see Ziolkowski, "Put in No-Man's Land."

93. Guibert, *Autobiographie*, 424: "Pater tuus Amorreus, et mater tua Cettea."

94. Ibid., 422: "paterna et avita nequitia in exitium matris semper ecclesiae redundavit."

95. For the extended narrative of Guibert's mother and her influence on her son, see Guibert, *Self and Society* 1.12–19; 63–101; *Autobiographie*, 74–169.

96. Guibert, *Autobiographie*, 422: "Judaei cujusdam studio fratrem proprium cupiditate comitatus veneno occiderat."

97. Ibid.: "linguam diacono cuidam a gutture exemptam succidi fecit oculosque convelli."

98. Ibid.: "Judaeum ignis assumpsit. Et ipsa pridie quam caput jejunii sequebatur, postquam eximie coenaverat, in ipso sui somni nocte primordio paralisi percussa, officia linguae perdidit, totius corporis invalitudinem incurrit, quodque potissimum est, nil deinceps quod ad Deum pertineret sapuit, et de caetero porcum vixit. Cui etiam justo Dei judicio, quasi pro medela, pene lingua desecta est. Sic se ab initio quadragesimae usque ad octavas Paschae, cum diem clausit, habuit."

99. For an analysis of such an economy of bodily transgression and retribution in other, later medieval texts, see Kruger, "Bodies."

100. Guibert, *Autobiographie*, 424: "non modo ad parentem regeneravit utrumque, sed multo deteriora peregit."

101. Ibid.: "Ipse Judaeorum et haereticorum perfidiam tantopere coluit, ut quod Judaeis metu fidelium impraesumptibile erat, ipse diceret de Salvatore nefaria....Cum Judaeos attollerat, a Judaeis pro insano habebatur, dum verbo sectas eorum approbaret, et nostra inpromptu sequeretur."

102. Ibid., 424, 426: "Nocte paschali se in ecclesia ad vigilandum contulerat.... 'Pulchras,' ait, 'mulieres, quae istic coexcubant, libenter attendo.'"

103. Ibid., 426: "Certe cum conjugem juvenculam speciosam haberet, ea contempta, rugosissimam ita affectabat anum, ut, cum intra domum cujusdam Judaei lectum sibi et illi saepius apparari faceret, nunquam tamen stratu cohiberi poterat, sed in aliquem angulum turpem, aut certe intra apothecam aliquam prae furore libidinis se cum illa sordidissima contrudebat."

104. Ibid.: "Quid, quod cum uxore sua parasitastrum quendam, extinctis jam nocte lucernis, sub specie sui cubitum ire mandavit, ut adulterii sui crimen impingeret!"

105. On this action as an attempt to "dismiss" his wife—and as part of a larger aristocratic pattern of such "repudiations"—see Duby, *Knight*, 154.

106. Guibert, *Autobiographie*, 426: "Quae cum non esse comitem ex corporis qualitate sentiret,—erat enim comes foede pruriginosus,—suo quo valuit nisu et pedissequarum auxilio, scurram dure cecidit." Again, as with the story of the monk and the nun who becomes a dog, we are here close to the traditions of folk narrative and the plots of *fabliau*.

107. Ibid.: "Non sanctimonialem, non monacham a sua abusione excluserat."

108. Ibid., 428: "A multis discretioribus te didici omnes foeminas debere esse communes, et hoc nullius momenti esse peccatum." As Duby notes: "The words Guibert attributes to [Jean] are those that had been attributed to the heretics of Orleans a hundred years before" (*Knight*, 56).

109. Guibert, *Tractatus*, 490.

110. Ziolkowski, "Put in No-Man's Land," 119.

111. The opposition of the Virgin to Jean's action and the involvement of devils in his downfall are both characteristic as well of stories of *Jewish* transgression and punishment.

112. Guibert, *Autobiographie*, 426: "Hujus putidissimi blasphemias cum pati jam Virgo mater, omnium regina, non posset, redeunti ei ab expeditione regia, collegarum suorum daemonum ad urbem jam propinquanti ingens globus apparuit. Qui hirta coma, sensu effero, domum veniens, ea nocte conjuge repulsa, cum anu praedicta concubuit, in qua et lethali morte decubuit."

113. Ibid., 426, 428: "[C]lericum...super urinarum suarum consideratione consuluit; qui, ei de morte respondens, cum de sua anima et de perpetratis libidinibus eum conveniret."

114. Ibid., 428: "nihil aliud quam rabiem postea dixit aut fecit."

115. Ibid.: "Nam astantem sibi conjugem pede volens propellere, cuidam militi... impegit grandem adeo, ut eum everteret. Tenebantur ergo insanissimi hominis manus, ne se suosque disiceret."

116. Ibid.: "clandestina serpat." Guibert's famous treatment of the heresy at Bucy is discussed in a variety of contexts by Trachtenberg, *Devil and the Jews*, 205; Cohn, *Europe's Inner Demons*, 49; Moore, *Origins*, 67–69; Duby, *Knight*, 148; Bullough, "Postscript," 209–10; Moore, *Formation*, 36, 64, 94, 122–23, 124–27, 129–30; Ginzburg, *Ecstasies*, 76; and Richards, *Sex, Dissidence and Damnation*, 59.

117. Guibert, *Autobiographie*, 430: "pro eucharistia."

118. Ibid.: "videas viros mulieribus cohabitare sine mariti conjugisque nomine, ita ut vir cum femina, singulus cum singula, non moretur, sed viri cum viris, feminae cum feminis cubitare noscantur, nam viri apud eos in foeminam coitus nefas est."

119. The sense of the "righteous" Christian self that we thus might read over against the "Judaizing" and "heretical" tendencies of a Jean of Soissons seems consistent with the Anselmian psychological scheme that Rubenstein (*Guibert of Nogent*, esp. Chapters 2 and 3) sees Guibert developing in his earlier exegetical works and deploying in the structure of his *Memoirs:* here, "Affection" and "Will" must be properly subsumed to "Reason" if the Christian subject is to attain "Understanding," or the possibility of a contemplation of the divine. Abulafia, "Theology," also ties an Anselmian psychology to Guibert's treatment of Jews, and particularly their failure to "rise above a literal understanding of the Bible" and leave behind "the rut of carnality" (33).

120. Guibert, *Autobiographie*, 2: "inveterata pravitatum studia, necdum sub defatigati corporis torpore cessantia . . . perseverantissimarum impuritatum mearum."

121. Ibid., 4, 6: "Pecco siquidem, sed, ratione recepta, in affectum cordis transisse me poenitet, tamque stercorosis cophinis mens graviter invita succumbit."

122. Ibid., 2: "et creberrimos ad te miserationis internae, quos tamen inspirasti, recursus."

123. Rubenstein, *Guibert of Nogent*, 116.

124. Guibert, *Autobiographie*, 430: "in ypogeis aut penetralibus abditis."

125. Ibid., 248: "arma / praesumunt et in quandam ecclesiam compellentes, utrum vi nescio an dolo inde recutiunt, et gladiis indiscrete sexus et aetates addicunt." Guibert notes, however, that Jews who converted to Christianity were spared. For a brief discussion of this passage, see Moore, *Formation*, 29–30.

126. For a discussion of Guibert's *Gesta* in the context of other chronicles of the First Crusade, see Daniel, *Arabs*, 120–26. For a recent treatment of Guibert's depiction of Muslims, see Tolan, *Saracens*, esp. 135–47. For consideration of the *Gesta* in the context of Guibert's larger career, see Rubenstein, *Guibert of Nogent*, esp. 95–101.

127. Guibert, *Gesta*, 130; 692: "Hujus nefariae institutionis obscuritas Christianum tunc nomen obtexit; et adhuc per Orientis pene universi, Affricae, AEgypti, AEthyopiae, Libiae, et juxta nos Hispaniae remotissimos sinus obliterat."

128. As Southern suggests, Western writers in the early twelfth century "had a few facts" about Muhammad's life "derived ultimately from Byzantine writers" (*Western Views*, 29); these included "his marriage to a rich widow, his fits, his Christian background, and his plan of general sexual license as an instrument for the destruction of Christendom" (29–30). Southern sees Guibert's account as typical of "the picture of Mahomet and his followers which became current in northern Europe in the first half of the twelfth century" (ibid., 29–30 n. 26; and see 31). For further discussion of the (mis)representation of

Muhammad's life by chroniclers like Guibert, see Daniel, *Arabs*, 235–40, and Tolan, *Saracens*, esp. 135–69.

129. Guibert, *Gesta*, 129; 690: "eversis obtutibus, facie tabida, labiis spumantibus, dentium ejus stridoribus ipsa terreri." For the association of the marriage bed and Muhammad's epilepsy, see ibid., 128; 690: "At quum saepius utrorumque commercia lecti unius urna susciperet, propheta coepit egregius morbo epilensiae, quem caducum vulgo dicimus" [But since more often the vessel of one bed received their mutual intercourse, that extraordinary prophet began to suffer from the disease of epilepsy, which we commonly call falling sickness].

130. Ibid., 129; 691: "quotienscumque prophetarum Deus inlabitur mentibus, tota corporis humani massa concutitur, quia ferre non praevalet carnis infirmitas, quum ei se applicat divina majestas."

131. Ibid., 129; 691: "totum jam non modo tolerabile, sed etiam sacrosanctum et spectabile arbitratur quicquid prius foedum ac despicabile putabatur."

132. See the discussion of Western representations of Muhammad's death in Daniel, *Islam*, 125–29, and Tolan, *Saracens*, 142–43. On visual representations of (a monstrous) Muhammad's death, see Strickland, *Saracens, Demons, and Jews*, 190–91. Southern notes that the account of "Mahomet's death and destruction by pigs during one of his fits" is "a hateful elaboration of some details in the Byzantine tradition" (*Western Views*, 31).

133. On the significance of pigs in medieval interreligious polemics, see Fabre-Vassas, *Singular Beast,* and Enders, "Homicidal Pigs."

134. Guibert here alludes to the conclusion of Horace's *Epistles* I.iv; later in the passage (in a section I do not quote), he also cites Horace's *Odes* III.30.

135. Rubenstein reads a significant change in Guibert's tone here: "Guibert thus gives an alternate, almost credible, account of Islam....At the very least, this passage points to an ability, if not a habit of mind, to think about alien groups on two levels—a literary level and a realistic, critical level" (*Guibert of Nogent*, 122). But clearly any such change is momentary; by the end of the passage, Guibert is again strongly mocking Muslim belief and practice.

136. Guibert, *Gesta*, 130; 692–93: "Sed hunc tantum tamque mirificum legislatorem quis exitus de medio tulerit, dicendum est. Quum subitaneo ictu epylenseos saepe corruerat, quo eum diximus superius laborare, accidit semel, dum solus obambulat, ut morbo elisus eodem caderet; et inventus, dum ipsa passione torquetur, a porcis in tantum discerpitur, ut nullae ejus praeter talos reliquiae invenirentur. Ecce legifer optimus, dum Epicureum, quem veri Stoici, Christi scilicet cultores, occiderant, porcum resuscitare molitur, immo prorsus resuscitat, porcus ipse porcis devorandus exponitur: ut obscoenitatis magisterium obscoenissimo, uti convenit, fine concludat. Talos jure reliquit, quia perfidiae ac turpitudinis vestigia deceptis miserabiliter animabus infixit.... Quod si Manichaeorum sunt vera repurgia sectae, ut in omni quod comeditur pars quaedam maneat commaculata Dei, et dentium comminutione, et stomachi concoctione pars ipsa Dei purgetur, et purgata jam in angelos convertatur, qui ructibus et ventositate extra nos prodire dicantur: sues de hujus carnibus pastas quot credimus angelos effecisse et magnis hinc inde flatibus emisisse? Sed omissis jocularibus quae pro sequacium derisione dicuntur, hoc est insinuandum: quod non eum Deum, ut aliqui aestimant, opinantur; sed hominem justum eumdemque patronum, per quem leges divinae tradantur. Hunc coelitus assumptum astruunt; et solos talos relictos ad suorum fidelium monimentum, quos etiam infinita veneratione revisunt: porcorum vero esum, justa prorsus ratione, contemnunt, qui morsibus eorum dominum consumpserunt."

137. See the section headings in the *PL* text of Guibert's *Gesta* (689, 687); these do not appear in the *Recueil* text, but they do accurately describe the contents of that text (125–27).

138. Guibert, *Gesta*, 128; 689–90.

139. On the letter, see Boswell, *Christianity*, 279 n. 33. The Greek version translated by Boswell (367–69) differs significantly from the Latin version presented by Guibert, who in fact notes that, rather than insert the letter itself, he will offer some of what it says, "clothed in my words" [verbis . . . vestita meis] (*Gesta*, 131; 693). See Daniel's comment that "[d]ifferent versions of the *Letter of the Emperor of Constantinople* are variations on a pornographic theme" (*Arabs*, 126).

140. "Mathomarias" is a variant form of "Mahomeria, Machomeria, Mahummaria," all attested in du Cange, *Glossarium*, and glossed as "templum Mahometicum"; see the entry "Mahum."

141. The Latin "commercia" here is the same word Guibert uses, a few pages earlier, to describe the "commerce" of Muhammad's marriage bed; see n. 129 above.

142. Guibert, *Gesta*, 131–32; 693–94: "'De ecclesiis querimonia est, quas siquidem Gentilitas eversa Christianitate tenebat, in quibus equorum ac mulorum ceterorumque animalium catabula construebat. Quod in tantum verum fuit, ut etiam fana sua, quae Mathomarias vocant, inibi instituerent, et infinitae turpitudinis commercia exercerent, ut non jam basilicae, sed meritoria et scenae fierent. Porro de catholicorum necibus frustra agerem, quum mortuis in fide vitae aeternalis videretur instare concambium; superstites sub miseri jugo famulatus vitam gererent, ipsis, ut arbitror, mortibus acriorem. Virgines enim fidelium deprehensae publicum fieri praecipiebantur scortum, quum nusquam pudori deferretur ac honestati conjugum. Matres correptae in conspectu filiarum, multipliciter repetitis diversorum coitibus vexabantur, quum filiae assistentes carmina praecinere saltando nefaria inter hujusmodi cogerentur. Eadem statim passio, quod dici quidem et dolor et pudor est, revolvebatur ad filias, quae etiam foeditas obscenis infelicium matrum cantionibus ornabatur. Totius denique nominis reverentia Christiani prostibulo tradebatur. Quumque sexui femineo non parcitur, quod tamen excusari poterit pro competenti natura, in masculinum, pecualitate transgressa, solutis humanitatum legibus, itur.' — Unde, ut unius execranda et penitus intolerabili auribus majestate flagitii illa, quae in mediocres et infimos defurebat, petulantia panderetur, dicit quemdam eos abusione Sodomitica interemisse episcopum. — 'Et quomodo praeceps et omnibus omnino vesaniis praeferenda libido, quae semper consilii frontisque fugax perpetuo impetu agitur, et quo crebrius extinguitur eo vivaciori flamma iterato succenditur, erga humana se temperet, quae brutorum animalium inauditis et ori Christiano vetitis commixtionibus sordet? Et quum sit miseris permissa suo ipsorum arbitrio multiplicitas feminarum, parum est apud eos nisi et dignitas tantae spurcitiae volutabro commaculetur marium. Nec mirum si Deus exoletam eorum nequitiam et in clamorem versam impatienter tulerit, tantaque funestorum habitatorum execramenta, more antiquo, terra vomuerit.'" I have consulted Boswell's translation of the last two sentences of this passage (*Christianity*, 280). He renders the final sentence, "Nor is it surprising that God has impatiently borne their ancient evil and the cry against it and that the land has vomited forth such execrations from its dead inhabitants," noting, "[t]he Latin is unusual" (ibid., 280 n. 37). Levine translates: "It is not surprising that God could not tolerate their ripe wantoness [*sic*], and turned it into grief, and the earth, in its ancient way, cast out the excrement of such destructive inhabitants" (Guibert, *Deeds of God*, 37).

143. I cite here a heading from the *PL* edition—"Quam perversa imperatoris mens" (695)—not in the *Recueil* text; see *Recueil*, 133.

144. Guibert, *Gesta*, 133; 695: "quia, edicto celebri, de pluribus universorum filiabus unam per omne imperium suum prostitui juberet, et fisco proprio lucrum foedissimae passionis inferret. Nec minus illud, quod de pluribus filiis unum eunuchizari, data praecepti auctoritate, mandaverit."

145. Ibid., 133; 695–96: "et corpora marium ademptis virilibus enervia ac effeminata reddiderit, quae usibus militiae jam non habeantur utilia; immo ad detrimenti cumulum, abscidatur in ipsis propago futura, cujus incrementis sperari valerent contra hostes auxilia."

146. Ibid., 124; 685: "Honores amplissimi, castellorum et urbium dominia spernebantur; uxores pulcherrimae quasi quiddam tabidum vilescebant; omni gemma gratiores quondam promiscui sexus pignorum fastidiebantur aspectus."

147. For more on Guibert's belief that "the crusade cleansed knighthood of its impurities" (222), see Duby, *Three Orders*.

148. For a recent treatment of the affect of disgust, see Menninghaus, *Disgust*.

149. I have consulted both the *PL* text of Guibert, *De pignoribus sanctorum*, and the Corpus Christianorum edition, *De sanctis et eorum pigneribus*. For a recent, full discussion of the text, see Rubenstein, *Guibert of Nogent*, 124–30, 138–52, 158–72.

150. Ibid., esp. Chapter 6.

151. Kimḥi, *Book of the Covenant*, 36–37.

152. Guibert, *Tractatus*, 496: "Quare zelo vehementi non efferar, cum videam, eos qui conjugia pulcherrima et honesta deserunt, et anus etiam sub maritis agentes, jamque rugosissimas assectantur." Compare Guibert, *Self and Society* 3.16; 210–11; *Autobiographie*, 426.

153. Abulafia, "Theology," 30, 34–35; Guibert, *Tractatus*, 513: "furta, et foenora" (also see 506, 524).

154. Ibid., 499: "putidissime et nequam."

155. Ibid., 492: "Nullus, inquiunt, nisi qui desipiat, credit Deum ad uteri feminei sese demittere voluisse vilitatem."

156. Ibid.

157. Ibid., 499: "Dei Filius in carnem veniens, si competentia corpori membra habuit, membrorum compositio non nocuit. Frustraque non pudeat quod ipsum non puduit. Et quid eum puderet, ubi nihil non sanctum fuit! Si quidquid est, bonum est, nisi ubi peccatum est, membra quae per se bona sunt, cum peccatum non est, sancta sunt. Membra nostra imbecillitati nostrae sunt administratoria, etcum aures, ora vel nares superfluis capitum egerendis inserviunt, caetera quid mali faciunt, quae inferius intestinorum pondus exponunt?"

158. Ibid.: "si spuerit, si nares emunxerit, si pituitas oculorum vel aurium digitis hauserit."

159. Ibid.: "intellige quia qua honestate superiora haec fecerit, et residua, peregerit. Aut dic mihi, ille tuus, qui Abrahae apparuit Deus, ea quae comedit in quem alium [*f.* alvum] deposuit? quomodo etiam, aut si factum est, quod consequens fuit? Contremisco dum de his disputo; sed vos, filii diaboli, me cogitis. Deus a vobis exigat, qui novit, quo affectu id ago. Breviter accipite Deum humiliter omnia hominis suscepisse, et nihil hominis veritum praeter peccata fuisse."

160. Albert of Aix, *Historia Hierosolymitana* 1.26, 292: "Unde, nescio si vel Dei judicio aut aliquo animi errore, spiritu crudelitatis adversus Judaeorum surrexerunt populum, per quascumque civitates dispersos, et crudelissimam in eos exercuerunt necem, et praecipue in regno Lotharingiae, asserentes id esse principium expeditionis suae et obsequii contra hostes fidei christianae. Haec strages Judaeorum primum in civitate Coloniensi a civibus acta est: qui subito irruentes in modicam manum illorum, plurimos gravi vulnere detruncaverunt; domos et synagogas eorum subverterunt, plurimum pecuniae illorum inter se dividentes."

161. For pertinent bibliography, see n. 52 above.

162. *Chronicle of Rabbi Eliezer bar Nathan*, in Eidelberg, *Jews and the Crusaders*, 86–87.

163. Eidelberg, *Jews and the Crusaders*, 32–33.

164. Guibert, *Tractatus*, 499.

165. The Hebrew used to describe the Jewish martyrdom is "kiddush ha-Shem" [sanctification of the Name].

166. Albert of Aix, *Historia Hierosolymitana* 1.27, 293: "Judaei vero, videntes Christianos hostes in se suosque parvulos insurgere, et nulli aetati parcere, ipsi quoque in se suosque confratres, natosque, mulieres, matres et sorores irruerunt, et mutua caede se peremerunt. Matres pueris lactentibus, quod dictu nefas est, guttura ferro secabant, alios transforabant, volentes potius sic propriis manibus perire, quam incircumcisorum armis exstingui."

167. *Chronicle of Solomon bar Simson*, in Eidelberg, *Jews and the Crusaders*, 68.

168. See the quotation at n. 166 above.

169. See Cohen, "Jews as the Killers."

170. Yuval's essay, "Vengeance and Damnation," prompted critical essays in *Zion*, n.s., 59 (1994), to which Yuval responded, in the same volume. Several of the essays in *Jews and Christians in Twelfth-Century Europe* build on and respond to Yuval's work.

171. Wolfson, "Martyrdom, Eroticism, and Asceticism."

172. Marcus, "Dynamics," identifies "two opposite trends in Jewish-Christian social relations" during this period: "One trend was an increase in the possibilities for individuals to make new choices among different religious groups. Such a choice might also include crossing over the boundary to join the other religious culture as a convert. The other trend, which occurred at the same time, and in some ways was stimulated by the dangers perceived in the first, involved an upsurge of each religious culture's sense of group solidarity and identity. This included an increased hostility toward members of the other camp" (32).

3. Becoming Christian?

1. On medieval ideas of the sexed and gendered body, see Cadden, *Meanings*, and Jacquart and Thomasset, *Sexuality and Medicine*. On medieval ideas of body and racial difference, see Friedman, *Monstrous Races*.

2. On whether "race" might be a useful category of analysis in premodern contexts, see "Race and Ethnicity in the Middle Ages," esp. the essays by Hahn ("Difference"), Bartlett ("Medieval and Modern"), and Jordan ("Why 'Race'?").

3. See, for instance, Spelman, *Inessential Woman;* Butler, *Bodies;* Stoler, *Race and the Education;* and Pellegrini, *Performance Anxieties*. For medievalist essays that take feminist and queer inquiry in a variety of directions, see *Queering the Middle Ages*.

4. For the most part, in the discussion in this chapter, I bracket the category of class, highlighting instead the interactions of gender, sexuality, religion, and (quasi) race. Certainly, however, the anomalous class position of Jews—as *servi* or serfs to the aristocracy, but also as, from the viewpoint of the Christian peasantry, economically privileged—is significant in shaping Jewish-Christian interactions. I take up questions linked to class position more explicitly in chapter 4 below.

5. Butler, *Bodies*, 168.

6. In my discussion, I use the terms (quasi) race, (quasi-)racial, etc., to indicate medieval constructions similar but not identical to modern, Western ideas of race.

7. Moore, *Formation*, 99. See also Boswell, *Christianity;* Richards, *Sex, Dissidence and Damnation;* and Cohen, *Living Letters*.

8. Lorde, *Zami*, 72–80.

9. For fuller analysis, see Kruger, *AIDS Narratives*, esp. 45–59, and Harper, *Are We Not Men?* 3–38, esp. 22–38.

10. As Sedgwick, *Epistemology*, 43, notes, however, with changes in biomedical technology, the notion that the biological is the essential and hence unchangeable is currently subject to a strong challenge.

11. For one treatment of Michael Jackson as a Black American cultural phenomenon, see Harper, *Are We Not Men?* 74–99, esp. 88–94.

12. See Sells, *Bridge Betrayed*.

13. On the sex/gender system, see the particularly influential treatment of Gayle Rubin, "Traffic in Women." On the (anti)essentialist movements of feminist thought, see Spelman, *Inessential Woman*, and Fuss, *Essentially Speaking*.

14. See especially Butler, *Gender Trouble* and *Bodies*.

15. Again see Butler's work, as well as Sedgwick's treatment of social construction (*Epistemology*, 40–44).

16. See especially the work of Fausto-Sterling, *Sexing the Body*.

17. See, for a variety of perspectives, Bornstein, *Gender Outlaw;* Feinberg, *Transgender Warriors;* Prosser, *Second Skins;* and Halberstam, *Female Masculinity*.

18. Sedgwick, *Epistemology*, esp. the "axiomatic" introduction and Chapter 1.

19. For the original reports of research findings, see LeVay, "Difference," and Hamer et al., "Linkage." For popularizing accounts of the science involved in these reports, see LeVay, *Sexual Brain*, and Hamer and Copeland, *Science of Desire*.

20. Such a "cure" is indeed called "reparative" or "conversion therapy" and is often explicitly linked with Christian religious indoctrination. See, for instance, the Exodus International Web site, http://www.exodus-international.org.

21. See, for just one instance, the marriage announcement of Janis Ian and Patricia Snyder, which notes that "Ms. Ian . . . divorced her husband in 1986" and then, in the following paragraph, that "she has known she was gay since the age of 9" (Campbell, "Weddings/Celebrations").

22. Thus, erotic/pornographic Internet stories and Web sites emphasizing such a straight-to-gay sexual conversion have proliferated; see, for instance, the large collection of stories in the "Nifty Erotic Stories Archive," http://www.nifty.org/nifty/index.html. Bisexuality—a category that touches simultaneously both the hetero- and homosexual—would seem in some ways an answer to fantasies of sexual conversion: it is not that one changes sexuality but that the bisexual potential is present in the individual all along. But discourses of bisexuality themselves also sometimes depend upon ideas of conversion—the discovery within of new, unexpected resources of sexual identity. On the complex, fiercely contested ground of bisexuality, see the essays collected in *Bisexuality*.

23. See Cadden, *Meanings*, and Jacquart and Thomasset, *Sexuality and Medicine*.

24. See Laqueur, *Making Sex*, esp. 7, 18–19, 123–30, 136. For one important consideration of the one-sex model in a medieval context, see Clover, "Regardless of Sex." For a wide-ranging treatment of metamorphosis in medieval culture, see Bynum, *Metamorphosis*.

25. See Bynum (*Jesus as Mother*; "'. . . And Woman His Humanity'"; *Holy Feast*; and *Fragmentation*) for an important body of work on the gendered complexities of medieval Christian thought and practice.

26. On the paradox of a "natural" "vitium contra naturam" [sin against nature], see Boswell, *Christianity*, esp. chapter 11, as well as Jordan, "Homosexuality"; Cadden, "Sciences/Silences"; and Jordan, *Invention*, 67–91, 94–99, 110–11, 126–27, 143–47.

27. Damian, *Opusculum septimum: Liber Gomorrhianus*, 161: "Heu! pudet dicere, pudet tam turpe flagitium sacris auribus intimare; sed si medicus horret virus plagarum, quis curabit adhibere cauterium? Si is, qui curaturus est, nauseat, quis ad incolumitatis statum pectora aegrota reducat? Vitium igitur contra naturam velut cancer ita serpit, ut sacrorum hominum ordinem attingat." Though I here provide my own translation, published translations are available: Damian, *Book of Gomorrah*, and Letter 31, in *Letters 31–60*.

28. Damian, *Liber Gomorrhianus*, 161: "Et nisi quantocius sedis apostolicae vigor occurrat, non est dubium, quin effrenata nequitia cum restringi voluerit, a cursus sui impetu desistere nequeat."

29. For some examples, see Friedman, *Monstrous Races*; Mellinkoff, *Outcasts*; and Strickland, *Saracens, Demons, and Jews*. For an important body of work on the medieval uses of monstrosity, see *Monster Theory* and Cohen, *Of Giants*.

30. Friedman, *Monstrous Races*, 65.

31. Ibid., 72–73.

32. See, for just one instance, Baron, *Social and Religious History*, 4:92.

33. Alfonsi, *Diálogo*, 60: "Quod si inipso tempore, quo peccatum est a vobis commissum, totam Iudaicam progeniem funditus delevisset, multis temporum transactis curriculis culpa oblivione deleta a nullo mortalium sciretur, sicque et infamiae obprobrium et

malorum evitaretis periculum, sicut et de multis contigit gentibus et regibus, quorum gesta temporum sunt vetustate deleta. Est et alia causa, propter quam deus Iudaicam noluit perdere gentem. Videbat enim quosdam de vestro semine quandoque in se credituros atque salvandos et ideo propter eos noluit omnino vestram disperdere styrpem"; my translation. The text is also available in the *PL*: Alfonsi, *Dialogi*, 575.

34. For important recent work on medieval Christianity and conversion, see Morrison, *Understanding Conversion* and *Conversion and Text*.

35. See, for instance, the association of old age with a repudiation of immoral behavior in such vernacular works as *The Parlement of the Thre Ages* and Langland's *Piers Plowman*, and the parody of such a movement in Chaucer's *Merchant's Tale*.

36. On Abelard and Guibert, see chapter 2 above, and the bibliography provided there. See Kempe, *Book*; Julian, *Book*.

37. On Paul and his conversion, see Boyarin, *Radical Jew*, and Segal, *Paul the Convert*.

38. Acts 9:1–9, 17–20: "Saulus autem adhuc inspirans minarum et caedis in discipulos Domini accessit ad principem sacerdotum / et petiit ab eo epistulas in Damascum ad synagogas ut si quos invenisset huius viae viros ac mulieres vinctos perduceret in Hierusalem / et cum iter faceret contigit ut adpropinquaret Damasco et subito circumfulsit eum lux de caelo / et cadens in terram audivit vocem dicentem sibi Saule Saule quid me persequeris / qui dixit quis es Domine et ille ego sum Iesus quem tu persequeris / sed surge et ingredere civitatem et dicetur tibi quid te oporteat facere viri autem illi qui comitabantur cum eo stabant stupefacti audientes quidem vocem neminem autem videntes / surrexit autem Saulus de terra apertisque oculis nihil videbat ad manus autem illum trahentes introduxerunt Damascum / et erat tribus diebus non videns et non manducavit neque bibit . . . et abiit Ananias et introivit in domum et inponens ei manus dixit Saule frater Dominus misit me Iesus qui apparuit tibi in via qua veniebas ut videas et implearis Spiritu Sancto / et confestim ceciderunt ab oculis eius tamquam squamae et visum recepit et surgens baptizatus est / et cum accepisset cibum confortatus est fuit autem cum discipulis qui erant Damasci per dies aliquot / et continuo in synagogis praedicabat Iesum quoniam hic est Filius Dei." The conversion account is retold by Paul, with differences, at Acts 22 and 26.

39. Bodleian Library, Lat. liturg. e.39, in which the illustration appears, is the Breviary of Chertsey Abbey; the manuscript dates to the first quarter of the fourteenth century, 1307 or later. The illustration appropriately introduces the text for the Feast of the Conversion of St. Paul (25 January). A color version is available on the Bodleian Library Web site: http://www.bodley.ox.ac.uk/dept/scwmss/wmss/medieval/jpegs/lat/liturg/e/1500/ 03900806.jpg. The horse, which appears in this and other medieval and early modern illustrations of the conversion, is an addition to the biblical account. Many other artistic treatments of the theme survive. Most famous is Caravaggio's "Conversion on the Way to Damascus" (1600), but there are also many earlier examples. See, for instance, the St. Paul Window at Chartres Cathedral; the sketch of a lost twelfth-century illumination from a volume commissioned by Herrad of Landsberg (reproduced as Figure 1 in Morrison, *Understanding Conversion*, viii) and the thirteenth-century illumination from Princeton University Library, Garrett 39, fol. 266v (Figure 2, Morrison, *Understanding Conversion*, 12); the Northern Italian illuminated leaf on vellum, ca. 1270, in the Ellin Mitchell Gallery, reproduced

on the Humanities Interactive Web site, http://www.humanities-interactive.org/medieval/
songglory/exo71_13e.html; and the several thirteenth-, fourteenth-, and fifteenth-century
examples found at the Biblical Art on the WWW Web site, http://www.biblical-art.com/
index.htm.

40. On the implication of horses in medieval identity constructions, see Kolve,
Chaucer and the Imagery, 236–62, and Cohen, *Medieval Identity Machines*, 35–77.

41. Quoted in Moore, *Origins*, 126.

42. See Southern's discussion of the beguines of Cologne, *Western Society*, 319–31.
For an overview of the literature on "the swelling numbers of women attracted to both ortho-
dox and heterodox movements in the twelfth to the fourteenth centuries," see Bynum,
Jesus as Mother, 182–83 n. 33. For a fine recent treatment of the beguine movement, see
Simons, *Cities of Ladies*.

43. Kempe, *Book*, trans. Windeatt, 153, 168; also see 172; ed. Meech and Allen: "'for
I trowe þow art comyn hedyr to han a-wey owr wyuys fro us & ledyn hem wyth þe'" (I.48,
116); "women cam rennyng owt of her howsys with her rokkys, crying to þe pepil, 'Bren-
nyth þis fals heretyk,'" "'forsake þis lyfe þat þu hast, & go spynne & carde as oþer women
don'" (I.53, 129; also see I.54, 133).

44. For a few Middle English examples of the conflation of Judaism and Islam, see
the Towneley Herod play, where Herod is described as "the heynd kyng . . . of Jury" "By
grace of Mahowne" (*Towneley Plays*, 16.14–16); the Croxton *Play of the Sacrament*, where
the Jewish merchant Jonathas invokes "almighty Machomet" (149); Dunbar's "Fenyeit
Freir of Tungland," *Poems*, where a "Turk of Tartary" (line 5) is described also as a "jow"
(line 31). For the conflation of Jews and Muslims in a very different (legal) context, see
Oldradus de Ponte, *Jews and Saracens*, esp. 21–22. For bibliography on the depiction of
Islam as a Christian "heresy," see chapter 2, n. 21, above. For a particularly rich and suggestive discussion of accusations against Jews that linked them to Muslims, to heretics,
and to lepers, see the first two chapters in Ginzburg, *Ecstasies*.

45. For one example specifically addressed to Jews, see the Fourth Lateran Council,
in Grayzel, *Church*, 310–11. The earlier Council of Montpellier (1195) legislates against
both "Judei" and "Saraceni" [Jews and Saracens] exercising power over Christians; ibid.,
298–99.

46. Mirrer, "Representing 'Other' Men," 173. Baron observes that, in a later period
in Spanish literature, Cervantes spoke of the Jews "as the *gente afeminada*" (*Social and Religious History*, 11:54); that "With many Spanish authors the diminutive, *judihuelo*, stood for
both a little Jewish boy and a coward" (ibid.); and that "In his *Reprobación del amor mun-
dano o Carbacho*, written in 1438, Alphonso Martínez de Toledo, 'archpriest' of Talavera, on
several occasions uses the term *judio* as a synonym for *coward or cowardly*, placing Jews on
a par with women and priests" (ibid., 11:341–42 n. 3).

47. Polo, *Travels*, 306.

48. See Baron, *Social and Religious History*, 11:154, 11:342 n. 3, and Cohen, *Under
Crescent*, 35, 47. Baron notes that "The popular mind saw no conflict between . . . allegations
of Jewish proneness to violence and the growingly accepted view that Jews were effeminate and cowardly, a view which doubtless gained in currency with the spreading prohibitions for Jews to bear arms. Even in Spain, where Jews often continued to conduct them-

selves as *hidalgos*, denigration of Jewish courage was even applied to the sixteenth-century *conversos*" (*Social and Religious History*, 11:154). One might in fact argue that the very idea of a Jewish "proneness to violence," and of a strong Muslim military threat to Europe, necessitated emasculating depictions of Jewish and Muslim men. For an examination of how, in a very different context, male bodies are constructed as simultaneously threatening and debilitated, see Kruger, *AIDS Narratives*, Chapter 2.

49. Shapiro, *Shakespeare and the Jews*, has recently examined the significance of circumcision, including the affiliations of circumcision with emasculation, in Elizabethan culture; see esp. 113–30.

50. Cohen, *Under Crescent*, 35.

51. Quoted in Brundage, *Law, Sex*, 66. Certain traditions within Judaism explain circumcision in a similar way; see, most notably, Maimonides, *Guide for the Perplexed* III.49, 378: "As regards circumcision, I think that one of its objects is to limit sexual intercourse, and to weaken the organ of generation as far as possible, and thus cause man to be moderate." Boyarin, "'This We Know,'" notes this passage (486–87 n. 37), comparing Maimonides' position to a similar reading of circumcision in Philo (485–87). He points out as well that the traditional circumcision ceremony involves addressing the circumcised boy with the second-person *feminine* pronoun (496): as Boyarin suggests, "circumcision is understood . . . as feminizing the male" (495; and see the more extensive discussion, 494–97).

52. On the importance of eunuchry for the realignment of ideas about masculinity in late antique Christianity, see Kuefler, *Manly Eunuch*.

53. For a brief overview of the "extremely important function" of eunuchs "in the Byzantine state" (16), see Bullough, "Formation," 16–17.

54. See above, chapter 2, at nn. 145–46.

55. See the spurious letter of the Greek emperor Alexius Comnenus to Count Robert of Flanders, translated in Boswell, *Christianity*, 367–68. Also see Guibert, *Gesta*, 131–32; 693–94; discussed in chapter 2 above. The idea that Muslims forcibly circumcised "Christian boys and youths," expressed here, might be seen as related to the persistent Christian questioning of the legality of forced baptism; at least some canonists argued that Christians might indeed take Jewish children from their parents and make them Christian. See Dahan, *Intellectuels chrétiens*, 143–52, esp. 149–52.

56. Biberman, *Masculinity, Anti-Semitism*, has recently argued that it is not until the Renaissance that ideas of the effeminacy of Jewishness develop, and that before the elaboration of the idea of the "Jew-sissy" the dominant Christian construction of the Jew is as hypermasculine and violent—the "Jew-devil." But the medieval evidence seems to me to suggest an effeminizing of Jewishness simultaneous with, indeed mutually constitutive of, a sense of uncontrolled Jewish violence.

57. Quoted in Trachtenberg, *Devil and the Jews*, 149.

58. Abelard, *Dialogue*, 47. A similar idea persists into the Renaissance and is expressed, for instance, by Thomas Browne, who argues in *Pseudodoxia Epidemica* that "Jewish women 'desire copulation' with Christians 'rather than [with men of] their own nation, and affect Christian carnality above circumcised venery'" (quoted in Shapiro, *Shakespeare and the Jews*, 37).

59. See Caesarius, *Dialogue*, 1:102. Jewish male bodily deficiency here provides the opportunity for a Jewish woman to escape the watchful eye of her father and have sex with a Christian clerk since, "on the night of the Friday before your Easter... the Jews are said to labour under a sickness called the bloody flux, with which they are so much occupied, that they can scarcely pay attention to anything else at that time." Gilman, *Jewish Self-Hatred*, identifies Thomas of Cantimpré (thirteenth century) as the first to present a "'scientific' statement of the phenomenon" of Jewish male menstruation (74). On belief in this phenomenon, see also Trachtenberg, *Devil and the Jews*, 50, 149, 228 n. 27 (Trachtenberg discusses the more general belief that Jews suffered diseases of bleeding [50–51], and he places that belief in relation to the blood accusations made against Jews [140–55]); Poliakov, *Histoire*, 160; Baron, *Social and Religious History*, 11:153–54; Shapiro, *Shakespeare and the Jews*, 37–38, 241–42 n. 116; Katz, "Shylock's Gender"; Resnick, "Medieval Roots." Shapiro also notes, in Renaissance writers, the idea that "Jewish men were sometimes capable of breast-feeding": "Samuel Purchas writes that 'if you believe their *Gemara* (can you choose?), a poor Jew having buried his wife and not able to hire a nurse for his child had his own breasts miraculously filled with milk, and became nurse himself.' Purchas also cites a Midrashic tradition regarding the Book of Esther that the orphaned Esther had been breast-fed by Mordechai" (*Shakespeare and the Jews*, 38). Johnson argues that the "bloody flux" of the earlier medieval texts refers to an anal bleeding "exegetically linked to Jewish deicidal bloodguilt," and that the trope is not "gendered" until the 1494 Tyrnau accusations ("Myth," 273). But while Johnson's argument is in many ways compelling, it seems to me that in a text like Caesarius's the bloody flux indeed undermines the Jewish man's masculinity (e.g., by making the father neglect his paternal duties); while not explicitly described as feminine, it still serves a gendered, feminizing function.

60. The problem that the circumcision of Christ's own body posed in relation to denigrations of the circumcised bodies of medieval Jews—an association of Christ's perfect body with the debased, "feminized" bodies of Jews—was partly solved by depictions that made the circumcision a prefiguration of the crucifixion, one more Jewish attack on Christ's divinized humanity, and an attack thus affiliated with Christ's salvific submission to violence. For one depiction of Christ's circumcision as Jewish attack, see Mellinkoff, *Outcasts*, Plate II.23, and the discussion at 1:43 and 1:106–7.

61. Shapiro, *Shakespeare and the Jews*, 102. Shapiro discusses both medieval and early modern instances (100–111). As he notes, "the one feature of the myth of ritual murder most peculiar to English versions (it was nowhere near as central to accusations made elsewhere in Europe) was that Jews circumcised their young male victims" (111).

62. Lipman, *Jews of Medieval Norwich*, 59–62.

63. Tovey, *Anglia Judaica*, 65–66; emphasis in original. As Tovey points out, "*Bonefand* pleaded *not guilty*, and was very honourably acquitted" (65; emphasis in original). Tovey dates the accusation to the fourth year of the reign of King John (1199–1216).

64. Baron, *Social and Religious History*, 11:85–86. Also see Simonsohn, *Apostolic See*, 1:334–35. For more on the regulation of Christian public space vis-à-vis Jews, see Jordan, "Problems."

65. Moore, *Formation*, 97; also see 38–39.

66. See Baron, *Social and Religious History*, 11:86. A direct connection between Jewish "usury" and female prostitution was made in the Renaissance (see Shapiro, *Shakespeare and the Jews*, 99–100 and 256 n. 38).

67. Paris, *Chronicles*, 95. The association of circumcision and debasement of currency persisted at least until the eighteenth century: "In brave Edward's days they (the Jews) were caught in a gin, / For clipping our coin, now to add sin to sin, / As they've got all our pelf, they'd be clipping our skin. / Those foes to the pork of old England" (quoted in Shapiro, *Shakespeare and the Jews*, 210). Note further the association, in Langland's *Piers Plowman*, of a debased coin, the "Loscheborw" (17.72, 17.82, 17.168), with "leccherye and oþer lustes of synne" (17.79) and with a Muhammad whom Langland depicts as a Christian "heretic": "Me fynde wel þat Macometh was a man ycristened / And a cardinal of court, a gret clerk withalle, / And pursuede to haue be pope, prince of holy chirche. / Ac for he was lyk a Lossheborw y leue oure lord hym lette" (17.165–68).

68. Paris, *Chronicles*, 215.

69. Caesarius, *Dialogue*, 1:106.

70. Work on medieval Jewish women's lives and their representation in both mainstream Jewish and Christian traditions is still at a relatively early stage. See Alvarez Perez, "Martyrs and Moneylenders," for one extensive treatment of how we might recover access to medieval Jewish women's experiences, and for further bibliography.

71. Chaucer, *Riverside Chaucer* II.359–62. The other non-Christian mother-in-law of the tale, Donegild, is similarly "mannysh" (II.782). On the medieval Semiramis—a female usurper of properly male authority—see Samuel, "Semiramis," and Parr, "Chaucer's Semiramis."

72. See, for instance, Adler, *Jews of Medieval England*, 17–42.

73. Boccaccio, *Decameron*, 169–91; quotation at 170.

74. Ibid., 191.

75. Caesarius, *Dialogue*, 1:102, 104–5.

76. Ibid., 1:104.

77. Ibid., 1:107; compare 1:109.

78. Ibid., 1:107. Also see Shapiro's suggestion that, in the Renaissance, "conversion is not quite the same for Jewish women as it is for Jewish men": "In the world of fiction, the marriage and conversion of Jewish women usually go hand in hand. . . . In contrast, Jewish men who convert to Christianity are never married off to Christian women. And where Jewish women are always depicted as young and desirable, male Jewish converts are invariably old and impotent, condemned to remain unwed and at the periphery of the Christian community. . . . To early modern Englishmen, the fantasy of Christian men marrying converting Jewesses was far more appealing than the idea of Jewish men, even converted ones, marrying Christian women" (*Shakespeare and the Jews*, 132).

79. On literary accusations of sodomy, see Burgwinkle, *Sodomy*. On the history of sodomy as a theological category, see Jordan, *Invention*. An important new project on sodomy is Scanlon's *At Sodom's Gate*.

80. Boswell, *Christianity*, 381–89, at 386.

81. *Gíslasaga*, 3–4.

82. On the *Roman d'Eneas*, see Gaunt, "From Epic to Romance," and Burgwinkle, "Knighting."

83. Ellis, *Studies*, 35–36.

84. Marie, *Lais*, 112 (lines 280–82); the accusation scene spans lines 259–302.

85. Ibid., 113 (lines 284–85).

86. Ibid. (line 283).

87. Schibanoff, "Chaucer's Lesbians," 12. Also see Lemay, "Human Sexuality," 196, and the more recent discussion of the complex medieval discourses circulating around the clitoris in Lochrie, *Heterosyncrasies*. For wide-ranging consideration of medieval female same-sex desire, see *Same Sex Love and Desire among Women in the Middle Ages*.

88. See Boswell, *Christianity*, 138–43, 305, 316–18, 356–58; Strickland, *Saracens, Demons, and Jews*, 147–48, 153–54.

89. See the discussion in chapter 2 above.

90. For a fuller discussion, see Kruger, "Bodies."

91. See Trachtenberg, *Devil and the Jews*, 50–52.

92. See Langmuir, *Toward a Definition*, 246–47.

93. Rubin, *Gentile Tales*, 45.

94. Paris, *Chronicles*, 214–15.

95. On the linkage of "sodomy" and "heresy," see Boswell, *Christianity*, 283–86, and on the bodily corruptions associated with homosexuality, 210–13, 359–63, 375–78.

96. Boswell, *Christianity*: on Chrysostom, 359–63; Cantor, 375–78; Damian, 210–13.

97. See Ginzburg, *Ecstasies*, 33–62, and Nirenberg, *Communities*, Chapters 2–4, for discussion of the events of 1320–21.

98. Damian, *Liber Gomorrhianus*, 162: "egregias civitates."

99. Boswell suggests in a (perhaps too sweeping) formulation that "the fate of Jews and gay people has been almost identical throughout European history, from early Christian hostility to extermination in concentration camps" (*Christianity*, 15).

100. On Christian injunctions against intermarriage and sex with Jews or Muslims, see Grayzel, *Church*, 184–85, 198–99, 204–5, 208–9, 210; Marcus, *Jew*, 39, 102; Baron, *Social and Religious History*, 3:50, 3:142–43, 3:189, 4:9, 5:133, 11:77–87; Simonsohn, *Apostolic See*, 1:130–32, 147–49, 527–28, 529; 2:1089; and Cohen, *Under Crescent*, 34–35, 129–30. There were also, of course, Jewish injunctions against intermarriage and interfaith sex; see Baron, *Social and Religious History*, 3:142–43, 5:100, and Cohen, *Under Crescent*, 109. Muslim law was more lenient toward intermarriage with *dhimmis* ("people of the Book," including both Jews and Christians); see Cohen, *Under Crescent*, 133.

101. Grayzel, *Church*, 308–9: "In nonnullis ecclesie provinciis a Christianis Judeos, seu Saracenos habitus distinguit diversitas; sed in quibusdam sic quedam inolevit confusio, ut nulla differentia discernantur. Unde contingit interdum quod per errorem Christiani, Judeorum, seu Saracenorum, et Judei seu Saraceni Christianorum mulieribus commisceantur. Ne igitur tam damnate commixtionis excessus per velamen (-tum) hujusmodi erroris, (ulterius) excusationis possint habere diffugium, statuimus, ut tales utriusque sexus in omni Christianorum provincia, et omni tempore qualitate habitus publice ab aliis populis distinguantur cum et per Moysen hoc ipsum eis legatur iniunctum." For

more on legislation concerning distinctive clothing, including the badge, see Grayzel, *Church*, 61–62, 156–57, 166–67, 168–69, 206–7, 258–59, 282–83, 294–95, 314–15; Marcus, *Jew*, 138; Simonsohn, *Apostolic See*, 1:99, 101, 103, 105, 111, 117, 118, 132–34, 141–43, 145–47, 174–75, 185–86, 199, 200–201, 209, 227–29, 268–70, 388–89, 431–32, 445–46, 460, 518–24, 530–31, 536–38; 2:555–56, 593–602, 624–27, 629–34, 635–36, 637, 669–71, 685, 719, 730–34, 739–40, 809–10, 811, 819, 858–59, 977–98, 983, 984–85, 1043–44, 1055–56, 1057–58, 1060–61, 1071–73, 1106–7; and Cohen, *Under Crescent*, 64, 129–30. Bolton argues that Lateran IV "represented a watershed" in the church's attitude toward all "deviants" ("Tradition and Temerity," 79).

102. Grayzel, *Church*, 106–7: "[C]um in Lateranensi concilio sit statutum, ut Judei, nec sub alendorum puerorum obtentu, nec pro servitio, nec alia qualibet causa, in domibus suis habere permittantur mancipia christiana, sed excommunicentur qui cum eis presumpserint habitare, ipsi et servos Christianos habere non dubitant, et nutrices, cum quibus eas interdum abominationes exercent, quas te potius punire convenit quam nos deceat explicare." In reading this passage, Dahan, *Intellectuels chrétiens*, admits that Innocent III's "formule sibylline" [Sibylline formula] makes us think of the sexual, but argues that "the theme of the libertine Jew" [le thème du juif libertine] had not yet been established and that the point here is one more of "religious conduct" [la conduite religieuse] than of sexual danger (162). Though I would agree that the implications of this papal injunction are not *simply* sexual, the combination of "abominatio" (evoking, as it does, Leviticus and its sexual [and, admittedly, other] "abominationes") with the trope of unspeakability, developing at this same moment with regard to sodomy (see Jordan, *Invention*, 106, 111, 133, 150–51), certainly suggests a sexual component to the pope's concern.

103. Grayzel, *Church*, 252–53: "faciunt Christianas filiorum suorum nutrices in contumeliam fidei Christiane, cum quibus turpia multa committunt." On the injunctions against Jewish ownership or employment of Christians, also see ibid., 296–97, 314–15; Baron, *Social and Religious History*, 4:11, 4:16–17, 5:133, 11:86–87; and Simonsohn, *Apostolic See*, 1:50, 60, 84, 86–88, 141–43, 145–47, 180–82, 225–26, 239–40, 243–44, 262–64.

104. Chazan, *Daggers*, 31. Also see Dahan, *Intellectuels chrétiens*, 160–79.

105. See Trachtenberg, *Devil and the Jews*, 187; Baron, *Social and Religious History*, 3: 189, 11:78, 11:80, 11:82; and Chazan, *Daggers*, 35.

106. Trachtenberg, *Devil and the Jews*, 167. Baron, however, interprets the event differently: "The romantic interest was not the compelling motive in his conversion. Even at his trial before the Council of Oxford in 1222 no one stressed the fact that he had a Jewish consort; according to contemporary chroniclers, he was prosecuted only for apostasy, the desecration of the host, defilement of the crucifix, and blasphemies against the Virgin" (*Social and Religious History*, 11:84).

107. Trachtenberg, *Devil and the Jews*, 187; also see Baron, *Social and Religious History*, 11:80, 11:82.

108. For useful readings of Damian's work, see Fliche, *Réforme grégorienne*, 1:175–264; Leclercq, *Saint Pierre Damien*; Berger, "St. Peter Damian"; Little, "Personal Development"; Boyd, "Disrupting the Norm"; Leyser, "Cities of the Plain"; Jordan, *Invention*, 45–66; Scanlon, "Unmanned Men"; and Burgwinkle, *Sodomy*, 53–65.

109. Jordan, *Invention*, Chapter 3.

110. Thus, for instance, Peter's letter is extensively used in the disputations of Ceuta and Majorca *(Disputationen)*.

111. Damian, Letter 31, 2:6; *Book of Gomorrah*, 27. In the discussion that follows, as here, I generally cite Blum's translation from Damian, *Letters*, noting where I have adopted a different translation; I also, however, provide page references to Payer's translation *(Book of Gomorrah)*. I provide the Latin text from the *PL (Liber Gomorrhianus)* but have also consulted the more recent MGH edition *(Briefe)*; I note significant differences between the *PL* and MGH texts. The passage here reads: "Quoddam autem nefandum [*Briefe:* nefandissimum (287)] et ignominiosum valde vitium in nostris partibus inolevit" (161).

112. Damian, Letter 31, 2:6–7; *Book of Gomorrah*, 29; *Liber Gomorrhianus*, 161.

113. My translation; Blum has "eminent cities" (Letter 31, 2:8) and Payer "famous cities" *(Book of Gomorrah*, 32). *Liber Gomorrhianus*, 162: "egregias civitates."

114. See, for instance, the depiction of the area around the Dead Sea in Mandeville, *Travels*, 89–90.

115. See, for instance, the disputation of Majorca, *Disputationen*, 214–16.

116. For the dating of Peter's letters, see Blum's notes in Damian, *Letters*. In the discussion of Letter 1 below, I cite Blum's translation, giving references as well to the Latin edition of the *PL* and noting passages where the text of the MGH edition *(Briefe)* differs.

117. Damian, Letter 1, 1:38; 41: "fides autem omnium virtutum sit proculdubio fundamentum; ubi fundamentum quatitur, tota mox aedificii fabrica praecipitium ruitura minatur."

118. See, for instance, Damian, Letter 1, 1:81, where the Jewish interlocutor is told that he is being punished for the "incurable crime" of "hav[ing] killed Christ"; "insanabilis culpa . . . quia Christum Dei Filium occidisti" (66). Compare, for just one of many possible instances, Letter 31, 2:6 ("criminal vice"); *Book of Gomorrah*, 29 ("criminal wickedness"); *Liber Gomorrhianus*, 161 ("nequitiae scelere").

119. Damian, Letter 1, 1:81; 66: "Hoc enim profundissimum vestrae iniquitatis baratrum omnium flagitiorum transcendit modum, omnium superat immanitatem criminum."

120. Damian, Letter 31, 2:8; *Book of Gomorrah*, 32; *Liber Gomorrhianus*, 162: "Hoc nempe flagitium inter caetera crimina non immerito deterrimum creditur."

121. Damian, Letter 1, 1:63; 55: "poterat forsitan malitia Judaeorum veritati contradicere." Damian, Letter 31, 2:22, 2:53; *Book of Gomorrah*, 52, 91; *Liber Gomorrhianus*, 170 ("dogma suae perversitatis"), 189 ("perversorum hominum querela").

122. Damian, Letter 1, 1:57, 1:63; 52 ("inverecundae mentis audacia"), 55 ("Impudentissimum"). Damian, Letter 31, 2:6, 2:37; *Book of Gomorrah*, 27, 71; *Liber Gomorrhianus*, 161 ("cum tantae libertatis saevit audacia"), 180 ("arroganter usurpet [*Briefe:* usurpat (316)]").

123. Damian, Letter 1, 1:43, 1:83; 44 ("Tu autem nolim [*Briefe:* noli (69)] mihi, ut vester mos est, subdolis tergiversationibus, velut in variarum te formarum monstra convertas [*Briefe:* convertes (69)], nisi [*Briefe:* non (69)] ut lubricus anguis, cum captus fueris, manus evadere gestias"), 68 ("ab invisibilium te insidiis hostium misericorditer protegat"). Damian, Letter 31, 2:7, 2:16; *Book of Gomorrah*, 29, 43; *Liber Gomorrhianus*, 161 ("Hos itaque corruendi gradus artifex diaboli machinatio reperit"), 167 ("Ut autem diabolicae machinatione [*Briefe:* machinationis (297)] argumenta non lateant, sed quae in officina

veteris malitiae secreto fabricantur, in lucem me pallificante procedant" [for "secreto fabricantur," *Briefe* reads "inter suos secretarios fabricat" (297)]).

124. Damian, Letter 1, 1:39; 42 ("insaniam"). Damian, Letter 31, 2:14, 2:22, 2:25, 2:28; *Book of Gomorrah*, 39, 52, 56, 60; *Liber Gomorrhianus*, 166 ("insania"), 170 ("quis tam vesane desipiat"), 172 ("scenicis deliramentis"), 174 ("energumenis").

125. Damian, Letter 1, 1:81; 66: "insanabilis culpa."

126. Damian, Letter 31, 2:8, 2:14, 2:33, 2:50; *Book of Gomorrah*, 30, 39, 67, 88; *Liber Gomorrhianus*, 162, 166, 177, 188 ("vulnus," "plaga").

127. Ibid., 2:24, 2:28, 2:46; 53, 60, 83; 171, 174, 185 ("venenum," "virus").

128. Ibid., 2:15, 2:36, 2:40, 2:52; 40, 69, 75, 89; 166 ("pestem"), 179 ("Pestis illa Gomorrhiana"), 181 ("de peste immunditiae"), 189 ("pestis").

129. Ibid., 2:31; 64; 176 ("pestilentissima Sodomorum regina").

130. Ibid., 2:17, 2:27, 2:36–37; 43, 59, 70–71; 167, 174 ("lepra"), 179 ("leprosus," "lepra").

131. Damian, Letter 1, 1:38; 41 ("Christi miles"). Damian, Letter 31, 2:52; *Book of Gomorrah*, 89; *Liber Gomorrhianus*, 189 ("Dei militem").

132. Damian, Letter 1, 1:39, 1:82; 42 ("sagitta," "spicula"), 67–68 ("sagittarum fasciculum in pharetram," "arma," "clypeum," "bella"). Damian, Letter 31, 2:52; *Book of Gomorrah*, 89; *Liber Gomorrhianus*, 189: "acutissimis verborum spiculis," "cuneorum acie."

133. Damian, Letter 1, 1:43; 44 (the Latin is quoted above, n. 123); I have slightly modified Blum's translation.

134. Damian, Letter 31, 2:31; *Book of Gomorrah*, 64; *Liber Gomorrhianus*, 176: "pestilentissima Sodomorum regina."

135. Ibid., 2:32; 64; 176: "venenatissimus coluber."

136. Ibid., 2:42; 78; 183: "Serpens enim iste, quem nostrae disputationis sude frangere nitimur, quadriceps est."

137. Ibid., 2:30; 63; 175: "Hoc siquidem vitium mors est corporum, interitus est animarum, carnem polluit, mentis lumen exstinguit, Spiritum sanctum de templo humani pectoris ejicit, incentorem luxuriae diabolum introducit."

138. Damian, Letter 1, 1:81; 66.

139. Damian, Letter 31, 2:30; *Book of Gomorrah*, 63; *Liber Gomorrhianus*, 175: "coelestis Jerusalem civem tartareae Babylonis facit haeredem."

140. Ibid., 2:32; 65; 177: "a superna patria exsul."

141. Damian, Letter 1, 1:81; 65: "omnium gentium pedibus videmini servitute substrati."

142. Damian, Letter 31, 2:52; *Book of Gomorrah*, 89; *Liber Gomorrhianus*, 189: "captivus ... servierat."

143. See Burgwinkle, *Sodomy*, for an analysis that recognizes the strong ambivalences of Peter's *Liber*.

144. See Wheatley, "'Blind' Jews," on medieval traditions of actual and metaphorical blindness.

145. Damian, Letter 1, 1:43, 1:82; 44, 66 ("ignorantiae velamen").

146. Ibid., 1:65; 57: "Ecce qui post tam perspicuam exemplorum lucem adhuc testimoniis indiget, restat ut ad contemplandum radiantem in meridie solem lucernae lumen efflagitet. Nam cum tot astrorum coelestium radios coram te, Judaee, videas enitescere, miror, quae tam densae tenebrae caecitatis locum etiam in vacuis oculorum orbibus valeant obtinere."

147. Ibid., 1:43, 1:82; 44 ("mentis tuae tenebris"), 66 ("errorum tenebris").

148. Jerome, *Liber*, 828: "Sodoma ... pecus, silens, vel caecitas, vel similitudo eorum."

149. Guibert, *Moralia*, 118, 143.

150. Pseudo-Alcuin, *Liber*, 1194: "caecitas mentis."

151. Jacquart and Thomasset, *Sexuality and Medicine*, 56, quoting the fifteenth-century *Problemata Varia Anatomica*. Damian shows himself familiar with the sort of medical lore that leads to such a conclusion; see Letter 31, 2:40; *Book of Gomorrah*, 75; *Liber Gomorrhianus*, 181.

152. See, for instance, ibid., 2:13–14, 2:17, 2:22, 2:34; 38–39, 44, 52, 68; 165–66, 167, 170, 178.

153. See, for instance, ibid., 2:5–6, 2:30, 2:34; 27, 63, 68; 161, 175, 178.

154. See, for instance, ibid., 2:18, 2:25, 2:27–28, 2:29; 45, 56, 59, 61; 168, 172, 174, 175.

155. Ibid., 2:33; 66; 177: "immunditiae sordibus."

156. Ibid., 2:32; 65; 177: "fit sibi coelum ferreum, et terra aenea; neque illuc potest pondere criminis gravatus assurgere."

157. Ibid., 2:12; 37; 165: "amissis interioribus oculis." I quote Payer's translation here; Blum has "after losing the sight furnished by their conscience."

158. Damian, Letter 1, 1:82; 66: "desere Judaicae caecitatis errorem, et te ad Evangelicae gratiae dirige veritatem." In the opening of this letter, Peter also expresses a hope for Jewish conversion (1:39; 41).

159. Ibid., 1:81 (my emphasis); 66: "insanabilis culpa," "irremediabilis poena."

160. Damian, Letter 31, 2:44; *Book of Gomorrah*, 81; *Liber Gomorrhianus*, 184: "Exsurge, exsurge, quaeso, expergiscere, o homo, qui miserae voluptatis sopore deprimeris; revivisce tandem, qui lethali coram inimicis tuis gladio corruisti."

161. Ibid., 2:9–10; 33; 163: "etiamsi honestis moribus polleat, si psalmodiae studio ferveat, si in amore orationis enitescat, et omnino religiosam vitam sub approbatae famae testimonio ducat; reatus quidem indulgentiam plene potest accipere, ad ecclesiasticum vero ordinem nequaquam permittitur aspirare." Also see ibid., 2:30; 62; 175.

162. Shapiro, *Shakespeare and the Jews*, 170–71. On the *foetor judaicus*, see further Trachtenberg, *Devil and the Jews*, 47–50.

163. Laqueur, *Making Sex*, 124.

164. For the highly influential distinction between a system of sexual *acts* and a modern sexuality based on coalesced identities, see Foucault, *History of Sexuality*. For a nuanced reading of Foucault's argument, see Halperin, "Forgetting Foucault."

165. On chaste or spiritual marriage, see Elliott, *Spiritual Marriage*.

166. Chaucer, *Riverside Chaucer*, VIII.373, 376. In subsequent references to Chaucer, I give fragment and line numbers from the *Riverside Chaucer* parenthetically in my text. On the reconfiguration of "the body and society" within early Christianity, see Brown's influential account, *Body and Society*.

167. On the battle over the "true" interpretation of Franciscan spirituality, see Burr, *Spiritual Franciscans*.

168. It is in part because of this model of ideal(ized) Christian identity separate from the heterosexually based family that we cannot—as Lochrie, *Heterosyncrasies*, strongly argues—think of medieval culture as in any way unproblematically "heteronormative."

169. Elliott, *Spiritual Marriage*, 298.

170. For recent gendered readings of the *Man of Law's Tale*, see Schibanoff, "Worlds Apart"; Frantzen, *Before the Closet*, 259–66; and Robertson, "'Elvyssh' Power." For the interesting suggestion that we should read the tale's mothers-in-law as evoking the *Jewish* mother-in-law of Ecclesia, Synagoga, see Rose, "Jewish Mother-in-Law."

171. For widows as disruptive of gendered social structures, we need look no further than Chaucer's own Wife of Bath.

172. Recall the association, noted above, of the sultaness with Semiramis as the prototype of inappropriately masculine female rulers.

173. 1 Corinthians 11:3.

174. Of course, the *Man of Law's Tale* itself stands between historiographical and fictional genres; its principal source is Nicholas Trivet's Anglo-Norman Chronicle, the pertinent sections of which are printed in Bryan and Dempster, *Sources and Analogues*.

175. See, for instance, Nolte, "Gender and Conversion," and Goodman, "Marriage and Conversion." Goodman touches on the Constance story.

176. Baron, *Social and Religious History*, 3:10.

177. Grayzel, *Church*, 88–91. Also see Simonsohn, *Apostolic See*, 1:72–73. In the inverse situation, where one of two married Christians apostatized, the spouse who remained Christian was not allowed to remarry.

178. Simonsohn, *Apostolic See*, 2:755–56.

179. Grayzel, *Church*, 18–19, 88–89, 100–101; Simonsohn, *Apostolic See*, 1:65, 72, 79.

180. Simonsohn, *Apostolic See*, 1:241, my emphasis: "quae de Sarracenis aut Judaeis *traxerunt originem.*"

181. Baron, *Social and Religious History*, 11:79.

182. The sense here seems to demand the opposite of the Latin *erumptiam*, which I have translated as "breaking out." The point is that Petrus would prefer to undergo perpetual imprisonment and death rather than consummate a marriage with the "heretical" Blancha.

183. Simonsohn, *Apostolic See*, 2:1051: "Sane, pro parte dilecti filii Petri dela Cavalleria, minoris dierum, civitatis Cesaraugustane, nobis nuper oblata petitio continebat, quod dudum ipse cum Blancha Palau, civitatis Valencie, que habita erat et reputata Christiana, matrimonium per verba legittime de presenti contraxit, carnali copula minime subsecuta; verum, quia manifeste deprehendit, quod dicta Blancha Iudaice insanie et Iudeorum ritibus et cerimonialibus heretica est et heretice vivit, et ita relatu fidedignorum perhibetur, quod mater ipsius Blanche de gente Iudeorum veniens, eadem heretica pravitate laborans, ipsam dictam Blancham instruxit et imbuit, prefatus Petrus, verus Catolicus, potius perpetue carceris erumptiam [sic] et omne mortis periculum subire paratus est, quam velit huiusmodi matrimonium consumare, ne forsan sua procreanda proles matris insaniam prosequeretur, et ex Christiano Iudeus crearetur, pro parte dicti Petri nobis fuit humiliter supplicatum, ut matrimonium ipsum nullum fuisse et esse declarari, vel si forsan matrimonium dici potest, ut et illud ex premissis causis dissolvere, prefatoque Petro, ut alteri nubere possit, concedere, aliasque sibi et statui suo in premissis opportune providere, de benignitate apostolica dignaremur."

184. Baron, *Social and Religious History,* 3:248.

185. Ibid., 4:10–11.

186. Simonsohn, *Apostolic See,* 2:845–47.

187. For one treatment of this love triangle, see Mongan, "Between Knights."

188. Malory, *Works,* 473; subsequent references are given parenthetically in the text.

189. *Sir Orfeo,* 459.

190. See, for instance, the framing of Alfonsi's *Dialogi* in BL Additional 15404: "petri alfunsi / uiri / illustris et / ex iudeo christiani / catholici" (fol. 31r), "Explicit liber Petri alfunsi uiri illustris et ex iudeo christiani catholici" (fol. 144r).

191. See Hermann, *Opusculum,* 70.

192. For the naming "Friar Paul, called Christian," see the 1267 papal bull cited in Cohen, "Mentality," 36; Simonsohn, *Apostolic See,* 1:234.

193. Baron, *Social and Religious History,* 3:39.

194. See ibid., 3:176; Simonsohn, *Apostolic See,* 2:935–37, 979–80. For varied and extensive consideration of conversos in the Iberian context, see "Inflecting the Converso Voice," and the response, in "Letters on 'Inflecting.'"

195. On the "relapse" of converts, see Baron, *Social and Religious History,* 3:39, 3: 247, 4:5; Simonsohn, *Apostolic See,* 1:42, 80–81, 244–45, 248–49, 266, 267–68, 271–72, 273–74, 275–76, 285–86, 303–4, 334, 371, 384–85, 394–96, 405–7, 408–10, 422–23, 433–36, 497–98; 2:824–27, 999–1001.

196. Cohen, "Mentality," 23.

197. For a comparison of the motives behind these three conversions, see ibid.

198. See Boyarin, "'This We Know,'" for more on the origins of this formulation.

199. Dinshaw, *Chaucer's Sexual Poetics,* 22; also see Lampert, *Gender and Jewish Difference.* The work of Bynum has problematized, in our reading of medieval culture, a simple identification of body with femaleness and soul or spirit with maleness; see, most recently, *Resurrection.* Still, a series of analogical dichotomies—body/spirit, female/male, Jewish/Christian—underpins certain crucial medieval understandings.

200. Kruger, *Dreaming,* 154–65. For further bibliography on Hermann, see chapter 1, n. 52 above.

201. Thus, for instance, Hermann poses the Jews' foolishness and "old wives' tales" (*Opusculum,* 113: "stultas et aniles . . . fabulas") against the nourishing sweetness of his own growing Christian knowledge (113: "mellifluam . . . spiritualium allegoriarum dulcedinem").

202. Ibid., 101–3: "concupiscentias," "carnis voluptate," "carnis delectationem."

203. Ibid., 98: "ipse [diabolus] mihi in meam ruinam mulierem matrimonio copulavit."

204. Ibid., 101: "Nos tibi semper monita salutis dabamus, quibus te aliquando consensurum et in Christum nostre salutis auctorem crediturum sperabamus; et ecce contra spem nostram tuas potius sequi concupiscentias elegisti ac desperata salute perditioni te ad integrum tradidisti."

205. Ibid., 102: "cepi cum summa illic carnis voluptate iacere, quo me ante timueram precipitare."

206. Ibid., 103: "propter modicam carnis delectationem in tantam me perditionis voraginem precipitassem."

207. Ibid., 108: "meritis ipsarum et precibus tanta repente cordi meo christiane fidei claritas infulsit, ut ab eo totius pristine dubietatis et ignorantie tenebras penitus effugaverit, congrua nimirum vicissitudine, ut per feminam lapsum femine precibus sublevarent."

4. MERCHANTS, CONVERTS, JEWS

1. The formulation I develop here obviously shares much with Prosser's treatment of transsexuality (and autobiography) as working through interlinked questions of identity and conversion, and with her emphasis on transsexual identity as an identity of transition *(Second Skins)*. I also have in mind Freccero's influential treatment of Dante's "poetics of conversion" *(Dante)*.

2. I cite Mieth's recent edition, Alfonsi, *Diálogo,* but I have also consulted the edition of the *Dialogi* in the *PL,* and I provide references to both editions. Translations are my own. For discussion of Peter's life and work, and for further bibliography, see Blumenkranz, "Jüdische und christliche Konvertiten," esp. 272–75; Septimus, "Petrus Alfonsi"; Cohen, "Mentality," esp. 23–29; Tolan, *Petrus Alfonsi*; Abulafia, *Christians and Jews in the Twelfth-Century Renaissance,* 91–93, 100–101, 103, 116–17, 120, 125–26; *Estudios*; Stone, "Ramon Llull"; Cohen, *Living Letters,* 201–18; Biddick, *Typological Imaginary,* 23–27.

3. This opening scene follows a "Proemium" and "Prologus" that introduce the text in a general way, outlining the *Dialogi*'s twelve *tituli* and emphasizing especially its *compositor*'s status as convert, giving the text's most historically detailed account of Moses/Peter's conversion (Alfonsi, *Diálogo,* 5–8; *Dialogi,* 535–38). The *PL* text does not include the list of *tituli,* following a different manuscript tradition here than does Mieth: compare BL Harley 3707, fol. 165v, which does not have the list, to BL Additional 15404, fol. 32r–v, or BN lat. 3359a, fol. 3r, both of which do.

4. Alfonsi, *Diálogo,* 8; *Dialogi,* 537–38: "A tenera igitur pueritiae aetate quidam michi perfectissimus adheserat amicus nomine Moyses, qui a primaeva aetate meus consocius fuerat et condiscipulus. Ad hunc cum pervenisset sermo, quod ego paterna lege relicta, Christianam delegissem fidem, relicto suae stationis loco, ad me festinus pervenit, in ipso adventu quendam vultum ferens hominis indignantis et increpans salutavit me more non amici, sed quasi alieni et sic exorsus est: / Vah, Petre Alfunse, multum pertransivit temporis, ex quo ad te venire, te videre, tecum loqui et commorari sollicitus fui, sed meus affectus caruit effectu, usque modo cum te leto dei gratia video vultu. / Nunc tuam michi, queso, patefacias intentionem, et propter quid vel antiquam deserueris vel novam legem delegeris, pandas rationem."

5. Ibid., 7; 538: "In tutandis etiam Christianorum rationibus nomen, quod modo Christianus habeo, posui, rationibus vero adversarii confutandis nomen, quod ante baptismum habueram, id est Moysen."

6. For overviews of medieval Christian-Jewish debate, and for further bibliography, see Berger, *Jewish-Christian Debate*; Schreckenberg, *Christlichen Adversus-Judaeos-Texte (1.–11. Jh.), (11.-13. Jh.),* and *(13.-20. Jh.); Contra Iudaeos*; Abulafia, *Christians and Jews in Dispute*; and Dahan, *Christian Polemic.*

7. See above, Introduction, n. 42.

8. Crispin, *Works*, 9; Hunt, "Disputation," 153; *Disputationen*.

9. We might perhaps see certain precedents in the writings of the convert Paul and, later, in the confessional writings of a convert like Augustine *(Confessions)*. But these texts are not, of course, staged as *dialogues*, even when they might dramatize, as Augustine certainly does, self-alienation.

10. For overviews of medieval Boethian traditions, see Means, *Consolatio Genre*, and Cherniss, *Boethian Apocalypse*.

11. Alain, *Plaint* VI.pr.3, 116–17.

12. Boethius, *Consolation* I.pr.3, 138; my translation.

13. Ibid. I.pr.3, 138; my translation.

14. Ibid. I.pr.1, 130; my translation.

15. See Tolan's brief consideration of Peter's "life and times," which includes a discussion of Peter's Andalusian education (*Petrus Alfonsi*, 3–11).

16. Alfonsi, *Diálogo*, 5; *Dialogi*, 536: "Omnipotens suo nos spiritu inspiravit et me ad rectam semitam direxit, tenuem prius albuginem oculorum et post grave corrupti animi velamentum removens."

17. Ibid., 11; 540: "video eos [Iudeos] solam legis superficiem attendere et litteram non spiritualiter sed carnaliter exponere, unde maximo decepti sunt errore."

18. Ibid., 7; 541: "Iudei verba prophetarum carnaliter intelligunt et ea falso exponunt."

19. For some of the most striking instances of the opposition between Jewish and Christian modes of reading, see ibid., 29–31, 89 (where Peter refers explicitly to Pauline doctrine, 2 Corinthians 3:6), 111–12, 116–17, 133–34, 137–40, 186–90; 553–54, 596, 611–12, 615, 627–28, 630–32, 666–68. But these are only particularly striking instances; the opposition is in fact prominent throughout the text.

20. Compare the military metaphors in Damian, discussed above, chapters 1 and 3. Also see works such as Raymond Martini's *Pugio Fidei* [*Dagger of Faith*] and Theobald of Saxony's *Pharetra fidei contra Iudaeos* [*Quiver of Faith against the Jews*], and the opening of Rupert of Deutz's *Anulus*, where the author speaks of "arming" the Christian with reason (Arduini, *Ruperto di Deutz*, 184).

21. Alfonsi, *Diálogo*, 9; *Dialogi*, 539 (my emphasis): "uterque in alterne rationis *campo* discurramus."

22. Ibid., 10; 539: "tuo namque ipsius gladio occidere te multum cupio."

23. Ibid., 5; 535.

24. See n. 5 above.

25. Alfonsi, *Diálogo*, 20; *Dialogi*, 546: "Magnae cecitatis velamen de pectore meo educens veritatis lucernam clarissime infudisti, quare digna a deo compensetur retributio tibi." Compare ibid., 5; 536, cited above at n. 16.

26. Ibid., 91; 597: "Hactenus Iudaicae gentis fides quam inanis et inconstans in omnibus esset," "in quanto permanserim hactenus errore."

27. Ibid.: "Sed cum paternam reliqueris fidem, miror, cur Christianorum et non pocius Sarracenorum, cum quibus semper conversatus atque nutritus es, delegeris fidem."

28. On the material Peter presents regarding Islam, see Septimus, "Petrus Alfonsi."

29. Alfonsi, *Diálogo*, 92–93; *Dialogi*, 598: "Licet...eis eodem tempore quatuor legitimas habere uxores et qualibet repudiata aliam semper accipere, ita tamen, ut nunquam quaternarium numerum transeant....Empticias vero atque captivas, quotcumque voluerit, habere licitum erit....Conceditur insuper eis de propria cognatione habere uxores, ut sanguinis proles accrescat et fortius inter eos amicitiae vinculum vigeat."

30. Ibid., 101–2; 604: "Quod de uxoribus utique dixisti licere quatuor accipere et qualibet repudiata aliam ducere, hoc nulla quidem precipitur ratione, neque enim nisi causa filios procreandi preceptum est uxorem accipere. Quod autem aempticias et captivas quotlibet possunt habere, hoc quidem quantum ad vos adulterium est, quia multociens pater emit aliquam stupratam a filio, et contra filius vel frater a patre corruptam vel a fratre."

31. Ibid., 98; 602: "Munditia autem de ablutione membrorum pertinebat cultoribus stellae Veneris, qui, volentes eam orare, ad modum feminae se aptabant, ora et oculos tingentes."

32. Ibid., 102; 604–5: "Mahometus valde feminas diligebat et pernimium luxuriosus erat, et, sicut ipsemet professus est, vis luxuriae quadraginta hominum in eo manebat."

33. Ibid., 146 (compare 158); 636 (compare 645): "Stultissime omnium, o Moyses"; 147; 637: "Non est gens in toto mundo stolidior vobis."

34. Ibid., 11; 540: "de eo [i.e., deo] tales protulere sententias, que non aliud nisi verba videntur iocantium in scolis puerorum vel nentium in plateis mulierum."

35. Ibid., 50; 567: "Hoc itaque est, quod tibi superius dixi, verba doctorum vestrorum non aliud videri quam verba iocantium in scolis puerorum vel nentium in plateis mulierum."

36. Ibid., 110–11; 611. See Figure 4 and the fuller discussion below.

37. Ibid., 193: "Multum certe suae tibi deus dedit sapientiae et te magna illustravit ratione, quem vincere nequeo, immo tu obiectiones meas confutasti ratione." The text in the *PL* is somewhat different, though the overall sense is similar: "Multum certe tibi dedit Deus sapientiae, et te plurima illustravit ratione, quod in te Scripturae intelligentia tanta sit, ut te superare nequeam, imo quod contradicam non habeam" (*Dialogi*, 671).

38. Tolan, *Petrus Alfonsi*, 41.

39. The first four and last three *tituli* of the *Dialogi* all end with Peter praying for Moses's enlightenment and conversion. The fifth *titulus* also ends with Peter voicing a prayer, though here it is for his own freedom from error and for the capacity to complete his argument aright (*Diálogo*, 103; *Dialogi*, 606). *Tituli* vi–ix do not include the formulaic prayer.

40. Ibid., 193; 671–72: "Hoc procul dubio donum est Spiritus Sancti, quem in baptismo recipimus, qui et corda nostra illuminat, ne falsum quid credere presumamus. Quod si tu, quod credimus, ipse etiam crederes et baptizari te faceres, eandem Spiritus Sancti illustrationem haberes, ut, quae vera sunt, cognosceres et, quae falsa, respueres. Nunc autem quoniam super te pietatem habeo, dei misericordiam imploro, ut Spiritus sui plenitudine te illustret et finem meliorem quam principium tibi prestet. Amen."

41. Ibid., 8; 537: "paterna lege relicta."

42. Tolan, *Petrus Alfonsi*, 95.

43. See ibid., 98–103, 182–98. I have myself examined the following manuscripts (I give the *sigla* used by Tolan in parentheses after each manuscript designation). From the twelfth century: BL Harley 3707 (L1), BL Harley 3861 (L2), BN lat. 10624 (P1), BN lat. 10722 (P2), BN lat. 5080 (P3), BN lat. 14069 (P4), BN lat. 15009 (P5), BN lat. 18104 (P8); the last three might be from the early thirteenth century. From the thirteenth century: BL Royal 15.C.ii (L3), BL Additional 15404 (L4), BN lat. 3359a (P6); the last might be from the early fourteenth century. From the fourteenth century: BN lat. 16523 (P7), BN lat. 2134 (P9). From the sixteenth century: BN lat. 3394 (P10).

44. Tolan, *Petrus Alfonsi*, 131.

45. Ibid., 100.

46. Ibid., 101.

47. Hunt discusses Alfonsi's influence in England ("Disputation"); Tolan's discussion of the *Dialogi* as "a medieval *auctoritas*" clearly shows its widespread use (*Petrus Alfonsi*, 95–131).

48. See the discussion in ibid., 123–26. The portion of Vincent de Beauvais's *Speculum historiale* dependent on the *Dialogi* is Book 25, chapters 118–45, columns 1043–55.

49. Only a fragmentary text survives, but a copy of this translation seems to have been part of the library of Pedro de Luna, Pope Benedict XIII, who presided over the early fifteenth-century Tortosa disputation (chapter 5 below); see Tolan, *Petrus Alfonsi*, 126–29, and Ainaud de Lasarte, "Una versión catalana." An abridged text was also translated into German in the nineteenth century "for the express purpose of converting the Jews" (Tolan, *Petrus Alfonsi*, 131).

50. See the discussion in ibid., 108–15.

51. See, for one clear instance, BN lat. 3394, which presents only *titulus* v of the *Dialogi*, alongside Latin and French translations of Quranic material and the *Contarietas alfolica* (or *Liber denudationis*); on the last, a Christian apology originally written in Arabic and then translated into Latin, see Burman, "Influence."

52. See Tolan, *Petrus Alfonsi*, 113–21. That the *Dialogi* was sometimes received specifically as a source of Talmudic material is made clear by several manuscripts that gather it together with other texts on the Talmud—e.g., Burgo de Osma, Biblioteca Capitular 35 (28), and Prague, Archiv Prazského hradu O.XLVIII (Tolan, *Petrus Alfonsi*, 185, 196). For more on the Burgo manuscript, see Millás Vallicrosa, "Tratado"; Cantera Burgos, "Textos."

53. BN lat. 15009. The manuscript consists of what were originally two separate manuscripts; the second begins at fol. 144r, as does the text of Honorius's *Imago mundi*. Gildas's *De Anglia* follows (beginning at fol. 160v). "Megacosmus magistri Bernardi" begins at fol. 187r and his "microcosmus" at fol. 194r. The "liber petri alfunsi contra iudeos" then follows, at fol. 205r; it ends at fol. 255r. The manuscript concludes with short occasional texts.

54. BL Royal 15.C.ii. The Guillaume de Conches text begins at fol. 100v (following texts by Seneca) and ends at fol. 115r. The *Dialogi* begins at fol. 116r.

55. Tolan, *Petrus Alfonsi*, 121–23.

56. The *Dialogi* begins at fol. 145r.

57. Bern, Bürgerbibliothek Cod. 188 and Cod. 111 both contain Gilbert Crispin's *Disputatio*, as do Klosterneuberg Stiftsbibliothek 826; Lisbon, Biblioteca Nacional Acobaça

148 (CCXLI); and Biblioteca Pública Municipal do Porto 34 (43). See Tolan, *Petrus Alfonsi*, 184, 188–89, 190, 195. Odo of Cambrai's *Disputatio* appears in Harvard College Library, Judaica 16; see Tolan, *Petrus Alfonsi*, 187–88. BN lat. 10624 has Guibert's *De incarnatione* ("contra iudeos et iudaizantes"), beginning at fol. iv. Peter's text begins, with no title or attribution, at fol. 63v.

58. See the description of Troyes, Bibliothèque Municipale 1720, in Tolan, *Petrus Alfonsi*, 197.

59. Bern, Bürgerbibliothek Cod. iii, mentioned above in n. 57, contains, in addition to Alfonsi and Crispin, a copy of the Emperor of Constantinople's letter to Robert of Flanders and Robertus Monachus's *Historia belli sacri*, as well as a *Historia de inventione sanctae Crucis*. Chartres, Bibliothèque de la Cathédral 127 (130) contains Baldric [Baudri] of Dole's history of the First Crusade, as does BL Harley 3707 (here, the text of the *Dialogi* is truncated). Tolan, *Petrus Alfonsi*, 186, 189.

60. Manuscripts that place Peter's *Dialogi* (or sections of it) in proximity to texts attacking heresy include Charleville, Bibliothèque Municipale 113 (Alain de Lille's *Contra haereticos*, which treats Jews, "pagans" [Muslims], and heretics together); Klosterneuberg Stiftsbibliothek 826; Munich, Bayerische Staatsbibliothek 6502; Oxford, Merton College 175 (formerly K.3.3); Prague, Archiv Prazského hradu C.XCV (including, again, Alain de Lille). Tolan, *Petrus Alfonsi*, 186, 188–89, 191, 193, 196.

61. BL Additional 15404. Bonaventure's *Lignum vitae* begins at fol. 3r, the "uita Iude symonis scariothis" at fol. 19r, the "De natiuitate dignitate morte et supplicio pylati presidis iudee" at fol. 23r, and the *Dialogi* at fol. 31r.

62. Alfonsi, *Diálogo*, 15; *Dialogi*, 543: "Vos deum caput, brachia et totam corporis formam habere contenditis."

63. Ibid., 110–11; 611: "Trinitas quidem subtile quid est et ineffabile et ad explanandum difficile, de qua prophetae non nisi occulte loquuti sunt et sub velamine, quodadusque venit Christus, qui de tribus una personis, fidelium illam mentibus pro eorum revelavit capacitate. Si tamen attendas subtilius et illud dei nomen, quod in Secretis secretorum explanatum invenitur, inspicias, nomen, inquam, trium litterarum quamvis quatuor figuris, una namque de illis geminate bis scribitur, si, inquam, illud inspicias, videbis, quia idem nomen et unum sit et tria. Sed quod unum, ad unitatem substantiae, quod vero tria, ad trinitatem respicit personarum. Constat autem nomen illud his quatuor figuris 'i' ['yod'] et 'e' ['he'] et 'v' ['vav'] et 'e' ['he'], quarum si primam tantum coniunxeris et secundam, 'i' ['yod'] scilicet et 'e' ['he'], erit sane nomen unum. Item si secundam et terciam, 'e' ['he'] scilicet et 'v' ['vav'] iam habebis alterum. Similiter si terciam tantum copulaveris atque quartam, 'v' ['vav'] scilicet et 'e' ['he'], invenies et tercium. Rursum si omnes simul in ordinem conexeris, non erit nisi nomen unum, sicut in ista patet geometrica figura."

64. For a reproduction of Alfonsi's diagram of the triune Tetragrammaton using the Roman alphabet, see the figure from BN lat. 5080, fol. 185v, in *Diálogo*, 111. Among the manuscripts I have examined, the following all use the Roman alphabet to represent the Hebrew terms of the text: BL Harley 3861 (fol. 53v), BL Royal 15.C.ii (fol. 151r), BL Additional 15404 (fol. 94v), BN lat. 10624 (fol. 133v), BN lat. 10722 (fol. 45v), BN lat. 5080 (fol. 185v), BN lat. 16523 (fol. 34r–v; here, "i – e – v – e" are used in the text, but, though space has been left for the diagram of the trinitarian Tetragrammaton, that diagram has not

been copied). The following partial texts of the *Dialogi* do not include the section of *titulus* vi in which Peter discusses the Trinity and Tetragrammaton: BL Harley 3707, BN lat. 18104, BN lat. 3359a, BN lat. 2134, BN lat. 3394.

65. In addition to BN lat. 15009, fol. 232r, from which Figure 4 is taken, BN lat. 14069, fol. 84v, also here uses Hebrew rather than Roman lettering. Both of these are manuscripts that Tolan dates to the late twelfth or early thirteenth century; while he suggests that BN lat. 14069 is probably copied from BN lat. 5080, he notes that the trinitarian diagram seems to have been copied from BN lat. 15009 (*Petrus Alfonsi*, 194).

66. Mellinkoff, *Outcasts*, 1:95–117, and vol. 2: Figures II.23, 24, 26; III.4, 33, 43; IV.1–24; VII.12.

67. The diagram also reproduces the Hebrew word "adonay" [my Lord], in Roman characters, above the Tetragrammaton, suggesting perhaps some knowledge of Jewish ritual practice, where, in place of the unpronounceable Tetragrammaton, one substitutes the word "adonai." On the left side of the diagram, the scribe repeats in Roman characters the demonstration (made with Hebrew characters in the body of the diagram) of the three "nomina" contained within the single "nomen" of the Tetragrammaton itself.

68. The text of the *Dialogi* concludes at BN lat. 15009, fol. 255r; after the *explicit*, the rest of the page is blank. On the verso of this same folio begins a text that Delisle identifies as a "Catalogue des rois de France" (*Inventaire*, 65); the *incipit* is "Priamus et Antenor interfecerunt primarium ducem de romano senatu." This text ends at fol. 256v, with the name "philippus" (that is, Philip Augustus, who reigned 1180–1223). Fol. 257r, at the base of which the Hebrew alphabet appears, seems originally to have ended the manuscript, since it contains the following colophon: "Iste liber est sancti victoris parisiensis quicumque eum furatus fuerit uel celauerit uel titulum istum deleuerit anathema sit" [This book is of Saint Victor of Paris: cursed be whoever might steal it or hide it or delete this inscription]. In various (presumably somewhat later) hands following the colophon, historical material (largely regarding France, England, and the Normans) is recorded. On the following page (fol. 257v) a poetic text "De cismate grandimontanorum" (according to Delisle, "Satyre contre l'ordre de Grammont"), again probably added after the bulk of the manuscript was written, begins; it ends at fol. 258r. Fols. 258v and 259r are blank, and the manuscript concludes (fol. 259v) with an accurate list of the manuscript's contents.

69. For a particularly full account of this shift, see Cohen, *Living Letters*.

70. See the bibliography given in chapter 2, nn. 65–68.

71. See chapter 2, n. 64.

72. On relapse, see chapter 1, n. 54; chapter 3, n. 195.

73. See Langmuir, *Toward a Definition*, 197–208; Cohen, *Living Letters*, 219–70; Chazan, "Twelfth-Century Perceptions" and *Medieval Stereotypes*, 41–57.

74. For particularly full and influential treatments of this thirteenth-century moment, see Cohen, *Friars*, and Chazan, *Daggers*.

75. Foucault, *History of Sexuality*, 98.

76. Thus, as Cohen notes, the Dominican Raymond de Peñaforte set up, in North Africa and Spain, schools of Arabic and Hebrew intended to train missionaries (*Friars*, 107–8). Cohen also treats in detail the knowledge of Hebrew by one important Franciscan scholar, Nicholas of Lyra (*Friars*, 170–80).

77. On the *Extractiones de Talmut*, see Cohen, *Friars*, 65, 74; Dahan, *Intellectuels chrétiens*, 258–59; Dahan, "Traductions latines." The original compilation is in BN lat. 16558; as Cohen notes, copies of parts of the text are widely distributed in European libraries (*Friars*, 65 n. 25). Also see Millás Vallicrosa, "Extractos"; Dahan, "Rashi."

78. I have consulted the text of Martini, *Pugio Fidei*, in the 1687 Leipzig edition. For a useful introduction to Raymond's thought and missionizing activity, see Cohen, *Friars*, 129–69; for earlier work on Raymond, see Berthier, "Maître orientaliste," and Bonfil, "Nature of Judaism."

79. Martini, *Pugio Fidei*, 685: "ut ait Magister *Petrus Alphonsi*, qvi fuit in Hispania priusqvam fieret Christianus; magnus Rabinus apud Judaeos; tres literae priores hujus nominis, scilicet 'yod – he – vav' indicant in Deo hoc nomine vocato tres esse 'midot'; id est, proprietates a seipsis invicem differentes ex sua diversitate, qvam habent tam in figura, qvam in nomine, ut praedictum est. Una vero earum qvae repetitur, & in fine nominis ponitur, qvae est 'he,' & est prima in hoc nomine 'havayah' Essentia; indicat trium 'midot' id est, proprietatum, vel personarum unitatem Essentiae."

80. Ibid., 685–89: "ostenditur manifeste qvod *hoc est nomen super omne nomen*, ut ait *Apostolus Paulus ad Philipp. 2. v. 9*" (689).

81. Ibid. III.iii.21–23. Emphasizing the work's closing consideration of the ultimate conversion of the Jews, in the 1687 Leipzig edition, is that edition's inclusion, following the *Pugio*, of a text of Hermann of Cologne's "de sua conversione opusculum."

82. One might draw a useful comparison here to the later system of power/knowledge that Said, *Orientalism*, has described as "orientalism."

83. Thus, for instance, Pope Innocent IV wrote in 1247: "Despite the fact that, among other things, Divine Scriptures pronounces the law 'Thou shalt not kill,' and despite the fact that it prohibits the Jews, while solemnizing the Passover, to touch any dead body, nevertheless they are falsely accused that during this very festival they share the heart of a murdered child" [Scriptura divina inter alia mandata legis dicente; "Non occides," ac prohibente illos in solemnitate paschali quicquam morticinium non contingere, falso imponunt eisdem quod in ipsa solemnitate se corde pueri communicant interfecti] (Grayzel, *Church*, 268, 271).

84. See the detailed accounts provided, for the fifteenth and sixteenth centuries, in Hsia, *Myth* and *Trent 1475*. But also see Shatzmiller, *Shylock Reconsidered*, for the sense that Christians and Jews lived intimately intertwined lives and that, in the 1317 trial investigated here, at least some Christians were ready to defend the honor of a Jewish neighbor and business associate, even though he was a member of a strongly denigrated profession, moneylending.

85. Thomas of Monmouth, *Life and Miracles*, 93–94; see the discussion in Langmuir, *Toward a Definition*, 224–26. For additional instances, and for a recognition of the complexity of the convert's position in relation to accusations of Jewish crime, see Rubin, *Gentile Tales*, 84–88, 123, 129, 182–84, 186–87; Hsia, *Trent 1475*, 95–104; Hsia, *Myth*, 67–70, 120–23.

86. See the discussion in chapter 2.

87. Gower, *Vox Clamantis* V.11.687–88; *Major Latin Works*, 211; *Complete Works*, 4: 220: "O quam Iudeus domini sacra sabbata seruat, / Non vendens nec emens, nec sibi lucra petens!"

88. Chaucer, *Riverside Chaucer* VI.474–75.

89. Kempe, *Book* I.44, 105; trans. Windeatt, 143.

90. Ibid. I.52, 124; 163.

91. For different perspectives on such changes, see *Cambridge Economic History*, vols. 1–3; Southern, *Western Society*; Lopez, *Commercial Revolution*; Duby, *Early Growth*; Little, *Religious Poverty*; and Bartlett, *Making*.

92. For an overview of the Jews' role in the European "commercial revolution," see Little, *Religious Poverty*, 42–57. On Jewish moneylending, see Jordan, "Jews on Top," "Aspect," and "Women and Credit"; Shatzmiller, *Shylock Reconsidered*; Alvarez Perez, "Martyrs and Moneylenders."

93. See Dahan, *Intellectuels chrétiens*, 209–16, on the legal status of usury.

94. See, for instance, Paris, *Chronicles*, 95.

95. Little, *Religious Poverty*, 56.

96. For important historical work on medieval mercantilism, see Thrupp, *Merchant Class*; Lopez and Raymond, *Mediterranean Trade*; Goitein, *Mediterranean Society*; Baldwin, *Masters, Princes, and Merchants*; Braudel, *Mediterranean*; and Le Goff, *Time* and *Your Money*.

97. Langland, *Piers Plowman* C.IX.22 and C.IX.26; for the whole passage, see C.IX.22–42. And see the discussion in Smith, *Arts of Possession*, Chapter 4.

98. On Jews in Langland's poem, see Narin van Court, "Hermeneutics," and Goldstein, "'Why Calle Ye Hym Crist.'"

99. For Gower's defense of mercantilism, see *Mirour de l'Omme* 25192–212, *Complete Works*, vol. 1, and compare *Vox Clamantis* V.11, *Major Latin Works*, 210. For the association of merchants with usury, see *Mirour* 7285–7320; for their association with fraud ("Triche"), 25237–60.

100. For a different and fuller reading of the *Shipman's Tale* as an exploration of new social organizations, see Burger, "Queer Theory."

101. Many readings of the *Prioress's Tale* consider its representation of Jews. For one particularly influential treatment, see Fradenburg, "Criticism, Anti-Semitism."

102. For a treatment of both the Croxton *Play* and the *Prioress's Tale*, see Kruger, "Bodies."

103. For a treatment of *The Merchant of Venice* in relation to earlier, medieval discourses, see Lampert, *Gender and Jewish Difference*, Chapter 5.

104. Wallace, *Premodern Places*, 181–202, quotations at 195 n. 6, 188, 181.

105. Burger, *Chaucer's Queer Nation*, esp. Chapters 2–3.

106. I have consulted both Limor's MGH edition of the two texts, *Disputationen*, and Dahan's edition and French translation of the Majorca disputation—Contardo, *Disputatio*. I cite *Disputationen* unless otherwise indicated; translations are my own. On the disputations, also see Limor, "Missionary Merchants." The Majorca disputation is discussed briefly in the context of the history of Majorca (Abulafia, *Mediterranean Emporium*, 140) and of Genoese merchants (Kedar, *Merchants*, 40–41).

107. *Disputationen*, 137 ("sapientissimum Iudeum Mo Abraym nomine"), 169 ("sapientissimos Iudeos doctoresque in sinagogis Iudeorum"), 264 ("quidam Iudeus, qui doctor erat in synagogis, qui et ipse sapientissimus erat in Hebrayco et in dictamine summus"); also see 192, 204, 260.

108. For an overview of the history of Genoa and of Genoese trade, see Epstein, *Genoa*.

109. See Baer, *History of the Jews*, 1:76–77, and Limor, "Missionary Merchants," 36–37.

110. Baer, *History of the Jews*, 1:138–39, 141–42.

111. On the manuscript of the Ceuta disputation, see *Disputationen*, 39–40; on the manuscripts and printed texts of Majorca, 42–115.

112. Limor, "Missionary Merchants," and *Disputationen*, 1–34.

113. Soifer, " 'You Say,' " has recently argued, however, that the Ceuta disputation differs significantly from earlier disputational texts in its insistent focus on the Messiah; she sees Ceuta, because of this difference, as a significant turning point in the literature of Jewish-Christian debate.

114. *Disputationen*, 205: "bonis armis munitus, ut suam possit partem viriliter defensare."

115. See Ferruolo, *Origins*, and Weijers, *"Disputatio."*

116. Limor notes, *Disputationen*, 164 n. 138: "Hier erscheint zum ersten Mal das Motiv des Kaufmanns als Held, ein entscheidendes Charakteristikum dieser Disputation. Weiter ausgebaut wird das Motiv in der Disputation zu Mallorca (S. 229; 232; 254; 263f.; 266), wo sowohl der Beruf des Disputanten wie sein Vorzug vor gelehrten Geistlichen hervorgehoben werden" [Here appears for the first time the motif of the merchant as hero, a definitive characteristic of this disputation. The motif is further developed in the disputation of Majorca (pp. 229, 232, 254, 263f., 266), where both the occupation of the disputant and his precedence over learned clerics are emphasized].

117. Ibid., 137 and 166.

118. Ibid., 164: "Vere testificor tibi, quod, si possibile esset, ut Christiani omnes convenirent in unum, et his omnibus que tibi opposui eis opposuissem, / non michi videtur tam sapienter posse respondere quemadmodum tu solus michi respondisti."

119. Ibid., 169.

120. Ibid., 229: "diem adventus Messie."

121. Ibid.: "Sed si omnes clerici et fratres Predicatores et Minores et doctores et sapientes Christianorum insimul essent, hoc facere non possent. Et tu, qui mercator es, credis hoc facere? Te ipsum decipis!"

122. They place the disputation, however, at "Gerona" rather than at Barcelona, an understandable error, since Gerona was home to the Jewish disputant Naḥmanides. Dahan also notes—Contardo, *Disputatio*, 189 n. 101—that the Barcelona debate "avait été précédé de discussions plus informelles à Gérone" [had been preceded by more informal discussions at Gerona]. On the Barcelona disputation, also see chapter 5 below.

123. *Disputationen*, 229–30: "Et volumus tibi dicere et affirmare, quod in tempore domini Iacobi boni regis Aragonum, qui fuit pater domini Petri et avus istius domini Alfonsi qui nunc regnat, fuerunt apud Geronam fratres Predicatores et Minores, et frater Paulus qui fuit Iudeus, et multi alii peritissimi Christiani, et etiam quam plures legum doctores, et disputaverunt cum nostris Iudeis. Finis qualis fuit, interroga eos qui affuerunt, et scies, si finis fuit bonus pro Christianis an non." Inghetto interestingly here professes ignorance of the Barcelona disputation, asking the Jews to provide him with a text and translation of the proceedings (230).

124. Ibid., 254: "Bonus predicator esses, quia bene scires ponere verba et deaurare ea. Sed, per deum, dic nobis, si fuisti frater Minor vel Predicator, vel si clericus es, et unde tibi hec que nobis dixisti et dicis!"

125. Ibid., 254–55. This passage is cited below, n. 170.

126. Limor, "Missionary Merchants," suggests that "The world of commerce and the world of the missionaries were in general closely interconnected. . . . In the accounts of thirteenth-century voyages, the missionaries generally followed in the wake of the merchants, and people often connected the two activities" (45). Of course, many of the thirteenth-century missionaries were friars.

127. As Limor notes—*Disputationen*, 291 n. 354, and "Missionary Merchants," 44, 49, 50 n. 12—Inghetto's statements may sometimes be read as approaching the heretical.

128. *Disputationen*, 187: "qui predicant et seducunt gentes"; see also 229, 256–57.

129. Ibid., 187.

130. Ibid., 281: "Docete eum in testamento novo et in fide catholica."

131. Ibid., 166: "'Libentissime hoc [i.e., Christianum me facere et batizare] facerem et adimplerem, nisi timerem. Quoniam Mussumuti isti mali et pessimi sunt valde, et si hoc forte scirent, nos et vos in periculo mortis erimus; et tantum pro me per totum mundum nollem evenire. Sed in hoc non dubito, immo omnino credo, quod dominus Iesus Christus, qui per suam gratiam spiritum sanctum per te mittere dignatus est, ipse me in suo sanctissimo flumine, in quo ille baptizatus fuit, me concederit baptizari.' Quibus expletis, con filiis et fratribus / atque sororibus ac cognatis in navem Ianuensium ascendit, et Hierosolimam perrexit, Christi nomine se in Iordane flumine baptizavit, ipso prestante, qui cum patre et spiritu sancto vivit et regnat deus per infinita secula seculorum. Amen."

132. Ibid., 264: "doctor . . . sapientissimus . . . in Hebrayco et in dictamine summus."

133. Ibid., 282: "quamplures Iudei de melioribus et maioribus qui essent Maiorice."

134. Ibid.: "quoniam de consilio vestro multum indigent."

135. Ibid.

136. Ibid.: "navis magna domini regis."

137. Ibid., 283.

138. Ibid.: "Et hoc dicens subito apparuit circa navem barcha piscatorum. Et visa barcha gavisus fuit valde et dixit marinariis: 'Per deum, vocate barcham illam.' Et tunc marinarii vocaverunt barcham et dixerunt illis de barcha: 'Pro deo, prohycite hominem istum ad terram,' quoniam si dixissent Iudeum istum, non iam venissent. Venerunt ergo et levaverunt eum et portaverunt ad terram. Et cum appropinquaret ad terram, voluit solvere ipsis quid petissent; ipsi vero nichil accipere voluerunt, dicentes ei: 'Ite in nomine domini! Maius servicium isto faceremus vobis.'"

139. Ibid., 284: "Secundum vero miraculum fuit in baptissmo, quia qui sui patrini fuerunt una cum Ingeto volebant vocare nomen eius Iohannem. Et ad introytum ecclesie, quando presbyter dixit: 'Quomodo vocabitur?' Responderunt: 'Iohannes vocabitur.' Et dixit ipse: 'Non, domini mei! Placeat vobis, quod nomen meum vocetur: Philippus!' Et sic vocatum fuit nomen eius Philippus. Et ea pro quibus pervenit ad baptismum incepta fuerunt in festo beatorum apostolorum Phyllipi et Iacobi."

140. Ibid., 285.

141. Ibid., 254, 183–84.

142. See, for instance, ibid., 173, 176, 183, 208, 216, 248.

143. See, for instance, ibid., 165, 183, 187, 219, 249.

144. Ibid., 285: "Et recesserunt Iudei insimul Hebrayce loquentes, valde confusi quid dicere nescientes"; also see 239, 241.

145. See, for instance, ibid., 200, 216, 217, 218.

146. Ibid., 242, 292.

147. For some instances, see ibid., 217, 234, 282, 292.

148. See, for instance, the long passage associating merchants with "Triche" [Fraud] in Gower's *Mirour de l'Omme* (25237–60) or the more subtle suggestions, in Chaucer's portrait of the Canterbury Merchant, of an underhanded concealment of his true situation.

149. See, for instance, *Disputationen*, 141, 149, 157–60, 171, 173, 174, 197, 220–22, 252, 258–59.

150. Jewish physicians were common in many medieval contexts, and they were both admired for their expertise and feared; they were several times prohibited from practicing on Christian patients. See, for instance, Grayzel, *Church*, 74–75, 318–19, 332–33, 336–37. And note the prominence of a charlatan-physician, though not a Jewish one, in the anti-Jewish Croxton *Play*. The Jewish physician's double status as especially expert and especially dangerous continued into the Renaissance; see, for instance, the case of Elizabeth I's Jewish physician, Roderigo Lopez, who was executed on charges that he intended to poison the queen (Shapiro, *Shakespeare and the Jews*, 71–73).

151. *Disputationen*, 287: "Domine Ingete, si vos possetis hunc converti facere, bonum medicum haberetis."

152. Ibid., 262: "Veritas est, quod iste pannus est viridis, et ille niger, et ille alius rubeus, et iste vester blavus, et quod hec domus hedificata est lapidum et lignorum."

153. Ibid: "Hec non est veritas, ymmo humanitas transitoria et que mutari potest. Veritas vero mutari non potest."

154. Ibid., 288: "Amor filiorum et cupiditas usure et peccatum illud maledictum."

155. For evidence of late medieval (fifteenth-century) associations between merchants and usury, see Carroll, "'In the Name,'" and Mormando, *Preacher's Demons*, 182–91.

156. *Disputationen*, 215–16; see also 212, 245, 251.

157. Ibid., 214–15: "in spe vivitis, quod Messias veniet, et hec spes vana est sicut flos qui floret et fructum non producit, et sperando gaudetis, et gaudium vestrum nichil est nichilque boni habens, et est sicut fenum tectorum quod priusquam evellatur exaruit. Et vere impletum est in vobis hoc quod dicit propheta: *Nisi dominus reliquisset nobis semen quasi Sodoma fuissemus et quasi Gomorra similes essemus,* quia in veritate bene estis Sodoma et Gomorra quantum in potentia. Sed vos, qui remansistis, ad testimonium nostrum estis, et de vobis non fit mencio sicut non essetis."

158. See ibid., 222, 225.

159. Ibid., 296: "novus miles ... Christi."

160. See, for the various locations, ibid., 169, 180, 207 ("in quadam domo cuiusdam magni Iudei, in qua multitudo magna librorum erat"), 235, 262, 266 ("extra civitatem"), 267, 274, 278, 285–86, 287, 289, 300.

161. Ibid., 179: "Christianus efficiar et baptizabor.... Iudeus efficiar et circumcidar."

162. Ibid., 265: "Est in terra ista quidam mercator Ianuensis, cui non possumus in lege resistere, nec magister noster maior. Et dicit ipse, quod si nos possumus ei monstrare quod Ierusalem debeat rehedificari per Iudeos, quod ipse Iudeus erit et circumcisionem accipiet."

163. Ibid., 180: "quoniam mortuus esset, nec hoc facere auderet timore mortis."

164. Ibid., 180–81: "Non curetis de morte mea, quoniam dico vobis in certa veritate et in fide bona, quod si vos michi monstrare poteritis Messiam non venisse, Iudeus ero. Et si mille vitas haberem, omnes perderem pro salvando animam meam, quia aliud non quero nisi viam veritatis."

165. Ibid., 179–80.

166. Ibid., 300: "Domum vacuam paratam habemus, in qua non intrabit aliquis, nisi vos cum sociis vestris et ego solus."

167. Ibid., 170–71.

168. Dahan here translates "avec ce fameux Angelo" [with this famous Angelo] (Contardo, *Disputatio*, 227), Limor "jener jüdische Engel" [that Jewish angel] (*Disputationen*, 255 n. 255). Kedar, "R. Yeḥiel," translates "with that Jewish angel" (354). Dahan summarizes and considers Kedar's suggestion that this "angel" is Rabbi Yeḥiel of Paris, chief Jewish spokesman at the disputation of Paris in 1240.

169. For theories as to the identity of the figure named here, see Dahan (Contardo, *Disputatio*, 39–42) and Limor (*Disputationen*, 255–56 n. 255). Dahan suggests that "Balaafeç" may be read as Hebrew "Ba'al ha-hefez" or "Ba'al hefez," i.e., "maître du désir (ou de désir)" [master of the desire (or of desire)] or as the author of a Hebrew work entitled "Hefez" (41). Limor proposes that the name may be a form of Hebrew "Baal-Shem" (literally, "master of the Name"), meaning, Limor suggests, "the Kabbalist" (256 n. 255).

170. *Disputationen*, 254–55: "Nec clericus sum neque fui, nec alicuius religionis umquam fui. Ymmo mercator sum. Sed hec que scio didici a Iudeis et per gratiam dei et Messie domini nostri Yesu Christi. Et bene dico vobis, quod in tempore meo cum multis Iudeis habui conflictum, et specialiter in Provincia et in Alexandria Egypti cum illo angelo Iudeo, quem Iudei de Syria vocabant 'regem Ierusalem,' similiter et cum illo beloasem [*var.* Balaafez] de Babillonia, qui est, si vivit, maximus doctor inter Iudeos."

171. Ibid., 230: "Tamen multum rogo vos, quod si in scriptis habetis disputationem illam, quod michi exemplo tradatis, quia desidero magno desiderio, ut habeam translatum ipsius."

172. Ibid., 210: "Dixerunt Iudei: 'Non vadas per ambages! De quo incepimus loqui, loquamur! Revertamur ad Ysayam!'"

173. Ibid., 211: "Dixerunt Iudei: 'Si vis respondere nobis, responde, aut surgamus et eamus ... hec verba sunt hominis subtrahentis se a veritate et reverti volentis in fabulis.'"

5. Staying Jewish?

1. *Disputationen*, 247–48: "Quia invenio, quod impii et iniqui—id est Samaritani, publicani et peccatores et gentiles—conversi fuerunt in tempore Christi et etiam post tempus Christi usque nunc, quoniam nos Christiani de gentilibus nati sumus sive maior pars Christianorum."

2. Ephesians 2:1–2, 4–5: "et vos cum essetis mortui delictis et peccatis vestris / in quibus aliquando ambulastis secundum saeculum mundi huius secundum principem potestatis aeris huius.... Deus autem qui dives est in misericordia propter nimiam caritatem suam qua dilexit nos / et cum essemus mortui peccatis convivificavit nos Christo gratia estis salvati."

3. On the Jewish hat as a marker in medieval visual representations, see Mellinkoff, *Outcasts*, 1:41, 46, 48, 49, 59–94, 102, 214, 217, 231–33.

4. In the original context of Acts 18, it is Apollos not Paul who refutes the Jews in Achaia, but clearly the illustration conflates Apollos and Paul (whose missionary activity is described earlier in Acts 18 and, immediately following 18:28, in Acts 19).

5. *Disputationen*, 275: "O, Iudee, vos nescitis quid dicatis! Quoniam si baptismum accipietis, vocabimini 'canis filius canis,' tam a Christianis quam a Iudeis. Et in paupertate eritis, et qui hodie vobis dabit obolum, in toto uno anno non dabit vobis alium; et sic multam necessitatem habebitis et forsitan in desperatione cito cadere posscetis."

6. Stacey, "Conversion."

7. The phrases quoted here from the disputation of Tortosa—*Disputa*, 2:25 ("populus dure cervicis," "obstinacionis macula cordis")—are common in medieval Christian anti-Jewish polemic.

8. Marcus, *Jew*, 34–35.

9. Chaucer here refers to Alfonsi, *Scholar's Guide*, 42.

10. See the fuller discussion in chapter 2 above.

11. Simonsohn, *Apostolic See*, 1:42. See also the discussion of these events in Chazan, *European Jewry*, 137, 325 n. 2.

12. Eidelberg, *Jews and the Crusaders*, 68.

13. For some of the (often contentious) scholarship on conversos, New Christians, and Marranos, see Baer, *History of the Jews*, esp. 2:244–99 (but much of vol. 2 touches on questions about conversion); Netanyahu, *Marranos* and *Origins* (Netanyahu positions himself especially against Baer); "Inflecting the Converso Voice," and "Letters on 'Inflecting.'"

14. The text is cited more fully in chapter 3, n. 183, above.

15. Cohen, *Friars*, 59; Cohen concludes that, given the current state of the evidence, "one cannot be sure about the extent of the actual burning" of Maimonides' texts (58). Also see the account in Baer, *History of the Jews*, 1:96–110.

16. See Cohen, *Friars*, 52–53.

17. Ibid., 54–55 (quoting Rabbi David Kimḥi of Narbonne and Judah and Abraham ibn Ḥasdai of Barcelona). See also Rosenthal, "Talmud," 61–62, and Baer, *History of the Jews*, 1:400–401.

18. Augustine, *City of God* 18.46, 827; *De civitate dei*, 644: "prophetias nos non finxisse de Christo."

19. Rosenthal, "Talmud," 62.

20. Grayzel, *Church*, 240–43: "universos libros Judeorum Regni tui ... capi" (242), "in qua tot abusiones, et nefaria continentur, quod pudori referentibus, et audientibus sunt horrori" (240). The text of these documents is also available in Simonsohn, *Apostolic See*, 1:171–74.

21. Rosenthal, "Talmud," 76, 150–66. Rosenthal here analyzes both the summary of charges made against the Talmud at Paris that is included in an appendix to the *Extractiones de Talmut* and Rabbi Yeḥiel's account of the Paris disputation (74–75).

22. Ibid., 76 and 145–50.

23. Grayzel, *Church*, 240–41: "Si vera sunt, que de Judeis in regno Francie, et aliis provinciis commorantibus asseruntur, nulla de ipsis esset poena sufficiens, sive digna; ipsi enim sicut accepimus, lege veteri, quam Dominus per Moysen in scriptis edidit, non contenti, immo penitus pretermittentes eadem, affirmant legem aliam, que Talmut, id est Doctrina, dicitur, Dominum edidisse ac verbo Moysi traditam; et insertam eorum mentibus mentiuntur tamdiu sine scriptis servatam, donec quidam venerunt, quos Sapientes, et scribas appellant, qui eam, ne per oblivionem a mentibus hominum laberetur, in scripturam, cujus volumen in immensum excedit Textum Biblie, redegerunt." The text is also in Simonsohn, *Apostolic See*, 1:172.

24. Cohen, *Friars*, 75.

25. Rembaum, "Talmud," 210–11.

26. Cohen, *Friars*, 76.

27. Ibid., 63. For more on the trial and burning of the Talmud at Paris, see Loeb, "Controverse de 1240"; Tuilier, "Condamnation"; Chazan, "Condemnation"; *Brûlement*.

28. Cohen, *Friars*, 75. Rembaum, "Talmud," looks closely at changes in papal attitudes toward the Talmud during the 1240s, and later.

29. Maccoby, *Judaism on Trial*, 148.

30. Ibid., 115; also translated in Rankin, *Jewish Religious Polemic*, 188.

31. Maccoby, *Judaism on Trial*, 189; *Disputa*, 2:8: "quod iudeus de necessitate tenetur credere omnia in Talmut contenta, sive sint glose legis, iudicia, cerimonie, vel sermones aut annunciaciones, glose, addiciones, sive invenciones, facte super dicto Talmut; nec licet iudeo aliquid negare de illo."

32. Maccoby, *Judaism on Trial*, 209; *Disputa*, 2:457: "magnum scelus vos commisisse vel perpetrasse, cum negaveritis vestri Talmud auctoritates."

33. Hermann, *Opusculum*, 76–83.

34. Stein, "Jewish-Christian Disputations," 17–22.

35. On the second debate at Paris, see Shatzmiller, *Deuxième controverse*; Golb, *Jews*, 495–507.

36. For an introductory discussion of the three disputations, and for partial translations of both Latin and Hebrew accounts of the debates, see Maccoby, *Judaism on Trial*. Cohen, *Friars*, discusses Paris and Barcelona at some length (60–85, 108–28); Baer, "Disputations," presents an influential account of the same two debates.

37. On the dissemination of the *Vikuaḥ*, see Chazan, *Barcelona*, 138–39.

38. On Nicholas Donin, see Grayzel, *Church*, 339–40; Merchavia, "Did Nicholas Donin Instigate?"; Cohen, *Friars*, 60–76.

39. On Pablo Christiani's career, see Rosenthal, "Religious Disputation"; Shatzmiller, "Paulus Christiani"; Cohen, *Friars*, 103–28; Chazan, *Daggers*, 43–48, 70–71, 76–77, 83–85, 90–98, 102–37; Chazan, "Chapter Thirteen"; Shatzmiller, *Deuxième controverse*, esp. 15–22.

40. On Geronimo de Santa Fe, see Pacios Lopez's introduction to *Disputa*, 1:40–51.

41. Chazan, "Barcelona 'Disputation,'" 824 n. 1.

42. Maccoby, *Judaism on Trial*, 153.

43. Ibid., 102; also translated by Rankin, *Jewish Religious Polemic*, 179.

44. Maccoby, *Judaism on Trial*, 168. Also see the Catalan translation, *Crònica*, 29.

45. Rembaum reviews suggestions "that the 1240 Paris 'disputation' was a form of inquisitorial trial" ("Talmud," 204). Also see Rosenthal, "Talmud," and Stein, "Jewish-Christian Disputations," 7.

46. On the role of converts in the compilation of the *Extractiones de Talmut* and other texts connected to the 1240 Paris disputation, see Dahan, "Traductions latines"; Rosenthal, "Talmud," 74–75; Maccoby, *Judaism on Trial*, 163; Rembaum, "Talmud," 205; and Stein, "Jewish-Christian Disputations," 17.

47. Grayzel, *Church*, 200–201: "districtius inhibentes ne de fide, vel ritu suo cum Christianis presumant aliquatenus disputare, ne sub pretextu disputationis hujusmodi in erroris laqueum, quod absit, simplices delabantur." The text is also in Simonsohn, *Apostolic See*, 1:141–43.

48. *Disputationen*, 263–66.

49. For an important discussion of ideas of Jewish immutability and their implications for conversion to Christianity, see Elukin, "From Jew to Christian?"

50. Grayzel, *Church*, 310–11: "Quidam, sicut accepimus, qui ad sacri undam baptismatis voluntarii accesserunt, veterem hominem omnino non exuunt, ut novum perfectius induant: cum prioris ritus reliquias retinentes, Christiane religionis decorem tali commixtione confundant. Cum autem scriptum sit. 'Maledictus homo qui terram dobus viis ingreditur' et indui vestis non debeat lino lanaque contexta; statuimus ut tales per prelatos ecclesiarum ab observantia veteris ritus omnimodo compescantur, ut quos Christiane religioni libere voluntatis arbitrium obtulit, salutifere coactionis necessitas in ejus observatione conservet; cum minus malum existat viam Domini non agnoscere, quam post agnitam retroire."

51. It is significant that the policing of Jewish texts often coincides temporally and spatially with orthodox Christian concern about "heretical" activity, where, from the perspective of the church, a certain movement of "anticonversion" is at work within Christianity. Moore, *Formation*, gives an overview of such a pattern of "coincidence."

52. Chazan, *Barcelona*, gives a particularly full account of the Barcelona disputation. Also see Kayserling, "Disputation"; Loeb, "Controverse de 1263"; Denifle, "Quellen zur Disputation"; Roth, "Disputation of Barcelona"; Cohen, "Reflections"; Grossinger, "Disputation"; Cohen, *Friars*, 108–28.

53. Maccoby, *Judaism on Trial*, 128–29; also translated in Rankin, *Jewish Religious Polemic*, 197–98. On the identity of Arnold of Segarra, see Cohen, *Friars*, 123. Similar interventions by the friars attending the debate also occur elsewhere. See, for instance, the involvement of the Franciscan Peire de Genova (Peter of Genoa); Maccoby, *Judaism on Trial*, 108–9; Rankin, *Jewish Religious Polemic*, 183.

54. For a typical account from a Jewish perspective, see "Naḥmanides," 775.

55. The letter is dated ca. 1266 by Simonsohn, *Apostolic See*, 1:230–32; the citation is at 1:231: "districtionis severitas manifestet et ipsius exemplo aliorum audacia compescatur."

56. On Naḥmanides' emigration, see Chazan, *Barcelona*, 98–99; Chazan concludes that "the rabbi's decision for emigration could have been the result of the discomfort

occasioned by the Dominican efforts [to prosecute him] or, alternatively, of spiritual factors that had nothing to do with his involvement in the Barcelona debate" (99).

57. See Tolan, *Petrus Alfonsi*, 126–29.

58. On the accounts of the debate, see *Disputa*, 1:31–40.

59. Ibid., 2:19: "Anno a nativitate Domini millesimo quadringentesimo decimo tercio, die septima mensis februarii, Pontificatus sanctissimi in Christo patris et domini, domini Benedicti, divina providencia Pape terciidecimi anno decimo nono, illustrissimo ac serenissimo rege Aragonensi domino Ferdinando, sub anno primo dominii sui principante, in civitate Dertusensi, eiusdem regni, ex mandato prefati domini nostri Pape, omnes maiores doctores, sive Rabini, qui in regionibus dicti regni, inter iudeorum aliamas sunt reperti, fuere pariter congregati, ut errores propter quos ab actibus Messie actenus deviabant, ipsis presertim nondum venisse Messiam asserentibus . . . amonerentur: Et ad probandum . . . Dominum nostrum Iesum Christum Dei filium, omnium redemptorem, verum esse Messiam, a Deo promissum et a prophetis prenunciatum . . . reducerentur."

60. Maccoby, *Judaism on Trial*, 170.

61. Ibid., 168.

62. *Convivencia* is a controversial formulation in medieval Iberian studies. For the recent influential argument that "*Convivencia* was predicated upon violence; it was not its peaceful antithesis" (245), see Nirenberg, *Communities*. For other views, see *Convivencia* and Menocal, *Ornament*.

63. See Carreras y Candi, *L'Aljama de Juhéus*, and, for a briefer overview, the article on "Tortosa" in the *Encyclopaedia Judaica*. Carreras y Candi treats the Tortosa disputation at 89–102.

64. On the history of the *Reconquista*, see O'Callaghan, *Reconquest*.

65. The quotation is from Netanyahu, *Origins*, 169. On Abner of Burgos/Alfonso de Valladolid, see also Baer, *History of the Jews*, 1:327–54. Alfonso is the author of the Hebrew *Moreh Zedek* [*Teacher of Righteousness*], which considers "the reasons which prevented Jews from taking the path to Christian 'repentance'" and "attempt[s] to find in talmudic literature support for the basic teachings of Christianity" (ibid., 1:333, 334). The *Moreh Zedek* was translated into Spanish as the *Mostrador de justicia*; an incomplete copy is preserved in BN esp[agnol] 43.

66. On Paul of Burgos, see Baer, *History of the Jews*, 2:139–50, and Netanyahu, *Origins*, 168–206.

67. Paul of Burgos, *Scrutinium scripturarum*, BN nouv. acq. lat. 1379: "Scrutinium scripturarum veterum editum a Rabi paulo episcopo Burgensis Neophito aduersus Judeos" (fol. 1r); "Explicit prima pars huius operis dialogica inter Saulum et paulum" (fol. 6v).

68. Baer, *History of the Jews*, 2:141; Netanyahu, *Origins*, 172.

69. Baer, *History of the Jews*, 2:139–50. See Lorki, *Apologetische Schreiben*, for the text of the *Iggeret* [*Letter*] to Paul.

70. Baer, *History of the Jews*, suggests, however, that Lorki was the pope's physician even before his conversion (2:171).

71. Netanyahu, *Origins*, 202–3.

72. Ibid., 203. See the first appendix in volume 1 of *Disputa* for a detailed summary of Geronimo's treatise; Pacios Lopez here gives the following title (from the 1552 Zurich

edition of the text): "Of Geronimo of Santa Fe, a Jew converted to Christianity, two books, of which the first assails the faith and religion (of the Jews), and the second indeed the Talmud. By mandate of the Lord Pope Benedict XIII, an account made in the year of the Lord 1412, in the month of August, in Spain" [Hieronimi de Sancta Fide, Iudaei ad christianismum conversi, libri duo, quorum prior fidem et religionem (Iudaeorum) impugnat, alter vero Talmud. Ad mandatum Domini Papae Benedicti XIII, facta relatione anno Domini 1412, mense Augusto, in Hispania] (1:345). Also see Orfali, "Portuguese Edition."

73. For an introduction to Vincent Ferrer, see the article in *Catholic Encyclopedia* ("St. Vincent Ferrer"). For a detailed overview of Ferrer's written work, see Brettle, *San Vicente Ferrer*.

74. Ghéon, *St. Vincent Ferrer*, 39.

75. Quoted in Paris, *End of Days*, 32.

76. The events of 1391 and their aftermath are treated in detail in Baer, *History of the Jews*, 2:95–169. On the legislation of 1393, see ibid., 2:125. Carreras y Candi, *L'Aljama de Juhéus*, 77–88, treats the events of 1391 in Tortosa.·

77. Netanyahu, *Marranos*, 243 (with fuller discussion at 238–48, 255–74). Also see Netanyahu, *Origins*, 1095–1102; Baer, *History of the Jews*, 2:246; Paris, *End of Days*, 96.

78. On Ferrer's activity during these years, see Baer, *History of the Jews*, 2:166–72, 196, 223–24, 230–32; Netanyahu, *Origins*, 183–91, 198–203.

79. *Disputa*, 2:252: "multum venerabilis ac famosissimi patris et religiosi, dominique mei, singularissimi fratris Vincencii, ordinis Predicatorum, hic presentis." The text here indicates that Vincent will preach to the Jewish disputants on the New Testament and "Catholic doctors" outside the formal context of the disputation.

80. See Baer, *History of the Jews*, 2:166–69; Netanyahu, *Origins*, 191–201; Paris, *End of Days*, 92.

81. Netanyahu, *Origins*, 192; also see Baer, *History of the Jews*, 2:167.

82. Netanyahu, *Origins*, 193; also see Baer, *History of the Jews*, 2:168.

83. Netanyahu, *Origins*, 193; also see Baer, *History of the Jews*, 2:168.

84. Netanyahu, *Origins*, 194.

85. Ibid., 195; also see Baer, *History of the Jews*, 2:168.

86. Netanyahu, *Origins*, 195.

87. Baer, *History of the Jews*, 2:168.

88. Netanyahu, *Origins*, 202; also see Baer, *History of the Jews*, 2:166–67, 170–73.

89. *Disputa*, 2:595–608.

90. Simonsohn, *Apostolic See*, 2:593–602; Netanyahu, *Origins*, 205; Paris, *End of Days*, 113–14. The text of the papal bull and the text presented within the transcript of the disputation of Tortosa (*Disputa*, 2:597–608) are essentially identical, and both conclude with the statement that they were promulgated at Valencia. It is possible that the later (1415) text has been inserted into the transcript of the disputation as a concluding "session," but the text does insist that the papal decree was read aloud on November 12–13, 1414 (*Disputa*, 2:595).

91. Simonsohn, *Apostolic See*, 2:553.

92. Ibid., 2:554.

93. Ibid., 2:571.

94. Ibid., 2:585.

95. Ibid., 2:586, 591, 611.

96. Ibid., 2:610.

97. Ibid., 2:587, 592.

98. Ibid., 2:588, 602–9.

99. Ibid., 2:589, 590, 615.

100. Netanyahu, *Origins*, 190.

101. Ibid., 182–83.

102. *Disputa*, 2:597–98: "Nos itaque, quos licet immeritos, celestis agricola vinee sue dignatus est hiis impacatis temporibus preesse custodes, quamvis aliis grandibus et arduis negociis, unionem Sancte Matris Ecclesie, et extirpacionem pestiferorum scismatum concernentibus, que illam omnino devastare conantur, quam plurimum occupati, quantum in nobis fuit, Domino cooperante, huic insercioni dedimus operam efficacem." The reference to grafting of course evokes Romans 11:16–24, which also uses the verb "inserere."

103. *Disputa*, 2:599: "Nos, eorum vestigia imitantes."

104. Ibid.: "predecessores nostri Gregorius IXus. et Innocencius IVus. prefatos libros Talmud, . . . propter errores et hereses in eo contentos, comburi iusserunt."

105. Maccoby, *Judaism on Trial*, 170.

106. *Disputa*, 2:86: "Perfecta dicta dieta, divina gracia que illuminat omnem hominem venientem in hunc mundum misericorditer inspirante in decem iudeos notabiles, quinque videlicet de Aliama ville Montissoni, duos vero de Aliama loci de Falçet, unum de Aliama loci de Mora, unumque notabilem studentem talmudistam de Aliama ville Alcanicii, qui a cunabulis de domo paterna ac scolla sua continue Talmut audiendo nunquam discesserat, quemdam eciam iuvenem de civitate Calataiubii, se ipsam illustrative effudit. / Qui omnes pariter decem, magna cum devocione magnaque humilitate, genibusque flexis ante scabellum pedum Sanctissimi Domini nostri Pape Benedicti XIII prostrati, confessi sunt dicentes unanimiter: Evidenter enim videmus atque clare cognoscimus raciones magistri Ieronimi fore veras, et responsa rabinorum iudeorum nullius penitus esse valoris. Ideo Sanctitatem vestram, Pater beatissime, ac clementissime Domine, maxima cum devocione, maximaque cum humilitate supplicamus atque requirimus quatenus vestra Sanctitas benignissima nos faciat baptizari, ut valeamus acquirere nostrarum salutem animarum."

107. Ibid.: "honorifice ac solempniter fecit eos baptizari . . . uxores ac eorumdem familie usque ad numerum triginta animarum et ultra, in fonte baptismatis a lepra iudaica fuerunt mundate."

108. Ibid., 2:102, 151, 598 ("super tria millia hominum").

109. Ibid., 2:572: "plures vanitates, cavillaciones, decepciones, hereses, turpitudines, et errores innumeri"; "sex species abhominacionum." Also see the "Indice de Materias" that precedes the account of the disputation proper: "abhominaciones, hereses, immundicie et vanitates que in libro Talmut continentur" (ibid., 2:8; translated in Maccoby, *Judaism on Trial*, 189).

110. *Disputa*, 2:572: "ut legi contradicerent Iesu Christi."

111. See, for instance, Trachtenberg, *Devil and the Jews*, 15, 17.

112. For one example, see *Disputa*, 2:110.

113. Ibid., 2:117: "legis destruccio et casus . . . heresis manifeste."

114. Ibid., 2:19.

115. Simonsohn, *Apostolic See*, 2:575.

116. *Disputa*, 2:570: "de bonis temporalibus et fortune vos estis prosperati usque nunc valde, tam viventes deliciose et quiete cum officiis delicatis, quam eciam in habendo habunde lucra magna absque labore, per viam usurariam, et eciam tenendo sinagogas sumptuosas, tenendo adhuc personas et vitam christianorum in posse vestrum per officium medicine, et cirurgie, et eorum pecunias per officium cursorie, aliarumque administracionum."

117. Ibid., 2:571: "Messiam venisse . . . Salvatoris nostri Iesu Christi."

118. Ibid., 2:570: "sunt excitati sanctissimus Dominus Noster Papa et Princeps serenissimus rex noster. Et viso quod sustinere hoc esset valde iniustum et irracionabile, et manifeste venire contra divinum servicium, et cum anexa et unica voluntate unanimiter restringere, et in illo ordine et regula qualiter debeatis vivere iuxta habitum et regulam captivorum."

119. Ibid., 2:40–41: "magister Salomon Ysach, quod rabi Astruch minus bene et insufficienter responderat dixit."

120. Ibid., 2:41: "dictus magister Salomon cessat loqui."

121. Ibid., 2:37: "Tunc vero, pluribus inconvenientibus ex dictis rabi Iucef datis, atque inde secutis, atque vocatis, copiosa mu[l]titudo iudeorum inibi astancium, dicta glosa rabi Iucef tamquam a disona, vana, nulliusque comodi disce[]dencium, ac dictum rabi Iucef in hoc quam plurimum vacillantem deridencium, super hoc iudicarunt convictum." Pacios Lopez corrects the text's "discendencium" to "discedencium" (2:619); I have corrected "muititudo" to "multitudo."

122. Ibid., 2:550: "quod prius concesserant, impudenter negaverunt." The text here is from the summary of earlier stages of the disputation presented in session sixty-two; compare 2:59–60.

123. Ibid., 2:550: "circumspiciens variacionem eorumdem, et quod id quod uno die concedebant, alio certe negabant, non immerito duxit ordinandum, precipiens quod raciones cuiuslibet partis in scriptis manifeste et publice offerrentur taliter quod nullo modo negarentur." Compare 2:60.

124. Ibid., 2:60: "notario apostolico."

125. Ibid., 2:75.

126. Ibid., 2:131.

127. Crispin, *Works,* 9: "tacito mei et ipsius nomine, scripsi sub persona Iudei cum Christiano de fide nostra disceptantis."

128. *Disputa*, 2:91: "pertinaciter," "perfidiose," "inverecunde."

129. Maccoby, *Judaism on Trial,* 172.

130. Ibid., 169.

131. Ibid., 178.

132. Ibid.

133. *Disputa*, 2:43: "Ad hec autem dictus rabi Mathatias nichil respondit."

134. Ibid., 2:44: "Tunc quidem dictus rabi se amplius nichil scire respondere publice confessus est."

135. Ibid., 2:47: "Ad que omnia dictus rabi silencium pro responsione accepit."

136. Ibid., 2:50: "Tunc autem rabi Ferrer tacuit."

137. Ibid., 2:123: "Iudeus . . . respondet quod ipse adheret eius responsis superius factis . . . dicens quod ad presens nichil aliud sibi occurrit responsum propter eius insufficienciam et intellectus infirmitatem et ignoranciam. Et cum hoc eius responsionibus ultimum finem imponit, sicut ille cuius sciencia ultra non transcendit."

138. Ibid., 2:140: "sibi met in presenti materia nullam possunt attribuere ignoranciam, quoniam ce[r]tum est ipsos sapienciores esse et maiores rabini qui sunt ad presens in toto regno. Et esto quod non sint antiquorum sufficienciam ymitantes, saltem non potest negari eos dicta antiquorum bene ac sufficienter intelligere, et insuper aliquid ultra super eo videre. / Accidit eis sicut parvulo super collum gigantis sedenti vel equitanti." Pacios Lopez corrects "cedtum" to "certum" (2:620).

139. Ibid., 2:183: "responsum iudeorum, tam longum tamque prolixum factum in hiis que a propria deviant materia, et tam succinctum tamque breve super factis interrogacionibus ipsis iudeis super presenti materia, ubi tota vertitur informacionis medulla."

140. Netanyahu, *Origins*, 204.

141. *Disputa*, 2:593: "Et ego Astruch Levi, cum debita humilitate, subieccione ac reverencia reverendissime paternitatis et dominacionis Domini Cardinalis, aliorumque reverendorum Patrum et Dominorum hic presencium, respondeo dicens: Quod licet auctoritates talmudice, qua[s] contra Talmut, tam per reverendum meum Dominum elemosinarium, quam per honorabilem magistrum Ieronimum allegate, sicut ad literam iacent, male sonent, partim quia prima facie videntur heretice, partim contra bonos mores, partim quia sunt erronee; et quamvis per tradicionem meorum magistrorum habuerim quod ille habeant, aut possint alium sensum habere, fateor tamen illum me ignorare. Idcirco dictis auctoritatibus nullam fidem adhibeo, nec auctoritatem aliqualem, nec illis credo, nec easdem defendere intendo. Et quamcumque responsionem per me superius datam huic mee ultime responsioni obviante illi, revoco et pro non dicta habeo, in eo solum in quo huic contradicit."

142. Ibid.: "Omnibus iudeis et rabinis tocius congregacionis aliamarum ibidem presencium, rabi Ferrer et rabi Iuçef Albo dumtaxat exceptis, magna voce clamantibus et dicentibus: Et nos in dicta cedula concordamus et illi adheremus."

143. Ibid., 2:595: "sentenciam contra dictum Talmud . . . et quasdam constituciones vel ordinaciones . . . contra iudeos."

144. Ibid., 2:598: "super tria millia hominum."

145. Ibid.: "tam assiduis altercacionibus, quam crebris informacionibus, tum in nostra presencia, tum in absencia per illos quos ad hoc deputavimus insistentes, actum est ut, Deo inspirante, eorum quam plurimi sacrum baptisma puro corde reciperent et mente devota, suis se codicibus convictos publice confitentes, illum in quem sui predecessores transfixerant, Christum Iesum scilicet Nazarenum, verum Messiam et Salvatorem suum et Dominum cognoscentes."

146. Baer, *History of the Jews*, 2:211–17.

147. This is of course one of the crucially contentious questions in scholarship on the conversos and the Inquisition: were, in fact, many converts still practicing Jews (which would then give the Inquisition a "rational" basis); or were most, in fact, "true" converts (which would show the Inquisition operating from largely "irrational," racist premises)? It is along this general fault line that the differences between Baer and Netanyahu emerge.

148. Eidelberg, *Jews and the Crusaders*, 68.

149. *Disputa*, 2:19: "Et licet in dicta Curia prefati domini Pape, sint quam plurimi sacre theologie magistri et doctores, sapiencia, sciencia, ac discrecione non modica preful-gentes, placuit dicto domino nostro Pape in conclusionibus supra dictis, discretum virum et honorabilem magistrum Ieronimum de Sancta Fide, sue beatissime persone medicus, ad iudeorum informacionem esse specialiter deputatum."

150. Ibid.: "in veteris Testamenti Biblia, glosisque eiusdem, necnon Talmut cunc-tisque tractatibus iudeorum . . . copiose fundatum."

151. Maccoby, *Judaism on Trial*, 168.

152. Ibid., 171.

153. Ibid., 173.

154. See Baer, *History of the Jews*, 2:232–34. Baer discusses Jucef Albo's work along-side two other significant post-Tortosa Hebrew texts, Rabbi Shem Tov's *Sefer ha-Emunot* [*The Book of Beliefs*] and Rabbi Shlomo Alami's *Iggeret Musar* [*The Letter of Ethics*] (2:234–43). On Alami, also see Gutwirth, "Social Tensions," esp. 1–58.

155. Cited in Baer, *History of the Jews*, 2:216–17. For more on Bonafed, see Gutwirth, "Social Criticism"; Bejarano Escanilla, "Šělomoh Bonafed"; Gutwirth, "Leer"; Sáenz-Badillos, "Šelomoh Bonafed."

BIBLIOGRAPHY

❖

ABBREVIATIONS

BL   British Library
BN   Bibliothèque Nationale
PL   J.-P. Migne, ed. *Patrologiae cursus completus, Series Latina.* 221 vols. Paris, 1841–79.
RSV Revised Standard Version

PRIMARY SOURCES

Abelard, Peter. *Dialogue of a Philosopher with a Jew, and a Christian.* Trans. Pierre J. Payer. Toronto: Pontifical Institute of Mediaeval Studies, 1979.

———. *Dialogus inter philosophum, iudeum et christianum.* Ed. Rudolf Thomas. Stuttgart: F. Frommann, 1970.

———. *Ethical Writings: Ethics and Dialogue between a Philosopher, a Jew, and a Christian.* Trans. Paul Vincent Spade. Indianapolis: Hackett Publishing, 1995.

Alain de Lille. "Contra Paganos." [*De fide catholica,* Book Three.] Ed. Marie-Thérèse d'Alverny. In *Islam et Chrétiens du Midi,* 325–50.

———. *De fide catholica.* PL 210, 305–430.

———. *The Plaint of Nature.* Trans. James J. Sheridan. Toronto: Pontifical Institute of Mediaeval Studies, 1980.

Albert of Aix [Alberti Aquensis]. *Historia Hierosolymitana.* In *Recueil des historiens des croisades,* 4:265–713.

pseudo-Alcuin. *Liber de divinis officiis.* PL 101, 1173–1286.

Alfonsi, Peter. *Dialogi contra Iudaeos.* PL 157, 535–672.

———. *Dialogi contra Iudaeos.* Manuscripts: BL Additional 15404; BL Harley 3707; BL Harley 3861; BL Royal 15.C.ii; BN lat. 2134; BN lat. 3359a; BN lat. 3394; BN lat. 5080; BN lat. 10624; BN lat. 10722; BN lat. 14069; BN lat. 15009; BN lat. 16523; BN lat. 18104.

———. [Pedro Alfonso de Huesca]. *Diálogo contra los Judíos.* Intro. John Tolan. Ed. Klaus-Peter Mieth. Trans. Esperanza Ducay. Coord. M.ª Jesús Lacarra. Huesca: Instituto de Estudios Altoaragoneses, 1996.

———. *The Scholar's Guide: A Translation of the Twelfth-Century "Disciplina Clericalis" of Pedro Alfonso.* Trans. Joseph Ramon Jones and John Esten Keller. Toronto: Pontifical Institute of Mediaeval Studies, 1969.

Alfonso de Valladolid [Abner of Burgos]. *Mostrador de justicia.* MS BN esp[agnol] 43.

Arduini, Maria Ludovica. *Ruperto di Deutz e la controversia tra Christiani ed Ebrei nel secolo XII, con testo critico dell'Anulus seu dialogus inter Christianum et Iudaeum.* Ed. Rhabanus Haacke. Rome: Nella Sede dell'Istituto, Palazzo Borromini, 1979.

Augustine. *Concerning the City of God against the Pagans.* Trans. Henry Bettenson. Harmondsworth: Penguin, 1984.

———. *Confessions.* Trans. R. S. Pine-Coffin. Harmondsworth: Penguin, 1961.

———. *De civitate dei.* Ed. Bernard Dombart and Alphonse Kalb (with emendations by the editors of CCSL). Corpus Christianorum, Series Latina, 47–48. Turnhout: Brepols, 1955.

———. *De Genesi contra Manichaeos. PL* 34, 173–220.

Berger, David, ed. and trans. *The Jewish-Christian Debate in the High Middle Ages: A Critical Edition of the Niẓẓaḥon Vetus.* Philadelphia: Jewish Publication Society of America, 1979.

Bible. *The Holy Bible.* RSV. New York: Harper & Brothers, 1952.

———. *The Holy Bible, Translated from the Latin Vulgate* [Douai-Rheims]. New York: P. J. Kenedy & Sons, 1950.

Biblia Sacra iuxta Vulgatam Versionem. Ed. Robertus Weber, with Bonifatio Fischer, Iohanne Gribomont, H. F. D. Sparks, and W. Thiele. 2nd ed. 2 vols. Stuttgart: Württembergische Bibelanstalt, 1969.

Biblia Sacra Latina ex Biblia Sacra Vulgatae Editionis, Sixti V. et Clementis VIII. London: Samuel Bagster and Sons, 1904.

Biblical Art on the WWW. http://www.biblical-art.com/index.htm.

Boccaccio, Giovanni. *The Decameron.* Trans. G. H. McWilliam. Harmondsworth: Penguin, 1972.

Bodleian Library. "The Conversion of St. Paul on the Road to Damascus." http://www.bodley.ox.ac.uk/dept/scwmss/wmss/medieval/jpegs/lat/liturg/e/1500/03900806.jpg.

Boethius. *The Theological Tractates.* Trans. H. F. Stewart and E. K. Rand. *The Consolation of Philosophy.* Trans. I. T. (1609). Rev. H. F. Stewart. Loeb Classical Library. Cambridge: Harvard University; London: William Heinemann, 1962 [1918].

Bryan, W. F., and Germaine Dempster, eds. *Sources and Analogues of Chaucer's Canterbury Tales.* Chicago: University of Chicago Press, 1941.

Caesarius of Heisterbach. *The Dialogue on Miracles.* Trans. H. von E. Scott and C. C. Swinton Bland. 2 vols. London: George Routledge and Sons, 1929.

Campbell, Colin. "Weddings/Celebrations: Vows" [Janis Ian and Patricia Snyder]. *New York Times,* 7 September 2003, Sunday Style 15.

Chaucer, Geoffrey. *The Riverside Chaucer.* Ed. Larry D. Benson. 3rd ed. Boston: Houghton Mifflin, 1987.

Contardo, Inghetto. *Disputatio contra Iudeos: Controverse avec les juifs.* Ed. and trans. Gilbert Dahan. Paris: Les Belles Lettres, 1993.

———. Also see *Disputationen zu Ceuta (1179) und Mallorca (1286),* below.

Crispin, Gilbert. *The Works of Gilbert Crispin, Abbot of Westminster.* Ed. Anna Sapir Abulafia and G. R. Evans. London: Oxford University Press, for The British Academy, 1986.

La Crònica en Hebreu de la Disputa de Tortosa. Ed. Jaume Rieri i Sans. Barcelona: Fundació Salvador Vives Casajuana, 1974.

Croxton. *Play of the Sacrament.* In *Medieval Drama,* ed. David Bevington, 754–88. Boston: Houghton Mifflin, 1975.

Dame Sirith. In *Early Middle English Verse and Prose,* 2nd ed., ed. J. A. W. Bennett and G. V. Smithers, 77–95. Oxford: Clarendon Press, 1968.

Damian, Peter. *Book of Gomorrah: An Eleventh-Century Treatise against Clerical Homosexual Practices.* Trans. Pierre J. Payer. Waterloo, Ont.: Wilfrid Laurier University Press, 1982.

———. *Die Briefe des Petrus Damianus.* Vol. 1: *Letters 1–40.* Ed. Kurt Reindel. Munich: Monumenta Germaniae Historica, 1983.

———. *Letters.* Vol. 1: *Letters 1–30.* Vol. 2: *Letters 31–60.* Trans. Owen J. Blum. 2 vols. Washington, DC: Catholic University of America Press, 1989–90.

———. *Opusculum secundum: Antilogus contra Judaeos, ad Honestum virum clarissimum* and *Opusculum tertium: Dialogus inter Judaeum requirentem, et Christianum e contrario respondentem. Ad eundem Honestum.* PL 145, 41–68.

———. *Opusculum septimum: Liber Gomorrhianus, ad Leonem IX Rom. Pont.* PL 145, 159–90.

Dante. *The Divine Comedy.* Ed. and trans. Charles S. Singleton. 6 vols. Princeton: Princeton University Press, 1970–75.

La Disputa de Tortosa. Ed. Antonio Pacios Lopez. 2 vols. Madrid: Instituto "Arias Montano," 1957.

Disputatio Ecclesiae et Synagogae. In *Thesaurus novus anecdotorum,* vol. 5, ed. Edmond Martène and Ursin Durand, cols. 1497–1506. Paris: Lutetiae Parisiorum, 1717.

Die Disputationen zu Ceuta (1179) und Mallorca (1286): Zwei antijüdische Schriften aus dem mittelalterlichen Genua. Ed. Ora Limor. Munich: Monumenta Germaniae Historica, 1994.

The Dream of the Rood. Ed. Michael J. Swanton. Exeter: University of Exeter Press, 1996.

Dunbar, William. *The Poems of William Dunbar.* Ed. W. Mackay Mackenzie. London: Faber and Faber, 1932.

Eidelberg, Shlomo, ed. and trans. *The Jews and the Crusaders: The Hebrew Chronicles of the First and Second Crusades.* Hoboken: KTAV, 1996 [1977].

Ellis, Havelock. *Studies in the Psychology of Sex.* Vol. 1, Part 4: *Sexual Inversion.* New York: Random House, 1936.

Exodus International, North America. http://www.exodus-international.org or http://www.exodus.to/default2.asp.

Extractiones de Talmut. Manuscript: BN lat. 16558.

The Getty Museum. http://www.getty.edu.

Gíslasaga. The Saga of Gisli the Outlaw. Trans. George Johnston. Toronto: University of Toronto Press, 1963.

Gower, John. *The Complete Works of John Gower.* Ed. G. C. Macauley. 4 vols. Oxford: Clarendon Press, 1899–1902.

———. *Vox Clamantis.* In *The Major Latin Works of John Gower: The Voice of One Crying and the Tripartite Chronicle.* Trans. Eric W. Stockton. Seattle: University of Washington Press, 1962.

Grayzel, Solomon. *The Church and the Jews in the XIIIth Century: A Study of Their Relations during the Years 1198–1254, Based on the Papal Letters and the Conciliar Decrees of the Period.* Rev. ed. New York: Hermon Press, 1966 [1933].

Guibert of Nogent. *Autobiographie.* Ed. and trans. Edmond-René Labande. Paris: Société d'Édition "Les Belles Lettres," 1981.

———. *De pignoribus sanctorum.* PL 156, 607–80.

————. *De sanctis et eorum pigneribus.* Ed. R. B. C. Huygens. Corpus Christianorum, Continuatio Mediaevalis 127. Turnhout: Brepols, 1993. 79–175.

————. *De vita sua, sive monodiarum libri tres.* PL 156, 837–962.

————. *The Deeds of God through the Franks: A Translation of Guibert of Nogent's Gesta Dei per Francos.* Trans. Robert Levine. Woodbridge: Boydell Press, 1997.

————. *Dei Gesta per Francos, et cinq autres textes.* Ed. R. B. C. Huygens. Corpus Christianorum, Continuatio Mediaevalis 127A. Turnhout: Brepols, 1996.

————. *Gesta Dei per Francos.* PL 156, 679–837.

————. *Gesta Dei per Francos.* In *Recueil des historiens des croisades,* 113–263.

————. *A Monk's Confession: The Memoirs of Guibert of Nogent.* Trans. Paul J. Archambault. University Park: Pennsylvania State University Press, 1996.

————. *Moralia in Genesim.* PL 156, 19–338.

————. *Self and Society in Medieval France: The Memoirs of Abbot Guibert of Nogent.* Ed. John F. Benton. Trans. C. C. Swinton Bland. New York: Harper & Row, 1970.

————. *Tractatus de incarnatione contra judaeos.* PL 156, 489–528.

Guillaume de Lorris and Jean de Meun. *Le Roman de la rose.* Ed. Daniel Poirion. Paris: Garnier-Flammarion, 1974.

ha-Levi, Judah. *The Kuzari (Kitab al-Khazari): An Argument for the Faith of Israel.* Trans. Hartwig Hirschfeld. New York: Schocken Books, 1964 [1905].

Hamer, Dean H., Stella Hu, Victoria L. Magnuson, Nan Hu, and Angela M. L. Pattatucci. "A Linkage between DNA Markers on the X Chromosome and Male Sexual Orientation." *Science* 261 (16 July 1993): 321–27.

Hermann of Cologne [Hermannus quondam Judaeus]. *Opusculum de conversione sua.* Ed. Gerlinde Niemeyer. Monumenta Germaniae Historica. Weimar: Hermann Böhlaus Nachfolger, 1963.

————. Also see Morrison, Karl. *Conversion and Text,* below (Secondary Sources).

Horace [Q. Horatius Flaccus]. *Opera.* Ed. Edward C. Wickham. 2nd ed. Rev. H. W. Garrod. Oxford: Clarendon Press, 1975 [1901].

Humanities Interactive. "The Conversion of St. Paul." http://www.humanities-interactive .org/medieval/songglory/ex071_13e.html.

Jerome. *Liber de nominibus Hebraicis.* PL 23, 771–858.

Julian of Norwich. *A Book of Showings to the Anchoress Julian of Norwich,* 2 parts, *The Short Text* and *The Long Text.* Ed. Edmund Colledge and James Walsh. Toronto: Pontifical Institute of Mediaeval Studies, 1978.

Kempe, Margery. *The Book of Margery Kempe.* Ed. Sanford Brown Meech and Hope Emily Allen. Early English Text Society, O.S. 212. London: Oxford University Press, 1940.

————. *The Book of Margery Kempe.* Trans. B. A. Windeatt. London: Penguin, 1985.

Kimhi, Joseph. *The Book of the Covenant.* Trans. Frank Talmage. Toronto: Pontifical Institute of Mediaeval Studies, 1972.

Kushner, Tony. *Angels in America: A Gay Fantasia on National Themes.* Part Two: *Perestroika.* New York: Theatre Communications Group, 1994.

Langland, William. *Piers Plowman by William Langland: An Edition of the C-Text.* Ed. Derek Pearsall. Berkeley and Los Angeles: University of California Press, 1978.

LeVay, Simon. "A Difference in Hypothalamic Structure between Heterosexual and Homosexual Men." *Science* 253 (30 August 1991): 1034–37.

Lorde, Audre. *Zami: A New Spelling of My Name*. Trumansburg, NY: Crossing Press, 1982.

Lorki, Joshua. *Das apologetische Schreiben des Josua Lorki an den Abtrünnigen Don Salomon ha-Lewi (Paulus de Santa Maria). Iggeret R. Yehoshua ha-Lorki.* Ed. L. Landau. Antwerp: Verlag von Teitelbaum & Boxenbaum, 1906.

Maccoby, Hyam, ed. and trans. *Judaism on Trial: Jewish-Christian Disputations in the Middle Ages*. London: Littman Library of Jewish Civilization, 1993 [1982].

Maimonides, Moses. *The Guide for the Perplexed*. Trans. M. Friedlander. 2nd ed. New York: Dover, 1956 [1904].

Malory, Thomas. *Works*. Ed. Eugène Vinaver. Oxford: Oxford University Press, 1971.

Mandeville, John. *The Travels of Sir John Mandeville*. Trans. C. W. R. D. Moseley. Harmondsworth: Penguin, 1983.

Marcus, Jacob R., ed. *The Jew in the Medieval World: A Source Book: 315–1791*. New York: Atheneum, 1981 [1938].

Marie de France. *The Lais of Marie de France*. Trans. Robert Hanning and Joan Ferrante. Durham, NC: Labyrinth, 1982.

Marlowe, Christopher. *The Jew of Malta*. Ed. David Bevington. Manchester: Manchester University Press, 1997.

Martini, Raymond. *Pugio Fidei adversus Mauros et Judaeos*. Leipzig, 1687. Reprint, Farnborough, Hampshire: Gregg Press, 1967.

Melville, Herman. *Moby Dick*. Ed. Harrison Hayford and Hershel Parker. New York: W. W. Norton, 1967.

"Nifty Erotic Stories Archive." http://www.nifty.org/nifty/index.html.

Odo of Cambrai [= Tournai]. *Disputatio contra Iudaeum Leonem nomine de adventu Christi filii Dei*. PL 160, 1103–12.

———. *On Original Sin and A Disputation with the Jew, Leo, Concerning the Advent of Christ, the Son of God*. Trans. Irven M. Resnick. Philadelphia: University of Pennsylvania Press, 1994.

Oldradus de Ponte. *Jews and Saracens in the Consilia of Oldradus de Ponte*. Ed. and trans. Norman Zacour. Toronto: Pontifical Institute of Mediaeval Studies, 1990.

Paris, Matthew. *Chronicles of Matthew Paris: Monastic Life in the Thirteenth Century*. Ed. and trans. Richard Vaughan. Gloucester: Alan Sutton; New York: St. Martin's Press, 1986 [1984].

The Parlement of the Thre Ages: An Alliterative Poem on the Nine Worthies and the Heroes of Romance. In *Select Early English Poems*, vol. 2, ed. I. Gollancz. London: H. Milford, Oxford University Press, 1915.

Paul of Burgos. *Scrutinium scripturarum*. Manuscript: BN nouv. acq. lat. 1379.

Polo, Marco. *The Travels*. Trans. Ronald Latham. Harmondsworth: Penguin, 1958.

Pontifical Biblical Commission. *The Jewish People and Their Sacred Scripture in the Christian Bible*. Intro. Joseph Cardinal Ratzinger. Vatican City: Libreria Editrice Vaticana, 2001. http://www.vatican.va/roman_curia/congregations/cfaith/pcb_documents/rc_con_cfaith_doc_20020212_popolo-ebraico_en.html.

Rankin, Oliver Shaw. *Jewish Religious Polemic of Early and Later Centuries, A Study of Documents Here Rendered in English.* New York: KTAV Publishing House, 1970.

Recueil des historiens des croisades, Historiens occidentaux. Vol. 4. L'Academie des Inscriptions et Belles-Lettres. Paris: Imprimerie Nationale, 1879. Reprint, Farnborough, Hampshire: Gregg Press, 1967.

Rijksmuseum, Amsterdam. http://www.rijksmuseum.nl/index.jsp.

Rupert of Deutz. *Dialogus inter christianum et judaeum.* PL 170, 559–610.

———. Also see Arduini, *Ruperto di Deutz,* above.

Shakespeare, William. *The Merchant of Venice.* Ed. M. M. Mahood. Cambridge: Cambridge University Press, 1987.

Simonsohn, Shlomo, ed. *The Apostolic See and the Jews.* Vol. 1: *Documents: 492–1404* and vol. 2: *Documents: 1394–1464.* Toronto: Pontifical Institute of Mediaeval Studies, 1988–89.

Sir Orfeo. Ed. A. J. Bliss. London: Oxford University Press, 1954.

Theobald of Saxony. *Pharetra fidei contra Iudaeos.* Ed. J. C. Wolf. *Bibliotheca Hebraea* 4 (1733): 555–67.

Thomas of Monmouth. *The Life and Miracles of St. William of Norwich.* Ed. Augustus Jessopp and Montague Rhodes James. Cambridge: Cambridge University Press, 1896.

Tovey, D'Blossiers. *Anglia Judaica: Or the History and Antiquities of the Jews of England.* Oxford, 1738. Reprint, New York: Burt Franklin, 1967.

The Towneley Plays. Ed. Martin Stevens and A. C. Cawley. 2 vols. Early English Text Society, S.S. 13–14. Oxford: Oxford University Press, 1994.

Ugolino di Monte Santa Maria. *The Little Flowers of St. Francis.* Trans. Raphael Brown. Garden City, NY: Image Books, 1958.

Vincent de Beauvais [Vincentius Bellovacensis]. *Speculum historiale.* Vol. 4 in *Speculum quadruplex, sive speculum maius.* Douai, 1624. Reprint, Graz: Akademische Druck-u. Verlagsanstalt, 1965.

SECONDARY SOURCES

Abulafia, Anna Sapir. "The *ars disputandi* of Gilbert Crispin, Abbot of Westminster (1085–1117)." In *Ad Fontes: Opstellen aangeboden aan Prof. Dr. C. van de Kieft,* ed. C. M. Cappon et al., 139–52. Amsterdam: Verloren, 1984. Reprint, Abulafia, *Christians and Jews in Dispute,* chapter VI.

———. "An Attempt by Gilbert Crispin, Abbot of Westminster, at Rational Argument in the Jewish-Christian Debate." *Studia Monastica* 26 (1984): 55–74. Reprint, Abulafia, *Christians and Jews in Dispute,* chapter VIII.

———. "Bodies in the Jewish-Christian Debate." In *Framing Medieval Bodies,* ed. Sarah Kay and Miri Rubin, 123–37. Manchester: Manchester University Press, 1994.

———. "Christian Imagery of Jews in the Twelfth Century: A Look at Odo of Cambrai and Guibert of Nogent." *Theoretische Geschiedenis* 16 (1989): 383–91. Reprint, Abulafia, *Christians and Jews in Dispute,* chapter X.

———. *Christians and Jews in Dispute: Disputational Literature and the Rise of Anti-Judaism in the West (c. 1000–1150).* Aldershot: Ashgate Variorum, 1998.

———. *Christians and Jews in the Twelfth-Century Renaissance.* London: Routledge, 1995.

———. "Christians Disputing Disbelief: St. Anselm, Gilbert Crispin and Pseudo-Anselm." In *Religionsgespräche im Mittelalter,* 131–48. Reprint, Abulafia, *Christians and Jews in Dispute,* chapter V.

———. "Gilbert Crispin's Disputations: An Exercise in Hermeneutics." In *Les mutations socio-culturelles au tournant des XI–XII siècles,* ed. Raymonde Foreville, 511–20. Paris: Centre National de la Recherche Scientifique, 1984. Reprint, Abulafia, *Christians and Jews in Dispute,* chapter VII.

———. "The Ideology of Reform and Changing Ideas Concerning Jews in the Works of Rupert of Deutz and Hermannus Quondam Iudeus." *Jewish History* 7 (1993): 43–63. Reprint, Abulafia, *Christians and Jews in Dispute,* chapter XV.

———. "*Intentio Recta an Erronea?* Peter Abelard's Views on Judaism and the Jews." In *Medieval Studies in Honour of Avrom Saltman,* ed. Bat-Sheva Albert, Yvonne Friedman, and Simon Schwarzfuchs, 13–30. Ramat-Gan: Bar-Ilan University Press, 1995.

———. "St. Anselm and Those Outside the Church." In *Faith and Identity: Christian Political Experience,* ed. David Loades and Katherine Walsh, 11–37. Oxford: B. Blackwell, for the Ecclesiastical History Society, 1990. Reprint, Abulafia, *Christians and Jews in Dispute,* chapter IV.

———. "Theology and the Commercial Revolution: Guibert of Nogent, St. Anselm and the Jews of Northern France." In *Church and City 1000–1500: Essays in Honour of Christopher Brooke,* ed. David Abulafia, Michael J. Franklin, and Miri Rubin, 23–40. Cambridge: Cambridge University Press, 1992. Reprint, Abulafia, *Christians and Jews in Dispute,* chapter XI.

———. "Twelfth-Century Renaissance Theology and the Jews." In *From Witness to Witchcraft,* 125–39.

Abulafia, David. *A Mediterranean Emporium: The Catalan Kingdom of Majorca.* Cambridge: Cambridge University Press, 1994.

Adler, Michael. *Jews of Medieval England.* London: Jewish Historical Society of England, 1939.

Ainaud de Lasarte, Juan. "Una versión catalana desconocida de los *Dialogi* de Pedro Alfonso." *Sefarad* 3 (1943): 359–76.

Alexander, Sidney. *Marc Chagall: A Biography.* New York: G. P. Putnam's Sons, 1978.

Alvarez Perez, Rosa. "Martyrs and Moneylenders: Retrieving the Memory of Jewish Women in Medieval Northern France." PhD Diss., The City University of New York, 2005.

Anchel, Robert. "The Early History of the Jewish Quarters in Paris." *Jewish Social Studies* 2 (1940): 45–60.

Auerbach, Erich. "Figura." In *Scenes from the Drama of European Literature,* trans. Ralph Manheim, Catherine Garvin, and Erich Auerbach, 11–76. Minneapolis: University of Minnesota Press, 1984 [1954].

Baer, Yitzhak. "The Disputations of R. Yeḥiel of Paris and of Naḥmanides" (Hebrew). *Tarbiz* 2 (1931): 172–87.

———. *A History of the Jews in Christian Spain.* Trans. Louis Schoffman, et al. 2 vols. Philadelphia: Jewish Publication Society, 1992 [1961–66].

Baldwin, John W. *Masters, Princes, and Merchants: The Social Views of Peter the Chanter and His Circle*. 2 vols. Princeton: Princeton University Press, 1970.

Baron, Salo Wittmayer. *A Social and Religious History of the Jews*. 2nd ed. 18 vols. New York: Columbia University Press, 1952–83.

Bartlett, Robert. *The Making of Europe: Conquest, Colonization and Cultural Change, 950–1350*. Princeton: Princeton University Press, 1993.

———. "Medieval and Modern Concepts of Race and Ethnicity." In "Race and Ethnicity in the Middle Ages," 39–56.

Bauman, Zygmunt. "Allosemitism: Premodern, Modern, Postmodern." In *Modernity, Culture, and "the Jew,"* ed. Bryan Cheyette and Laura Marcus, 143–56. Stanford: Stanford University Press, 1998.

Bejarano Escanilla, Ana María. "Šĕlomoh Bonafed, poeta y polemista hebreo (s. XIV–XV)." PhD Diss., University of Barcelona, 1991.

Benton, John F. "Consciousness of Self and Perceptions of Individuality." In *Renaissance and Renewal in the Twelfth Century*, 263–95.

Berger, David. "The Attitude of St. Bernard of Clairvaux toward the Jews." *Proceedings of the American Academy for Jewish Research* 40 (1972): 89–108.

———. "Gilbert Crispin, Alan of Lille, and Jacob ben Reuben: A Study in the Transmission of Medieval Polemic." *Speculum* 49 (1974): 34–47.

———. "St. Peter Damian: His Attitude toward the Jews and the Old Testament." *Yavneh Review* 4 (1965): 80–112.

Berthier, André. "Un maître orientaliste du XIIIe siècle: Raymond Martin O.P." *Archiv fratrum praedicatorum* 6 (1936): 267–311.

Beyond the Persecuting Society: Religious Toleration before the Enlightenment. Ed. John Christian Laursen and Cary J. Nederman. Philadelphia: University of Pennsylvania Press, 1998.

Biberman, Matthew. *Masculinity, Anti-Semitism, and Early Modern English Literature: From the Satanic to the Effeminate Jew*. Aldershot, Hampshire: Ashgate, 2004.

Biddick, Kathleen. "The ABC of Ptolemy: Mapping the World with the Alphabet." In *Text and Territory*, 268–93.

———. "Paper Jews: Inscription/Ethnicity/Ethnography." *Art Bulletin* 78 (1996): 594–99.

———. *The Typological Imaginary: Circumcision, Technology, History*. Philadelphia: University of Pennsylvania Press, 2003.

Bisexuality: A Critical Reader. Ed. Merl Storr. London and New York: Routledge, 1999.

Blumenkranz, Bernhard. "Augustin et les Juifs; Augustin et le Judaïsme." *Recherches augustiniennes* 1 (1958): 225–41.

———. "La *Disputatio Judei cum Christiano* de Gilbert Crispin, Abbé de Westminster." *Revue du Moyen Âge Latin* 4 (1949): 237–52.

———. *Die Judenpredigt Augustins: Ein Beitrag zur Geschichte der jüdisch-christlichen Beziehungen in den ersten Jahrhunderten*. Paris: Études Augustiniennes, 1973 [1946].

———. "Jüdische und christliche Konvertiten im jüdisch-christlichen Religionsgespräch des Mittelalters." In *Judentum im Mittelalter: Beiträge zum christlich-judischer Gespräch*, ed. Paul Wilpert, 264–82. Berlin: Walter de Gruyter, 1966.

———. *Le Juif médiéval au miroir de l'art chrétien*. Paris: Études Augustiniennes, 1966.

Blurton, Heather F. "Guibert of Nogent and the Subject of History." *Exemplaria* 15 (2003): 111–31.

Boas, George. *Essays on Primitivism and Related Ideas in the Middle Ages*. Baltimore: Johns Hopkins Press, 1948.

Bolton, Brenda. "Tradition and Temerity: Papal Attitudes to Deviants, 1159–1216." In *Schism, Heresy, and Religious Protest*, ed. Derek Baker, 79–91. Cambridge: Cambridge University Press, 1972.

Bonfil, Reuven. "The Nature of Judaism in Raymond Martini's *Pugio fidei*" (Hebrew). *Tarbiz* 40 (1971): 360–75.

Bornstein, Kate. *Gender Outlaw: On Men, Women, and the Rest of Us*. New York: Routledge, 1994.

Boswell, John. *Christianity, Social Tolerance, and Homosexuality: Gay People in Western Europe from the Beginning of the Christian Era to the Fourteenth Century*. Chicago: University of Chicago Press, 1980.

Boyarin, Daniel. *Dying for God: Martyrdom and the Making of Christianity and Judaism*. Stanford: Stanford University Press, 1999.

———. *A Radical Jew: Paul and the Politics of Identity*. Berkeley and Los Angeles: University of California Press, 1994.

———. "'This We Know to Be the Carnal Israel': Circumcision and the Erotic Life of God and Israel." *Critical Inquiry* 18 (1992): 474–505.

Boyd, David Lorenzo. "Disrupting the Norm: Sodomy, Culture, and the Male Body in Peter Damian's *Liber Gomorrhianus*." *Essays in Medieval Studies* 11 (1994): 63–73.

Braudel, Fernand. *The Mediterranean and the Mediterranean World in the Age of Philip II*. Trans. Siân Reynolds. 2 vols. New York: Harper and Row, 1972.

Brettle, S. *San Vicente Ferrer und sein literarischer Nachlass*. Munster: Aschendorff, 1924.

Brogan, Kathleen. *Cultural Haunting: Ghosts and Ethnicity in Recent American Literature*. Charlottesville: University Press of Virginia, 1998.

Brown, Peter. *The Body and Society: Men, Women and Sexual Renunciation in Early Christianity*. New York: Columbia University Press, 1988.

Le Brûlement du Talmud à Paris, 1242–1244. Ed. Gilbert Dahan, with Élie Nicolas. Paris: Éditions du Cerf, 1999.

Brundage, James A. *Law, Sex, and Christian Society in Medieval Europe*. Chicago: University of Chicago Press, 1987.

Bullough, Vern L. "Formation of Medieval Ideals: Christian Theory and Christian Practice." In *Sexual Practices and the Medieval Church*, 14–21.

———. "Postscript: Heresy, Witchcraft, and Sexuality." In *Sexual Practices and the Medieval Church*, 206–17.

Burger, Glenn. *Chaucer's Queer Nation*. Minneapolis: University of Minnesota Press, 2003.

———. "Queer Theory." In *Chaucer: An Oxford Guide*, ed. Steve Ellis, 432–47. Oxford: Oxford University Press, 2005.

Burger, Glenn, and Steven F. Kruger, eds. *Queering the Middle Ages*. Minneapolis: University of Minnesota Press, 2001.

Burgwinkle, William. "Knighting the Classical Hero: Homo/Hetero Affectivity in *Eneas*." *Exemplaria* 5 (1993): 1–43.

————. *Sodomy, Masculinity, and Law in Medieval Literature: France and England, 1050–1230*. Cambridge: Cambridge University Press, 2004.

Burman, Thomas. "The Influence of the *Apology of al-Kindî* and *Contrarietas alfolica* on Ramon Lull's Late Religious Polemics, 1305–1313." *Mediaeval Studies* 53 (1991): 197–228.

Burns, Robert I. "Christian-Islamic Confrontation in the West: The Thirteenth-Century Dream of Conversion." *American Historical Review* 76 (1971): 1386–1434.

Burr, David. *The Spiritual Franciscans: From Protest to Persecution in the Century after Saint Francis*. University Park: Pennsylvania State University Press, 2001.

Bush, Jonathan A. "'You're Gonna Miss Me When I'm Gone': Early Modern Common Law Discourse and the Case of the Jews." *Wisconsin Law Review* 5 (1993): 1225–85.

Butler, Judith. *Bodies That Matter: On the Discursive Limits of "Sex."* New York: Routledge, 1993.

————. *Gender Trouble: Feminism and the Subversion of Identity*. New York: Routledge, 1990.

————. "Melancholy Gender/Refused Identification." In *Constructing Masculinity*, ed. Maurice Berger, Brian Wallis, and Simon Watson, 21–36. New York: Routledge, 1995.

————. *The Psychic Life of Power: Theories in Subjection*. Stanford: Stanford University Press, 1997.

Bynum, Caroline Walker. "'...And Woman His Humanity': Female Imagery in the Religious Writing of the Later Middle Ages." In *Gender and Religion: On the Complexity of Symbols*, ed. Caroline Walker Bynum, Stevan Harrell, and Paula Richman, 257–88. Boston: Beacon Press, 1986.

————. *Fragmentation and Redemption: Essays on Gender and the Human Body in Medieval Religion*. New York: Zone Books; Cambridge: MIT Press, 1992.

————. *Holy Feast and Holy Fast: The Religious Significance of Food to Medieval Women*. Berkeley and Los Angeles: University of California Press, 1987.

————. *Jesus as Mother: Studies in the Spirituality of the High Middle Ages*. Berkeley and Los Angeles: University of California Press, 1982.

————. *Metamorphosis and Identity*. New York: Zone Books; Cambridge: MIT Press, 2001.

————. *The Resurrection of the Body in Western Christianity, 200–1336*. New York: Columbia University Press, 1995.

Cadden, Joan. *Meanings of Sex Difference in the Middle Ages: Medicine, Science, and Culture*. Cambridge: Cambridge University Press, 1993.

————. "Sciences/Silences: The Natures and Languages of 'Sodomy' in Peter of Abano's *Problemata* Commentary." In *Constructing Medieval Sexuality*, 40–57.

The Cambridge Economic History of Europe. Ed. M. M. Postan and H. J. Habakkuk. 2nd ed. 8 vols. Cambridge: Cambridge University Press, 1965–89.

Cantera Burgos, Francisco. "Textos de polémica antijudaica y judeo-catalano-aragoneses en un manuscrito de Burgo de Osma." *Revista de filogía española* 48 (1966): 135–44.

Carlebach, Elisheva. *Divided Souls: Converts from Judaism in Germany, 1500–1750*. New Haven: Yale University Press, 2001.

Carreras y Candi, Francesch. *L'Aljama de Juhéus de Tortosa*. Barcelona: La Renaxensa, 1928.

Carroll, Margaret D. "'In the Name of God and Profit': Jan van Eyck's Arnolfini Portrait." *Representations* 44 (1993): 96–132.

Cassou, Jean. *Chagall*. Trans. Alisa Jaffa. New York and Washington: Frederick A. Praeger, 1965.

Castle, Terry. *The Apparitional Lesbian: Female Homosexuality and Modern Culture*. New York: Columbia University Press, 1993.

The Catholic Encyclopedia. 15 vols. New York: Robert Appleton, 1907–14. Internet: New Advent. http://www.newadvent.org/cathen/.

Chaucer and the Jews: Sources, Contexts, Meanings. Ed. Sheila Delany. New York: Routledge, 2002.

Chazan, Robert. *Barcelona and Beyond: The Disputation of 1263 and Its Aftermath*. Berkeley and Los Angeles: University of California Press, 1992.

———. "The Barcelona 'Disputation' of 1263: Christian Missionizing and Jewish Response." *Speculum* 52 (1977): 824–42.

———. "Chapter Thirteen of the *Maḥazik Emunah:* Further Light on Friar Paul Christian and the New Christian Missionizing." *Mikhael* 12 (1991): 9–26.

———. "The Condemnation of the Talmud Reconsidered (1239–1248)." *Proceedings of the American Academy for Jewish Research* 55 (1988): 11–30.

———. *Daggers of Faith: Thirteenth-Century Christian Missionizing and Jewish Response*. Berkeley and Los Angeles: University of California Press, 1989.

———. *European Jewry and the First Crusade*. Berkeley and Los Angeles: University of California Press, 1987.

———. "From the First Crusade to the Second: Evolving Perceptions of the Christian-Jewish Conflict." In *Jews and Christians in Twelfth-Century Europe*, 46–62.

———. *God, History, and Humanity: The Hebrew First Crusade Chronicles*. Berkeley and Los Angeles: University of California Press, 2000.

———. *Medieval Stereotypes and Modern Antisemitism*. Berkeley and Los Angeles: University of California Press, 1997.

———. "Twelfth-Century Perceptions of the Jews: A Case Study of Bernard of Clairvaux and Peter the Venerable." In *From Witness to Witchcraft*, 187–201.

Chenu, Marie-Dominique. *Nature, Man, and Society in the Twelfth Century: Essays on New Theological Perspectives in the Latin West*. Ed. and trans. Jerome Taylor and Lester K. Little. Chicago: University of Chicago Press, 1968.

Cherniss, Michael. *Boethian Apocalypse: Studies in Middle English Vision Poetry*. Norman: Pilgrim Books, 1987.

Chism, Christine. *Alliterative Revivals*. Philadelphia: University of Pennsylvania Press, 2002.

Cigman, Gloria. "The Jew as an Absent-Presence in Late Medieval England." 17th Sacks Lecture. Oxford Centre for Postgraduate Hebrew Studies. 29 May 1991.

Clover, Carol J. "Regardless of Sex: Men, Women, and Power in Early Northern Europe." In *Studying Medieval Women: Sex, Gender, Feminism*, ed. Nancy F. Partner, 61–85. Cambridge: Medieval Academy of America, 1993. [Originally in *Speculum* 68 (1993): 363–87.]

Cohen, Jeffrey J. *Medieval Identity Machines*. Minneapolis: University of Minnesota Press, 2003.

———. *Of Giants: Sex, Monsters, and the Middle Ages*. Minneapolis: University of Minnesota Press, 1999.

———. "Was Margery Kempe Jewish? Storms and Screams in The Book of Margery Kempe." Lecture, Medieval Club of New York. 3 February 2003.

Cohen, Jeremy. *The Friars and the Jews: The Evolution of Medieval Anti-Judaism.* Ithaca: Cornell University Press, 1982.

———. "The Hebrew Chronicles of the First Crusade in Their Christian Cultural Context." In *Juden und Christen zur Zeit der Kreuzzüge,* ed. Alfred Haverkamp, 17–34. Sigmaringen: Jan Thorbecke Verlag, 1999.

———. "The Jews as the Killers of Christ in the Latin Tradition, from Augustine to the Friars." *Traditio* 39 (1983): 1–27.

———. *Living Letters of the Law: Ideas of the Jew in Medieval Christianity.* Berkeley and Los Angeles: University of California Press, 1999.

———. "The Mentality of the Medieval Jewish Apostate: Peter Alfonsi, Hermann of Cologne, and Pablo Christiani." In *Jewish Apostasy in the Modern World,* ed. Todd M. Endelman, 20–47. New York: Holmes and Meier, 1987.

———. "The Muslim Connection or On the Changing Role of the Jew in High Medieval Theology." In *From Witness to Witchcraft,* 141–62.

———. "The 'Persecutions of 1096'—From Martyrdom to Martyrology: The Sociocultural Context of the Hebrew Crusade Chronicles" (Hebrew). *Zion,* n.s., 59 (1994): 169–208.

———. "Scholarship and Intolerance in the Medieval Academy: The Study and Evaluation of Judaism in European Christendom." *American Historical Review* 91 (1986): 592–613. Reprint, *Essential Papers on Judaism and Christianity in Conflict,* 310–41.

———. "*Synagoga conversa:* Honorius Augustodunensis, the Song of Songs, and Christianity's 'Eschatological Jew.'" *Speculum* 79 (2004): 309–40.

———. "A 1096 Complex? Constructing the First Crusade in Jewish Historical Memory, Medieval and Modern." In *Jews and Christians in Twelfth-Century Europe,* 9–26.

Cohen, Mark R. *Under Crescent and Cross: The Jews in the Middle Ages.* Princeton: Princeton University Press, 1994.

Cohen, Martin A. "Reflections on the Text and Context of the Disputation of Barcelona." *Hebrew Union College Annual* 35 (1964): 157–92.

Cohn, Norman. *Europe's Inner Demons.* New York: New American Library, 1977 [1975].

Cole, Penny J. *The Preaching of the Crusades to the Holy Land, 1095–1270.* Cambridge: Medieval Academy of America, 1991.

Constructing Medieval Sexuality. Ed. Karma Lochrie, Peggy McCracken, and James A. Schultz. Minneapolis: University of Minnesota Press, 1997.

Contra Iudaeos: Ancient and Medieval Polemics between Christians and Jews. Ed. Ora Limor and Guy G. Stroumsa. Tübingen: J. C. B. Mohr [Paul Siebeck], 1996.

Convivencia: Jews, Muslims, and Christians in Medieval Spain. Ed. Vivian B. Mann, Thomas F. Glick, and Jerrilynn D. Dodds. New York: George Braziller and The Jewish Museum, 1992.

Coupe, M. D. "The Personality of Guibert de Nogent Reconsidered." *Journal of Medieval History* 9 (1983): 317–29.

Cowdrey, H. E. J. *The Cluniacs and the Gregorian Reform.* Oxford: Clarendon Press, 1970.

Dahan, Gilbert. *The Christian Polemic against the Jews in the Middle Ages.* Trans. Jody Gladding. Notre Dame: University of Notre Dame Press, 1998 [1991].

———. "La connaissance de l'hébreu dans les correctoires de la Bible du XIIIᵉ siècle: Notes préliminaires." In *Rashi 1040–1990: Hommage à Ephraïm E. Urbach,* ed. Gabrielle Sed-Rajna, 567–78. Paris: Éditions du Cerf, 1993.

———. *L'exégèse chrétienne de la Bible en Occident médiéval, XIIᵉ–XIVᵉ siècle.* Paris: Éditions du Cerf, 1999.

———. *Les intellectuels chrétiens et les Juifs au Moyen Âge.* Paris: Éditions du Cerf, 1990.

———. "Rashi, sujet de la controverse de 1240: Édition partielle du ms. Paris, BN lat. 16558." *Archives juives* 14 (1978): 43–54.

———. "Les traductions latines de Thibaud de Sézanne." In *Brûlement du Talmud à Paris,* 95–120.

d'Alverny, Marie-Thérèse. "Alain de Lille et l'Islam: Le 'Contra Paganos.'" In *Islam et Chrétiens du Midi,* 301–24.

———. "Translations and Translators." In *Renaissance and Renewal in the Twelfth Century,* 421–62.

Daniel, Norman. *The Arabs and Mediaeval Europe.* 2nd ed. London: Longman, 1979.

———. *Islam and the West: The Making of an Image.* Rev. ed. Oxford: Oneworld, 1993.

Daniélou, Jean. *From Shadows to Reality: Studies in the Biblical Typology of the Fathers.* Trans. Wulstan Hibberd. London: Burns & Oates, 1960 [1950].

Delany, Sheila. "Editor's Introduction." In *Chaucer and the Jews,* viii–xi.

de Lauretis, Teresa. *The Practice of Love: Lesbian Sexuality and Perverse Desire.* Bloomington: Indiana University Press, 1994.

Delisle, Léopold. *Inventaire des manuscrits de l'abbaye de Saint-Victor conservés à la Bibliothèque Impériale, sous les numéros 14232–15175 du fonds latins.* Paris: Auguste Durand et Pedone-Lauriel, 1869.

de Lubac, Henri. *Exégèse médiévale: Les quatre sens de l'écriture.* 2 parts, 4 vols. Paris: Aubier, Éditions Montaigne, 1959–64.

Denifle, Heinrich. "Quellen zur Disputation Pablos Christiani mit Mose Nachmani zu Barcelona 1263." *Historisches Jahrbuch* 8 (1887): 225–44.

Derrida, Jacques. *Limited Inc.* Ed. Gerald Graff. Trans. Samuel Weber and Jeffrey Mehlman. Evanston: Northwestern University Press, 1988.

———. *Specters of Marx: The State of the Debt, the Work of Mourning, and the New International.* Trans. Peggy Kamuf. New York: Routledge, 1994 [1993].

Despres, Denise L. "The Protean Jew in the Vernon Manuscript." In *Chaucer and the Jews,* 145–64.

Dinshaw, Carolyn. *Chaucer's Sexual Poetics.* Madison: University of Wisconsin Press, 1989.

Dollimore, Jonathan. *Sexual Dissidence: Augustine to Wilde, Freud to Foucault.* Oxford: Clarendon Press, 1991.

Douglas, Mary. *Purity and Danger: An Analysis of the Concepts of Pollution and Taboo.* London: Routledge & Kegan Paul, 1966.

Dove, Mary. "Chaucer and the Translation of the Jewish Scriptures." In *Chaucer and the Jews,* 89–107.

Dronke, Peter. *Poetic Individuality in the Middle Ages: New Departures in Poetry, 1000–1150.* Oxford: Clarendon Press, 1970.

Duby, Georges. *The Early Growth of the European Economy: Warriors and Peasants from the Seventh to the Twelfth Century.* Trans. Howard B. Clarke. Ithaca: Cornell University Press, 1974 [1973].

———. *The Knight, the Lady, and the Priest: The Making of Modern Marriage in Medieval France.* Trans. Barbara Bray. New York: Pantheon Books, 1983.

———. *The Three Orders: Feudal Society Imagined.* Trans. Arthur Goldhammer. Chicago: University of Chicago Press, 1980.

du Cange, Charles du Fresne. *Glossarium mediae et infimae Latinitatis.* Editio nova. 1883. Reprint, Paris: Librairie des sciences et des arts, 1937–38.

Edelman, Lee. *Homographesis: Essays in Gay Literary and Cultural Theory.* New York: Routledge, 1994.

Einbinder, Susan. "Signs of Romance: Hebrew Prose and the Twelfth-Century Renaissance." In *Jews and Christians in Twelfth-Century Europe,* 221–33.

Elliott, Dyan. *Spiritual Marriage: Sexual Abstinence in Medieval Wedlock.* Princeton: Princeton University Press, 1993.

Elukin, Jonathan M. "The Discovery of the Self: Jews and Conversion in the Twelfth Century." In *Jews and Christians in Twelfth-Century Europe,* 63–76.

———. "From Jew to Christian? Conversion and Immutability in Medieval Europe." In *Varieties of Religious Conversion,* 171–89.

Emmerson, Richard K., and Ronald B. Herzman. *The Apocalyptic Imagination in Medieval Literature.* Philadelphia: University of Pennsylvania Press, 1992.

Encyclopaedia Judaica. 16 vols. Jerusalem: Keter; New York: Macmillan, 1971.

Enders, Jody. "Homicidal Pigs and the Antisemitic Imagination." *Exemplaria* 14 (2002): 201–38.

Epstein, Steven A. *Genoa and the Genoese, 858–1528.* Chapel Hill: University of North Carolina Press, 1996.

Essential Papers on Judaism and Christianity in Conflict, From Late Antiquity to the Reformation. Ed. Jeremy Cohen. New York: New York University Press, 1991.

Estudios sobre Pedro Alfonso de Huesca. Ed. María Jesús Lacarra. Huesca: Instituto de Estudios Altoaragoneses, 1996.

Evans, Austin P. "The Albigensian Crusade." In *A History of the Crusades,* 2:277–324.

Fabre-Vassas, Claudine. *The Singular Beast: Jews, Christians, and the Pig.* Trans. Carol Volk. New York: Columbia University Press, 1997.

Fausto-Sterling, Anne. *Sexing the Body: Gender Politics and the Construction of Sexuality.* New York: Basic Books, 2000.

Feinberg, Leslie. *Transgender Warriors: Making History from Joan of Arc to Dennis Rodman.* Boston: Beacon Press, 1996.

Ferguson, Chris D. "Autobiography as Therapy: Guibert de Nogent, Peter Abelard, and the Making of Medieval Autobiography." *Journal of Medieval and Renaissance Studies* 13 (1983): 187–212.

Ferruolo, Stephen C. *The Origins of the University: The Schools of Paris and Their Critics, 1100–1215.* Stanford: Stanford University Press, 1985.

Fliche, Augustin. *La réforme grégorienne.* 2 vols. Paris: E. Champion, 1924–37. Reprint, Geneva: Slatkine Reprints, 1978.

Foucault, Michel. *The History of Sexuality.* Vol. 1: *An Introduction.* Trans. Robert Hurley. New York: Vintage Books, 1980 [1976].

Fradenburg, Louise O. "Criticism, Anti-Semitism, and the *Prioress's Tale.*" *Exemplaria* 1 (1989): 69–115.

France, John. "Patronage and the Appeal of the First Crusade." In *The First Crusade: Origins and Impacts,* ed. Jonathan Phillips, 5–20. Manchester: Manchester University Press, 1997.

Frantzen, Allen J. *Before the Closet: Same-Sex Love from "Beowulf" to "Angels in America."* Chicago: University of Chicago Press, 1998.

Freccero, John. *Dante: The Poetics of Conversion.* Ed. Rachel Jacoff. Cambridge: Harvard University Press, 1986.

Fredriksen, Paula. "Divine Justice and Human Freedom: Augustine on Jews and Judaism, 392–398." In *From Witness to Witchcraft,* 29–54.

———. "*Excaecati occulta justitia Dei:* Augustine on Jews and Judaism." *Journal of Early Christian Studies* 3 (1995): 299–324.

Freud, Sigmund. *The Ego and the Id.* Trans. Joan Riviere. London: Hogarth Press, Institute of Psycho-analysis, 1950 [1927].

———. *Moses and Monotheism.* Trans. Katherine Jones. New York: A. A. Knopf, 1939.

———. "Mourning and Melancholia" (1917). Trans. Joan Riviere. In *Collected Papers,* 4: 152–70. London: Hogarth Press, Institute of Psycho-analysis, 1956 [1925].

Friedman, John Block. *The Monstrous Races in Medieval Art and Thought.* Cambridge: Harvard University Press, 1981.

From Witness to Witchcraft: Jews and Judaism in Medieval Christian Thought. Ed. Jeremy Cohen. Wiesbaden: Harrassowitz Verlag, 1996.

Füglister, Robert L. *Das Lebende Kreuz: Ikonographisch-ikonologische Untersuchung der Herkunft und Entwicklung einer spätmittelalterlichen Bildidee und ihrer Verwurzelung im Wort.* Einsiedeln: Benziger Verlag, 1964.

Fukuyama, Francis. *The End of History and the Last Man.* New York: Free Press, 1992.

Funkenstein, Amos. "Basic Types of Christian Anti-Jewish Polemics in the Later Middle Ages." *Viator* 2 (1971): 373–82.

———. "Changes in the Patterns of Christian Anti-Jewish Polemics in the Twelfth Century" (Hebrew). *Zion,* n.s., 33 (1968): 125–44.

Fuss, Diana. *Essentially Speaking: Feminism, Nature, and Difference.* New York: Routledge, 1989.

———. "Inside/Out." In *Inside/Out: Lesbian Theories, Gay Theories,* ed. Diana Fuss, 1–10. New York: Routledge, 1991.

Gaunt, Simon. "From Epic to Romance: Gender and Sexuality in the *Roman d'Enéas.*" *Romanic Review* 83 (1992): 1–27.

Gauss, Julia. "Anselm von Canterbury: Zur Begegnung und Auseinandersetzung der Religionen." *Saeculum* 17 (1966): 277–363.

———. "Die Auseinandersetzung mit Judentum und Islam bei Anselm." In *Die Wirkungsgeschichte Anselms von Canterbury,* vol. 2, ed. Helmut Kohlenberger, 101–9. Frankfurt: Minerva, 1975.

Ghéon, Henri. *St. Vincent Ferrer.* Trans. F. J. Sheed. New York: Sheed and Ward, 1939.

Gilman, Sander. *Jewish Self-Hatred: Anti-Semitism and the Hidden Language of the Jews.* Baltimore: Johns Hopkins University Press, 1986.

———. *The Jew's Body.* New York: Routledge, 1991.

Ginzburg, Carlo. *Ecstasies: Deciphering the Witches' Sabbath.* Trans. Raymond Rosenthal. New York: Pantheon Books, 1991 [1989].

Goitein, S. D. *A Mediterranean Society: The Jewish Communities of the Arab World as Portrayed in the Documents of the Cairo Geniza.* 5 vols. Berkeley: University of California Press, 1967–88.

Golb, Norman. *The Jews in Medieval Normandy: A Social and Intellectual History.* Cambridge: Cambridge University Press, 1998.

———. "Notes on the Conversion of European Christians to Judaism in the Eleventh Century." *Journal of Jewish Studies* 16 (1965): 69–74.

Goldstein, R. James. "'Why Calle Ye Hym Crist, Siþen Iewes Called Hym Iesus?' The Disavowal of Jewish Identification in *Piers Plowman* B Text." *Exemplaria* 13 (2001): 215–51.

Goodman, Jennifer R. "Marriage and Conversion in Late Medieval Romance." In *Varieties of Religious Conversion,* 115–28.

Graboïs, Aryeh. "Un chapitre de tolérance intellectuelle dans la société occidentale au XIIᵉ siècle: Le 'Dialogus' de Pierre Abélard et le 'Kuzari' d'Yehudah Halévi." In *Pierre Abélard, Pierre le Vénérable: Les courants philosophiques, littéraires et artistiques en Occident au milieu du XIIᵉ siècle,* ed. René Louis, Jean Jolivet, and Jean Châtillon, 641–54. Paris: Éditions du Centre National de la Recherche Scientifique, 1975.

———. "Le dialogue religieux au XIIᵉ siècle: Pierre Abélard et Jehudah Halévi." In *Religionsgespräche im Mittelalter,* 149–67.

———. "The *Hebraica Veritas* and Jewish-Christian Intellectual Relations in the Twelfth Century." *Speculum* 50 (1975): 613–34.

Grayzel, Solomon. "The Confession of a Medieval Jewish Convert." *Historia Judaica* 17 (1955): 89–120.

Gregg, Joan Young. *Devils, Women, and Jews: Reflections on the Other in Medieval Sermon Stories.* Albany: State University of New York Press, 1997.

Grossinger, Hermine. "Die Disputation des Nachmanides mit Fra Pablo Christiani, Barcelona 1263." *Kairos,* n.s., 19 (1977): 257–85; 20 (1978): 1–15, 161–81.

Grossman, Avraham. "The Jewish-Christian Polemic and Jewish Biblical Exegesis in Twelfth Century France (On the Attitude of R. Joseph Qara to Polemic)" (Hebrew). *Zion,* n.s., 51 (1985): 29–60.

Guldan, Ernst. *Eva und Maria: Eine Antithese als Bildmotif.* Graz: Verlag Hermann Böhlaus, 1966.

Gurevich, Aaron. *The Origins of European Individualism.* Trans. Katherine Judelson. Oxford: Blackwell, 1995.

Gutwirth, Eleazar. "Leer a Bonafed en su entorno." In *La sociedad medieval a través de la litteratura hispanojudía,* ed. Ricardo Izquierdo Benito and Ángel Sáenz-Badillos, 341–57. Cuenca: Ediciones de la Universidad de Castilla-La Mancha, 1998.

———. "Social Criticism in Bonafed's Invective and Its Historical Background." *Sefarad* 45 (1985): 23–53.

———. "Social Tensions within Fifteenth Century Hispano-Jewish Communities." PhD Diss., University of London, 1978.

Haftmann, Werner. *Marc Chagall*. Trans. Heinrich Baumann and Alexis Brown. New York: Abradale Press, Harry N. Abrams, 1998 [1972].

Hahn, Thomas. "The Difference the Middle Ages Makes: Color and Race before the Modern World." In "Race and Ethnicity in the Middle Ages," 1–37.

Halberstam, Judith. *Female Masculinity*. Durham: Duke University Press, 1998.

Halperin, David. "Forgetting Foucault: Acts, Identities, and the History of Sexuality." *Representations* 63 (1998): 93–120.

Hamer, Dean H., and Peter Copeland. *The Science of Desire: The Search for the Gay Gene and the Biology of Behavior*. New York: Simon and Schuster, 1994.

Hanning, Robert W. *The Individual in Twelfth-Century Romance*. New Haven: Yale University Press, 1977.

Harper, Phillip Brian. *Are We Not Men? Masculine Anxiety and the Problem of African-American Identity*. Oxford: Oxford University Press, 1996.

Harris, E. "Mary in the Burning Bush: Nicolas Froment's Triptych at Aix-en-Provence." *Journal of the Warburg and Courtauld Institutes* 1, no. 4 (1938): 281–86.

Haskins, Charles Homer. *The Renaissance of the Twelfth Century*. Cambridge: Harvard University Press, 1927.

Heng, Geraldine. *Empire of Magic: Medieval Romance and the Politics of Cultural Fantasy*. New York: Columbia University Press, 2003.

A History of the Crusades. Ed. Kenneth K. Setton. Vol. 1: *The First Hundred Years*, ed. Marshall W. Baldwin. Vol. 2: *The Later Crusades, 1189–1311*, ed. Robert Lee Wolff and Harry W. Hazard. Madison: University of Wisconsin Press, 1969.

Hsia, R. Po-Chia. *The Myth of Ritual Murder: Jews and Magic in Reformation Germany*. New Haven: Yale University Press, 1988.

———. *Trent 1475: Stories of a Ritual Murder Trial*. New Haven: Yale University Press, in cooperation with Yeshiva University Library, 1992.

Hunt, R. W. "The Disputation of Peter of Cornwall against Symon the Jew." In *Studies in Medieval History Presented to Frederick Maurice Powicke*, ed. R. W. Hunt, W. A. Pantin, and R. W. Southern, 143–56. Oxford: Clarendon Press, 1948; reprint, 1969.

"Inflecting the Converso Voice" [cluster of essays]. *Corónica: A Journal of Medieval Spanish Language and Literature* 25, no. 1 (Fall 1996): 3–68.

Ingham, Patricia Clare. *Sovereign Fantasies: Arthurian Romance and the Making of Britain*. Philadelphia: University of Pennsylvania Press, 2001.

Iogna-Prat, Dominique. *Order and Exclusion: Cluny and Cristendom Face Heresy, Judaism, and Islam (1000–1150)*. Trans. Graham Robert Edwards. Ithaca: Cornell University Press, 1998.

Islam et Chrétiens du Midi (XIIᵉ–XIVᵉ s.). Ed. Edouard Privat. Toulouse: Centre d'Études Historiques de Fanjeaux, 1983.

Jacquart, Danielle, and Claude Thomasset. *Sexuality and Medicine in the Middle Ages*. Trans. Matthew Adamson. Princeton: Princeton University Press, 1988 [1985].

Jews and Christians in Twelfth-Century Europe. Ed. Michael A. Signer and John Van Engen. Notre Dame: University of Notre Dame Press, 2001.

Johnson, Willis. "The Myth of Jewish Male Menses." *Journal of Medieval History* 24 (1998): 273–95.

Jordan, Mark D. "Homosexuality, *Luxuria*, and Textual Abuse." In *Constructing Medieval Sexuality,* 24–39.

———. *The Invention of Sodomy in Christian Theology.* Chicago: University of Chicago Press, 1997.

Jordan, William Chester. "An Aspect of Credit in Picardy in the 1240s: The Deterioration of Jewish-Christian Financial Relations." *Revue des Études Juives* 142 (1983): 141–52.

———. "Jews on Top: Women and the Availability of Consumption Loans in Northern France in the Mid-Thirteenth Century." *Journal of Jewish Studies* 29 (1978): 39–56.

———. "Problems of the Meat Market of Béziers, 1240–1247—A Question of Anti-Semitism." *Revue des Études Juives* 135 (1976): 31–49.

———. "Why 'Race'?" In "Race and Ethnicity in the Middle Ages," 165–73.

———. "Women and Credit in the Middle Ages: Problems and Directions." *Journal of European Economic History* 17 (1988): 33–62.

Kantor, Jonathan. "A Psychohistorical Source: The *Memoirs* of Abbot Guibert of Nogent." *Journal of Medieval History* 2 (1976): 281–303.

Katz, D. S. "Shylock's Gender: Jewish Male Menstruation in Early Modern England." *Review of English Studies,* n.s., 50 (1999): 440–62.

Kayserling, M. "Die Disputation des Bonastruc mit Frai Pablo in Barcelona." *Monatsschrift für Geschichte und Wissenschaft des Judenthums* 14 (1865): 308–13.

Kedar, Benjamin Z. *Crusade and Mission: European Approaches toward the Muslims.* Princeton: Princeton University Press, 1984.

———. *Merchants in Crisis: Genoese and Venetian Men of Affairs and the Fourteenth-Century Depression.* New Haven: Yale University Press, 1976.

———. "R. Yeḥiel of Paris and Palestine" (Hebrew, with English summary). *Shalem* 2 (1976): 349–54.

Kolve, V. A. *Chaucer and the Imagery of Narrative: The First Five Canterbury Tales.* Stanford: Stanford University Press, 1984.

Kritzeck, James. *Peter the Venerable and Islam.* Princeton: Princeton University Press, 1964.

Kruger, Steven F. *AIDS Narratives: Gender and Sexuality, Fiction and Science.* New York: Garland, 1996.

———. "The Bodies of Jews in the Late Middle Ages." In *The Idea of Medieval Literature: Essays on Chaucer and Medieval Culture in Honor of Donald R. Howard,* ed. James Dean and Christian Zacher, 301–23. Newark: University of Delaware Press; London and Toronto: Associated University Presses, 1992.

———. *Dreaming in the Middle Ages.* Cambridge: Cambridge University Press, 1992.

———. "Medieval/Post-Modern: HIV/AIDS and the Temporality of Crisis." In *Queering the Middle Ages,* 252–83.

———. "The Spectral Jew." *New Medieval Literatures* 2 (1998): 9–35.

Kuefler, Mathew. *The Manly Eunuch: Masculinity, Gender Ambiguity, and Christian Ideology in Late Antiquity.* Chicago: University of Chicago Press, 2001.

Kwalbrun, Lara. "Playing God's Chosen: Protestants, Jews, and Sixteenth-Century Drama." PhD Diss., The City University of New York, 2003.

Lampert, Lisa. *Gender and Jewish Difference from Paul to Shakespeare*. Philadelphia: University of Pennsylvania Press, 2004.

Langmuir, Gavin I. *History, Religion, and Antisemitism*. Berkeley and Los Angeles: University of California Press, 1990.

———. *Toward a Definition of Antisemitism*. Berkeley and Los Angeles: University of California Press, 1990.

Laqueur, Thomas. *Making Sex: Body and Gender from the Greeks to Freud*. Cambridge: Harvard University Press, 1990.

Lawton, David. "Sacrilege and Theatricality: The Croxton *Play of the Sacrament*." *Journal of Medieval and Early Modern Studies* 33 (2003): 281–309.

Leclercq, Jean. *The Love of Learning and the Desire for God: A Study of Monastic Culture*. 3rd ed. Trans. Catharine Misrahi. New York: Fordham University Press, 1982.

———. *Saint Pierre Damien: Ermite et homme d'Église*. Rome: Storia e letteratura, 1960.

Le Goff, Jacques. *The Birth of Purgatory*. Trans. Arthur Goldhammer. Chicago: University of Chicago Press, 1984 [1981].

———. *The Medieval Imagination*. Trans. Arthur Goldhammer. Chicago: University of Chicago Press, 1988 [1985].

———. *Time, Work, and Culture in the Middle Ages*. Trans. Arthur Goldhammer. Chicago: University of Chicago Press, 1980 [1977].

———. *Your Money or Your Life: Economy and Religion in the Middle Ages*. Trans. Patricia Ranum. New York: Zone Books [MIT Press], 1988.

Lemay, Helen Rodnite. "Human Sexuality in Twelfth- through Fifteenth-Century Scientific Writings." In *Sexual Practices and the Medieval Church*, 187–205.

"Letters on 'Inflecting the Converso Voice.'" *Corónica: A Journal of Medieval Spanish Language and Literature* 25, no. 2 (Spring 1997): 159–205.

LeVay, Simon. *The Sexual Brain*. Cambridge: MIT Press, 1993.

Lewis, C. S. *The Allegory of Love: A Study in Medieval Tradition*. Oxford: Oxford University Press, 1936.

Leyser, Conrad. "Cities of the Plain: The Rhetoric of Sodomy in Peter Damian's 'Book of Gomorrah.'" *Romanic Review* 86 (1995): 191–211.

Limor, Ora. "Missionary Merchants: Three Medieval Anti-Jewish Works from Genoa." *Journal of Medieval History* 17 (1991): 35–51.

Lipman, V. D. *The Jews of Medieval Norwich*. London: Jewish Historical Society of England, 1967.

Lipton, Sara. *Images of Intolerance: The Representation of Jews and Judaism in the Bible moralisée*. Berkeley and Los Angeles: University of California Press, 1999.

Little, Lester K. "The Personal Development of Peter Damian." In *Order and Innovation in the Middle Ages: Essays in Honor of Joseph R. Strayer*, ed. William C. Jordan, Bruce McNab, and Teofilo F. Ruiz, 317–41, 523–28. Princeton: Princeton University Press, 1976.

———. *Religious Poverty and the Profit Economy in Medieval Europe*. Ithaca: Cornell University Press, 1978.

Lochrie, Karma. *Heterosyncrasies: Female Sexuality When Normal Wasn't*. Minneapolis: University of Minnesota Press, 2005.

Loeb, Isidore. "La controverse de 1240 sur le Talmud." *Revue des Études Juives* 1 (1880): 247–61; 2 (1881): 248–70; 3 (1881): 39–57.

———. "La controverse de 1263 à Barcelone entre Paulus Christiani et Moise ben Nahman." *Revue des Études Juives* 15 (1887): 1–18.

Lopez, R. S. *The Commercial Revolution of the Middle Ages, 950–1350.* Englewood Cliffs: Prentice-Hall, 1971.

Lopez, R. S., and Irving W. Raymond. *Mediterranean Trade in the Medieval World: Illustrative Documents Translated with Introduction and Notes.* New York: Columbia University Press, 1955.

Lotter, Friedrich. "The Position of the Jews in Early Cistercian Exegesis and Preaching." In *From Witness to Witchcraft,* 163–85.

Marcus, Ivan G. "Une communauté pieuse et le doute: Mourir pour la Sanctification du Nom *(Qiddouch ha-Chem)* en Achkenaz (Europe du Nord) et l'histoire de rabbi Amnon de Mayence." *Annales: Histoire, sciences sociales* 49 (1994): 1031–47.

———. "The Dynamics of Jewish Renaissance and Renewal in the Twelfth Century." In *Jews and Christians in Twelfth-Century Europe,* 27–45.

———. "From Politics to Martyrdom: Shifting Paradigms in the Hebrew Narratives of the 1096 Crusade Riots." *Prooftexts* 2 (1982): 40–52. Reprint, *Essential Papers on Judaism and Christianity in Conflict,* 469–83.

———. *Rituals of Childhood: Jewish Acculturation in Medieval Europe.* New Haven: Yale University Press, 1996.

McCracken, Peggy. *The Curse of Eve, The Wound of the Hero: Blood, Gender, and Medieval Literature.* Philadelphia: University of Pennsylvania Press, 2003.

Means, Michael H. *The Consolatio Genre in Medieval English Literature.* Gainesville: University of Florida Press, 1972.

Mellinkoff, Ruth. *Outcasts: Signs of Otherness in Northern European Art of the Late Middle Ages.* 2 vols. Berkeley and Los Angeles: University of California Press, 1993.

Menninghaus, Winfried. *Disgust: The Theory and History of a Strong Sensation.* Trans. Howard Eiland and Joel Golb. Albany: State University of New York Press, 2003.

Menocal, María Rosa. *The Ornament of the World: How Muslims, Jews, and Christians Created a Culture of Tolerance in Medieval Spain.* Boston: Little, Brown, 2002.

Merchavia, Ch. "Did Nicholas Donin Instigate the Blood Libel?" (Hebrew). *Tarbiz* 49 (1979–80): 111–21.

Metlitzki, Dorothee. *The Matter of Araby in Medieval England.* New Haven: Yale University Press, 1977.

Meyer, Franz. *Marc Chagall.* Trans. Robert Allen. New York: Harry N. Abrams, 1964.

Millás Vallicrosa, José Mª. "Extractos del Talmud y allusiones polemicas en un manuscrito de la biblioteca catedral de Gerona." *Sefarad* 20 (1960): 17–49.

———. "Un tratado anónimo de polémica contra los judíos." *Sefarad* 13 (1953): 4–34.

Mirrer, Louise. "Representing 'Other' Men: Muslims, Jews, and Masculine Ideals in Medieval Castilian Epic and Ballad." In *Medieval Masculinities: Regarding Men in the Middle Ages,* ed. Clare A. Lees, with Thelma Fenster and Jo Ann McNamara, 169–84. Minneapolis: University of Minnesota Press, 1994.

Misch, Georg. *Geschichte der Autobiographie.* 4 vols. Frankfurt: G. Schulte-Bulmke, 1955.

Momigliano, Arnaldo. "A Medieval Jewish Autobiography." In *History and Imagination:*

Essays in Honour of H. R. Trevor-Roper, ed. Hugh Lloyd-Jones, Valerie Pearl, and Blair Warden, 30–36. London: Duckworth, 1981.

Mongan, Olga Burakov. "Between Knights: Triangular Desire and Sir Palomides in Sir Thomas Malory's *The Book of Sir Tristram de Lyones*." *Arthuriana* 12 (2002): 74–89.

Monster Theory: Reading Culture. Ed. Jeffrey J. Cohen. Minneapolis: University of Minnesota Press, 1996.

Moore, R. I. *The Formation of a Persecuting Society: Power and Deviance in Western Europe, 950–1250*. Oxford: Basil Blackwell, 1987.

———. "Guibert of Nogent and His World." In *Studies in Medieval History Presented to R. H. C. Davis*, ed. H. Mayr-Harting and R. I. Moore, 107–17. London: Hambledon Press, 1985.

———. *The Origins of European Dissent*. Oxford: Basil Blackwell, 1985 [1977].

Mormando, Franco. *The Preacher's Demons: Bernardino of Siena and the Social Underworld of Early Renaissance Italy*. Chicago: University of Chicago Press, 1999.

Morris, Colin. *The Discovery of the Individual: 1050–1200*. New York: Harper & Row, 1972.

Morrison, Karl F. *Conversion and Text: The Cases of Augustine of Hippo, Herman-Judah, and Constantine Tsatsos*. Charlottesville: University Press of Virginia, 1992.

———. *Understanding Conversion*. Charlottesville: University Press of Virginia, 1992.

Le Moyen Âge et la Bible. Ed. Pierre Riché and Guy Lobrichon. Paris: Beauchesne, 1984.

Mundill, Robin R. *England's Jewish Solution: Experiment and Expulsion, 1262–1290*. Cambridge: Cambridge University Press, 1998.

Muñoz, José Esteban. *Disidentifications: Queers of Color and the Performance of Politics*. Minneapolis: University of Minnesota Press, 1999.

"Nahmanides." In *Encyclopaedia Judaica*, 12:774–82.

Narin van Court, Elisa. "The Hermeneutics of Supersession: The Revision of the Jews from the B to the C Text of *Piers Plowman*." *Yearbook of Langland Studies* 10 (1996): 43–87.

———. "Socially Marginal, Culturally Central: Representing Jews in Late Medieval English Literature." *Exemplaria* 12 (2000): 293–326.

Nederman, Cary J. *Worlds of Difference: European Discourses of Toleration, c. 1100–c. 1550*. University Park: Pennsylvania State University Press, 2000.

Netanyahu, B. *The Marranos of Spain from the Late 14th to the Early 16th Century, According to Contemporary Hebrew Sources*. 3rd ed. Ithaca: Cornell University Press, 1999 [1966].

———. *The Origins of the Inquisition in Fifteenth Century Spain*. 2nd ed. New York: New York Review Books, 2001 [1995].

Nirenberg, David. *Communities of Violence: Persecution of Minorities in the Middle Ages*. Princeton: Princeton University Press, 1996.

———. "The Specter of Judaism in the Age of Mass Conversion: Spain 1391–1492." Plenary address. Thirty-Eighth International Congress on Medieval Studies. Kalamazoo, Michigan. 9 May 2003.

Nolte, Cordula. "Gender and Conversion in the Merovingian Era." In *Varieties of Religious Conversion*, 81–99.

O'Callaghan, Joseph F. *Reconquest and Crusade in Medieval Spain*. Philadelphia: University of Pennsylvania Press, 2003.

O'Reilly, Jennifer. "The Rough-Hewn Cross in Anglo-Saxon Art." In *Ireland and Insular Art AD 500–1200*, ed. Michael Ryan, 153–58. Dublin: Royal Irish Academy, 1987.

Orfali, Moises. "The Portuguese Edition (1565) of Hieronymus de Sancta Fide's *Contra Iudeos.*" In *Contra Iudaeos,* 239–56.

Paris, Erna. *The End of Days: A Story of Tolerance, Tyranny, and the Expulsion of the Jews from Spain.* Amherst, NY: Prometheus Books, 1995.

Parr, Johnstone. "Chaucer's Semiramis." *Chaucer Review* 5 (1970): 57–61.

Patterson, Lee. *Chaucer and the Subject of History.* Madison: University of Wisconsin Press, 1991.

———. *Negotiating the Past: The Historical Understanding of Medieval Literature.* Madison: University of Wisconsin Press, 1987.

Pelikan, Jaroslav. *The Christian Tradition: A History of the Development of Doctrine.* 5 vols. Chicago: University of Chicago Press, 1971–89.

———. "A First-Generation Anselmian, Guibert of Nogent." In *Continuity and Discontinuity in Church History: Essays Presented to George Huntston Williams on the Occasion of His 65th Birthday,* ed. F. Forrester Church and Timothy George, 71–82. Leiden: Brill, 1979.

Pellegrini, Ann. *Performance Anxieties: Staging Psychoanalysis, Staging Race.* New York: Routledge, 1997.

Poliakov, Léon. *Histoire de l'anti-semitisme: Du Christ aux juifs de cour.* Vol. 1. Paris: Calmann-Lévy, 1955.

Prawer, Joshua. "The Autobiography of Obadyah the Norman, a Convert to Judaism at the Time of the First Crusade." In *Studies in Medieval Jewish History and Literature,* ed. Isadore Twersky, 110–34. Cambridge: Harvard University Press, 1979.

Prosser, Jay. *Second Skins: The Body Narratives of Transsexuality.* New York: Columbia University Press, 1998.

Rabinowitz, L. *The Social Life of the Jews of Northern France in the XII–XIV Centuries as Reflected in the Rabbinical Literature of the Period.* 2nd ed. New York: Hermon Press, 1972.

"Race and Ethnicity in the Middle Ages." Ed. Thomas Hahn. Special issue, *Journal of Medieval and Early Modern Studies* 31 (2001).

Religionsgespräche im Mittelalter. Ed. Bernard Lewis and Friedrich Niewöhner. Wiesbaden: Otto Harrassowitz, 1992.

Rembaum, Joel E. "The Talmud and the Popes: Reflections on the Talmud Trials of the 1240s." *Viator* 13 (1982): 203–23.

Renaissance and Renewal in the Twelfth Century. Ed. Robert L. Benson and Giles Constable, with Carol D. Lanham. Cambridge: Harvard University Press, 1982.

Resnick, Irven M. "Medieval Roots of the Myth of Jewish Male Menses." *Harvard Theological Review* 93 (2000): 241–63.

Richards, Jeffrey. *Sex, Dissidence and Damnation: Minority Groups in the Middle Ages.* London: Routledge, 1991.

Robertson, Elizabeth. "The 'Elvyssh' Power of Constance: Christian Feminism in Geoffrey Chaucer's *The Man of Law's Tale.*" *Studies in the Age of Chaucer* 23 (2001): 143–80.

Rose, Christine M. "The Jewish Mother-in-Law: Synagoga and the *Man of Law's Tale.*" In *Hildegard of Bingen: A Book of Essays,* ed. Maud Burnett McInerney, 191–226. New York: Garland, 1998. Reprint, *Chaucer and the Jews,* 3–23.

Rosenthal, Judah M. "A Religious Disputation between a Scholar Named Menachem and the Apostate and Dominican Friar Pablo Christiani" (Hebrew). *Hagut Ivrit ba-Amerika* 3 (1974): 61–74.

———. "The Talmud on Trial: The Disputation at Paris in the Year 1240." *Jewish Quarterly Review*, n.s., 47 (1956): 58–76, 145–69.

Roskies, David G. *Against the Apocalypse: Responses to Catastrophe in Modern Jewish Culture.* Cambridge: Harvard University Press, 1984.

Roth, Cecil. "The Disputation of Barcelona (1263)." *Harvard Theological Review* 43 (1950): 117–44.

Rubenstein, Jay. *Guibert of Nogent: Portrait of a Medieval Mind.* New York: Routledge, 2002.

Rubin, Gayle. "The Traffic in Women: Notes on the 'Political Economy' of Sex." In *Toward an Anthropology of Women,* ed. Rayna R. Reiter, 157–210. New York: Monthly Review Press, 1975.

Rubin, Miri. *Gentile Tales: The Narrative Assault on Late Medieval Jews.* New Haven: Yale University Press, 1999.

Ruether, Rosemary Radford. "The *Adversus Judaeos* Tradition in the Church Fathers: The Exegesis of Christian Anti-Judaism." In *Essential Papers on Judaism and Christianity in Conflict,* 174–89.

Sáenz-Badillos, Ángel. "Šelomoh Bonafed, último gran poeta de Sefarad, y la poesía hebrea." *eHumanista* 2 (2002): 1–22.

Said, Edward W. *Orientalism.* New York: Vintage Books, 1979 [1978].

Saltman, Avrom. "Hermann's *Opusculum de Conversione Sua:* Truth or Fiction?" *Revue des Études Juives* 147 (1988): 31–56.

Same Sex Love and Desire among Women in the Middle Ages. Ed. Francesca Canadé Sautman and Pamela Sheingorn. New York: Palgrave Macmillan, 2001.

Samuel, Irene. "Semiramis in the Middle Ages: The History of a Legend." *Medievalia et Humanistica* 2 (1944), 32–44.

Scanlon, Larry. *At Sodom's Gate: Medieval Writing, Postmodern Theory and the Regulation of Desire.* In progress.

———. "Unmanned Men and Eunuchs of God: Peter Damian's *Liber Gomorrhianus* and the Sexual Politics of Papal Reform." *New Medieval Literatures* 2 (1998): 37–46.

Schibanoff, Susan. "Chaucer's Lesbians: Drawing Blanks?" *Medieval Feminist Newsletter,* no. 13 (Spring 1992): 11–14.

———. "Worlds Apart: Orientalism, Antifeminism, and Heresy in Chaucer's *Man of Law's Tale.*" *Exemplaria* 8 (1996): 59–96.

Schiller, Gertrud. *Iconography of Christian Art.* Vol. 2: *The Passion of Jesus Christ.* Trans. Janet Seligman. Greenwich, CT: New York Graphic Society, 1972 [1968].

Schlauch, Margaret. "The Allegory of Church and Synagogue." *Speculum* 14 (1939): 448–64.

Schmitt, Jean-Claude. *La conversion d'Hermann le Juif: Autobiographie, histoire et fiction.* Paris: Éditions du Seuil, 2003.

———. *Les corps, les rites, les rêves, le temps: Essais d'anthropologie médiévale.* Paris: Gallimard, 2001.

———. *Ghosts in the Middle Ages: The Living and the Dead in Medieval Society.* Trans. Teresa Lavender Fagan. Chicago: University of Chicago Press, 1998 [1994].

Schreckenberg, Heinz. *Die christlichen Adversus-Judaeos-Texte und ihr literarisches und historisches Umfeld (1.-11. Jh.).* 3rd ed. Frankfurt: Peter Lang, 1994.

———. *Die christlichen Adversus-Judaeos-Texte (11.-13. Jh.): Mit einer Ikonographie des Judenthemas bis zum 4. Laterankonzil.* 2nd ed. Frankfurt: Peter Lang, 1991.

———. *Die christlichen Adversus-Judaeos-Texte und ihr literarisches und historisches Umfeld (13.-20. Jh.)*. Frankfurt: Peter Lang, 1994.

———. *The Jews in Christian Art: An Illustrated History*. Trans. John Bowden. New York: Continuum, 1996.

Sedgwick, Eve Kosofsky. *Between Men: English Literature and Male Homosocial Desire*. New York: Columbia University Press, 1985.

———. *Epistemology of the Closet*. Berkeley and Los Angeles: University of California Press, 1990.

———. *Tendencies*. Durham, NC: Duke University Press, 1993.

Segal, Alan F. *Paul the Convert: The Apostolate and Apostasy of Saul the Pharisee*. New Haven: Yale University Press, 1990.

Seiferth, Wolfgang S. *Synagogue and Church in the Middle Ages: Two Symbols in Art and Literature*. Trans. Lee Chadeayne and Paul Gottwald. New York: Frederick Ungar, 1970.

Sells, Michael A. *The Bridge Betrayed: Religion and Genocide in Bosnia*. Berkeley: University of California Press, 1996.

Septimus, Bernard. "Petrus Alfonsi on the Cult at Mecca." *Speculum* 56 (1981): 517–33.

Sexual Practices and the Medieval Church. Ed. Vern L. Bullough and James Brundage. Buffalo: Prometheus Books, 1982.

Shapiro, James. *Shakespeare and the Jews*. New York: Columbia University Press, 1996.

Shatzmiller, Joseph. *La deuxième controverse de Paris: Un chapitre dans la polémique entre chrétiens et juifs au Moyen Âge*. Paris: Éditions E. Peeters, 1994.

———. "Paulus Christiani: Un aspect de son activité anti-juive." In *Hommage à Georges Vajda: Études d'histoire et de pensée juives*, ed. Gérard Nahon and Charles Touati, 203–17. Louvain: Éditions Peeters, 1980.

———. *Shylock Reconsidered: Jews, Moneylending, and Medieval Society*. Berkeley: University of California Press, 1990.

Shepkaru, Shmuel. "To Die for God: Martyrs' Heaven in Hebrew and Latin Crusade Narratives." *Speculum* 77 (2002): 311–41.

Signer, Michael A. "God's Love for Israel: Apologetic and Hermeneutical Strategies in Twelfth-Century Biblical Exegesis." In *Jews and Christians in Twelfth-Century Europe*, 123–49.

Simon, Marcel. *Verus Israel: A Study of the Relations between Christians and Jews in the Roman Empire (135–425)*. Trans. H. McKeating. Oxford: Oxford University Press, 1986.

Simons, Walter. *Cities of Ladies: Beguine Communities in the Medieval Low Countries, 1200–1565*. Philadelphia: University of Pennsylvania Press, 2001.

Smalley, Beryl. *The Study of the Bible in the Middle Ages*. 2nd ed. Notre Dame: University of Notre Dame Press, 1964 [1952].

Smith, D. Vance. *Arts of Possession: The Middle English Household Imaginary*. Minneapolis: University of Minnesota Press, 2003.

Soifer, Maya. "'You Say That the Messiah Has Come…': The Ceuta Disputation (1179) and Its Place in Christian Anti-Jewish Polemics of the High Middle Ages." New York Interuniversity Doctoral Consortium Colloquium: "The Mediterranean in the Middle Ages." 16 April 2004.

Southern, R. W. *The Making of the Middle Ages*. New Haven: Yale University Press, 1959.

———. *Western Society and the Church in the Middle Ages*. Harmondsworth: Penguin, 1970.

———. *Western Views of Islam in the Middle Ages.* Cambridge: Harvard University Press, 1962.

Spelman, Elizabeth V. *Inessential Woman: Problems of Exclusion in Feminist Thought.* Boston: Beacon Press, 1988.

Stacey, Robert C. "The Conversion of Jews to Christianity in Thirteenth-Century England." *Speculum* 67 (1992): 263–83.

———. "Jews and Christians in Twelfth-Century England: Some Dynamics of a Changing Relationship." In *Jews and Christians in Twelfth-Century Europe,* 340–54.

Stein, S. "A Disputation on Moneylending between Jews and Gentiles in Me'ir b. Simeon's Milḥemeth Miṣwah (Narbonne, 13ᵗʰ Cent.)." *Journal of Jewish Studies* 10 (1959): 45–61.

———. "Jewish-Christian Disputations in Thirteenth-Century Narbonne." Inaugural Lecture, University College, London, 22 October 1964. London: H. K. Lewis, 1969.

Steinberg, Leo. *The Sexuality of Christ in Renaissance Art and in Modern Oblivion.* 2nd ed. Chicago: University of Chicago Press, 1996.

Stiefel, Tina. *The Intellectual Revolution in Twelfth-Century Europe.* New York: St. Martin's Press, 1985.

Stock, Brian. *The Implications of Literacy: Written Language and Models of Interpretation in the Eleventh and Twelfth Centuries.* Princeton: Princeton University Press, 1983.

———. *Myth and Science in the Twelfth Century: A Study of Bernard Silvester.* Princeton: Princeton University Press, 1972.

Stoler, Ann Laura. *Race and the Education of Desire: Foucault's History of Sexuality and the Colonial Order of Things.* Durham: Duke University Press, 1995.

Stone, Gregory B. "Ramon Llull vs. Petrus Alfonsi: Postmodern Liberalism and the Six Liberal Arts." *Medieval Encounters* 3 (1997): 70–93.

Strickland, Debra Higgs. *Saracens, Demons, and Jews: Making Monsters in Medieval Art.* Princeton: Princeton University Press, 2003.

Studies in Maimonides and St. Thomas Aquinas. Ed. Jacob I. Dienstag. New York: KTAV, 1975.

Text and Territory: Geographical Imagination in the European Middle Ages. Ed. Sylvia Tomasch and Sealy Gilles. Philadelphia: University of Pennsylvania Press, 1998.

Thrupp, Sylvia L. *The Merchant Class of Medieval London, 1300–1500.* Chicago: University of Chicago Press, 1948.

Timmer, David E. "Biblical Exegesis and the Jewish-Christian Controversy in the Early Twelfth Century." *Church History* 58 (1989): 309–21.

Timmermann, Achim. "The Avenging Crucifix: Some Observations on the Iconography of the Living Cross." *Gesta* 40 (2001): 141–60.

Tolan, John. *Petrus Alfonsi and His Medieval Readers.* Gainesville: University Press of Florida, 1993.

———. *Saracens: Islam in the Medieval Imagination.* New York: Columbia University Press, 2002.

Tomasch, Sylvia. "Judecca, Dante's Satan, and the Dis-placed Jew." In *Text and Territory,* 247–67.

———. "Postcolonial Chaucer and the Virtual Jew." In *The Postcolonial Middle Ages,* ed. Jeffrey Jerome Cohen, 243–60. New York: St. Martin's Press, 2000. Reprint, *Chaucer and the Jews,* 69–85.

"Tortosa." In *Encyclopaedia Judaica,* 15:1268–70.

Trachtenberg, Joshua. *The Devil and the Jews: The Medieval Conception of the Jew and Its Relation to Modern Anti-Semitism*. Philadelphia: Jewish Publication Society of America, 1983 [1943].

Tuilier, André. "La condamnation du Talmud par les maîtres universitaires parisiens et les attitudes populaires à l'égard des juifs au XIIIᵉ siècle." In *Études sur la sensibilité*, Actes du 102ᵉ Congrès National des Sociétés Savantes (Limoges, 1977), 2:199–214. Paris: Bibliothèque Nationale, 1979.

Ullmann, Walter. *The Individual and Society in the Middle Ages*. Baltimore: Johns Hopkins Press, 1966.

Vaccaro, Christopher T. "Crux Christi/Cristes Rod: Interpreting the Anglo-Saxon Cross." PhD Diss., The City University of New York, 2003.

Van Engen, John. "Ralph of Flaix: The Book of Leviticus Interpreted as Christian Community." In *Jews and Christians in Twelfth-Century Europe*, 150–70.

———. *Rupert of Deutz*. Berkeley and Los Angeles: University of California Press, 1983.

Varieties of Religious Conversion in the Middle Ages. Ed. James Muldoon. Gainesville: University of Florida Press, 1997.

Wallace, David. *Premodern Places: Calais to Surinam, Chaucer to Aphra Behn*. Oxford: Blackwell, 2004.

Walther, Ingo F., and Rainer Metzger. *Marc Chagall, 1887–1985: Painting as Poetry*. Trans. Michael Hulse. Cologne: Taschen, 1987.

Weijers, Olga. *La "Disputatio" dans les facultés des arts au moyen âge*. Turnhout: Brepols, 2002.

Wetherbee, Winthrop. *Platonism and Poetry in the Twelfth Century: The Literary Influence of the School of Chartres*. Princeton: Princeton University Press, 1972.

Wheatley, Edward. "'Blind' Jews and Blind Christians: Metaphorics of Marginalization in Medieval Europe." *Exemplaria* 14 (2002): 351–82.

Whitman, Jon. *Allegory: The Dynamics of an Ancient and Medieval Technique*. Cambridge: Harvard University Press, 1987.

Williams, A. Lukyn. *Adversus Judaeos: A Bird's Eye View of Christian Apologiae until the Renaissance*. Cambridge: Cambridge University Press, 1935.

Wolfson, Elliot R. "Martyrdom, Eroticism, and Asceticism in Twelfth-Century Ashkenazi Piety." In *Jews and Christians in Twelfth-Century Europe*, 171–220.

Yerushalmi, Yosef Hayim. *Zakhor: Jewish History and Jewish Memory*. Seattle: University of Washington Press, 1996 [1982].

Yuval, Israel J. "Vengeance and Damnation, Blood and Defamation: From Jewish Martyrdom to Blood Libel Accusations" (Hebrew). *Zion*, n.s., 58 (1993): 33–90.

Ziolkowski, Jan M. "Put in No-Man's Land: Guibert of Nogent's Accusations against a Judaizing and Jew-Supporting Christian." In *Jews and Christians in Twelfth-Century Europe*, 110–22.

Žižek, Slavoj. *The Sublime Object of Ideology*. London: Verso, 1989.

MEDIEVAL CULTURES